Social Support of Young People in and after Residential Care: Is Someone There for You?

Decades of research highlight the protective tole of strong, positive, and secure relationships for children and young people at risk, both in the community and in out-of-home care.

This volume offers an in-depth exploration of social support among young people in residential care and after leaving care, emphasizing its role in their well-being. Drawing on research from Australia, Brazil, Canada, Ghana, India, Ireland, Israel, Norway, the Netherlands, Portugal, Spain, and the United States, the contributions in this collection focus on the residential care setting while offering insights relevant to other out-of-home care contexts, such as foster care and educational residential facilities.

Academics and professionals working in social work, education, child protection, and child psychology will find this book a valuable resource.

Eunice Magalhães (Ph.D.) is a researcher at CIS-ISCTE and has been teaching topics related to related to child maltreatment, child protection, foster care, and residential care at ISCTE for the past years. Her research also focuses on the mental health and resilience of vulnerable groups.

Shalhevet Attar-Schwartz (Ph.D.) is a full professor at the School of Social Work and Social Welfare at the Hebrew University of Jerusalem. Her research focuses on child well-being and child welfare, with a particular emphasis on children and youth in out-of-home care, including residential care settings, family foster care, and adoption.

Routledge Advances in Social Work

Social Work, Social Welfare and Social Development in Nigeria
A Postcolonial Perspective
Mel Gray and Solomon Amadasun

International Perspectives on Parenting Support and Parental Participation in Children and Family Services
Edited by Carmel Devaney and Rosemary Crosse

Against Critical Thinking in Health, Social Care and Social Work
Reframing Philosophy for Professional Practice
Tom Grimwood

Challenging the Conventional Wisdom about Residential Care for Children and Youth
A Good Place to Grow
Bruce Henderson

Using Language, Fiction and Story in Social Work Teaching
Dara Sampson and Amanda Howard

Social Welfare Programs and Social Work Education at a Crossroads
New Approaches for a Post-Pandemic Society
Edited by Antonio López Peláez, Annaline Keet and Chung Moon Sung

Systems Complexity in Child Protection and Welfare
Policy, Leadership, Practice and Evaluation
Edited by Aisling Gillen, John Canavan, Carmel Devaney and Caroline McGregor

Utopian Thinking and Social Work
Chris Horsell

Social Support of Young People in and after Residential Care: Is Someone There for You?
An International Perspective
Edited by Eunice Magalhães and Shalhevet Attar-Schwartz

https://www.routledge.com/Routledge-Advances-in-Social-Work/book-series/RASW

Social Support of Young People in and after Residential Care: Is Someone There for You?

An International Perspective

Edited by Eunice Magalhães and Shalhevet Attar-Schwartz

Routledge
Taylor & Francis Group
LONDON AND NEW YORK

First published 2025
by Routledge
4 Park Square, Milton Park, Abingdon, Oxon OX14 4RN

and by Routledge
605 Third Avenue, New York, NY 10158

Routledge is an imprint of the Taylor & Francis Group, an informa business

British Library Cataloguing-in-Publication Data
A catalogue record for this book is available from the British Library

Library of Congress Cataloging-in-Publication Data
Names: Magalhães, Eunice, editor. | Attar-Schwartz, Shalhevet, editor.
Title: Social support of young people in and after residential care : is someone there for you? : an international perspective / edited by Eunice Magalhães and Shalhevet Attar-Schwartz.
Description: Abingdon, Oxon ; New York, NY : Routledge, 2025. | Series: Routledge advances in social work | Includes bibliographical references and index. |
Identifiers: LCCN 2024057885 (print) | LCCN 2024057886 (ebook) |
ISBN 9781032543529 (hardback) | ISBN 9781032543536 (paperback) |
ISBN 9781003424468 (ebook)
Subjects: LCSH: Social work with youth. | Youth--Institutional care. |
Social service--Psychological aspects. | Interpersonal relations.
Classification: LCC HV1421 .S635 2025 (print) | LCC HV1421 (ebook) |
DDC 362.7--dc23/eng/20250214
LC record available at https://lccn.loc.gov/2024057885
LC ebook record available at https://lccn.loc.gov/2024057886

ISBN: 978-1-032-54352-9 (hbk)
ISBN: 978-1-032-54353-6 (pbk)
ISBN: 978-1-003-42446-8 (ebk)

DOI: 10.4324/9781003424468

Typeset in Sabon
by SPi Technologies India Pvt Ltd (Straive)

Contents

Figures

Tables

Contributors

Shalhevet Attar-Schwartz (Ph.D.) is a full professor at the School of Social Work and Social Welfare at the Hebrew University of Jerusalem. Her research focuses on child well-being and child welfare, with a particular emphasis on children and youth in out-of-home care, including residential care settings, family foster care, and adoption.

Maria Manuela Calheiros (PhD) is a full professor at the Faculty of Psychology of Lisbon University. She has experience in the definition of public policies informed by her research in residential care through the design, implementation, and evaluation of intervention programs in this context.

Antonia Canosa is a social anthropologist and research fellow at the Centre for Children and Young People at Southern Cross University. Antonia's research interests include children's rights and participation and the ethical dimensions of research and practice with children.

Mark E. Courtney is the Samuel Deutsch Professor Emeritus in the Crown Family School of Social Work, Policy, and Practice. His fields of special interest are child welfare policy and services, the connection between child welfare services and other institutions serving marginalized populations, and the professionalization of social work. His current work includes studies of the adult functioning of former foster children and the influence of juvenile courts on the operation of the child welfare system.

Jorge F. del Valle is a full professor of Psychosocial Intervention at the Department of Psychology, University of Oviedo, Spain and the Family and Childhood Research Group director. His research focuses on program evaluation in residential and foster care, the needs assessments of vulnerable groups, and the development of tools and instruments to facilitate the work of professionals in these areas (SERAR, PLANEA, etc.).

Débora Dalbosco Dell'Aglio is a psychologist with a master's and PhD in Psychology (UFRGS, Brazil). She was an associate professor at the Graduate Program in Education at the Universidade La Salle, Unilasalle (Canoas, Brazil) and a full professor at the Graduate Program in Psychology at the Universidade Federal do Rio Grande do Sul (Porto Alegre, Brazil). Her research focuses on broad questions of human development, acting on topics such as adolescence, institutionalization, and sexual abuse.

Robert J. Flynn is an emeritus professor in the School of Psychology at the University of Ottawa in Canada. Much of his research has been concerned with the evaluation of service quality and effectiveness, with a particular focus on the educational tutoring and outcomes of young people in out-of-home care.

Adi Fridman-Teutsch (MSW) is a social worker specializing in therapy for children impacted by intimate partner violence. She currently serves at the Center for Treatment and Prevention of Domestic Violence within the Social Services Department of Modi'in-Maccabim-Re'ut.

Kwabena Frimpong-Manso is an associate professor at the University of Ghana. His research interests include care leaving, children and families, and child welfare systems.

Elena Gallitto is a senior researcher and data analyst. She is an experienced researcher with strong abilities in program evaluation, psychometric assessment, and statistical analysis. Her research focuses on designing and evaluating interventions for at-risk children and youth to improve developmental outcomes.

Laura García-Alba is a postdoctoral researcher at the Department of Psychology, University of Oviedo (Spain), currently collaborating with the Family and Childhood Research Group. Her research focuses on promoting successful transitions to adulthood of young people from residential childcare, especially on developing, implementing, and evaluating programs in this context. She is a co-author of the PLANEA Program.

Robbie Gilligan is a professor emeritus of Social Work and Social Policy at the School of Social Work and Social Policy, Trinity College Dublin, The University of Dublin. His research interests revolve around children in care, alternative care systems, transitions from care, and the longer-term progress of care leavers.

Anne Graham is a professor of Childhood Studies and Founding Director of the Centre for Children and Young People at Southern Cross University. Anne's research has always had a strong focus on children's rights, well-being, and safety and aims to improve policy and practice.

Emmanuel Grupper (PhD) was an associate professor at the Ono Academic College. He was a founding figure in the field of residential education in Israel. He passed away in April 2024.

Federica Gullo has a PhD in Education and Psychology, is a postdoctoral researcher at the Department of Psychology, University of Oviedo, Spain, and a member of the Family and Childhood Research Group. Her research focuses on the transition to adulthood from care, especially on care leavers' needs, the interventions carried out to support them, their results, the satisfaction with the received benefits, and differences in especially vulnerable groups.

Annemiek T. Harder (PhD) is a professor by special appointment of Evidence-Based Youth Care and Education at the Erasmus School of Social and Behavioural Sciences of the Erasmus University Rotterdam. Her research interests include youth with serious behavioral problems, residential youth care, treatment approaches for reducing delinquency, motivational interviewing (MI), evidence-based interventions, and 'what works' in youth care.

Adena Hoffnung-Assouline (PhD) is an adjunct lecturer at the Hebrew University's School of Social Work and Social Welfare and leads a national team developing training for child welfare workers at Israel's Ministry of Social Affairs. Her expertise includes out-of-home care, adoption, and trauma treatment for children.

Yisca Huri is a social worker specializing in youth and mental health who completed her PhD at the Hebrew University. Her research centers on young people's well-being, with a particular focus on new family structures.

Gurneet Kaur Kalra has a PhD in Social Work from Jamia Millia Islamia University, India. She is a trained Researcher and Social Worker and is committed to research and fieldwork practice. She is currently engaged as Manager, Research and Advocacy at Udayan Care and has authored numerous papers in national and international journals.

Erik J. Knorth (PhD) is a full professor emeritus of Child and Youth Care at the University of Groningen, Faculty of Behavioural and Social Sciences, Department of Child and Family Welfare. His research interests relate to children and youth with serious emotional and behavioral problems and their families, the quality of child and youth care services including residential and family foster care programs, decision-making by professionals, and theoretical issues on what works in child and youth care.

Jonathan D. Leipoldt (PhD) is a lecturer/researcher in Clinical Developmental Psychology at the University of Amsterdam, Faculty of Social and Behavioural Sciences, Programme group Developmental Psychology. His research interests include residential youth care, specifically the effects of contextual characteristics on treatment outcome indicators. In addition, he studies scholastic motivation of youth at risk for dropping out of school.

Mónica López López is an associate professor at the Faculty of Behavioural and Social Sciences of the University of Groningen, the Netherlands. Her research interests include child welfare inequalities, children and youth participation, and the experiences of LGBTQIA+ youth in care.

Eunice Magalhães (Ph.D.) is a researcher at CIS-ISCTE and has been teaching topics related to child protection, foster care, and residential care at ISCTE for the past years. Her research also focuses on the mental health and resilience of vulnerable groups.

Gerald P. Mallon is the Julia Lathrop Professor of Child Welfare at the Silberman School of Social Work at Hunter College in New York City. He is a child welfare practitioner, advocate, educator, and researcher, with a primary focus on LGBTQ+ youth in child welfare settings.

Eran Melkman is a faculty member at the School of Education at Tel Aviv University. He is a clinical social worker and child welfare researcher, specializing in vulnerable youth and young adults in out-of-home placements and the community. His work examines the development of risk and resilience across the life course of vulnerable young people in out-of-home care and in the community and the intersection between child welfare and schools.

Kiran Modi has a PhD in American Literature from IIT, Delhi. She founded Udayan Care, a non-profit organization in 1994, to focus on family strengthening and care reform which now works in 36 cities across India and has international chapters in the United States and Germany. She is a recipient of many prestigious awards, including the National Award for Child Welfare – India's highest commendation for a non-profit child welfare organization.

Tim Moore is an associate professor and deputy director at the Institute of Child Protection Studies at the Australian Catholic University. Through his participatory research, Tim aims to ensure that services and systems are informed and responsive to children and young people's needs and wishes.

Nathanael J. Okpych is an associate professor in the School of Social Work at the University of Connecticut. His work focuses on youth characteristics (e.g., social networks and social support), policies, and programs. His professional experience in social services and higher education dovetail to inform his research on factors that influence post-secondary education outcomes for youth with foster care experience.

Keunhye Park is an assistant professor at Michigan State University's School of Social Work. Park's research interests include child welfare services and policy, juvenile justice services and policy, educational experiences of marginalized youth, and the transition to adulthood among foster youth. Park's work builds upon her field practice in public schools, juvenile detention centers, state departments of children and family services, and research institutes.

June C. Paul is an assistant professor in the Social Work Department at Skidmore College. Their research focuses on intersectionality, disproportionality, and advancing strategies that provide more equitable and effective care and services for LGBTQ+ children, youth, and families involved in public and community-based systems.

Shulamit Pinchover (PhD) is an independent researcher and adjunct professor at Touro University. Her research explores the intersection of parent-child relationships, child health and development, and children's health services.

Leena Prasad is a trained lawyer based out of Delhi with a passion for advocacy on human rights and child protection and is currently the Director at Udayan Care.

Iriana Santos is an assistant professor at the Department of Education of the University of Cantabria, Spain. Her main area of research focuses on the quality evaluation of residential care programs, transition to adulthood from care, and unaccompanied young migrants. She also has a long experience in training residential workers and practitioners in childcare.

Netanel Shalem (MSW) is completing his PhD in parent–child contact in residential care at the School of Social Work and Social Welfare, the Hebrew University. He works in policy and service development for people with disabilities at the Ministry of Welfare and lectures at the University of Haifa.

Marianne Tevik Singstad holds a position as an associate professor in Health Sciences (Child Welfare) at the Regional Centre for Child and Youth Mental Health and Child Welfare at the Department of Mental Health at the Norwegian University of Science and Technology (NTNU), Norway. Her specific research interests are children and youth development, children and adolescents in residential youth care, child welfare, social relationships and social support, early prevention and intervention, and research on optimizing school social workers' role in primary schools.

Yafit Sulimani-Aidan serves as an associate professor at Tel Aviv University's School of Social Work. Her research is centered around resiliency, with a specific emphasis on the strengths that empower at-risk youth and young adults to thrive. Moreover, her work delves into the factors that improve case workers' capacity to offer effective support to young adults at risk during their transition to adulthood.

Mijntje ten Brummelaar is an assistant professor at the Faculty of Behavioural and Social Sciences of the University of Groningen, the Netherlands. The focus of her research is on participatory research and ethical research practices with children and youth.

Bruna Wendt is a psychologist with a master's degree and PhD in developmental psychology from the Universidade Federal do Rio Grande do Sul (UFRGS), Brazil. She is a professor at the Instituição Evangélica de Novo Hamburgo (IENH, Brazil) and a clinical psychologist, working with Cognitive-Behavioral Therapy and Schema Therapy. She is mainly interested in topics such as vulnerable children and adolescents, residential care, and positive parenting.

Introduction*

Eunice Magalhães and Shalhevet Attar-Schwartz

According to the United Nations International Children's Emergency Fund (UNICEF), over 2.7 million young people worldwide live in residential care (Petrowski et al., 2017), primarily due to parental abuse, neglect, orphanhood, or other adverse life circumstances. Many of these children exhibit a range of emotional, health, and functioning difficulties (e.g., Magalhães & Camilo, 2023). In addition, recent global conflicts have introduced new complexities to migration patterns, increasing the need for resources and support for young people in vulnerable situations. Therefore, fostering protective factors both during care and throughout the transition out of care is essential for building resilience and promoting positive adaptation, even in the face of past adversity. One of the most significant protective factors for care-experienced young people, fostering their well-being and functioning, is the presence of meaningful, supportive relationships (Ferreira et al., 2020; Magalhães & Calheiros, 2017).

The United Nations General Assembly Resolution, adopted on December 18, 2009, affirms that "every child and young person should live in a supportive, protective, and caring environment that promotes his/her full potential" (United Nations, 2009, p. 2). Consequently, when placement in alternative family settings is not feasible, it is critical for residential care settings (RCSs) to foster supportive relationships within group homes (e.g., with staff and peers) and in the broader community (e.g., with family members and other significant individuals). These supportive relationships play a vital role in enhancing young people's well-being (Assouline & Attar-Schwartz, 2020; Magalhães & Calheiros, 2017), which is especially crucial for those in vulnerable circumstances (Pinheiro et al., 2022a). The quality of meaningful relationships serves as a therapeutic resource, fostering both recovery and personal growth during care (Castro et al., 2023) as well as hope for the future (Babo et al., 2024).

* Some chapters in this collection were edited for grammar and style by Ms. Liza Hazan, as well as by AI tools, including ChatGPT-4 and DeepL. Following the use of such editing, the authors reviewed and refined the content as needed and take full responsibility for the final publication.

DOI: 10.4324/9781003424468-1

This edited collection offers empirical and conceptual insights into the social support of children and youth in residential care and after leaving care from an international perspective. It includes 15 chapters authored by 38 contributors from 12 countries, whose diverse insights have greatly enriched this work. We are especially grateful to the authors who contributed to the peer-review process, providing valuable feedback that strengthened this collection. The evidence presented here addresses the unique challenges surrounding support receipt for young people with residential care experience. It examines social support from a range of formal and informal sources and highlights the role of such support in fostering psychological health and well-being. Additionally, it outlines various interventions aimed at strengthening the support systems for children and youth in residential care and during their transition beyond it.

Children in residential care represent a vulnerable group, experiencing higher levels of emotional, behavioral, social, health, and educational difficulties than those who live with their biological families (Assouline & Attar-Schwartz, 2020; Gearing et al., 2015; Jozefiak et al., 2016). These challenges often stem from traumatic events preceding their placement, as well as the additional stress associated with entering residential care (Magalhães & Camilo, 2023; Magalhães et al., 2016). Prior experiences of poverty, family breakdown, and maltreatment place these youth at a significant social disadvantage, emphasizing the critical role of supportive relationships (Roche, 2020). Placement in residential care is an impactful event, involving separation from their birth families and the need to adjust to an unfamiliar environment. The care setting, which often includes multiple caregivers, high staff turnover, low level of normalization, and strict routines, as well as a concentration of peers with similar intensive needs, can further increase vulnerability (Lou et al., 2018; Pinheiro et al., 2022b). Nevertheless, mental health outcomes vary significantly among young people in residential care (Attar-Schwartz, 2008, 2009; Bell et al., 2013; Hagaman et al., 2010). While some young people fall within the clinical range of functioning difficulties, others demonstrate resilience across various domains (see Bell & Romano, 2015; Legault et al., 2006).

Social support and social networks have been shown to play a vital role in explaining the pronounced variance in mental health and resilience among youth in residential care (e.g., Assouline & Attar-Schwartz, 2020; Attar-Schwartz & Huri, 2019; Fridman-Teutsch & Attar-Schwartz, 2019; Magalhães & Calheiros, 2017; Singstad et al., 2020). Social connections within these settings are particularly beneficial for young people's psychological health, as they offer a sense of belonging that positively influences well-being (López et al., 2024). This support is especially critical given the multiple losses and heightened risks these children may encounter during out-of-home care, factors that can increase their likelihood of experiencing social exclusion later in life.

Young people leaving care represent one of the most vulnerable groups in society. The challenges faced by care leavers as they transition from care to independent living are widely acknowledged worldwide (Courtney et al., 2011; Modi et al., 2016; Sulimani-Aidan et al., 2013; Van Breda et al., 2020). Supportive relationships are known to play a crucial role in helping care leavers navigate this transition, manage the separation from significant others in care, and adapt successfully to their new, independent lives.

Recognizing that mental health encompasses more than the mere absence of symptoms (Magalhães, 2024), this book offers a diverse range of chapters focusing on different sources of support and developmental outcomes, including psychopathology, well-being, and happiness. Despite considerable variations in the use of residential care across countries—such as Portugal, where 97% of children in out-of-home placements are in residential care versus approximately 7% in Australia—and the diversity of services provided globally, meaningful and supportive relationships remain crucial for fostering secure attachments and prioritizing the well-being of children and youth in care (Holden et al., 2010). This collection provides a thorough analysis of social support from various sources, examining its contribution to the psychological functioning of young people in residential care during both their placement and post-placement phases.

This book is organized into five sections, providing a global perspective on social support in residential care and after leaving care with evidence from Australia, Brazil, Canada, Ghana, India, Ireland, Israel, Norway, the Netherlands, Portugal, Spain, and the United States. Rather than centering on a single context, it presents cross-cultural insights into social support for youth in residential care.

Part 1 addresses the conceptual and theoretical definitions and frameworks of social support among young people in residential care, highlighting key issues and challenges both during and after care. It includes two chapters that set the stage for the international perspectives presented in the collection. The opening chapter, by Attar-Schwartz et al., reviews the foundational concepts and theories related to social support and social networks of young people in and after residential care. It explores the distinctions between support sources (formal and informal) and types (such as instrumental, emotional, informational, and appraisal) and discusses the mechanisms that contribute to the positive impact of social support on young people in and after residential care. It further identifies specific conditions under which support is most beneficial for at-risk youth and offers practical and policy-related recommendations. A key conclusion of this chapter emphasizes the importance of adopting trauma-informed, relational, and interdependence perspectives in supporting young people in RCSs and throughout their transition to adulthood. This involves a shift from focusing solely on preparing youth for independent living toward fostering interdependence by tailoring programs that help young people establish lasting, supportive relationships that include both current connections and new ones formed throughout their lives. Such long-term networks of support are crucial, extending beyond their time in the care system and promoting their ongoing well-being and resilience.

Chapter 2, by Gilligan, applies a life course conceptual perspective to explore the role of supportive relationships in shaping the developmental trajectories of young people in residential care. It also highlights the ways in which significant adults can support young people with residential care experiences, particularly in relation to their motivations, sense of life purpose, and social skills. Through selected case examples of both alumni and young people still residing in residential care, the author provides valuable insights into successful trajectories, offering reflections on how meaningful support can contribute to positive development and resilience in these young people.

Part 2 of this book focuses on social support among young people during their stay in residential care, presenting empirical findings from various countries (Australia, Canada, Israel, Norway, and Portugal) regarding different sources of support and their contribution to young people's well-being while in care. This part consists of five chapters centered on the experiences of young people during their placement in residential care.

Chapter 3, by Magalhães and Calheiros, discusses the findings from a series of studies conducted in Portugal, focusing on the perspectives of adolescents in residential care. It examines the direct, moderating, and mediating effects of social support on various outcomes of young people's development, including psychopathology, well-being, and academic performance. The chapter also reflects on the implications of these findings for child welfare practice and policy, highlighting the need for qualified RCSs and skilled professionals who can foster supportive relationships with young people. Additionally, it emphasizes the importance of facilitating quality connections between young people, their relatives, and peers.

Chapter 4, by Attar-Schwartz and colleagues, presents findings from two quantitative studies on social support in Israeli RCSs, supervised by the Ministry of Education and the Ministry of Social Affairs and Social Security. Drawing on a range of theoretical perspectives, including social capital theory, attachment theory, and the stress-buffering hypothesis, these studies primarily focus on youth perspectives. The aim is to map their perceptions of different sources of social support, such as parents, siblings, grandparents, peers, and residential care staff, and to examine the relationship between social support and youth well-being and functioning. Additionally, various moderating models were tested to identify the conditions under which social support proves most beneficial.

The following chapters further explore the role of supportive relationships in youth safety, happiness, and well-being, with studies from Australia (Moore et al.), Norway (Singstad), and Canada (Gallitto & Flynn). Moore et al. conducted a qualitative study focusing on the perspectives of both youth and staff in residential care, revealing the central role of supportive relationships in fostering well-being. Their findings highlight key supportive practices within residential care that can positively influence young people's overall health. Singstad's chapter presents evidence from a quantitative study showing that social support is linked to emotional well-being and quality of life for both girls and boys in care. This chapter emphasizes the protective role of social support on adolescents' psychological health and discusses practical implications for improving support systems. The final chapter of this part, by Gallitto and Flynn, reports findings from the Ontario Looking After Children project. They introduce a new measure of social support and provide evidence of how the quality of relationships in out-of-home care is associated with youth mental health, well-being, and placement satisfaction.

Part 3 focuses on the social support and social networks of care leavers, specifically examining the role of various support sources in their transition from residential care to independent living. It presents evidence from the United States (Park et al.), Israel (Sulimani-Aidan), Ghana (Frimpong-Manso), and India (Modi et al.). Park et al. describe longitudinal evidence from the United States, comparing youth with and without congregate care experience. Their findings highlight the importance of strengthening young people's connections with their informal support networks, particularly their families. Sulimani-Aidan systematizes empirical evidence on the social networks of care leavers in Israel, discussing how these networks contribute to outcomes in adulthood. This highlights the need for continued practice and policy efforts to prevent social exclusion among care leavers. Frimpong-Manso presents a qualitative study from Ghana, using the framework method to examine how various types of social support are available to care leavers during their transition out of care. This study emphasizes the critical role of fostering connections with family and community networks. Finally, Modi et al. present a participatory study that captures the voices of stakeholders in the Indian out-of-home care system. Their chapter highlights the detrimental effects of the lack of support services on care leavers' well-being in India, calling for enhanced policy and practice to ensure adequate preparation and support for care leavers as they transition to independent living.

Part 4 explores the intersecting challenges faced by various groups of young people in residential care and after care, focusing on LGBTQIA+ youth (Lopez et al.) and migrant youth (Gullo et al.), through an intersectional lens. Lopez and colleagues conducted studies in the Netherlands, Spain, and the United States, offering cross-cultural insights into the experiences of LGBTQIA+ young people leaving care. They examine how unique challenges in the transition process contribute to health outcomes among these youth and emphasize the critical role of social support in fostering a successful transition. LGBTQIA+ youth in care often face various forms of oppression linked to complex mental health needs, making social support an essential protective factor for their well-being. Gullo et al. investigate the formal and informal support networks described by youth transitioning out of residential care in Spain, with a particular focus on unaccompanied young migrants. They discuss the heightened difficulty in securing support networks for these youth, underscoring the need for specialized approaches to bolster their social connections.

Part 5 presents two chapters that focus on fostering social support within residential care through targeted interventions and services. Knorth et al. review the literature on social support in Dutch residential care, examining the roles of both family and staff in creating a positive social group climate that can nurture support for young people in residential care. They discuss how an intentional social group climate can promote supportive relationships and help prepare youth for life beyond care. Wendt and Dell'Aglio focus on training staff in Brazilian RCSs through the *Cuida* program, which aims to enhance staff's skills in building supportive networks for children. Their chapter evaluates Cuida's impact on staff abilities to strengthen these networks, emphasizing that strong relationships during care can improve outcomes both in care and after transition. Both chapters highlight the importance of ongoing training, supervision, and aftercare services to help youth maintain supportive connections as they transition to adulthood.

In conclusion, this book provides evidence-based insights for practice and policy, guiding interventions by residential care staff. By integrating theory, empirical research, and established standards, we illustrate why and how supportive relationships are essential for young people's positive outcomes both during and after residential care. Residential care has a pressing need for a trauma-informed and relational approach that emphasizes interdependence over independence, helping youth build lasting and supportive relationships that extend beyond their time in care.

References

Assouline, A. A. H., & Attar-Schwartz, S. (2020). Staff support and adolescent adjustment difficulties: The moderating role of length of stay in the residential care setting. *Children and Youth Services Review*, *110*, 104761. https://doi.org/10.1016/j.childyouth.2020.104761

Attar-Schwartz, S. (2008). Emotional, behavioral and social problems among Israeli children in residential care: A multi-level analysis. *Children and Youth Services Review*, *30*(2), 229–248. https://doi.org/10.1016/j.childyouth.2007.09.009

Attar-Schwartz, S. (2009). School functioning of children in residential care: The contributions of multilevel correlates. *Child Abuse & Neglect*, *33*(7), 429–440. https://doi.org/10.1016/j.chiabu.2008.12.010

Attar-Schwartz, S., & Huri, Y. (2019). Grandparental support and life satisfaction among adolescents in residential care. *Children and Youth Services Review*, *96*, 70–78. https://doi.org/10.1016/j.childyouth.2018.11.033

Babo, F., Carvalho, H., Santos, B., Matos, P. M., & Mota, C. P. (2024). Affective relationships with caregivers, self-efficacy, and hope of adolescents in residential care. *Children and Youth Services Review*, *157*, 107438. https://doi.org/10.1016/j.childyouth.2024.107438

Bell, T., & Romano, E. (2015). Child resilience in out-of-home care: Child welfare worker perspectives. *Children and Youth Services Review*, *48*, 49–59. https://doi.org/10.1016/j.childyouth.2014.12.008

Bell, T., Romano, E., & Flynn, R. J. (2013). Multilevel correlates of behavioral resilience among children in child welfare. *Child Abuse & Neglect*, *37*(11), 1007–1020. https://doi.org/10.1016/j.chiabu.2013.07.005

Castro, E., Magalhães, E., & del Valle, J. F. (2023). A systematic review of non-specific and specific treatment factors associated with lower or greater internalising and externalising symptoms in therapeutic residential care. *Children and Youth Services Review*, *147*, 106840. https://doi.org/10.1016/j.childyouth.2023.106840

Courtney, M. E., Lee, J., & Perez, A. (2011). Receipt of help acquiring life skills and predictors of help receipt among current and former foster youth. *Children and Youth Services Review*, *33*(12), 2442–2451. https://doi.org/10.1016/j.childyouth.2011.08.026

Ferreira, S., Magalhães, E., & Prioste, A. (2020). Social support and mental health of young people in residential care: A qualitative study. *Anuario de Psicología Jurídica*, *30*, 29–34. https://doi.org/10.5093/apj2019a12

Fridman-Teutsch, A., & Attar-Schwartz, S. (2019). Commitment to school and learning among youth in residential care: The role of mother and father support and parents' divorce. *American Journal of Orthopsychiatry*, *89*(2), 201. https://doi.org/10.1037/ort0000364

Gearing, R. E., Brewer, K. B., Elkins, J., Ibrahim, R. W., MacKenzie, M. J., & Schwalbe, C. S. (2015). Prevalence and correlates of depression, posttraumatic stress disorder, and suicidality in Jordanian youth in institutional care. *The Journal of Nervous and Mental Disease*, *203*(3), 175–181. https://doi.org/10.1097/NMD.0000000000000267

Hagaman, J. L., Trout, A. L., Chmelka, M. B., Thompson, R. W., & Reid, R. (2010). Risk profiles of children entering residential care: A cluster analysis. *Journal of Child and Family Studies*, *19*, 525–535. https://doi.org/10.1007/s10826-009-9325-3

Holden, M. J., Izzo, C., Nunno, M., Smith, E. G., Endres, T., Holden, J. C., & Kuhn, F. (2010). Children and residential experiences: A comprehensive strategy for implementing a research-informed program model for residential care. *Child Welfare*, *89*(2), 131–149.

Jozefiak, T., Kayed, N. S., Rimehaug, T., Wormdal, A. K., Brubakk, A. M., & Wichstrøm, L. (2016). Prevalence and comorbidity of mental disorders among adolescents living in residential youth care. *European Child & Adolescent Psychiatry*, *25*, 33–47. https://doi.org/10.1007/s00787-015-0700-x

Legault, L., Anawati, M., & Flynn, R. (2006). Factors favoring psychological resilience among fostered young people. *Children and Youth Services Review*, *28*(9), 1024–1038. https://doi.org/10.1016/j.childyouth.2005.10.006

López, M. L., Martínez-Jothar, G., ten Brummelaar, M. D., Parra, L. A., Sobrino, B. S. R., & Mallon, G. P. (2024). "They told me that you can be with whomever you want, be who you are": Perceptions of LGBTQ+ youth in residential care regarding the social support provided by child welfare professionals. *Children and Youth Services Review*, *159*, 107498. https://doi.org/10.1016/j.childyouth.2024.107498

Lou, Y., Taylor, E. P., & Di Folco, S. (2018). Resilience and resilience factors in children in residential care: A systematic review. *Children and Youth Services Review*, *89*, 83–92. https://doi.org/10.1016/j.childyouth.2018.04.010

Magalhães, E. (2024). Dual-factor models of mental health: A systematic review of empirical evidence. *Psychosocial Intervention*. Ahead of print. https://doi.org/10.5093/pi2024a6

Magalhães, E., & Calheiros, M. M. (2017). A dual-factor model of mental health and social support: Evidence with adolescents in residential care. *Children and Youth Services Review*, *79*, 442–449. https://doi.org/10.1016/j.childyouth.2017.06.041

Magalhães, E., Calheiros, M. M., & Costa, P. (2016). To be or not to be a rights holder: Direct and indirect effects of perceived rights on psychological adjustment through group identification in care. *Children and Youth Services Review*, *71*, 110–118. https://doi.org/10.1016/j.childyouth.2016.10.039

Magalhães, E. & Camilo, C. (2023). Maltreatment history and internalizing and externalizing in out-of-home care: A three-level meta-analysis. *European Journal of*

Psychology Applied to Legal Context, *15*(2), 89–103. https://doi.org/10.5093/ejpalc2023a10.
Modi, K., Nayar-Akhtar, M., Ariely, S., & Gupta, D. (2016). Addressing challenges of transition from children's home to independence: Udayan Care's Udayan Ghars (Sunshine Children's Homes) & aftercare programme. *Scottish Journal of Residential Child Care*, *15*(1), 87–101.
Petrowski, N., Cappa, C., & Gross, P. (2017). Estimating the number of children in formal alternative care: Challenges and results. *Child Abuse & Neglect*, *70*, 388–398. https://doi.org/10.1016/j.chiabu.2016.11.026
Pinheiro, M., Magalhães, E., & Baptista, J. (2022b). Adolescents' resilience in residential care: A systematic review of factors related to healthy adaptation. *Child Indicators Research*, *15*(3), 819–837. https://doi.org/10.1007/s12187-021-09883-4
Pinheiro, M., Magalhães, E., Calheiros, M. M. & Macdonald, D. (2022a). Quality of relationships between residential staff and youth: a systematic review. *Child and Adolescent Social Work Journal*. https://doi.org/10.1007/s10560-022-00909-6
Roche, S. (2020). Conceptualising children's life histories and reasons for entry into residential care in the Philippines: Social contexts, instabilities and safeguarding. *Children and Youth Services Review*, *110*, 104820. https://doi.org/10.1016/j.childyouth.2020.104820
Singstad, M. T., Wallander, J. L., Lydersen, S., Wichstrøm, L., & Kayed, N. S. (2020). Perceived social support among adolescents in Residential Youth Care. *Child & Family Social Work*, *25*(2), 384–393. https://doi.org/10.1186/s12955-021-01676-1
Sulimani-Aidan, Y., Benbenishty, R., Dinisman, T., & Zeira, A. (2013). Care leavers in Israel: What contributes to better adjustment to life after care?. *Journal of Social Service Research*, *39*(5), 704–718. https://doi.org/10.1080/01488376.2013.834283
United Nations (2009). *Guidelines for the Alternative Care of Children*. Resolution adopted by the General Assembly on 18 December 2009.United Nations Digital Library. Available here https://digitallibrary.un.org/record/673583?v=pdf
Van Breda, A. D., Munro, E. R., Gilligan, R., Anghel, R., Harder, A., Incarnato, M., ... & Storø, J. (2020). Extended care: Global dialogue on policy, practice and research. *Children and Youth Services Review*, *119*, 105596. https://doi.org/10.1016/j.childyouth.2020.105596

Part 1

Conceptual and Theoretical Framework

1 Social Support and Social Networks of Young People in Residential Care and Post-Care

Conceptual Frameworks and Theoretical Insights

Shalhevet Attar-Schwartz, Eran Melkman and Eunice Magalhães

Introduction

Social support plays a crucial role in enhancing the well-being of children and youth (Brennan, 2008). Young people in out-of-home care settings, living far from their families, are at an elevated risk of experiencing low levels of social support (Perry, 2006). The challenges associated with placement in care—such as separation from birth families and the need to adapt to unfamiliar developmental environments—can intensify their vulnerabilities. Factors like high staff turnover, strict routines, and placement instability further amplify the need for stable, supportive, and protective relationships (Lou et al., 2018; Pinheiro et al., 2022).

This chapter reviews key conceptual and theoretical issues related to social support and social networks of young people in residential care settings (RCSs) and during their transition to independent living. It also addresses the contribution of social support to their mental health and functioning, exploring various interpretations and mechanisms that explain its significance. Furthermore, it explores practical implications from these theoretical insights and discusses selected interventions aimed at expanding social networks, thereby improving the well-being and developmental trajectories of these young people.

Social Support and Social Networks: Key Concepts and Dimensions

The literature on social support offers a wide array of conceptualizations and definitions reflecting the multifaceted nature of this construct. Tardy's (1985) classic five-dimensional framework serves as a foundational model, providing a structured approach to understanding social support through its key elements: direction, disposition, description or evaluation, content, and network.

Direction refers to the dual aspects of social support—its provision and reception. While both are important, research has predominantly focused on the dynamics and impact of received support (Magalhães et al., 2021; Tardy, 1985).

DOI: 10.4324/9781003424468-3

Disposition refers to the availability and actual utilization of support, delineating between potential support (in terms of quantity or quality) and its actual enactment. This dimension illuminates the nuanced interplay between the available support resources and the way young people in need engage with them.

Description concerns individuals' perceptions and evaluations of their social support, focusing on their satisfaction with it. *Content* encompasses various types of support, such as emotional, instrumental, informational, and appraisal support. Emotional support involves the expression of love, affection, and care; instrumental support covers practical assistance (e.g., financial aid and transportation); informational support encompasses guidance and advice; and appraisal support offers evaluative feedback. Research suggests that emotional, informational, and instrumental support are particularly important for young people in care (Evans et al., 2022; Magalhães & Calheiros, 2017).

Finally, *network* delineates the diverse sources from which social support is drawn, ranging from informal sources like family and friends to formal supports from professionals. This dimension underscores the breadth and complexity of individuals' support networks (Tardy, 1985). The concept of social network relates to the composition and size of the social group with whom people maintain close contact (Tracy & Whittaker, 1990).

In this chapter, we will address each of these dimensions, examining their interplay and significance in contributing to the well-being of young people in RCSs and after leaving care. We will also review theoretical models that offer further insights into the role of social support in promoting the mental health and well-being of young people in RCSs.

When discussing social support, it is essential to distinguish between perceived support—an individual's subjective assessment of the support they perceive is available to them if needed—and actual or received support, which refers to interpersonal interactions or exchanges of support (Kaul & Lakey, 2003). This distinction matters as research shows that these two constructs have relatively low correlations, suggesting they are often independent from one another (Uchino, 2009). Perceived support has been shown to have stronger associations with both physical and mental health outcomes than the level of actual support received (Uchino, 2004; Wills & Shinar, 2000). In contrast, the link between received support and outcomes tends to be weaker or inconsistent, partly because recipients may not always perceive supportive actions positively (Smith & Goodnow, 1999). Moreover, receiving support may evoke feelings of dependence, which may undermine the recipient's sense of autonomy (Bolger & Amarel, 2007). It may also foster feelings of indebtedness and disrupt the balance in relationships, even when the support is well intended and meets the recipient's needs (Newsom et al., 2005). Paradoxically, individuals reporting higher levels of received support may experience increased stress and dependency (Barrera, 1986).

It is equally important to consider the negative aspects of an individual's social connections alongside the positive ones. Scholars emphasize that conflict, rejection, criticism, and intrusiveness can significantly impact psychological and physical health, as well as academic achievement (Newsom et al., 2005; Silva et al., 2022). A substantial body of research suggests that the negative dimensions of interpersonal relationships may have a greater influence on mental health outcomes than positive interactions (Finch et al., 1999; Newsom et al., 2003). These negative interactions can be particularly harmful because they often reflect deeper relational issues. Furthermore, emotionally hurtful behaviors are more likely to occur in close relationships, such as those with spouses or family members (Akiyama et al., 2003; Fingerman et al., 2004), thereby amplifying the negative effects of such exchanges. The examination of negative interactions is especially relevant in the context of young people with care experience. In-depth interviews with care-experienced young adults reveal heightened levels of strain and conflict during their transition to adulthood, particularly in relationships with parents (Cashmore & Paxman, 2007; Dixon et al., 2006), but also with siblings (Parker, 2010), romantic partners (Cashmore & Paxman, 2007), and peers (Mendes & Meade, 2010; Munson et al., 2010). However, the effects of negative social interactions on these young people have rarely been explored. For instance, a study involving 345 Israeli residential and foster care leavers (Melkman, 2017) found no significant effects of negative interactions on well-being and functional outcomes, possibly because the participants were asked to report negative interactions only with individuals who provided them with support, where the likelihood of experiencing social strain was lower. More research is needed to fully understand how negative social interactions affect young people in care and after leaving care.

Examining the sources of support for young people in RCSs and after leaving care is a key focus throughout the chapters of this book. These vital support networks can arise from a range of sources, including the formal care system (such as caseworkers, RCS staff, or foster parents), nuclear and extended family, peer relationships, adult mentors, and connections from school and work. The formal child welfare system plays a pivotal role in providing crucial support to young people in care, with RCS staff often serving as the most accessible and approachable figures in their lives (Assouline & Attar-Schwartz, 2020). These staff members frequently act as surrogate or supplementary parental figures (Small & Dodge, 1988), offering a wide range of social support across multiple areas of life (Lanctôt et al., 2016; Sulimani-Aidan, 2016a, 2016b). This includes offering emotional support during times of distress (Harder et al., 2012), companionship, guidance, and valuable information (Assouline & Attar-Schwartz, 2020). They also assist with academic goals (Melkman et al., 2016a) and help to prepare young people for independent living (Melkman et al., 2016b). Given the close, long-term relationships formed with staff, these individuals often become "natural" mentors or "chosen family" (Collins et al., 2010; Greeson et al., 2015; Munson et al., 2010), continuing to provide support as young people transition out of care and into adulthood (Melkman, 2017).

When considering informal support for young people in care and aftercare, it is important to acknowledge that, despite the inherent challenges in maintaining strong parent–child bonds during their time in care (e.g., Nickerson et al., 2006), parents can still play a crucial role as primary sources of emotional, instrumental, and advocacy support for these children (Attar-Schwartz, 2019). While research on the relationship between the frequency of parent–child contact and the well-being of young people in care remains inconsistent (as reviewed by Attar-Schwartz, 2019), there is consistent evidence showing a positive link between the quality of contact and children's educational, behavioral, and psychosocial adjustment (e.g., Attar-Schwartz, 2008, 2009; Attar-Schwartz & Fridman-Teutsch, 2018; Fridman-Teutsch & Attar-Schwartz, 2019; Small et al., 2015).

It is important to recognize that child welfare research and practice often focus predominantly on mothers or treat parents as a singular unit (Attar-Schwartz, 2008, 2009; Delfabbro et al., 2002), thereby overlooking the significant role of fathers (for a comprehensive discussion, see Attar-Schwartz & Fridman-Teutsch, 2018; Harty & Ethier, 2022; McWey et al., 2010). This tendency contributes to the exclusion of fathers from the lives of children in the child welfare system, perpetuating the phenomenon of "ghost fathers" (Brown et al., 2009). Although studies that differentiate between maternal and paternal support generally show that mothers are perceived as more supportive on average (e.g., Arteaga & del Valle, 2003; Attar-Schwartz & Fridman-Teutsch, 2018; Pinchover and Attar-Schwartz, 2018), it is crucial to acknowledge that fathers can also serve as vital sources of support, especially for boys (Attar-Schwartz & Fridman-Teutsch, 2018; Davidson-Arad & Navaro-Bitton, 2015; Fridman-Teutsch & Attar-Schwartz, 2019; Vanschoonlandt et al., 2012). Therefore, facilitating positive and healthy relationships between children in RCSs and both parents is a critical yet challenging objective of residential treatment. This challenge is further complicated by the significant number of young people with care experience who seek to reconnect with their biological parents and families after leaving care (Collins et al., 2010).

It is essential to acknowledge the significance of family support providers beyond parents. Siblings often play a vital role, providing support that surpasses even that of parents (Collins et al., 2010; Ibrahim & Howe, 2011; Mc Mahon & Curtin, 2013; Melkman & Benbenishty, 2018; Pinchover & Attar-Schwartz, 2018). These enduring familial bonds are vital for young people's sense of identity and belonging, especially when parental relationships are severed due to abuse and neglect, death, substance use, mental health issues, or incarceration (Parker, 2010). Consequently, close relationships with siblings is associated with enhanced well-being among children in care (Attar-Schwartz, 2021; Davidson-Arad & Klein, 2011; Leichtentritt, 2013). However, studies investigating the impact of joint placement of siblings in RCSs are limited and yield mixed results (Katz & Hamama, 2018). Some research indicates that placing siblings together leads to fewer placement disruptions, reduced emotional and behavioral problems, and improved academic performance (Davidson-Arad & Klein, 2011; Hegar & Rosenthal, 2009; Tarren-Sweeney & Hazell, 2005). Conversely, other studies suggest that intact placements do not necessarily correlate with fewer externalizing problems (Hegar & Rosenthal, 2009) and that separation may alleviate sibling conflict, reducing both externalizing and internalizing behaviors (Linares, 2006).

In addition, grandparents can play a significant role in the lives of youth in RCSs, contributing positively to their well-being (Attar-Schwartz & Huri, 2019). Scholars highlight the importance of these key extended family members—along with aunts, uncles, cousins, and others—as natural mentors, especially during the critical transition period when young people exit the care system (Collins et al., 2010; Thompson et al., 2016). This underscores a vital message for professionals working within RCSs, as they often overlook these influential relatives, despite their enduring connections with the young people in care (Dixon et al., 2006).

Lastly, peers also play an important role in the perceived social support of youth, a phenomenon widely recognized in general contexts (Helsen et al., 2000), but even more pronounced in RCSs, where peer relationships become especially significant (see Arteaga & del Valle, 2003; Emond, 2014). Peers provide young people in care and after care unique resources, including emotional support, reinforcement of self-esteem, and instrumental assistance during times of crisis, such as homelessness (Broad, 2005; Parker, 2010; Perez & Romo, 2011). Notably, RCSs offer exceptional opportunities for establishing a broad network of peers, presenting a distinct advantage over other forms of care (Emond, 2002).

It is important to bear in mind that the quality of resources available through one's network—particularly socioeconomic resources—can significantly impact both the actual and perceived levels of support received. This idea is rooted in social capital theory, which refers to the resources and opportunities individuals gain through social connections, or the advantages derived from "who they know" (Bourdieu, 1986; Portes, 1998). For many young people in RCSs, familial hardship often limits the social capital their family members can provide. Furthermore, their placement in institutions alongside peers from similarly disadvantaged backgrounds may further constrain their access to networks with greater social capital, thereby reducing opportunities for acquiring compensatory resources.

Scholars have cautioned against the formation of "closed groups" with limited connections to broader social networks (Goffman, 1961; Granovetter, 1983). While a certain level of group closure can help foster bonding social capital, the absence of "bridging" ties—connections to more diverse networks—can restrict access to valuable information and resources, potentially resulting in resource depletion (Burt, 2001). For instance, young people raised in out-of-home care who primarily form social relationships with peers from similar backgrounds may find themselves in under-resourced networks, limiting their exposure to new opportunities and diverse forms of social capital.

Thus, a key objective is to foster group cohesion and bonding ties within the immediate community while also facilitating the development of bridging ties with individuals from different social contexts (Snow & Mann-Feder, 2013). Involvement in extracurricular activities or interest-based groups outside the residential setting—such as sports teams, art groups, or participation in national service and higher education institutions after leaving care—can help achieve this balance. Researchers consistently highlight the importance of continued education for care-experienced young people, as a means of providing them with supportive environments that promote socialization, personal growth, and access to diverse opportunities after leaving care (Kirk & Day, 2011; Salazar et al., 2011).

Research on social support among older adolescents in care and young adults has often focused on the size of care-experienced young people's networks or the quality of support they receive (Hiles et al., 2013). For example, research has shown that youth with more connections to institutional agents were more likely to enroll in college after leaving care (Okpych & Courtney, 2017), and those youth with at least one enduring relation (i.e., a relationship that persisted from age 17 while in care to age 21 after leaving care) were less likely to experience hardship outcomes such as homelessness in early adulthood (Okpych et al., 2023).

Nevertheless, several studies have highlighted that, despite having considerable resources available, many young people in and after care do not fully or effectively utilize these supports (Hines et al., 2005; Samuels & Pryce, 2008). In line with attachment theory (Mikulincer & Shaver, 2009), early experiences of disappointing or hurtful relationships often lead to the development of "survivalist self-reliance"—a coping mechanism that helps them navigate relational trauma and protect themselves from future loss and disappointment (Samuels & Pryce, 2008). While this self-reliance may have been protective in the past or in specific situations, it can also hinder care-experienced young people from fully engaging with or utilizing the resources available within their support networks. The extent and effectiveness with which individuals utilize their support networks has been a central focus of previous research examining the role of social ties in employment outcomes. Early studies suggested that individuals from disadvantaged backgrounds experience poorer economic and social outcomes due to their reliance on smaller, resource-scarce networks (Wilson, 1987). However, more recent studies challenge this view, arguing that these outcomes are not solely the result of smaller networks but rather stem from a diminished capacity to effectively mobilize existing ties. For example, during job-seeking, individuals from lower socioeconomic classes tend to activate a smaller portion of their networks, primarily relying on a close circle of friends and family who possess limited employment-related resources. In contrast, individuals from higher socioeconomic classes activate larger, more diverse parts of their network, giving them access to a broader range of resources and opportunities (Smith et al., 2012).

In line with these ideas, a study involving 345 care leavers in Israel, primarily from residential settings, revealed significant discrepancies between the reported potential size of their networks and the actual number of individuals they were likely to turn to in times of need. This gap effectively narrowed their mobilized support network (Melkman & Benbenishty, 2018). Other research has similarly highlighted the challenges faced by residential care leavers in seeking help and fully utilizing their supportive connections (Refaeli, 2017). Evidence indicates that youth in congregate care are less likely than their peers in kinship and non-kinship foster homes, as well as other placements, to have adequate emotional support. Additionally, youth in congregate care are less likely to nominate a peer they can turn to for support compared to those in kinship and non-kinship foster homes and therapeutic foster care (Okpych et al., 2018). On a practical level, scholars highlight that the ability to effectively mobilize support resources is often cultivated within the home environment during childhood. Stauber and Walther (2005) emphasize the importance of helping young people how to recognize and harness the potential of their social networks to mobilize these resources effectively. Additionally, trauma-informed approaches can be particularly beneficial in helping youth rebuild their trust in others and foster their willingness to seek support when needed (Okpych & Courtney, 2018).

Social Networks and Social Support of Care-Experienced Young People Over Time

In line with the life course theory, particularly the concept of "linked lives," it is essential to consider how social networks evolve over time and how relationships with family, friends, and other key individuals are interdependent throughout the life course (Elder, 1994). While new relationships can "shape" lives and create "turning points" that lead to behavioral changes (Elder et al., 2003, p.13), experiences of relational loss and network disruption—common among young people in care—can have detrimental impacts on their well-being. This is particularly true during the transition to adulthood, which often coincides with leaving care. During this emerging adulthood phase, which is characterized by significant life changes, personal relationship networks undergo significant shifts in size, composition, and quality (Bidart & Lavenu, 2005). These changes reflect the individual's unique trajectory during this formative phase—whether entering the job market, pursuing education, or traveling abroad—as well as their personal history.

While familial relationships tend to remain stable for most young people at this stage, relationships with peers often show much greater variability. These connections become more central during young adulthood but are more vulnerable to life transitions, such as changes in residence, military enlistment, or discharge, which make them more transient (Bidart & Lavenu, 2005). For instance, young people from middle- to high-socioeconomic backgrounds frequently transition to university after high school, where their social lives revolve around large groups of both new acquaintances from studies and old-school friends. The frequent interactions and activities in these environments help expand their social networks. In contrast, those who enter the job market immediately after high school—more common among individuals from lower socioeconomic backgrounds—often experience a contraction of their social circles. This is due to the loss of school friendships and the generally more limited and less established nature of work-related relationships (Degenne & Lebeaux, 2005). Moreover, navigating challenges, such as economic hardship, unemployment, or the illness of a loved one, particularly when combined with personal tendencies toward distrust or withdrawal—common in distressed populations—can further reduce the already limited social networks of these young people during this critical period (Bidart & Lavenu, 2005).

Young people from out-of-home care settings are particularly vulnerable to these challenges. For them, the sudden transition to adulthood, combined with a long-term history in alternative care, often limits the development of a stable support network that adequately meets their needs (Rosenfeld et al., 1997). They frequently experience repeated disruptions in their social connections, beginning with their initial separation from their biological family, neighborhood school, and childhood friends. They may then move between temporary or unsuccessful placements, as well as between different social workers, counselors, or foster parents. Such instability increases the likelihood of weak social networks (Collins, 2004; Perry, 2006), disconnection from formal services (Keller et al., 2007; McCoy et al., 2008), and a range of social, behavioral, and mental health challenges (James et al., 2004; Samuels & Pryce, 2008). Moreover, leaving out-of-home care typically leads to the cessation of many welfare services and the loss of relationships with professionals and caregivers (Courtney et al., 2001; McMillen & Raghavan, 2009). As a result, many young people exit care without the multidimensional, long-term support typically provided by stable networks of biological family and childhood friends (Avery & Freundlich, 2009; Samuels, 2009).

Recent research on youth in care and care leavers has explored the mediating role of social support in the relationship between adverse childhood experiences and later well-being and functioning. The findings indicate that experiences of maltreatment, familial adversity (e.g., parental incarceration), and frequent placement changes are linked to smaller, less-supportive social networks. These weakened networks, in turn, contribute to higher levels of psychological distress, loneliness, and reduced economic sufficiency and adjustment (Melkman, 2017; Melkman & Benbenishty, 2018; Salazar et al., 2011).

Enhancing Well-Being in Residential Care: Exploring Theoretical Perspectives on Social Support

Children in care face an elevated risk of encountering various psychosocial and educational challenges (e.g., Attar-Schwartz, 2008, 2009; Jackson &

Cameron, 2014; Shalem & Attar-Schwartz, 2022). Identifying protective factors for this population is essential to help mitigate the emergence of detrimental emotional, behavioral, and physical health outcomes (Gabrielli et al., 2023). Moreover, the transition to independence for these young people occurs amidst significant strain and adversity, often marked by separation, instability, loss, and vulnerability, leading to poor outcomes across various domains of adult life, including education, employment, and mental health (Taylor et al., 2024). As emphasized in prior literature and several chapters of this book (e.g., Attar-Schwartz et al.; Frimpong-Manso; Magalhães et al.; Sulimanin-Aidan), both formal and informal support systems play a crucial role in the lives of children and youth residing in care facilities and transitioning out of care. Social support emerges as a significant protective factor, closely associated with the well-being, emotional stability, behavioral patterns, and educational achievements of these individuals. In this section, we aim to elucidate the primary theoretical perspectives pertinent to comprehending the contribution of social support on the outcomes of young people in RCSs and during their transition out of care.

The theory of social interdependence offers valuable insights into the support mechanisms for young people in care and during their transition out of care (Allen, 2023). According to this theory, the outcomes and experiences of young people are shaped by reciprocal relationships among various factors (Allen, 2023). For example, in the context of care leavers, these relationships involve the dynamic between the young person, their caregiver, the broader social network, and the care system. Social interdependence serves as a foundational framework for numerous child welfare theories, including those related to social ecology, social capital, resilience, and life course perspectives (Storø, 2018). Johnson and Johnson (2005) suggest that social interdependence can be either positive or negative. For example, positive interdependence occurs when all parties—care leavers, caregivers, and the wider social network—collaborate to achieve common goals. Conversely, negative interdependence arises when these parties fail to collaborate or intentionally hinder each other's objectives. Interdependence means that both the youth's actions and those of others facilitate the youth's goal achievement. This contrasts with independence, where the youth achieve their goal alone, dependence, where another person facilitates the youth's achievement, and helplessness, where neither the youth not others support the youth's goals (aligned with theoretical assumptions from Johnson & Johnson, 2005). It is through partnership and mutual support that a positive transition experience can be facilitated (Allen, 2023).

In line with this recognition of the importance of environment and context to human development, Bronfenbrenner's social ecological theory (Bronfenbrenner, 1979) suggests that young people derive crucial developmental input and shape their identities through various microsystem-level sources of support, including family, peers, school, and in the context of our discussion, RCS staff (Assouline & Attar-Schwartz, 2020). In instances where one source of support may be lacking or weak, alternative sources have the potential to compensate, thereby enhancing young people's adaptability in the face of adverse circumstances (Bronfenbrenner, 1979; Gabrielli et al., 2023).

In addition, the social convoy model (Manalel & Antonucci, 2022) suggests that as individuals undergo a shift in their personal characteristics and encounter changes in their social environments, their social networks adapt to meet their evolving needs. According to this model, the influence of social relationships on health varies significantly, depending on the specific context, with some situations being more or less stressful (Manalel & Antonucci, 2022). Given that young people in care often experience a partial or complete loss of normative social support, particularly from biological parents, alternative sources of perceived social support may help mitigate this deficit, serving as protective factors (Gabrielli et al., 2023). As mentioned earlier, supportive siblings (Attar-Schwartz, 2021), extended family members such as grandparents (Attar-Schwartz & Huri, 2019), RCS youth workers (e.g., Assouline & Attar-Schwartz, 2020), and peers within care settings (Price & Brew, 1998; Pinchover & Attar-Schwartz, 2018) emerge as significant sources of support among children and youth in residential care.

However, it is essential to emphasize the lasting importance of parents as key attachment figures for children in care. Research grounded in attachment theory (Bowlby, 1969) consistently demonstrates that these children view their primary caregivers, who are oftentimes a child's biological parents, as their primary sources of support (Pinchover & Attar-Schwartz, 2018). Despite the availability of alternative sources of support, parents continue to play a critical role in meeting fundamental emotional needs and fostering a sense of security and belonging. Even in cases of maladaptive parenting, children tend to develop attachments with their abusive caregivers, albeit with varying degrees of quality (Baker et al., 2016; Bowlby, 1969). Within this theoretical framework, studies have revealed positive associations between the quality of contact between children in care and their parents and the children's emotional-behavioral functioning (Attar-Schwartz & Fridman-Teutsch, 2018; Moyers et al., 2006; Shalem & Attar-Schwartz, 2022). Research into the ability of children in RCSs to rehabilitate and form secure attachments with caregivers has uncovered challenges in forming such bonds, both within care environments and later in adulthood (Vorria et al., 2003; Zeanah et al., 2005). However, research indicates variability among children and RCSs in the ability to establish secure relationships with at least one staff member. Such attachments are associated with better well-being outcomes among children in RCSs (Shalem & Attar-Schwartz, 2022).

Insights drawn from attachment theory also shed light on the unique challenges faced by children in care as they transition to adulthood. Research grounded in attachment theory highlights the difficulties many care leavers experience in accepting help or forming close relationships, while others adopt extreme independence, keeping important people at a distance (Kools & Kools, 1999). This research suggests that the negative life events children experience in out-of-home care not only affect the size and quality of the support networks available to care leavers but also their ability to recognize, seek out, and appreciate the support these networks offer (Melkman, 2017; Samuels & Pryce, 2008; Stein, 2006b). Samuels and Pryce (2008), who interviewed 44 former foster youth from the Midwest Study in the United States, describe how these flawed interpersonal patterns become an integral part of their identity, creating "survivalist self-reliance," as mentioned earlier in this chapter. This process, shaped by multiple losses, traumas, and the absence of parental figures in their daily lives, leads many young people to give up expecting external help, reject any sign of dependence on others, and derive a strong sense of pride from their self-sufficiency. Conversely, several studies examining distinct profiles of care leavers found that resilient profiles and positive outcomes are often associated with early positive experiences within the biological family and later in care, greater placement stability, and a strong attachment to at least one adult (Keller et al., 2007; Sinclair et al., 2005; Stein, 2006a). These findings align with self-determination theory (Deci & Ryan, 2012), which emphasizes the crucial role of the environment in meeting basic human needs. Specifically, the basic psychological needs theory, a component of self-determination theory, identifies autonomy, relatedness, and competence as key psychological needs that mediate the relationship between environmental support and positive outcomes for young people (Deci & Ryan, 2012).

The positive relationship between social support for children in RCSs, both during their stay and after leaving care, and their well-being can be understood through the lens of social capital theories mentioned above. Both formal and informal figures within these young people's central microsystems act as forms of social capital (Rose et al., 2013), promoting their well-being and contributing to positive outcomes, including educational achievement (Fridman-Teutsch & Attar-Schwartz, 2019), as well as emotional and behavioral functioning (Attar-Schwartz & Huri, 2019; Attar-Schwartz, 2021). This aligns with Hirschi's (1969) social bond theory, which suggests that support from significant individuals motivates adolescents to invest more time and effort in their personal development, such as committing to academic success (Fridman-Teutsch & Attar-Schwartz, 2019).

Research indicates that the impact of social support on young people, both generally and within residential care, is more significant when they face heightened levels of stress. In such situations, perceived social support likely moderates the relationship between adverse life experiences—such as parental maltreatment or negative encounters within care—and emotional and behavioral adjustment (Gabrielli et al., 2023). An illustrative example of these findings is discussed in Chapter 4 by Attar-Schwartz and colleagues, who explore the moderating effect of peer victimization on the relationship between paternal support and emotional and behavioral adjustment difficulties among children in RCSs. These findings align with the stress-buffering hypothesis, which posits that social support plays a key role in helping individuals cope with adversity. According to this hypothesis, the positive influence of social support intensifies with increasing stress: the more adverse experiences one endures, the stronger the impact of social support on positive adjustment. Thus, social support is believed to be most effective in improving well-being under conditions of high stress (Anderson, 2004; Cohen & Hoberman, 1983; Cohen & Wills, 1985).

Beyond the stress-buffering hypothesis, two other models have been explored in the literature: the mediating effect model and the main effect model (Beeble et al., 2009; Cohen & Wills, 1985; Lepore et al., 1991). The main effect model suggests that supportive relationships enhance well-being and health independently of stress, suggesting that social support has a consistently positive impact. Several studies conducted among care-experienced young people have provided ample evidence for such compensating effects of social support (Cashmore & Paxman, 2007; Dinisman et al., 2013). For example, Singstad and her colleagues (Singstad et al., 2021) report the important compensating contribution of perceived social support to the quality of life of 400 adolescents residing in 86 residential institutions in Norway. In contrast, the mediating effect model highlights that prolonged exposure to stress can result in poorer mental health outcomes, especially when social support becomes inadequate or is perceived as threatening (Cohen & Wills, 1985; Lepore et al., 1991). Lending support to social support's mediating role, Melkman (2017) demonstrated that adverse childhood experiences in the lives of Israeli residential and foster care leavers considerably limited both the actual support at their disposal as well as impairing their subjective perception that existing support adequately addressed their needs and that these deficits in social support, in turn, explained the young peoples' psychological well-being.

Implications for Practice and Policy

Building on insights discussed in this chapter, it is evident that RCSs must provide high-quality interventions that foster supportive, meaningful, and nurturing relationships for young people in residential care. These relationships should be cultivated both within the RCSs—among peers and staff—and beyond it, extending to connections outside the RCSs. These interventions, both during and after care, should prioritize strengthening existing support networks—such as connections with parents and other family members—while also establishing new support resources, such as mentors outside the placement setting.

Additionally, efforts should be made to enhance young people's social skills, enabling them to develop, maintain, and benefit from these networks. Trauma-informed approaches are essential to address the attachment issues and the complex emotional needs of these young people as deep-seated and unresolved trauma significantly affects their capacity to trust, seek support, and form close relationships (Okpych & Courtney, 2018). It is crucial to identify groups at higher risk of having weaker social networks or insufficient support. Targeted efforts should therefore prioritize assessing and promoting diverse support networks tailored to the unique needs of different groups of young people in residential care and after care. This calls for significant changes in the training of RCS staff to better prepare them for these goals. Staff should be reliable and deeply attuned to both the current and past experiences of young people in care, fostering trusting relationships where youth feel genuinely supported and understood (Hiles et al., 2013).

As an initial step in strengthening social support networks for young people in RCSs and preparing for aftercare, it is essential to map out their existing support systems. This process involves identifying individuals who already provide meaningful support, recognizing positive relationships with the potential for further growth, such as with trusted adult figures, and pinpointing connections that may place a burden on the young person, such as strained relationships or situations where they feel responsible for supporting others (e.g., a parent with mental illness). In recent years, several practical tools have been developed to assist in mapping the care leavers' social networks and evaluating the support they provide, many of which can be easily integrated into social work practice (e.g., Blakeslee, 2015; Courtney et al., 2014). Actively involving young people in this mapping process is vital, particularly when determining the role of extended family members (Hiles et al., 2013). This approach can significantly enhance interventions aimed at strengthening relationships during their time in care and preparing them for their transition out of care, forming a key component of the individual's transition plan.

Globally, various models and programs have been developed to strengthen the social support networks of young people in care and during their transition to independent living. In this international collection, several authors highlight key strategies for achieving positive outcomes in RCSs. For instance, Wendt and Dell'Aglio describe the "Cuida" Program in Brazil, which equips RCS staff with essential skills through a positive parenting framework. They argue that training staff is one of the most effective ways to cultivate positive and protective relationships with children. A proactive approach to providing support—offering help before young people have to ask, without being overbearing—is essential for helping them transition successfully from care, rather than waiting passively for them to seek assistance (Hiles et al., 2013). Similarly, Knorth and colleagues discuss the importance of fostering a positive social climate within residential settings, suggesting that environments that prioritize support and self-determination, while balancing autonomy and relatedness, are more beneficial than those focused on strictness and control.

Other programs and models described in the literature aim to enhance the social support available to young people in RCSs and aftercare, tailored to their unique needs and life circumstances. One such example is the CARE Model, an internationally recognized, evidence-based approach that is trauma-informed and relationship-centered, designed to strengthen staff's relational skills (Holden & Sellers, 2019). The model focuses on improving the well-being and development of young people in residential settings through secure and supportive daily interactions with staff (Holden et al., 2015; Holden & Sellers, 2019). It acknowledges that both the children, who have often experienced trauma, and the staff, who may experience secondary traumatic stress, can benefit from a trauma-informed care approach (Holden et al., 2015; Salloum et al., 2018). The CARE Model is implemented by supporting RCS leaders to fully integrate its key principles—developmentally focused, family involvement, competency-centered, relationship-based, trauma-informed, and ecologically oriented—and to serve as facilitators of these principles within the organization (Holden et al., 2015). Staff members receive specialized training in these principles, enhancing their ability to build meaningful, supportive relationships with young people (Holden & Sellers, 2019). This comprehensive intervention not only enhances caregivers' relational skills but also leads to positive outcomes for the youth, including better emotional and behavioral functioning (Holden et al., 2015; Holden & Sellers, 2019). Nevertheless, it is crucial to retain skilled staff and reduce high work-related demands and turnover, as these factors can disrupt the close, trusting relationships between youth and staff. Such disruptions risk re-traumatizing the youth by undermining the stability and security that are essential for their emotional well-being.

Fostering enduring relationships for children in RCSs is essential for ensuring the stability they need once formal support from these settings ends (Family Rights Group, 2018). One initiative, Lifelong Links, employs trained professionals who work with children in care to identify supportive adults who can become part of their support network (Holmes et al., 2020). By nurturing these lasting relationships, young people can benefit not only in terms of improved mental health but also in fostering a stronger sense of identity and belonging (Family Rights Group, 2018; Holmes et al., 2020).

Current literature emphasizes that the transition of young people from care to adulthood should be approached from relational and interdependence perspectives, focusing more on fostering interdependence than solely preparing youth for independence (Antle et al., 2009). This represents a significant shift in the underlying philosophy that informs both policy and practice. A key example of this approach is the "Staying Close" program in England (Allen, 2023; Narey, 2016). This initiative extends both practical and emotional support from residential caregivers to young individuals as they transition out of care while providing "move-on" accommodation for these young people. By applying the theory of social interdependence as a framework for analysis, the Staying Close program has received positive evaluations and was subsequently expanded by the British government (Allen, 2023).

Accumulating evidence regarding the transition from care indicates that care leavers most significantly require assistance in practical support, guidance, and access to information resources (Hiles et al., 2013). While same-age peers often struggle to provide this level of support, adult figures are identified as the primary source of satisfaction in these areas. Care leavers face substantial needs related to financial matters, housing, employment opportunities, education, and everyday issues such as when to seek medical care. The limited presence of adult figures, particularly parents, in the lives of care-experienced young people limits their access to the unique forms of tangible support and guidance that peers or siblings may not readily provide. This underscores the critical importance of mentors in their lives. Recognizing this need has led to the implementation of various mentoring programs for young people in out-of-home care settings (Sulimani-Aidan, 2018). Research evaluating these mentoring programs suggests that due to the negative interpersonal experiences frequently encountered by many care-experienced young people, they may be hesitant to engage with formal mentors. This reluctance underscores the critical importance of "natural" mentors—trusted individuals from their existing social networks—who can provide more organic and meaningful support tailored to their needs (Sulimani-Aidan et al., 2020).

In sum, there is a clear need to apply trauma-informed, relational, and interdependence perspectives in supporting young people in RCSs and throughout their transition to adulthood. This calls for a shift away from focusing solely on preparing youth for independent living, toward fostering interdependence by tailoring programs that help young people establish lasting, healthy relationships with both existing and new individuals in their lives. These connections should extend beyond their time in the care system, promoting a long-term network of support.

References

Akiyama, H., Antonucci, T., Takahashi, K., & Langfahl, E. S. (2003). Negative interactions in close relationships across the lifespan. *Journals of Gerontology: Psychological Sciences*, *58B*, 70–79. https://doi.org10.1093/geronb/58.2.p70

Allen, D. (2023). 'Staying close': Enabling social interdependence for young people leaving residential care in England. *Children & Society*, 1–17. https://doi.org/10.1111/chso.12769

Anderson, N. B. (2004). Stress-buffering hypothesis. In *The encyclopedia of health & behavior* (Vol. 2, pp. 780–783). London, United Kingdom: SAGE Publications. https://doi.org/10.4135/9781412952576

Antle, B. F., Johnson, L., Barbee, A., & Sullivan, D. (2009). Fostering interdependent versus independent living in youth aging out of care through healthy relationships. *Families in Society*, *90*(3), 309–315. https://doi.org/10.1606/1044-3894.3890

Arteaga, A. B., & del Valle, J. F. (2003). Social support networks of adolescents in residential child care. A comparative analysis with normative population. *Psicothema*, *15*(1), 136–142.

Assouline, A. A. H., & Attar-Schwartz, S. (2020). Staff support and adolescent adjustment difficulties: The moderating role of length of stay in the residential care setting. *Children and Youth Services Review*, *110*, 104761. https://doi.org/10.1016/j.childyouth.2020.104761

Attar-Schwartz, S. (2008). Emotional, behavioral and social problems among Israeli children in residential care: A multi-level analysis. *Children and Youth Services Review*, *30*(2), 229–248. https://doi.org/10.1016/j.childyouth.2007.09.009

Attar-Schwartz, S. (2009). School functioning of children in residential care: The contributions of multilevel correlates. *Child Abuse & Neglect*, *33*(7), 429–440. https://doi.org/10.1016/j.chiabu.2008.12.010

Attar-Schwartz, S. (2019). Parental availability of support and frequency of contact: The reports of youth in educational residential care. *Children and Youth Services Review*, *101*, 317–328. https://doi.org/10.1016/j.childyouth.2019.04.016

Attar-Schwartz, S. (2021). Sibling Support: The Reports of Israeli Adolescents in Residential Care. In A. Buchanan, & A. Rotkirch (Eds.), *Brothers and sisters: Global perspectives on the longest enduring relationship* (pp. 141–152). London: Palgrave Macmillan, Cham. https://doi.org/10.1007/978-3-030-55985-4_8

Attar-Schwartz, S., & Fridman-Teutsch, A. (2018). Father support and adjustment difficulties among youth in residential care: The moderating role of peer victimization and gender. *American Journal of Orthopsychiatry*, *88*(6), 701–712. https://doi.org10.1037/ort0000287

Attar-Schwartz, S., & Huri, Y. (2019). Grandparental support and life satisfaction among adolescents in residential care. *Children and Youth Services Review*, *96*, 70–78. https://doi.org/10.1016/j.childyouth.2018.11.033

Avery, R. J., & Freundlich, M. (2009). You're all grown up now: Termination of foster care support at age 18. *Journal of Adolescence*, *32*(2), 247–257. https://doi.org/10.1016/j.adolescence.2008.03.009

Baker, A. J., Creegan, A., Quinones, A., & Rozelle, L. (2016). Foster children's views of their birth parents: A review of the literature. *Children and Youth Services Review*, *67*, 177–183. https://doi.org/10.1016/j.childyouth.2016.06.004

Barrera, M. (1986). Distinctions between social support concepts, measures, and models. *American Journal of Community Psychology*, *14*(4), 413–445. https://doi.org/10.1007/BF00922627

Beeble, M. L., Bybee, D., Sullivan, C. M., & Adams, A. E. (2009). Main, mediating, and moderating effects of social support on the well-being of survivors of intimate partner violence across 2 years. *Journal of Consulting and Clinical Psychology*, *77*(4), 718–729. https://doi.org/10.1037/a0016140

Bidart, C., & Lavenu, D. (2005). Evolutions of personal networks and life events. *Social Networks*, *27*(4), 359–376. https://doi.org10.1016/j.socnet.2004.11.003

Blakeslee, J. (2015). Measuring the support networks of transition-age foster youth: Preliminary validation of a social network assessment for research and practice. *Children and Youth Services Review*, *52*, 123–134. https://doi.org10.1016/j.childyouth.2015.03.014

Bolger, N., & Amarel, D. (2007). Effects of social support visibility on adjustment to stress: Experimental evidence. *Journal of Personality and Social Psychology*, *92*(3), 458. https://doi.org10.1037/0022-3514.92.3.458

Bourdieu, P. (1986). The forms of capital. *Handbook of theory and research for the sociology of education* (pp. 241–258). https://doi.org10.1002/9780470755679.ch15

Bowlby, J. (1969). *Attachment and loss: Vol. 1. Attachment*. New York: Basic Book

Brennan, M. A. (2008). Conceptualizing resiliency: An interactional perspective for community and youth development. *Child Care in Practice*, *14*(1), 55–64. https://doi.org/10.1080/13575270701733732

Broad, B. (2005). *Improving the health and well-being of young people leaving care*. Lyme Regis: Russell House Publishing.

Bronfenbrenner, U. (1979). Contexts of child rearing: Problems and prospects. *American Psychologist*, *34*(10), 844–850. https://doi.org/10.1037/0003-066X.34.10.844

Brown, L., Callahan, M., Strega, S., Walmsley, C., & Dominelli, L. (2009). Manufacturing ghost fathers: The paradox of father presence and absence in child welfare. *Child & Family Social Work*, *14*(1), 25–34. https://doi.org/10.1111/j.1365-2206.2008.00578.x

Burt, R. S. (2001). Structural holes versus network closure as social capital. In N. Lin, R. Burt, & C. Cook (Eds.), *Social capital: Theory and research* (pp. 31–56). Hawthorne, New York: Transaction Publishers.
Cashmore, J., & Paxman, M. (2007). *Longitudinal study of wards leaving care: Four to five years on*. Sydney, Australia: Social Policy Research Centre, University of New South Wales.
Cohen, S., & Hoberman, H. M. (1983). Positive events and social supports as buffers of life change stress. *Journal of Applied Social Psychology*, *13*, 99–125. https://doi.org/10.1111/j.1559-1816.1983.tb02325.x
Cohen, S., & Wills, T. A. (1985). Stress, social support, and the buffering hypothesis. *Psychological Bulletin*, *98*, 310–357. https://doi.org/10 .1037/0033-2909.98.2.310
Collins, M. (2004). Enhancing services to youths leaving foster care: Analysis of recent legislation and its potential impact. *Children and Youth Services Review*, *26*(11), 1051–1065. https://doi.org/10.1016/j.childyouth.2004.08.005
Collins, M. E., Spencer, R. & Ward, R. (2010). Supporting youth in the transition from foster care: Formal and informal connections. *Child Welfare*, *89*(1), 125–143. https://doi.org10.1353/csd.2004.0017
Courtney, M. E., Charles, P., Okpych, N. J., Napolitano, L., & Halsted, K. (2014). *Findings from the California Youth Transitions to Adulthood Study (CalYOUTH): Conditions of foster youth at age 17*. Chicago, IL: Chapin Hall at the University of Chicago.
Courtney, M. E., Piliavin, I., Grogan-Kaylor, A., & Nesmith, A. (2001). Foster youth transitions to adulthood: A longitudinal view of youth leaving care. *Child Welfare*, *80*(6), 685–717. http://www.jstor.org/stable/45400302
Davidson-Arad, B. & Klein, A. (2011). Comparative wellbeing of Israeli youngsters in residential care with and without siblings. *Children and Youth Services Review*, *33*, 215–219. https://doi.org/10.1016/j.childyouth.2011.06.022
Davidson-Arad, B. & Navaro-Bitton, I. (2015). Resilience among adolescents in foster care. *Children and Youth Services Review*, *59*, 63–70. https://doi.org/10.1016/j.childyouth.2015.09.023
Deci, E. L., & Ryan, R. M. (2012). Self-determination theory. In P. Lange, A. Kruglanski, & E. Higgins (Eds.), *Handbook of theories of social psychology* (pp. 416–436). London: Sage.
Degenne, A., & Lebeaux, M. O. (2005). The dynamics of personal networks at the time of entry into adult life. *Social Networks*, *27*(4), 337–358. https://doi.org/10.1016/j.socnet.2004.11.002
Delfabbro, P. H., Barber, J. G. & Cooper, L. (2002). The role of parental contact in substitute care. *Journal of Social Service Research*, *28*(3), 19–39. https://doi.org/10.1300/J079v28n03_02
Dinisman, T., Zeira, A., Sulimani-Aidan, Y., & Benbenishty, R. (2013). The subjective well-being of young people aging out of care. *Children and Youth Services Review*, *35*(10). 1705–1711. https://doi.org/10.1016/j.childyouth.2013.07.011
Dixon, J., Wade, J., Byford, S., Weatherly, H., & Lee, J. (2006). *Young people leaving care: A study of costs and outcomes. Report to the DfES*. New York: SWRDU, University of York.
Elder, G. H. (1994). Time, human agency, and social change: Perspectives on the life course. *Social Psychology Quarterly*, *57*(1), 4–15. https://doi.org/10.2307/2786971
Elder, G. H., Johnson, M. K., & Crosnoe, R. (2003). The emergence and development of the life course theory. In J. T. Mortimer, & M. J. Shanahan (Eds.), *Handbook of the life course* (pp. 3–19). New York: Springer.
Emond, R. (2002). Understanding the resident group. *Scottish Journal of Residential Child Care*, *1*, 30–40.

Emond, R. (2014). Longing to belong: Children in residential care and their experiences of peer relationships at school and in the children's home. *Child and Family Social Work*, *19*(2), 194–202. https://doi.org/10.1111/j.1365-2206.2012.00893.x
Evans, R., Katz, C. C., Fulginiti, A., & Taussig, H. (2022). Sources and types of social supports and their association with mental health symptoms and life satisfaction among young adults with a history of out-of-home care. *Children*, *9*, 520. https://doi.org/10.3390/children9040520
Family Rights Group (2018). *Lifelong links toolkit*. London: Department for Education.
Finch, J. F., Okun, M. A., Pool, G. J., & Ruehlman, L. S. (1999). A comparison of the influence of conflictual and supportive social interactions on psychological distress. *Journal of Personality*, *67*(4), 581–621. https://doi.org/10.1111/1467-6494.00066
Fingerman, K. L., Hays, E. L., & Birditt, K. S. (2004). The best of ties, the worst of ties: Close, problematic, and ambivalent social relationships. *Journal of Marriage and the Family*, *66*, 792–808. https://doi.org/10.1111/j.0022-2445.2004.00053.x
Fridman-Teutsch, A., & Attar-Schwartz, S. (2019). Commitment to school and learning among youth in residential care: The role of mother and father support and parents' divorce. *American Journal of Orthopsychiatry*, *89*(2), 201–2011. https://doi.org10.1037/ort0000364
Gabrielli, J., Runno, A., Chiu, H. Y., Bennett, A., Kanine, R., & Jackson, R. (2023). Perceived social support: Measurement differences in youth residing in the community versus youth residing in foster care. *Child Abuse & Neglect*, *137*, 1–12. https://doi.org/10.1016/j.chiabu.2023.106040
Goffman, E. (1961). *Asylums: Essays on the social situation of mental patients and other inmates*. New York: Doubleday
Granovetter, M. (1983). The strength of weak ties: A network theory revisited. *Sociological Theory*, *1*(1), 201–233. https://doi.org/10.2307/202051
Greeson, J. K. P., Garcia, A. R., Kim, M., Thompson, A. E., & Courtney, M. E. (2015). Development and maintenance of social support among aged out foster youth who received independent living services: Results from the Multi-Site Evaluation of Foster Youth Programs. *Children and Youth Services Review*, *53*, 1–9. https://doi.org/10.1016/j.childyouth.2015.03.016
Harder, A. T., Knorth, E. J., & Kalverboer, M. E. (2012). A secure base? The adolescent–staff relationship in secure residential youth care. *Child & Family Social Work*, *18*(3), 305–317. https://doi.org/10.1111/j.1365-2206.2012.00846.x
Harty, J. S., & Ethier, K. L. (2022). Fatherhood in foster care: A scoping review spanning 30 years of research on expectant and parenting fathers in state care. *Child and Adolescent Social Work Journal*, *39*(6), 693–710. https://doi.org/10.1007/s10560-022-00848-2
Hegar, R. L., & Rosenthal, J. A. (2009). Kinship care and sibling placement: Child behavior, family relationships, and school outcomes. *Children and Youth Services Review*, *31*, 670–679. https://doi.org/10.1016/j.childyouth.2009.01.002
Helsen, M., Vollebergh, W. & Meeus, W. (2000). Social support from parents and friends and emotional problems in adolescence. *Journal of Youth and Adolescence*, *29*(3), 319–335. https://doi.org/10.1023/A:1005147708827
Hiles, D., Moss, D., Wright, J., & Dallos, R. (2013). Young people's experience of social support during the process of leaving care: A review of the literature. *Children & Youth Services Review*, *35*(12), 2059–2071. https://doi.org/10.1016/j.childyouth.2013.10.008
Hines, A. M., Merdinger, J., & Wyatt, P. (2005). Former foster youth attending college: Resilience and the transition to young adulthood. *The American Journal of Orthopsychiatry*, *75*(3), 381–394. https://doi.org/10.1037/0002-9432.75.3.381
Hirschi, T. (1969). *Causes of delinquency*. Berkeley, CA: University of California Press.

Holden, M. J., Anglin, J. P., & Nunno, M. A. (2015). Engaging the total therapeutic residential care program in a process of quality improvement: Learning from the CARE model. In J. K. Whittaker, J. Fernandez Del Valle, & L. Holmes (Eds.), *Therapeutic residential care with children and youth: developing evidence-based international practice*. Philadelphia, PA: Jessica Kingsley

Holden, M. J., & Sellers, D. (2019). An evidence-based program model for facilitating therapeutic responses to pain-based behavior in residential care. *International Journal of Child, Youth and Family Studies*, *10*(2–3), 63–80. https://doi.org/10.18357/ijcyfs102-3201918853

Holmes, L., Neagu, M., Sanders-Ellis, D. & Harrison, N. (2020). *Lifelong links. Evaluation report*. London: Department for Education.

Ibrahim, R. W., & Howe, D. (2011). The experience of Jordanian care leavers making the transition from residential care to adulthood: The influence of a patriarchal and collectivist culture. *Children and Youth Services Review*, *33*(12), 2469–2474. https://doi.org/10.1016/j.childyouth.2011.08.019

Jackson, S., & Cameron, C. (2014). *Improving access to further and higher education for young people in public care: European policy and practice*. Jessica Kingsley Publishers.

James, S., Landsverk, J. & Slymen, D. J. (2004). Placement movement in out-of-home care: Patterns and predictors. *Children and Youth Services Review*, *26*(2), 185–206. https://doi.org/10.1023/B:MHSR.0000036487.39001.51

Johnson, D. W., & Johnson, R. T. (2005). New developments in social interdependence theory. *Genetic, Social, and General Psychology Monographs*, *131*(4), 285–358.

Katz, C., & Hamama, L. (2018). The sibling relationship in the context of child maltreatment: What do we know? What are the directions for the future?. *Trauma, Violence, & Abuse*, *19*(3), 343–351. https://doi.org10.1177/1524838016659878

Kaul, M., & Lakey, B. (2003). Where is the support in perceived support? The role of generic relationship satisfaction and enacted support in perceived support's relation to low distress. *Journal of Social and Clinical Psychology*, *22*, 59–78. https://doi.org10.1521/jscp.22.1.59.22761

Keller, T. E., Cusick, G. R., & Courtney, M. E. (2007). Approaching the transition to adulthood: Distinctive profiles of adolescents aging out of the child welfare system. *Social Service Review*, *81*(3), 453–484. https://doi.org10.1086/519536

Kirk, R., & Day, A. (2011). Increasing college access for youth aging out of foster care: Evaluation of a summer camp program for foster youth transitioning from high school to college. *Children and Youth Services Review*, *33*(7), 1173–1180. https://doi.org10.1016/j.childyouth.2011.02.018

Kools, S., & Kools, S. (1999). Self-protection in adolescents in foster care. *Journal of Child and Adolescent Psychiatric Nursing*, *12*(4), 139–152. https://doi.org/10.1111/j.1744-6171.1999.tb00063.x

Lanctôt, N., Lemieux, A., & Mathys, C. (2016). The value of a safe, connected social climate for adolescent girls in residential care. *Residential Treatment for Children & Youth*, *33*(3–4), 247–269. https://doi.org/10.1080/0886571X.2016.1207218

Leichtentritt, J. (2013). "It is difficult to be here with my sister but intolerable to be without her": Intact sibling placement in residential care. *Children and Youth Services Review*, *35*(5), 762–770. https://doi.org/10.1016/j.childyouth.2013.01.022

Lepore, S. J., Evans, G. W., & Schneider, M. L. (1991). Dynamic role of social support in the link between chronic stress and psychological distress. *Journal of Personality and Social Psychology*, *61*(6), 899–909. https://doi.org/10.1037/0022-3514.61.6.899

Linares, L. O. (2006). An understudied form of intra-family violence: Sibling-to-sibling aggression among foster children. *Aggression and Violent Behavior*, *11*, 95–109. https://doi.org/10.1016/j.avb.2005.07.001

Lou, Y., Taylor, E. P., & Di Folco, S. (2018). Resilience and resilience factors in children in residential care: A systematic review. *Children and Youth Services Review*, *89*, 83–92. https://doi.org/10.1016/j.childyouth.2018.04.010
Magalhães, E., & Calheiros, M. M. (2017). A dual-factor model of mental health and social support: Evidence with adolescents in residential care. *Children and Youth Services Review*, *79*, 442–449. https://doi.org/10.1016/j.childyouth.2017.06.041
Magalhães, E., Calheiros, M. M., Costa, P., & Ferreira, S. (2021). Youth's rights and mental health: The role of supportive relations in care. *Journal of Social and Personal Relationships*, *38*(3), 848–864. https://doi.org/10.1177/0265407520975507
Manalel, J. A., & Antonucci, T. C. (2022). Development of social convoys: Trajectories of convoy structure and composition from childhood through adulthood. *Developmental Psychology*, *58*(9), 1806–1815. https://doi.org/10.1037/dev0001390
Mc Mahon, C., & Curtin, C. (2013). The social networks of young people in Ireland with experience of long-term foster care: Some lessons for policy and practice. *Child and Family Social Work*, *18*(3), 329–340. https://doi.org/10.1111/j.1365-2206.2012.00849.x
McCoy, H., McMillen, J. C., & Spitznagel, E. L. (2008). Older youth leaving the foster care system: Who, what, when, where, and why? *Children and Youth Services Review*, *30*(7), 735–745. https://doi.org/10.1016/j.childyouth.2007.12.003
McMillen, J. & Raghavan, R. (2009). Pediatric to adult mental health service use of young people leaving the foster care system. *Journal of Adolescent Health*, *44*(1), 7–13. https://doi.org10.1016/j.jadohealth.2008.04.015
McWey, L. M., Acock, A. & Porter, B. E. (2010). The impact of continued contact with biological parents upon the mental health of children in foster care. *Children and Youth Services Review*, *32*(10), 1338–1345. https://doi.org10.1016/j.childyouth.2010.05.003
Melkman, E. (2017). Childhood adversity, social support networks and well-being among youth aging out of care: An exploratory study of mediation. *Child Abuse and Neglect*, *72*, 85–97. https://doi.org/10.1016/j.chiabu.2017.07.02
Melkman, E., Refaeli, T., & Benbenishty, R. (2016a). An empirical test of a model of academic expectations among youth in residential care. *Children and Youth Services Review*, *67*, 133–141. http://authors.elsevier.com/a/1TAw1hNfKZszo
Melkman, E., Refaeli, T., Bibi, B., & Benbenishty, R. (2016b). Readiness for independent living among youth on the verge of leaving juvenile correctional facilities. *International Journal of Offender Therapy and Comparative Criminology*, *60*(10), 1209–1225. https://doi.org/10.1177/0306624X15575117
Melkman, E. P., & Benbenishty, R. (2018). Social support networks of care leavers: Mediating between childhood adversity and adult functioning. *Children and Youth Services Review*, *86*, 176–187. https://doi.org/10.1016/j.childyouth.2018.01.040
Mendes, P., & Meade, S. (2010). *From dependence to independence: Examining the support needs and pathways of young people leaving state care in rural Victoria*. Melbourne: Department of Social Work, Monash University.
Mikulincer, M., & Shaver, P. R. (2009). An attachment and behavioral systems perspective on social support. *Journal of Social and Personal Relationships*, *26*(1), 7–19. https://doi.org10.1177/0265407509105518
Moyers, S. Farmer, E., & Lipscombe, J. (2006). Contact with family members and its impact on adolescents and their foster placements. *British Journal of Social Work*, *36*(4), 541–559. https://doi.org/10.1093/bjsw/bch270
Munson, M. R., Smalling, S. E., Spencer, R., Scott, L. D., & Tracy, E. M. (2010). A steady presence in the midst of change: Non-kin natural mentors in the lives of older youth exiting foster care. *Children and Youth Services Review*, *32*(4), 527–535. https://doi.org10.1016/j.childyouth.2009.11.005
Narey, M. (2016). *Residential care in England. Report of sir Martin Narey's independent review of children's residential care*. Crown copyright, London.

Newsom, J. T., Nishishiba, M., Morgan, D. L., & Rook, K. S. (2003). The relative importance of three domains of positive and negative social exchanges: A longitudinal model with comparable measures. *Psychology and Aging*, *18*(4), 746. https://doi.org10.1037/0882-7974.18.4.746

Newsom, J. T., Rook, K. S., Nishishiba, M., Sorkin, D. H., & Mahan, T. L. (2005). Understanding the relative importance of positive and negative social exchanges: Examining specific domains and appraisals. *The Journals of Gerontology Series B: Psychological Sciences and Social Sciences*, *60*(6), 304–312. https://doi.org10.1093/geronb/60.6.P304

Nickerson, A. B., Brooks, J. L., Colby, S. A., Rickert, J. M. & Salamone, F. J. (2006). Family involvement in residential treatment: Staff, parent, and adolescent perspectives. *Journal of Child and Family Studies*, *15*(6), 681–694. https://doi.org/10.1007/s10826-006-9041-1

Okpych, N. J., & Courtney, M. E. (2017). Who goes to college? Social capital and other predictors of college enrollment for foster-care youth. *Journal of the Society for Social Work and Research*, *8*(4), 563–593. https://doi.org/10.1086/694897

Okpych, N. J., & Courtney, M. E. (2018). The role of avoidant attachment on college persistence and completion among youth in foster care. *Children and Youth Services Review*, *90*, 106–117. https://doi.org/10.1016/j.childyouth.2018.05.014

Okpych, N. J., Feng, H., Park, K., Torres-García, A., & Courtney, M. (2018). Living situations and social support in the era of extended foster care: A view from the US. *Longitudinal and Life Course Studies*, *9*(1), 6–29. https://doi.org/10.14301/llcs.v9i1.449

Okpych, N. J., Park, S., Powers, J., Harty, J. S., & Courtney, M. E. (2023). Relationships that persist and protect: The role of enduring relationships on early-adult outcomes among youth transitioning out of foster care. *Social Service Review*, *97*(4), 619–674. https://doi.org/10.1086/724736

Parker, E. (2010). *The meaning and significance of sibling and peer relationships for young people looked after on behalf of local authorities* (Doctoral dissertation). UK: University of Warwick.

Perez, B. F., & Romo, H. D. (2011). "Couch surfing" of Latino foster care alumni: Reliance on peers as social capital. *Journal of Adolescence*, *34*(2), 239–248. https://doi.org10.1016/j.adolescence.2010.05.007

Perry, B. (2006). Understanding social network disruption: The case of youth in foster care. *Social Problems*, *53*(3), 371–391. https://doi.org10.1525/sp.2006.53.3.371

Pinchover, S., & Attar-Schwartz, S. (2018). Is someone there for you? Social support of youth in educational residential care from family, peers and staff. *The British Journal of Social Work*, *48*(8), 2195–2214. https://doi.org/10.1093/bjsw/bcx164

Pinheiro, M., Magalhães, E., & Baptista, J. (2022). Adolescents' resilience in residential care: A systematic review of factors related to healthy adaptation. *Child Indicators Research*, *15*(3), 819–837. https://doi.org/10.1007/s12187-021-09883-4

Portes, A. (1998). Social capital: Its origins and applications in modern sociology. *Annual Sociology*, *24*, 1–24.

Price, J. M., & Brew, V. (1998). Peer relationships of foster children: Developmental and mental health service Implications. *Journal of Applied Developmental Psychology*, *19*(2), 199–218. https://doi.org/10.1016/S0193-3973(99)80036-7

Refaeli, T. (2017). Narratives of care leavers: What promotes resilience in transitions to independent lives? *Children and Youth Services Review*, *79*, 1–9. https://doi.org/10.1016/j.childyouth.2017.05.023

Rose, R. A., Wooley, M. E., & Bowen, G. L. (2013). Social capital as a portfolio of resources across multiple microsystems: Implications for middle-school students. *Family Relations*, *62*, 545–558. https://doi.org/10.1111/fare.12028

Rosenfeld, A. A., Pilowsky, D. J., Fine, P., Thorpe, M., Fein, E., Simms, M. D., ... Nickman, S. (1997). Foster care: An update. *Journal of the American Academy of Child and Adolescent Psychiatry*, *36*, 448–457. https://doi.org10.1097/00004583-199704000-00006

Salazar, A. M., Keller, T. E., & Courtney, M. E. (2011). Understanding social support's role in the relationship between maltreatment and depression in youth with foster care experience. *Child Maltreatment*, *16*(2), 102–113. https://doi.org/10.1177/1077559511402985

Salloum, A., Choi, M. J., & Stover, C. S. (2018). Development of a trauma-informed self-care measure with child welfare workers. *Children and Youth Services Review*, *93*, 108–116. https://doi.org/10.1016/j.childyouth.2018.07.008

Samuels, G. M. (2009). Ambiguous loss of home: The experience of familial (im) permanence among young adults with foster care backgrounds. *Children and Youth Services Review*, *31*(12), 1229–1239. https://doi.org/10.1016/j.childyouth.2009.05.008

Samuels, G. M. & Pryce, J. M. (2008) 'What doesn't kill you makes you stronger': Survivalist self-reliance as resilience and risk among young adults aging out of foster care. *Children and Youth Services Review*, *30*(10), 1198–1210. https://doi.org10.1016/j.childyouth.2008.03.005

Shalem, N., & Attar-Schwartz, S. (2022). Good enough residential care setting: Child-parent contact and youth adjustment in the context of staff attitudes towards parent involvement. *Children and Youth Services Review*, *143*, 106687.

Silva, C., Carvalho, H., Magalhães, E., Attar-Schwartz, S., Ornelas, S. & Calheiros, M. (2022). Organizational social context and academic achievement of youth in residential care: The mediating role of youth-caregiver relationship quality. *Children and Youth Services Review*, *137*, https://doi.org/10.1016/j.childyouth.2022.106449

Sinclair, I., Baker, C., Wilson, K., & Gibbs, I. (2005). *Foster children, where they go and how they get on*. London: Jessica Kinsley.

Singstad, M. T., Wallander, J. L., Greger, H. K., Lydersen, S., & Kayed, N. S. (2021). Perceived social support and quality of life among adolescents in residential youth care: A cross-sectional study. *Health and quality of life outcomes*, *19*, 1–12. https://doi.org/10.1186/s12955-021-01676-1

Small, R. W., Bellonci, C. & Ramsey, S. (2015). Creating and maintaining family partnerships in residential treatment programs. In J. K. Whittaker, J. F. del Valle, & Holmes, L. (Eds.), *Therapeutic residential care for children and youth: Developing evidence-based international practice*. London: Jessica Kingsley.

Small, R. W., & Dodge, L. M. (1988). Roles, skills, and job tasks in professional child care: A review of the literature. *Child & Youth Care Quarterly*, *17*(1), 6–23. https://doi.org/10.1007/BF01089398

Smith, E. B., Menon, T., & Thompson, L. (2012). Status differences in the cognitive activation of social networks. *Organization Science*, *23*(1), 67–82. https://doi.org/10.1287/orsc.1100.0643

Smith, J., & Goodnow, J. J. (1999). Unasked-for support and unsolicited advice: Age and the quality of social experience. *Psychology and Aging*, *14*, 108–121.

Snow, K., & Mann-Feder, V. (2013). Peer-centered practice: A theoretical framework for intervention with young people in and from care. *Child Welfare*, *92*(4), 75.

Stauber, B., & Walther, A. (2005). De-standardized pathways to adulthood in Europe: Informal learning in informal networks. *Revista de Sociología*, *31*(1), 241–262.

Stein, M. (2006a). Research review: Young people leaving care. *Child and Family Social Work*, *11*(3), 276–279. https://doi.org/10.1111/j.1365-2206.2006.00439.x

Stein, M. (2006b). Young people aging out of care: The poverty of theory. *Children and Youth Services Review*, *28*(4), 422–434. https://doi.org/10.1016/j.childyouth.2005.05.005

Storø, J. (2018). To manage on one's own after leaving care? A discussion of the concepts: Independence versus interdependence. *Nordic Social Work Research*, *8*(1), 104–115. https://doi.org/10.1080/2156857X.2018.1463282
Sulimani-Aidan, Y. (2016a). "She was like a mother and a father to me": Searching for the ideal mentor for youth in care. *Child and Family Social Work*, *22*(2), 862–870. https://doi.org/10.1111/cfs.12306
Sulimani-Aidan, Y. (2016b). In between formal and informal: Staff and youth relationships in care and after leaving care. *Children and Youth Services Review*, *67*, 43–49. https://doi.org/10.1016/j.childyouth.2016.05.025
Sulimani-Aidan, Y. (2018). Present, protective, and promotive: Mentors' roles in the lives of young adults in residential care. *American Journal of Orthopsychiatry*, *88*(1), 69.
Sulimani-Aidan, Y., Melkman, E., & Greeson, J. K. (2020). The contribution of mentoring to the life skills of youth leaving care in Israel. *Child & Family Social Work*, *25*(2), 345–354. https://doi.org/10.1111/cfs.12690
Tardy, C. H. (1985). Social support measurement. *American Journal of Community Psychology*, *13*, 187–202. https://doi.org/10.1007/BF00905728
Tarren-Sweeney, M., & Hazell, P. (2005). The mental health and socialization of siblings in care. *Children and Youth Services Review*, *27*, 821–843. https://doi.org/10.1016/j.childyouth.2004.12.014
Taylor, D., Albers, B., Mann, G., Lewis, J., Taylor, R., Mendes, P., ... & Shlonsky, A. (2024). Systematic review and meta-analysis of policies and interventions that improve health, psychosocial, and economic outcomes for young people leaving the out-of-home care system. *Trauma, Violence, & Abuse*, 15248380241253041.
Thompson, A. E., Greeson, J. K., & Brunsink, A. M. (2016). Natural mentoring among older youth in and aging out of foster care: A systematic review. *Children and Youth Services Review*, *61*, 40–50. https://doi.org/10.1016/j.childyouth.2015.12.006
Tracy, E. M., & Whittaker, J. K. (1990). The social network map: Assessing social support in clinical practice. *Families in Society*, *71*(8), 461–470. https://doi.org/10.1177/104438949007100802
Uchino, B. N. (2004). *Social support and physical health: Understanding the health consequences of relationships*. New Haven, CT: Yale University Press.
Uchino, B. N. (2009). Understanding the links between social support and physical health: A life-span perspective with emphasis on the separability of perceived and received support. *Perspectives on Psychological Science*, *4*(3), 236–255. https://doi.org/10.1111/j.1745-6924.2009.01122.x
Vanschoonlandt, F., Vanderfaeillie, J., Van Holen, F., De Maeyer, S., & Andries, C. (2012). Mental health of foster children: Do biological fathers matter? *Child Welfare*, *91*, 149–166.
Vorria, P., Papaligoura, Z., Dunn, J., Van IJzendoorn, M. H., Steele, H., Kontopoulou, A., & Sarafidou, Y. (2003). Early experiences and attachment relationships of Greek infants raised in residential group care. *Journal of Child Psychology and Psychiatry*, *44*(8), 1208–1220. https://doi.org/10.1111/1469-7610.00202
Wills, T. A., & Shinar, O. (2000). Measuring perceived and received social support. In S. Cohen, L. Gordon, & B. Gottlieb (Eds.), *Social support measurement and intervention: A guide for health and social scientists* (pp. 86–135). New York, NY: Oxford University Press.
Wilson, W. J. (1987). *The truly disadvantaged: The inner city, the underclass, and public policy*. Chicago, Winerip: University of Chicago Press.
Zeanah, C. H., Smyke, A. T., Koga, S. F., Carlson, E., & Bucharest Early Intervention Project Core Group. (2005). Attachment in institutionalized and community children in Romania. *Child Development*, *76*(5), 1015–1028. https://doi.org/10.1111/j.1467-8624.2005.00894.x

2 Transformative Change for Children in Residential Care

Exploring the Potential of Support for Work, Recreation and Educational Opportunities from a Life Course Perspective

Robbie Gilligan

Introduction

'We were strictly supervised, we didn't have friends outside; we were always the kids from the home, the kids with problems, we never went out.' (Man, aged 34; quoted in Crous et al., 2021, p. 901). This pithy quote from a care-experienced adult in Spain is a reminder of how the world of residential care can sometimes be restrictive, isolating and stigmatizing. From this perspective, life within the residential setting may have immediate implications for the young person, in terms of identity formation (as they may face stigmatizing labels like – 'the kids from the home,' 'the kids with problems'), limitations on personal agency (due to strict supervision and routines), challenges in securing social connections and accessing social support (lack of 'friends outside'), and a sense of isolation and detachment from the world outside ('never went out'). Such negative effects may apply not only during the placement in the residential care setting but also reverberate into the future, potentially constraining later choices and perceptions across the life course. While this specific case serves as a resonant illustration of possible experiences in care settings, it is also important to recognize that generalizations cannot be drawn from a single case.

This is the recollection of one person, in one national context, from one care setting, in one time period – it does not offer us a general view that holds true across all circumstances. As we will see later in this chapter, it is also possible to present examples of positive experiences arising from life in residential care. Nevertheless, reflecting on such negative *and* positive cases helps pause for reflection both on what we mean by, and expect from, residential *care* and on the role support may play in the short term but also in ultimate outcomes in adult life. Similar to the term 'residential care,' the term 'support' is subject to varied interpretations across different professional and scholarly perspectives and contexts. In the following paragraphs, the key concepts relevant to the approach outlined in this chapter are unpacked.

DOI: 10.4324/9781003424468-4

Background

Residential Care

Countries exhibit considerable diversity in their models of residential care for children and youth, encompassing variations in the typical size of settings and numbers of young people served, as well as differences in their expectations of the role of these settings. Moreover, disparities exist in the utilization rates of such settings, resources allocated to the sector, frontline staff training levels, support provisions for children in care and care-experienced adults, the nature of care outcomes and the extent of revelations regarding abuse in residential settings, among other factors (see Whittaker et al., 2023). This variation is linked to the interplay of diverse economic, ideological and cultural influences (Courtney et al., 2009). Residential care continues to be a topic of extensive debate internationally. The field comprises an exceptionally wide range of models worldwide. This breadth of variation poses numerous challenges, leading to and stemming from significant disparities in resourcing, quality and child-centredness of care provision. While adopting the single term of residential care has certain advantages, it often masks critical differences in the approach taken across different settings even within a single country or jurisdiction.

Evidence highlighting poor quality provision, cost considerations and various other issues has meant that in many countries, there has been sustained pressure to shift away from residential or institutional care towards community-based options such as foster family care or family support services (Jones, 1993; Courtney et al., 2009). However, the question swiftly evolves into a more complex inquiry than simply what type of care works best. Neagu (2021) concludes from her qualitative study of adult 'graduates' of residential and foster family care, and adoption in Romania, that 'what matters is the quality of social interaction, and the opportunities children have to develop their capabilities' (p. 197) rather than the placement category. She discovered variation in outcomes both within as well as across care placement categories, leading her to emphasize the importance of the *quality* of care. A consistent thread running through the narratives of the adult participants in Neagu's study was the importance of relational support, broadly understood, as a key aspect of positive care experiences and outcomes.

Social Support

In human services, the term 'support' is understood in widely different ways. Focusing on residential care settings, empirical studies have revealed variance in the levels of social support provided to children and young people (e.g., Pinchover & Attar-Schwartz, 2018). While there is undoubtedly a need for research evidence on the value of support and the contextual factors influencing its effectiveness, there is also a need for strong engagement with the complex conceptual issues surrounding which forms of support, addressing what specific issues and assessed from which perspectives. What influences the seeking and receipt of support? What is the appropriate timeframe for assessing the impact of support? Is it to be judged primarily as to how it alleviates immediate challenges during the 'here and now' of the placement, or as to whether it has lasting effects on the longer-term developmental trajectory of the young person? These questions emphasize the multifaceted nature of understanding and implementing effective support mechanisms within residential care settings. While studies often focus on support within the confines of the residential placement period – aiming to address immediate challenges or promote capacities during this time – this chapter takes a conceptual approach to examine the types of support (both formal and informal) that may be more relevant to promoting longer-term transformative change throughout the life course of the young person. The chapter considers, for example, how carers and other adults can support and facilitate opportunities for the young person to develop interests and talents, enhance their ambitions and aspirations, expand their social networks, build confidence, refine their social skills and cultivate social capital. It also suggests that, under the right conditions, influencing and sustaining participation in activities such as work experience and recreational activities may have the potential to shift developmental trajectories. For young people with positive experiences and outcomes in residential care, a likely key influence is the receipt of various types of social support from different actors in their lives (e.g., Magalhães, & Calheiros, 2017; Singstad et al., 2021). The concept of social capital reminds us of the importance of access to such actors by enhancing their presence in the social networks of young people in residential care (Alarcón & Mirković, 2023).

Life Course Perspective

An important dimension of understanding the effects of any formal or informal social intervention, such as support in residential care, lies in observing developments *over time*, extending long after the formal intervention or informal process has been enacted. Understanding the effectiveness of a supportive action or intervention requires more than observing changes in the immediate or early aftermath. It is also necessary to consider its sustained longer-term effect. In the case of residential care, a reasonable evaluative question from a life course perspective is whether and how an 'intervention' – any form of supportive effort – has affected the developmental *trajectory* over time. Life course theory is a widely accepted approach which among other things illuminates connections between experiences in childhood and adolescence and outcomes in later adult life and thus has special relevance for the field of child welfare (Brady & Gilligan, 2018). It provides a range of interacting principles and concepts which assist us to better understand the evolving dynamics in the life course over time and their underlying influences. Given the typical pressure for brevity in chapters such as this, I will focus on three elements drawn from the comprehensive set of life course principles and concepts. These are selected on the basis of their special relevance to the present discussion: (1) *Trajectory*: this relates to the overarching arc or pathway of development, which can be conceptualized at a particular point of observation, based on past and current trends, thus offering possible insights into the scope of potential future developments. (2) *Turning points*: these are understood as influential events, processes or other factors that precipitate long-term shifts in the arc of trajectory. Thus, where such turning points occur later assessments of a given trajectory may reveal outcomes that differ – either positively or negatively – from what might have been expected based solely on an appraisal of the pre-turning point pathway; (3) *Linked lives*: this concept underscores the potential power of shared connections between individuals through family, community or other ties. These connections can give rise to interactions with potential for considerable mutual influence and enduring commitments. Consider a life course perspective applied to a 16-year-old young person in state care with a sustained record of educational underachievement prior to and during placement in care. It is reasonable to expect that such a pattern of underachievement would continue into the future. However, the introduction of a new-found motivation for learning – perhaps stemming from the influence of a new carer with a strongly developing bond with the young person and a deep belief in the value of education, a renewed relationship with a birth relative who encourages educational commitment and/or the influence of a very committed teacher over several years – could spark an unexpected shift in academic performance. Importantly, this improvement proves to be sustained over the longer term. This combination of factors prompts what can later be observed as a turning point in the trajectory, a shift in the pathway when seen in retrospect. In this example, such a shift is influenced and sustained by relationship(s) with one or more of the carers, relatives or teachers, exemplifying the principle of 'linked lives' within the parlance of life course theory.

Integrating Residential Care Practices, Relational Support and Youth Participation in Work, Recreation and Education

While young people may be placed in state care for their own protection, it is important that the agenda of care stretches beyond risk reduction to the promotion of the young person's development. There may be many influences contributing to positive development for the young person within the residential care setting, including education. However, the focus of this chapter is on the specific value of support gained through work and recreation (informal education) opportunities particularly those occurring outside the care setting. Two issues arise in terms of the young person benefiting: the timeliness, relevance and accessibility of the opportunity for support for the young person and the young person's readiness to engage with that opportunity.

Reflecting on conditions relevant to support for young people in care, van Breda (2022) argues for the importance of cultivating their problem-solving and relationship-building skills. Based on his study of long-term resilient outcomes among care leavers in South Africa, he introduces the concept of a supportive relations triangle to capture the three key dimensions of support for young people in care and care leavers – support from formal services, support from individuals willing to offer support through relationships and the young person's capacity and willingness to *engage with* the support offered. The capacity of young persons to avail themselves of support is an important issue that may arguably receive less attention than mere access to support in academic and professional discourses.

With our current focus on promoting participation in work and recreation within the residential care setting, the question arises: how do care workers and other positive actors support young people in residential care to engage with – and sustain engagement with – opportunities to participate in work and recreation? Additionally, how do they identify and address barriers hindering such participation? Embracing such an approach requires a shift towards a more outward-facing orientation by both the worker and the young person, extending beyond the confines of the care setting. This shift is necessary since in most cases the relevant resources and opportunities lie waiting to be tapped in the world *beyond* the care setting, the same world where the young person will ultimately live their future life. Relevant to this point is the evidence that earlier work experience and 'real world experience' may be an important positive influence on care leavers' capacity to manage the transitions from the care setting to the wider world (Garcia-Alba et al., 2023, pp. 180–181).

Next, we consider the methodology employed for the chapter, which includes a review of data followed by a discussion of the wider potential relevance of the data. The data presented is drawn from in-depth case studies purposefully selected. These case studies are chosen with the aim of synthesizing themes previously introduced, namely children's experience in residential care settings, the importance of support in their adaptation and development, the value of a life course perspective in discerning key long-term influences on positive development and the importance of recreational and work-related experiences for young persons during their time in the residential care setting and beyond.

Methodology

The chapter is primarily built around three carefully selected case examples of adult 'graduates' of residential care who were provided with varying degrees of support during their time within the care setting. This support served to nurture their talents and interests ultimately leading to transformative outcomes over their life course – specifically, the development of careers in their respective areas of recreational interest. There are also two supplementary examples drawn from cases of children while still in care that speak about issues related to progress through work experience, recreation and education. The author has a long-standing interest in learning from successful outliers and outcomes in the field of child and youth welfare, where less success might be typically more expected. Consequently, the author has long been accumulating relevant features of such case examples.

The following criteria were used for selection of the adult cases in this chapter: (1) history of residential care placement as a child (up to age 18), (2) availability of published narrative data that relates to aspects of the person's care experience and post-care journey over the life course, (3) inclusion of attention to the role of recreational interests and talents during their time in care and how these link to their adult life and (4) incorporation of the person's reflection on their care experience, including the effects of care practices at the time and their enduring effects on their life trajectory. The nature of the data in the public domain allows reasonable interpretation of these issues based on the data and narrative content, thus facilitating a life course perspective on the person's trajectory of development.

There are many challenges inherent in obtaining qualitative life course data through conventional research such as the limited number of available (public) examples due to various ethical and logistical issues. The analysis here of published accounts of what are to a greater or lesser degree 'celebrity' cases provides an avenue for examining factors linked to the potential influence of the care process and setting on later life course trajectories. It should be noted that while these cases may now be termed 'celebrity' cases, they were unexceptional at the time of interest for the purpose of this chapter. The purpose here is to understand what factors facilitated and supported the transition of these young persons from being children in care to adults achieving success in their chosen careers.

The Cases

The Professional Footballer

Paul McGrath stands as a beloved and highly regarded Irish professional footballer, having left an indelible mark on the sport throughout the 1980s and 1990s. His exceptional performances for celebrated English football clubs, Manchester United and Aston Villa, along with his contribution as an international player for the Republic of Ireland have solidified his status as a sporting icon. Even years after his retirement, supporters privileged enough to have witnessed him play live still marvel as they recall his talent and skill.

Born to a Nigerian father and Irish mother, Paul grew up as a black boy in the predominantly then white city of Dublin. Much of his childhood was spent in a children's home in south Dublin, where he honed his footballing skills in the local schoolboy leagues. Paul is generous in acknowledging the support of those who helped him on his journey to sporting stardom. While the progress of young individuals through the care system is typically cloaked in the rules of confidentiality surrounding official files recording their progress, the case of Paul McGrath offers a rare glimpse into aspects of his life in care and afterwards, thanks to insights published in his biography (McGrath & Dervan, 1994). Paul underscores the pivotal role of Mr. Johnson, the head teacher at the school affiliated with the children's home, in his footballing journey. Not only did Mr. Johnson find opportunities for Paul to display and develop his talents on local underage teams while in the Home but he also invested considerable efforts ensuring that Paul had access to a supportive network of coaches upon leaving the children's home. Additionally, Mr. Johnson facilitated the involvement of adults willing to support his progress personally both on and off the football pitch (McGrath & Dervan, 1994). This example illustrates numerous instances of support for Paul's progress from a young boy, with each piece of the puzzle playing a crucial role. However, as highlighted in the wider literature on youth transitions and care transitions, support in this formative period is especially critical (Adley & Jupp Kina, 2017; Hiles et al., 2013; Palmer et al., 2022).

In this context, while Mr. Johnson played a significant role, there were also many other actors who played their part in Paul's journey. However, it could be argued that sustaining Paul's early trajectory towards elite football represented the critical turning point process (Gilligan, 2009). The narrative that unfolds is intertwined with its preceding events; without the groundwork laid before, there would be no subsequent progression. Likewise, without the subsequent developments, the full story we now appreciate would not exist. This serves as an important reminder that the process of support, regardless of its specific manifestation, often unfolds over an extended period, with its final effects involving the concerted efforts of numerous actors.

For children in care, the care setting clearly plays a central role in their narrative, but there often exists a wider 'system' of influence at play. Support flows not only through the efforts of caregivers and other positive actors but also through the young person's own agency – the purposeful engagement and actions they undertake. Support is rarely a single isolated action; rather, it unfolds as an iterative process over time. In retrospect, however, it becomes easier to identify key turning points – a moment, a period, a process that represents a significant shift in the narrative's development.

A key phase in this progression often occurs during the transition out of the care setting and the parallel transition from childhood to adulthood after reaching the age of 18. In Paul's story, we witness the continuous flow of support over time, orchestrated by multiple actors (including a staff member from the care setting), as well as the iterative process of gradual progress up the ladder of sporting success, with his abilities maturing with age and attracting greater attention. We also observe the agency of the young person and the relevance of turning points in the narrative, both past and future. Additionally, the significance of Paul's chronological age cannot be overlooked at age 18, a point marking the end of his formal time in care, his transition to early adulthood and further steps towards his future as a professional footballer. Overall, his journey through the care setting also represented his progress from being a skilful young person playing football to an elite young adult player on a much grander stage.

As Paul made the transition from care, he required assistance in gaining attention as a potential candidate for elite football. He also needed a sustaining environment to continue to nurture and support his development as a footballer. While Mr. Johnson may not have articulated his intentions in quite these terms, it is clear from Paul's account that Mr. Johnson had a good intuitive understanding of what was needed, reaching out from the children's home and orchestrating various types of relevant support. While all other supportive actors were important, Mr. Johnson emerged as a key figure in curating and scaffolding Paul's sporting progress. However, there was yet another pivotal figure in this narrative – Paul himself. Without his agency and determined efforts, there would be no great story to recall. The support offered required Paul's personal commitment and agency to achieve its full effect. Without his active engagement, the supportive efforts would have ultimately turned to dust. But in the process of gradually becoming recognized and 'embedded' as a promising elite footballer in the making, something changed, something shifted in his trajectory of development. A turning point had occurred in Paul's status and identity. Gilligan (2009) has proposed that turning points depend on four elements each discernible in the narrative of Paul McGrath as a young footballer and a boy in a residential care centre (*opportunity* (to take part in competitive football), *readiness* (timeliness of the opportunity), agency (willingness of the person to engage with the opportunity and *sustaining context* (provided by the coaches and others who cultivated his talent over time) (Gilligan, 2009).

The chain of support in Paul's football journey is comprised of many parts and is built over time – a common trajectory for most successful athletes. However, the sources and meaning of this support may be more significant for the young person, where they are also growing up in care or adjusting to the transition from care. In the absence of key support figures, Paul's story could have been very different. Care-experienced young people may often have less access to viable alternative sources of support. It is well established that being in out-of-home care is often linked to weaker social networks compared to young people not in care (Perry, 2006). Paul's progress in football is a powerful example of how recreational opportunities in the outside world may help protect and promote a positive social network for the young person.

The significance of early work experience is also highlighted in Paul's journey. The young Paul gradually acquired the fresh identity of a capable and ultimately professional footballer, a transformation supported by success and ongoing support. Such experiences have the power to revitalize identities, bringing with them renewed confidence and opening up new opportunities (Gilligan & Brady, 2023). There is evidence that early work experience, before the age of 18, can significantly contribute to career advancement later in life (Soyez et al., 2024). From this perspective, the coaching and additional support Paul received before turning 18 emerge as vital and indeed essential foundations for his later success. Overall, Paul McGrath's journey as seen through a life course lens illustrates the transformative potential of the purposeful and ongoing support of talents and interests. A range of actors each played their part in the iterative project of assisting Paul to navigate his life's sporting and personal challenges. Moving forward, we now proceed to the second case, which will be shorter in length as much of the argument has already been elucidated through the detailed review of Paul McGrath's experience.

The International Rock Star

During periods of difficulty in her childhood, Sinead O'Connor, the well-known singer, now sadly deceased, spent some time in state care in Ireland. According to her account, she generally did not have positive recollections of this period, although there were some exceptions. Notably, she acknowledged the positive role of Sister Margaret, a Roman Catholic nun, in her progress. Sister Margaret served as a residential worker in the religious-run centre where Sinead was placed for a time. Sister Margaret had sought to 'reach' Sinead in a deeper and more thoughtful way, leaving a lasting impression. She had nurtured Sinead's musical talents by buying her first guitar and arranging music lessons with a teacher to assist Sinead develop her guitar-playing skills (O'Connor, 2022). Indeed, somewhat humorously, Sinead attributed her tendency to run away from the centre to Sister Margaret's gift of the guitar, which had ignited her desire to immerse herself in the city's music scene. One of Sinead's earliest public performances was singing at her music teacher's wedding. Additionally, Sister Margaret enabled Sinead to take part in some recording sessions at a recording studio. Ultimately, Sinead went on to become an international star thanks to her magical singing talent, her charismatic, larger-than-life personality and the agency she displayed as a teenager in her pursuit of her talent and interest.

Sinead had noticed that the centre encouraged the development of aptitudes that might lead on to opportunities in the world outside. The provision of the guitar, the music classes and the recording sessions fitted into that framework. In her own unique way, Sister Margaret was bridging a pathway for Sinead from the Centre into an adult world that might fit her talents and personality. Sister Margaret played a pivotal role in opening a door for Sinead into her future musical career.

The Professional Musician

In each of the narratives of both Sinead and Paul, there is a delicate balance struck between the level of support provided and the degree of individual agency exerted. The successful outcomes in both Sinead's and Paul's journeys testify to some kind of sweet spot where support and agency intersect effectively. Evon Brennan's story, however, exemplifies a slightly different type of balance between support and agency. She was placed in two different residential care settings in Ireland in her adolescence. Her account highlights the importance of her own agency and the role of passive or tacit support from the caring adults in the setting. While resounding support for her musical talent may have been lacking, there appears to have been a degree of begrudging acceptance, if not active encouragement, or at the very least no overt obstruction. Overall, it could be argued that Evon had to use her own agency to curate her own independent journey to the wider world of music. Music became the channel through which Evon rebelled against what she deemed as the stifling atmosphere of the care setting and the prescribed identity it sought to enforce upon her. She applied her newfound passion and skill in music as a means to construct a new identity and discover a wider purpose in life beyond the confines of the centre.

> It was at the second home that I discovered a passion for music. I remember our first concert, with an audience of nuns all shrouded in black, listening to songs we had written about not having a boyfriend. I loved sneaking out to hear bands play, even though the nuns often locked the windows, so we had to stay out all night.
>
> (Brennan, 2007)

Evon's personal agency shines through in this account of her gradual induction into the world of music and performance. Despite the scrutiny of the adults in authority at the Home, she recounts how she actively made decisions to shape her identity around her passions and abilities.

> Music, sport, having a twin and being mischievous were the things that kept me sane. I loved playing the piano and practised for hours, often falling asleep with my head on the lid. Practice time was in a room on my own, where I composed, dreamed and scribbled down ideas. I kept this part of myself hidden for fear it would be stopped.
>
> (Brennan, 2007)

Talent and agency made a powerful combination for Evon as she proceeded in her self-curated progress through her adolescence in care. She quietly built her confidence in the room where she played her piano until she fell asleep. Her own motivation had to sustain her in the absence of guidance from her carers.

> I'd always been quite musical...and wanted to do something in that area, but I didn't really have the confidence to do it, because it was always considered by the nuns as noise. I had piano lessons for a while, and loved playing, but that stopped very quickly. Piano playing was an escape into my own world, but there were lots of question marks in

> terms of how I would go about pursuing it. There was no explanation from the nuns as to what to do or how to go about that – it was just a matter of getting out and getting a job.
>
> (Evon Brennan in interview: Clayton-Lea, 2006)

In the examples of Paul McGrath and Sinead O'Connor, their own agency and support from a key actor within the care setting helped them to achieve positive progress right into adult life. In the case of Evon, support was less visible, more ambivalent or tacit. In the absence of overt support, Evon drew instead on her own agency and the energy and encouragement she received through her association with the world of music outside the care setting.

These three case examples depict individuals whose talents and performances (and support) enabled them to transcend the challenges associated with spending part of their youth in residential care. With the benefit of hindsight, each narrative can be analysed to reflect on the influences and outcomes across the life course – from their time in care to adulthood. We can discern the overall effects of support from both within the care system and from numerous external sources. While not every young person in care possesses the innate talent to achieve stardom or recognition on public platforms, nor do they necessarily receive the same range of support and supporters (Paul and Sinead), the three stories illustrate the potential of support and its many possible sources for care-experienced young people, from both inside and outside the care system. Considering this potential, we must also acknowledge the relevance of support in the lives of young people embarking on different, perhaps less-publicized pathways into and hopefully through the world of work. While these narratives may be considered more 'ordinary' or 'typical' and lack the glamour of fame or publicity, they are still remarkable in their own way. In the following sections, I present two further examples from the cases of children where they were still living in residential care settings before the age of 18.

The stories of these two young people still under 18 and in residential care illustrate how transformative change can also arise in seemingly low-key and ordinary ways. In the two 'humble' examples presented here, one is publicly available, while for the other certain identifying details, including, necessarily, the source (to whom I express gratitude) and country, are omitted.

For 'Michael,' a boy in residential care in Israel, learning to swim was, ultimately, the pivotal step in a turning point process that led him from illiteracy at age 12 to securing a place in higher education (Refaeli & Strahl, 2014). While he is reported to have had experienced a troubled family life and many placement moves since first entering alternative care, the paper reporting his reading journey does not identify the specific reasons behind the delay in his learning to read. Swimming lessons outside the institution exposed the boy to children beyond the care setting, to peers who were not in care. This contact revealed to him that they were able to read, unlike himself, a discovery which motivated him to pursue learning to read at such a late stage in his life. Opening up the opportunity of learning to swim might not seem like a form of 'support' in a conventional sense, yet it proved to be the catalyst that motivated the boy to seek to learn to read at a late stage in order to be like other 'normal' children. As seen in other examples, the support provided in bridging pathways to experiences beyond the residential care environment led to transformative changes over time. Seen from a life course perspective, Michael's journey from illiteracy and residential care to higher education began with swimming classes arranged by his residential centre in the wider community. These served as a platform for Michael to realize that he was out of step with his peers in the community due to his inability to read. Michael took it upon himself to learn to read partly by enlisting the support of caregivers in the setting – a process that marked a transformative turning point in both his educational and broader life trajectory (Refaeli & Strahl, 2014). Three sets of actors are visible in the change effort: the peers from the wider community at the swimming pool who were serendipitously involved, those caretakers in the care setting whose help Michael enlisted in his personal learning to read the project, especially one with whom he identified strongly (and those who had organized the swimming sessions outside the centre) and Michael himself exercising his own agency for his chosen purpose.

The second example concerns a teenager growing up in a residential care setting where he felt that the staff perceived him as disinterested and disaffected. He attended school outside the centre. A school requirement to undertake work experience within the school schedule led him to a work placement in a small independently owned bakery. Despite the negative perceptions that he felt were held about him by staff in the care setting, the boy thrived in the bakery. He enjoyed his time there hugely, getting on very well with his mentor, the owner. The work schedule of the bakery required him to get up very early each morning to catch a bus to the bakery and to be in time for the start of the bakery day. At the end of the formal placement, the boy remained in the bakery as a part-time worker. While we don't know the ultimate outcome of the boy's story, there are hints in his commitment, discipline and enjoyment and in his retaining a part-time job there that provide some grounds for optimism. nd differences when the story is compared to the earlier accounts. The opportunity arose through a school requirement, the main driver of progress was the boy's personal agency and commitment, matching well with the supportive inclination of the bakery owner. He transformed into a reliable and engaged trainee, responding to the encouragement of the baker and the chance to move beyond the view of him held within the care centre. The opening at the bakery provided him with the chance to disrupt and challenge any negative narrative about himself and literally reinvent himself to cultivate a new identity featuring threads of competence, reliability and engagement. Moreover, these elements echo similar themes of cultivating positive identity through engagement with the outside world in the earlier stories.

Reflections on the Described Journeys

While the five stories have many differences, one shared aspect of importance is that the impetus for growth and development in the cases stemmed from engagement *with the world outside*. While active facilitation and support were prominent in the first two stories, those of Paul McGrath, the professional footballer, and Sinead O'Connor, the singer, the third story, revolving around Evon Brennan, the professional musician, depended heavily on Evon's own determination and agency. Through her proactive efforts, she essentially curated her own journey into the world of music and performance. On the whole, the role of the centre staff seems to have been largely passive or neutral. They may not have been particularly enthusiastic about her music, but they also did not assert outright opposition to it.

The two cases of children still in residential care show examples of children being agentic in pursuit of their own choices to acquire new identities as readers or assistant bakers. In these latter two cases, they had the support of mentors, a teacher/carer and a baker running his own business who had taken on the boy as a trainee as part of his school-based work experience programme.

This final story, depicting the young person who pursued a career as a baker, shows how progress depended on the efforts of the school, the young person and the baker. While the role of the centre staff remains unmentioned, it is notable that they did not appear to hinder the opportunity in any way. Their apparent passivity in this regard is not to be underestimated as it can be seen as a significant contribution to facilitating the opportunity. Support can manifest itself in various forms, ranging from active and energetic to silent and inert, depending on the circumstances. However, regardless of its form, support remains support, even if it amounts only to the absence of overt opposition.

It cannot be assumed that a disposition to support is always the default position of care centre staff. Given the possible tensions in the relationship between the boy and the staff in the baker story, leaving him free to use his own agency to engage with the bakery opportunity may be said to have been an inspired choice whether deliberate or not. This example is also a reminder of how support may be played out *systemically*, rather than within one single linear or dyadic relationship. While the relational nature of support for young people in care is undoubtedly important, the accounts show how multiple actors may sometimes be active in what become developmental processes within the wider ecology of the care setting. In the bakery example, the boy, the baker and the schoolteachers each played an active role; in the footballing example, a teacher from the care setting and football coaches from the wider community played vital roles and in the music examples, the influence of different actors is discernible.

It is easy to assume that frontline carers have the most influence over outcomes for young people in care. They are undoubtedly important, but in this chapter, the focus is on the significance of other actors whose role is easily overlooked or ignored. These five cases are a highly selective sample. No claim can be made that they are representative – but they are *real.* The five examples of successful progress are illustrative and instructive as to the relevance of other actors beyond care staff specifically.

Discussion and Conclusion

What can we learn from the cases? Firstly, it is evident that support at the personal level is inherently relational. Where it occurs, support takes effect through a bidirectional process. While the support may be offered or provided, its impact is truly felt when the prospective recipient opts into the process through agentic engagement. Mr. Johnson, for example, sought to open up a pathway for the young Paul McGrath towards a niche in the world of elite football. He did so in the course of his work in the care centre. However, that support only took effect because Paul was engaged with that purpose, motivated to follow that same path. Moreover, this relational dynamic occurs within a wider system which can either help or hinder the process. Both Mr. Johnson and Paul relied on the backing of wider networks of football coaches, talent scouts and local teams (and presumably being facilitated to some degree by other carers in the centre). These networks provided additional avenues for engagement, bolstering the broad goal of nurturing Paul's talent.

In the case of Sinead O'Connor, Sister Margaret insightfully sought to tap into Sinead's interest in music as a way to find a common purpose with her in the care setting. Responding through her own agency, Sinead embraced this 'offer' from Sister Margaret, and as with Mr. Johnson and Paul, the wider world outside provided a wider context or 'system' – this time the music 'scene' in Dublin which proved a magnetic draw for the budding young singer and musician. Sister Margaret's subtle and supportive efforts worked because they resonated with the interests of the young woman in her care. Evon Brennan's story presents a unique twist compared to the narratives of Paul McGrath and Sinead O'Connor. Unlike them, Evon didn't have a caregiver within the care facility who actively advocated for the development of her musical talents. Although Evon possessed both interest and talent, she lacked a dedicated champion to nurture her potential. Consequently, she took it upon herself to proactively cultivate her own skills and carve out her identity as a musician beyond the confines of the care setting. Her journey sheds light on a nuanced approach to support within care facilities. While the nuns overseeing Evon's care didn't actively push for her musical progression, they also didn't hinder it. Their stance suggests a form of tacit support, allowing Evon the freedom to pursue her passion without interference. This underscores the notion that support within care settings can manifest itself in various forms, sometimes requiring the young person to take the reins and exert agency proactively in pursuing their aspirations.

An important aspect of the three initial stories is how these young people found the motivation, and in two cases, the support from a caregiver, to craft their own public identity as footballers, singers, or musicians – a public identity that extended beyond their status as 'child in care' in their care settings. According to recognition theory (see Smith et al., 2017), having their new public identities acknowledged and affirmed by peers and leaders within their respective sports or music communities would have served as an important source of encouragement and motivation for their progress. Again, this underlines the significance of the wider systemic context (inclusive of and beyond the care setting) within which adult support and agentic effort by the young person may play out.

Outward-facing support involves engaging with resources in the community beyond the setting or facilitating such engagement by the young person. Drawing on a key concept derived from social capital theory, caregivers can act as 'bridging agents' (Alarcón & Mirković, 2023) between the inner world of the care setting and the outer world beyond its boundaries. Bridging support helps build social capital by linking the young person to connections and resources that may otherwise be beyond their social reach, thereby opening doors to new connections and possibilities in areas like work, education and recreation. In this sense, bridging support can be seen as having a dual action in the context of residential care: it encompasses the support experience itself and the subsequent support stemming from the additional connections activated through this bridging support.

It is, of course, unrealistic to expect in every instance that bridging support will deliver all-encompassing and enduring transformative change or resolve all of the life challenges faced by the young person. The argument is not that the child's issues are thereby fully resolved but that the trajectory following placement may be positively shifted by advantageous experiences linked to the resources and opportunities in the outside world. Life may be better to some degree in at least one domain of living subsequent to these experiences, but all of the issues may not be fully resolved or settled. This depends on other developments during and after the placement which may exert (or not) influence on later outcomes across other domains.

Nevertheless, the above-mentioned five case examples demonstrate powerfully the *potential* for transformative change under the right conditions and how a trajectory shift in even one life domain as in our cases, clearly has the power to shift developments across the life course in significant ways. Such developments, we have seen, may often be linked to how support widens the repertoire of valued identities to which the young person can lay claim.

Support for his passion for football opened up a career in professional sport for Paul. Similarly, support for her love of singing at a critical point in her life opened up a major international career in popular music for Sinead O'Connor in her adulthood. Likewise, her own devotion to music while she was in care settings sowed the seeds of a rewarding career as a performer and songwriter for Evon Brennan. It might be objected that not everyone possesses the exceptional talent showcased in these cases, and this is a fair point. But this does not actually negate the essence of the argument. Facilitating young people to pursue their talents and interests in the world beyond the care setting may open up new possibilities in the short term (as in the internship in the bakery) but also other low-key opportunities that may also play out in transformative ways over the life course. The internship in the bakery has the potential to open a lifetime of satisfying work, positive identity and income as a baker. The example from the bakery reminds us that becoming a celebrity is not the outcome in every case, but for the purposes of this chapter, examples from the lives of celebrities have been accessible because they have felt free to share their stories in the public domain. Overall, on the basis of the patterns in the cases reviewed, there seem to be four conditions relevant for support to be activated in relation to children from residential centres in participating in a regular activity (tailored to them) outside the centre (an activity that proves influential in later development). These are i) the efforts by the adult in curating/supporting the external activity; ii) engagement by the young person with this offer and the young person finding a 'work around' when this support is not overtly forthcoming; iii) support or tolerance of the activity by the centre leadership and iv) active willingness on the part of external actors who are linked to the activity (e.g., sport coaches, team members, fellow musicians and mentors at the workplace) to facilitate or encourage the young person's involvement.

In this chapter, the case has been made for a life course and outward-facing understanding of social support and its importance in the lives of children in residential care settings. We have seen the significance for the young person of having a 'curated' or bridging link to the outside world. From the examples presented, the 'curator' of support may be a worker from the care setting, or an external actor such as a teacher or workplace manager, or in the absence of such curators or champions, we have also seen how the young person can apply their own agency in achieving access to the opportunities and motivation offered in the world beyond the care setting. In addition, we have seen how support may be expressed in different ways, from the enthusiastic to the silent, and how support exerts its effect in combination with the agency and engagement of the young person. The examples show how the world outside the setting may be rich with opportunities for the young person to discover and build on talents and connections (through early activity in the worlds of work (internships, volunteering, part-time work etc.) or recreation) that may have potential to be transformative in their longer-term effect (see Soyez et al., 2024). A life course perspective sensitive to the power of support through established and new wider social connections (linked lives) has the potential to enhance the young person's trajectory of development and thus the positive and enduring impact of residential care in the lives of children and young people.

References

Adley, N., & Jupp Kina, V. (2017). Getting behind the closed door of care leavers: Understanding the role of emotional support for young people leaving care. *Child & Family Social Work*, *22*(1), 97–105. https://doi.org/10.1111/cfs.12203

Alarcón, X., & Mirković, B. (2023). "Those bridges that help you get there": How natural mentors improve social support and social capital of unaccompanied immigrant youths leaving residential rare. *Residential Treatment for Children & Youth*, *41*(17), 1–25. https://doi.org/10.1080/0886571X.2023.2241816

Brady, E., & Gilligan, R. (2018). The life course perspective: An integrative research paradigm for examining the educational experiences of adult care leavers?. *Children and Youth Services Review*, *87*, 69–77. https://doi.org/10.1016/j.childyouth.2018.02.019

Brennan, E. (2007). I was raised by nuns. *The Guardian* February 18th I was raised by nuns | Family | The Guardian

Clayton-Lea, T. (2006) Singing songs of strength and survival *Irish Times* September 16th (interview with Evon Brennan) Singing songs of strength and survival. *The Irish Times*.

Courtney, M. E., Dolev, T., & Gilligan, R. (2009). Looking backward to see forward clearly: A cross-national perspective on residential care. In M. Courtney, & D. Iwaniec (Eds.), *Residential care of children: Comparative Perspectives* (pp. 191–208). Oxford University Press https://doi.org/10.1093/acprof:oso/9780195309188.003.0012

Crous, G., Montserrat, C., Gallart-Mir, J., & Matás, M. (2021). 'In the end you're no longer the kid from the children's home, you're just yourself': Resilience in care leavers over 25. *European Journal of Social Work*, *24*(5), 896–909. https://doi.org/10.1080/13691457.2021.1918063

García-Alba, L., Gullo, F., & del Valle, J. F. (2023). Readiness for independent living of youth in residential childcare: A comparative study. *Child & Family Social Work*, *28*(1), 171–183. https://doi.org/10.1111/cfs.12951

Gilligan, R. (2009). Positive turning points in the dynamics of change over the life course. In J. A. Mancini, & K. A. Roberto (Eds.), *Pathways of human development: Explorations of change* (pp. 15–34). Lanham, MA: Lexington Books

Gilligan, R., & Brady, E. (2023). What helps adult care leavers return to education? Exploring the relevance of learner identity and the life course perspective. *Journal of Youth Studies*, *26*(10), 1373–1386. https://doi.org/10.1080/13676261.2022.2098706

Hiles, D., Moss, D., Wright, J., & Dallos, R. (2013). Young people's experience of social support during the process of leaving care: A review of the literature. *Children and Youth Services Review*, *35*(12), 2059–2071 https://doi.org/10.1016/j.childyouth.2013.10.008

Jones, M. B. (1993). Decline of the American orphanage, 1941–1980. *Social Service Review*, *67*(3), 459–480.

Magalhães, E., & Calheiros, M. M. (2017). A dual-factor model of mental health and social support: Evidence with adolescents in residential care. *Children and Youth Services Review*, *79*, 442–449. https://doi.org/10.1016/j.childyouth.2017.06.041

McGrath, P. & Dervan, C. (1994) *Ooh Aah Paul McGrath – The black pearl of Inchicore* Edinburgh: Mainstream Publishing

Neagu, M. (2021) *Voices from the silent cradles: Life histories of Romania's looked-after children*. Bristol: Bristol University Press.

O'Connor, S. (2022) *Rememberings* London: Penguin Random House

Palmer, A., Norris, M., & Kelleher, J. (2022). Accelerated adulthood, extended adolescence and the care cliff: Supporting care leavers' transition from care to independent living. *Child & Family Social Work*, *27*(4), 748–759. https://doi.org/10.1111/cfs.12922

Perry, B. L. (2006). Understanding social network disruption: The case of youth in foster care. *Social Problems*, *53*(3), 371–391. https://doi.org/10.1525/sp.2006.53.3.371

Pinchover, S., & Attar-Schwartz, S. (2018). Is someone there for you? Social support of youth in educational residential care from family, peers, and staff. *British Journal of Social Work*, *48*, 2195–2214. https://doi.org/10.1093/bjsw/bcx164

Refaeli, T., & Strahl, B. (2014). Turning point processes to higher education among care leavers. *Social Work & Society*, *12* (1).

Singstad, M. T., Wallander, J. L., Greger, H. K., Lydersen, S., & Kayed, N. S. (2021). Perceived social support and quality of life among adolescents in residential youth care: A cross-sectional study. *Health and Quality of Life Outcomes*, *19*, 1–12. https://doi.org/10.1186/s12955-021-01676-1

Smith, M., Cameron, C., & Reimer, D. (2017). From attachment to recognition for children in care. *British Journal of Social Work*, *47*(6), 1606–1623 https://doi.org/10.1093/bjsw/bcx096

Soyez, V., Gilligan, R., Arnau-Sabatès, L., Johansson, H., Hojer, I., Pazlorova, H., Sjöblom, Y., & Stoddart, J. (2024). Early work experiences, social inclusion and transition to adulthood: The voice of care-experienced young adults. *Journal of Social Work*. https://doi.org/10.1177/14680173231225423

van Breda, A. D. (2022). The contribution of supportive relationships to care-leaving outcomes: A longitudinal resilience study in South Africa. *Child Care in Practice*, 1–16. https://doi.org/10.1080/13575279.2022.2037516

Whittaker, J. K., Holmes, L., del Valle, J., & James, S. (2023) *Revitalizing residential care for children and youth – Cross-national trends and challenges*. New York: Oxford University Press.

Part 2

Social Support While in Residential Care

3 Social Support and Psychological Functioning

A Review of Empirical Evidence in the Portuguese Context

Eunice Magalhães and Maria Manuela Calheiros

Introduction

Residential care aims to protect children and young people who were victims of child abuse and neglect and who need services that can foster supportive and meaningful relationships (Magalhães & Calheiros, 2017; Pinheiro et al., 2022). Children and young people in out-of-home care have often experienced complex relational trauma, which requires trauma-informed care practices and models (Bailey et al., 2018). Trauma-informed care settings are those that are able to provide trusted and supportive relationships, which improve young people's relational skills, which in turn positively impact their social and emotional adjustment and mitigate their behavioral problems (Holden et al., 2015). In addition, ensuring quality relationships with peers, family, and significant others is fundamental to fostering young people's well-being and mental health in residential care.

As such, in this chapter, we intend to describe and discuss a set of findings from research projects we developed with children and adolescents in residential care in Portugal, in which the role of supportive relationships in their psychological adjustment was explored.

The Portuguese Out-of-home Care System

Contrasting with most European countries, out-of-home care in the Portuguese system is mainly based on residential care (96.5% of children and youth are placed in residential settings and merely 3.5% in family foster care) (ISS, 2022). Historically, the Portuguese system is based on an institutional perspective of alternative care, with the first 16 years of the Portuguese child protection system (from 1999 to 2015) involving residential care homes based on the young people's age and the expected length of stay in care (longer or temporary) instead of their developmental needs. Until the 80s and before the Portuguese law of Child Protection (1999), the institutional model was dominant (large-scale institutions with nonqualified staff) merely addressing young people's basic care needs. Gradually, the qualification for residential care settings was implemented in the Portuguese context

DOI: 10.4324/9781003424468-6

(particularly in 2007) to replace the institutional model of residential care with a specialized system that is able to address young people's needs (Rodrigues et al., 2013).

In 2015, a major amendment in Portuguese law brought significant changes to the out-of-home care system. First, family foster care was underlined particularly regarding children younger than six years. Second, the residential care system was organized in terms of how they address young people's needs: a) Emergency settings, b) settings to address young people's therapeutic or educational needs (i.e., with severe mental health problems or cognitive disabilities), and c) autonomy apartments (Law No. 142, 2015). In the last 15 years, we have had a decrease of around 48% children and young people in the out-of-home care system. This decrease may suggest a significant investment in the Portuguese system focused on family intervention, either to prevent the young people's removal from their family environment and their placement in care or to promote family reunification. In fact, children who have left the out-of-home care system have been mostly reunified with their birth family (nuclear or extended). Moreover, there has been a significant increase in specialized residential settings: the last five years have witnessed a growth of 124% in specialized settings (for young people with emotional and behavioral problems, unaccompanied minors) as well as a 127% increase in autonomy apartments (ISS, 2022). This increase may be due to worldwide social changes (i.e., refugee movements and the need to take care of unaccompanied minors) but also to the profile of young people in residential care in Portugal (mostly teenagers, and many of them revealing significant emotional and behavioral difficulties). Although Portugal is investing efforts and resources in a more specialized model of child protection, specialized settings are still a marginal alternative residential care context in the Portuguese system, since most children and young people are placed in generalist residential care settings (84.1%), while only 2.5% are placed in therapeutic settings, 0.7% in emergency settings, and 2.2% in autonomy apartments (ISS, 2022). In 2021, 6,369 children and young people were in the out-of-home care system in Portugal, most of whom are males (52%), aged over 12 years (70%), and placed in residential care by previous neglect (70%). Some of these young people show developmental and mental health difficulties: behavioral problems (26%), mental disabilities (7%), diagnosed mental health problems (4.8%), or substance use (2.6%). Around 38% have regular psychological intervention, 28% have pharmacological treatment, and 26% have regular psychiatric intervention (ISS, 2022).

The institutional model of residential care in Portugal has been progressively changing to be comprised of smaller settings, involving more qualified professionals and specialized or therapeutic contexts (Rodrigues et al., 2013). Despite this progress, we need a more successful way to make these residential contexts effectively protective of children and young people's needs, such as by fostering meaningful and supportive social relationships.

The Role of Social Support on Psychological Functioning

The role of supportive relationships in people's health and well-being has been discussed considering three different types of models: the main effect model, the stress-buffering model, and the mediating effect model (Beeble et al., 2009; Cohen et al., 2000; Lepore et al., 1991).

Regardless of current stressors, the main effect model posits that support fosters positive affect and a sense of belonging, which enable positive results for both physical and mental health. According to Cohen et al. (2000), supportive networks offer resources or information to address a variety of issues, which has a good impact on health. To be more precise, these main effects of support on mental health are explained by the Relational Regulation Theory (Lakey & Orehek, 2011). According to this theory, people may control their emotions and behaviors through routine social contacts and group activities (rather than through interactions during stressful situations), which has a beneficial effect on their well-being. When a variety of providers are accessible, the benefits of socially supportive contacts become even more apparent (Lakey & Orehek, 2011).

From another angle, the stress-buffering model proposes that support functions as a buffer or coping resource in the face of stressful events (Beeble et al., 2009; Cohen et al., 2000), in two ways: a) the perceived availability of social resources may influence the way people appraise the event (i.e., primary appraisal; people may perceive an event as less stressful or harmful) and their capacity to deal with (i.e., secondary appraisal; support fosters one's perceived capability to cope with difficulties); b) when people perceive an event as stressful, perceiving or receiving social support may buffer the negative stress-related cognitive, emotional, physiological, or behavioral responses, given that such support enables them to meet the demands posed by the stressor, thus preventing the development of physical or mental health difficulties (Cohen et al., 2000). The stress-buffering effect seems to be more likely reached when acute stress is experienced (in contrast to severe long-lasting stressful situations) (Beeble et al., 2009).

Finally, some classic theoretical approaches suggest, instead, that social support may be affected by the stressful event (Lepore et al., 1991), which is consistent with a perspective of social support as a mediator. This means that chronic and long-lasting stressful events can threaten social support (perceived and provided), given that people within individuals' social networks may be less available to provide support in the context of prolonged stress, which in turn may increase people's psychological difficulties (Lepore et al., 1991). As such, long-term exposure to stress may hinder the buffering effect of support and this worsening of perceived support may be associated with greater mental health difficulties (Lepore et al., 1991).

Based on these different mechanisms and roles of social support in mental health, in this chapter, we will describe and discuss a set of findings concerning these diverse possible roles of social support on different developmental outcomes of young people (i.e., self-representations, psychopathology, and academic performance) in residential care in Portugal.

A Review of Empirical Evidence in the Portuguese Context

Overview of the Studies' Methodologies

In this section, we will describe and synthesize a set of qualitative and quantitative findings obtained by our research team in the Portuguese context (cf. Table 3.1). Quantitative studies relied on gender-balanced samples of young people in residential care ranging from $n = 366$ to $n = 926$ and presenting a mean age range between $M = 14.82$ and $M = 16.26$. Most studies assessed supportive relationships through well-known self-reported questionnaires (e.g., *Social Support Questionnaire*, by Sarason et al., 1983; *The Network of Relationships Inventory–Relationship Quality Version* (NRI-RQV; Furman & Buhrmester, 1985, Buhrmester & Furman, 2008). Also, two studies (Magalhães & Calheiros, 2017; Magalhães et al., 2021) included an instrument that was specifically developed in the Portuguese context to assess formal social support (i.e., *Questionnaire of Institutional Support*, Calheiros et al., 2009; Calheiros & Paulino, 2007). Different outcomes were included in these studies, such as psychopathology (Magalhães et al., 2021; Silva, Calheiros et al., 2022), both psychopathology and well-being (Magalhães & Calheiros, 2017), self-representations (Calheiros et al., 2020), and academic achievement (Silva, Carvalho et al., 2022). Qualitative evidence was collected through individual interviews (Ferreira et al., 2020) and focus groups (Magalhães et al., 2018) using two different samples of 29 adolescents (M_{age} 14.79 and 15.17). Detailed information on the studies' methodologies is described in Table 3.1.

Main, Buffering, and Mediating Effects

Regarding the effects of social support on young people's outcomes, first, we will describe the main effects and then the buffering and mediating effects. Our quantitative studies have provided robust evidence about the positive association between support and psychological functioning of young people in residential care (Calheiros et al., 2020; Magalhães & Calheiros, 2017; Magalhães et al., 2021). Specifically, in a study with a large sample of young people in residential care (N = 926, from 71 residential care institutions), we have found that the quality of support from residential staff and friends evaluated through the NRI-RQV (Furman & Buhrmester, 1985; Buhrmester & Furman, 2008) were positively related to positive self-representations (e.g., adolescents described themselves as nice, friend, intelligent, or loved) and negatively with negative self-representations (e.g., adolescents described themselves as aggressive, depressed, traumatized, or neglected) (Calheiros et al., 2020). Also, Magalhães et al. (2021) with a sample of 366 adolescents assessed different dimensions of social support in residential care (e.g., esteem, emotional/relational, and instrumental). The authors found that staff support in residential care was associated with lower psychological difficulties, such as

Table 3.1 Characteristics of studies included in this chapter

Authors	*Design*	*Sample*	*Social support dimensions*	*Source of support*	*Instruments*	*Variables*	*Data analysis*
Magalhães & Calheiros, 2017	Quantitative, cross-sectional	*Young people* N = 369; 54% males Age: M = 14.75 *Residential settings* N = 59	Informal support: Availability Satisfaction Formal support: Esteem Emotional/ relational Evaluative/ informational	Informal support Formal support from staff in RC	Social support questionnaire (Sarason et al., 1983; Portuguese version, Moreira et al. (2002). Questionnaire of institutional support (Calheiros et al., 2009; Calheiros & Paulino, 2007).	Psychopathology: Antisocial behavior Anger control problems Emotional distress Positive self (difficulties) Well-being: Satisfaction with life Psychological Well-being	Test the dual-factor model (complete mental health, vulnerable, symptomatic but content, troubled): group comparison regarding the social support dimensions. Pearson correlations Mancova
Magalhães, et al., 2018	Qualitative, cross-sectional	*Young people* N = 29; 52% males Age: M = 15.17 *Residential settings* N = 6	N/A	Informal support (peers) Formal support from staff in RC	Focus group script	Psychopathology: Internalizing and externalizing	Qualitative analysis based on grounded theory
Calheiros et al., 2020	Quantitative, cross-sectional	*Young people* N = 926; 46% females Age: M = 16.26 *Residential settings* N = 71	Companionship Intimate disclosure Satisfaction Emotional support	Informal Support (peers/ friends) Formal support from staff in RC	The network of relationships inventory–relationship quality version (NRI-RQV; Furman and Buhrmester, 1985, Buhrmester and Furman, 2008)	Social images (IV) Self-representations (DP) Social support (moderator)	Bivariate correlations Multiple regressions

Ferreira et al. 2020	Qualitative, cross-sectional	*Young people* N = 29; 76% males Age: M = 14.79 *Residential settings* N = 10	Network Availability Utilization Content Evaluation Provided Social Support	Informal support Formal support from staff in RC	Individual interview script	Positive psychological functioning Psychological functioning problems	Thematic analysis
Magalhães et al., 2021	Quantitative, cross-sectional	*Young people* N = 366; 53% males Age: M = 14.82	Formal support (general dimension)	Staff in RC	Questionnaire of institutional support (Calheiros et al., 2009; Calheiros & Paulino, 2007).	Rights perceptions (IV) Psychopathology (General dimension) (DP) Social support (moderator)	Bivariate correlations Regressions
Silva, Carvalho et al., 2022	Quantitative, cross-sectional	*Young people* N = 699; 51% males Age: M = 16.18 *Residential settings* N = 55	Support	Staff in RC	The social provisions version (SPV), of the network of relationship inventory (NRI-RQV; Furman and Buhrmester, 1985)	Organizational social context (IV) Academic achievement (DP) Social support (mediator)	Bivariate correlations Multilevel mediations
Silva, Calheiros et al., 2022	Quantitative, cross-sectional	*Young people* N = 378; 51% males Age: M = 16.20 *Residential settings* N = 29	Support	Staff in RC	The social provisions version (SPV), of the network of relationship inventory (NRI-RQV; Furman and Buhrmester, 1985)	Organizational social context (IV) Psychopathology (DP) Social support (mediator)	Bivariate correlations Multilevel mediations

lower antisocial behavior, anger control problems, emotional distress, and difficulties in self-esteem and sociability (Magalhães et al., 2021).

These findings are consistent with theoretical assumptions from the Relational Regulation Theory (Lakey & Orehek, 2011) revealing that young people in residential care might benefit from supportive ordinary social interactions within the care setting to be more able to regulate their affect and behaviors, which might positively impact their psychological functioning. Being loved and cared for by staff in residential care may contribute to young people's feelings that they are valued, which may positively impact their self-system, for example, self-esteem, self-concept, or self-representation (Thois, 2011).

Beyond these associations we have found between support and psychological outcomes, the literature has been suggesting the need to conceptualize mental health from the dual-factor models. This means that mental health involves more than the mere absence of psychopathology, including an optimal state of functioning (Greenspoon & Saklofske, 2001; Magalhães, 2024; Wang et al., 2011). As such, when we explored different mental health profiles with adolescents in residential care (N = 369; 59 residential care settings), according to the dual-factor model (i.e., adolescents' scores on well-being and psychopathology), we found that social support seems to be differently perceived by adolescents (Magalhães & Calheiros, 2017). Specifically, the Complete Mental Health group (high well-being and low psychopathology) showed the highest scores on formal and informal social support, and the Troubled group (low well-being and high psychopathology) revealed the lowest scores (Magalhães & Calheiros, 2017). This possibly means that supportive relationships contribute to less psychological distress but also to higher levels of well-being. Furthermore, our findings indicate that social support seems to be particularly important to foster the well-being component of mental health. Indeed, we found that the Complete Mental Health group and the Symptomatic but Content group (high well-being and high psychopathology) revealed similar results on social support dimensions, more than when we compared groups with low psychopathology – that is, the Complete Mental Health and the Vulnerable groups (low well-being and low psychopathology). This evidence might suggest the need to carefully think about intervention with this Vulnerable group, who are socially perceived as non-problematic (since they show low psychopathology), although their well-being and self-actualization are threatened (Magalhães & Calheiros, 2017). These results thus suggest that, even though young people in care may reveal psychological difficulties, providing supportive relationships seems to contribute to their well-being, self-actualization, and empowerment.

In addition to these main effects, the results of two of the studies described above (Calheiros et al., 2020; Magalhães et al., 2021) have also suggested that social support plays a buffering role in the association between young people's perceptions of their social images (i.e., their perceptions about others' representations of them) and self-representations (Calheiros et al., 2020). Specifically, the association between young people's perceptions of negative social images (e.g., perceptions that they are socially viewed as being aggressive, angry, depressed, and traumatized) and their self-representations (i.e., their perceptions about themselves as nice, friend, helpful, funny, intelligent, and competent) was buffered by residential caregivers' support (Calheiros et al., 2020). These buffering effects revealed that the negative effect of perceived negative social images on self-representation was reduced or mitigated by higher support from staff in care.

In the same vein, in a study exploring the role of perceived rights in residential care as associated with mental health difficulties, we found that higher staff support may buffer the negative impact of less autonomy and contact with family on their psychological functioning (Magalhães et al., 2021). This means that social support from staff can counteract the negative effect of the absence of meaningful relationships with the birth family. Relationships in care that are stable, positive, and safe may provide a therapeutic milieu to these young people, thus being associated with lower emotional and behavioral difficulties (Castro et al., 2023; Petrie et al., 2006). This is even more critical as recent evidence suggests that, during adolescence, there is a new window of opportunity for adaptation, recovery, and psychological adjustment, when and if the residential care environment can provide supportive and secure relationships (Gunnar et al., 2019). In sum, the buffering effects of staff support are indicative that the relationships between young people and staff in residential care are therapeutic, protective, and have a significant impact on young people's adaptation when they are exposed to stressful events (e.g., others' devaluation of themselves).

Social support was also explored in our studies as a mediator in the relationship between organizational variables – that is, the social climate of the residential care settings – and psychological (Silva, Calheiros et al., 2022), and academic functioning (Silva, Carvalho et al., 2022). The study developed by Silva, Calheiros et al. (2022), was carried out with 378 youth and 54 caregivers from 29 generalist residential youth care settings. Silva, Carvalho et al. (2022) were based on a sample of 699 young people, their respective main residential caregivers (N = 242) and case managers (N = 168), from 55 residential care settings in Portugal. In both studies, the quality of youth–caregiver relationships was measured through the NRI–SPV (Furman & Buhrmester, 1985), which assesses youth's perceptions of the positive qualities of their close relationships (e.g., parents/caregivers; friends). In the present studies, participating youth rated their relationship with their main caregiver.

These studies showed that, on one hand, staff social support did not mediate the relationship between organizational social climate and people's academic functioning (Silva, Carvalho et al., 2022). On the other hand, results revealed that perceived staff support mediated the relationship between social climate (i.e., engagement, stress, and centralization) and youth's externalizing problems (Silva, Calheiros et al., 2022). This means that higher levels of caregiver perceptions of engagement (i.e., low depersonalization, personal accomplishment), stress (i.e., role conflict, role overload, and emotional exhaustion), and centralization (i.e., authority hierarchy) were associated with higher levels of staff support (affection, reliable alliance, enhancement of worth, intimacy, instrumental help, companionship, and nurturance) as perceived by adolescents, which, in turn, was associated with lower levels of youth's externalizing problems (Silva, Calheiros et al., 2022). These results suggest that engagement of staff in care may foster their supportive and quality relationships with young people, which in turn is associated with fewer behavioral problems. Also, a certain level of stress (if not excessive) can be a driver for staff's engagement in their professional role. As such, professionals who perceive more stress may be the ones who are more engaged with their work, which is associated with more positive supportive relationships and lower behavioral problems (Silva, Calheiros et al., 2022).

Finally, higher levels of authority hierarchy may enable staff in residential care to perceive higher control, coordination, and structure, which may be more effective in managing and dealing with stressful daily events, complex decision-making processes, and complex needs of youth and families (Silva, Calheiros et al., 2022). These results suggest that the organizational social climate impacts professional practices in residential care, namely their ability to establish supportive relationships with young people and foster their psychological functioning. Similarly, while caregivers' support mediated the relationship between social climate and externalizing behaviors, this was not the case for academic functioning, which might suggest that other variables (e.g., school-related factors) may be more helpful in explaining young people's academic outcomes.

In sum, mediating effects were found for the relationship between social climate and psychopathology. On the one hand, engagement or centralization may positively impact social support and the psychological functioning of young people. On the other hand, long-lasting stressful events (such as feelings of depersonalization or lower personal accomplishment) may threaten the capacity of staff in residential care to provide support to these young people, which in turn may increase their psychological difficulties (in line with theoretical assumptions previously described; Lepore et al., 1991).

The Voice of Young People in Residential Care

In addition to previous evidence based on quantitative studies, we have found additional insights from a qualitative and in-depth perspective focused on young people's experiences, meanings, and feelings (Ferreira et al., 2020; Magalhães et al., 2018). Regarding the perceived availability of support, the evaluation of the received social support, and the network of adolescents (e.g., family, friends, and staff) in the Portuguese residential care context, we developed a qualitative study through interviews with 20 young people in residential care. First, we found that almost all the participants (97%) feel that they have available support whenever they need it: "*I feel like I'm not that lonely and that there are people who can help me (...) I know that if anything happens to me, I can always count on them*" (Ferreira et al., 2020, pp. 31–32). Second, all the participants felt satisfied with the received social support (100%). However, some of these adolescents also pointed out less positive aspects of the received social support (24%), given that they were unsatisfied with the received support or identifying additional support needs.

In line with international evidence on this topic (e.g., Bravo & Del Valle, 2003), different sources of social support, mostly informal (from family and friends) but also formal (e.g., from staff in care or teachers at school) were identified (Ferreira et al., 2020). Family members and staff in residential care were considered the most important sources of support, providing instrumental (i.e., helping them with issues related to school or job), informational (i.e., advice and guidance), and emotional support (i.e., trust, empathy) (Ferreira et al., 2020). Moreover, in the study by Magalhães et al. (2018) through a focus group (N = 29), adolescents acknowledged that the support from staff in residential care is particularly helpful regarding their daily routines while in care (Magalhães et al., 2018). Specifically, while staff in residential care seem to be perceived as the most important providers of informational and instrumental support, emotional support seems to be provided by both the staff and young people's families (Ferreira et al., 2020). These findings are consistent with previous findings which revealed that families play a particularly important role in terms of affective and emotional support (Bravo & Del Valle, 2003).

Specifically, peer relationships were identified by youth as a significant source of support because, when they deem that their peers understand their current experiences in care, this seems to help these youth deal with the challenges of living in care, which is beneficial to their well-being (Magalhães et al., 2018). Considering the well-known developmental tasks during adolescence, young people's peer group is described as a particularly important context for healthy functioning in that stage, fostering young people's interpersonal, prosocial skills, and social developmental outcomes (Magalhães & Calheiros, 2015), which is particularly critical when young people have been exposed to adverse experiences (Grych et al., 2015; Pinheiro et al., 2021). Young people's feelings of being part of and supported by their peer group are well-described as a protective factor for mental health during adolescence (Magalhães & Calheiros, 2015; Magalhães et al., 2016; Tarrant, 2002).

Moreover, adolescents suggested that social support positively impacts their psychological functioning, by enhancing their perceived self-efficacy, well-being, and quality of life but also by helping them deal with their psychological, behavioral, or emotional difficulties (e.g., "*I was also a user of this [drug addict] because I also smoked drugs and had my issues and my own ways of solving them, but now because of some friends I quit drugs and the group home helped me and everything.*"; Ferreira et al., 2020, p. 32).

These findings are aligned with the dual-factor model of mental health assumptions, given that fostering protective and supportive relationships might provide a context for greater self-regulation, lower emotional and behavioral problems, and higher well-being (i.e., an optimal state of functioning) (Magalhães & Calheiros, 2017).

Finally, while the quantitative findings previously described the positive impact of support on mental health, our qualitative findings also revealed the need to think about the dialectic between support and autonomy (Ferreira et al., 2020). In some circumstances, support, especially when perceived as overprotective and unnecessary, may be found by adolescents as a factor that can undermine their autonomy and self-determination (e.g., "*There are things they do that I don't like, but they say that they are helping me, so… (…) they say they're helping me but I don't think so, but that's it.*" Ferreira et al., 2020, p. 32). Given that independence and autonomy are critical developmental tasks during adolescence (Christie & Viner, 2005), this finding calls for looking at support in care (particularly instrumental and informational) as a way of promoting social skills, self-determination, and empowerment, and preventing adolescents' dependence, which might hinder their adaptive development. In fact, some evidence suggests that supporting the autonomy of young people in residential care involves fostering their self-regulation (personal, emotional, and interpersonal skills) as well as self-care skills. Social support in this context is important in the sense that being warm and caring enables youth to build their capacity to be independent and emancipated (Calheiros et al., 2013).

Conclusions

The studies presented in this chapter highlighted that diverse sources of social support may play different roles in adolescents' developmental outcomes: main, buffering, and mediating effects. These three types of effects were found regarding staff support: main effects for self-representations and psychopathology; buffering effects on the relationship between young people's rights and psychopathology and social images and self-representations, and mediating effects in the associations between the organizational social climate and externalizing problems. Friends' support had main effects on positive and negative self-representations, and qualitative evidence also pointed out the importance of emotional support from family, which calls for additional insights regarding supportive relationships within the adolescents' family. In fact, the quantitative studies we have developed have focused primarily on support from staff and friends, and further research on the role of family support is lacking.

Overall, these results suggest that staff's social support in residential care may buffer the negative effect of variables related to the out-of-care context (e.g., social images, relationship, or contact with the birth family) but the social and organizational climate of the residential care homes seem to impact the supportive relationships in this context and therefore the psychological functioning of young people. Living (youth) and working (staff) in a residential care setting involves dealing with an organizational climate that involves persistent stress and may negatively impact the ability of staff to establish supportive and quality relationships with the youth. Contrarily, the ability of staff to be supportive seems to be positively impacted by a structured and predictable social and organizational climate, where professionals feel engaged with their tasks, roles, and work.

Despite the relevance and innovative nature of these results, it is important to highlight a set of limitations that require additional research efforts. First, the studies described in this chapter were all cross-sectional. Such cross-sectional designs do not allow causal conclusions. For example, we can conclude that social support reduces psychological difficulties among the youth, but it might also possibly be that youth with reduced problems receive more support from others, as it is easier to provide them with such support. Such limitations require further research evaluating both the support relationships and the psychological adjustment from longitudinal and developmental perspectives. Longitudinal designs enable us to identify patterns of behaviors across time and, thus, causal links could be identified.

Second, most of the studies presented here focused on examining the role of staff support. It can be said that not as much effort was expended on analyzing social support from other sources (e.g., family and peers). Given that the qualitative studies we developed have suggested that family and peers can be very important sources of support to young people's mental health in residential care, it is therefore necessary to develop further quantitative studies that enable us to test the communalities and specificities of social support from different sources (e.g., family, school, or peers) and its different effects (i.e., main, buffering, or mediating) regarding young people's mental health.

Concerning the evaluation of social support, most studies summarized and included here evaluated only the perceived support of young people in residential care, asking young people to report on their experiences regarding one or two specific sources (e.g., staff, peers) (Calheiros et al., 2020; Magalhães et al., 2021; Silva, Calheiros et al., 2022; Silva, Carvalho et al., 2022), while only one (qualitative) study (Ferreira et al., 2020) explored different aspects of social support (i.e., network, direction, disposition, content, and evaluation). In this sense, further studies exploring different aspects and sources of support (e.g., in and out of the residential care setting) and based on multiple informants (i.e., staff, young people, relatives, and teachers), it might allow a better understanding of the complexity of these relationships during the placement of youth in residential care as well as their effects on their developmental outcomes. Moreover, young people's outcomes were more discussed in terms of psychopathology (Magalhães et al., 2018; Magalhães et al., 2021; Silva, Calheiros et al., 2022) than in terms of their well-being or both (i.e., Ferreira et al., 2020; Magalhães & Calheiros, 2017). This calls for additional evidence from a more holistic approach to psychological health, including both positive and negative indicators of adjustment (Grych et al., 2015; Pinheiro et al., 2021).

Despite these limitations, these results are viewed as a promising body of evidence, obtained with quantitative and qualitative methods, and focusing on different outcomes. Based on this evidence, it is possible to identify a set of implications for professional practice in this context.

Implications for Practice and Policy

The results presented in this chapter suggest the need to plan residential services from an ecological and meaningful relationship-based perspective. According to Whittaker et al. (2016), residential care settings might involve a multidimensional living environment that offers treatment, education, socialization, support, and protection to children and youth with mental health or behavioral problems. In fact, residential homes need to respond to these complex mental health needs, which require a therapeutic milieu. Providing a therapeutic milieu means that young people can readily grasp the skills they need to achieve desirable developmental outcomes in the therapeutic environment, where daily life is predictable and relationships are reliable (Huefner & Ainsworth, 2021). As such, residential care services need to be able to provide an environment, where developing a close and trustworthy relationship with young people is critical (Huefner & Ainsworth, 2021). To be able to provide this therapeutic milieu, the availability of trained staff is imperative.

Residential staff should receive supervision and training (e.g., trauma-based intervention), given that young people who are placed in residential care frequently undergo extremely negative pre-care experiences, which might negatively impact their mental health. Therefore, it is very important that professional training on relationship skills and trauma-informed care address the complex needs of young people in residential care (Garcia Quiroga & Hamilton-Giachritsis, 2016; Izzo et al., 2020). Having qualified staff capable of responding to the young people's needs (e.g., in terms of affection, reliable alliance, instrumental help, or companionship) (Silva, Calheiros et al., 2022) may buffer the negative impact of previous traumatic experiences. Moreover, given that staff practices are affected by the organizational social climate, organizational implications must also be acknowledged. Residential care settings that are clearly structured are more able to engage staff in their challenging work. Moreover, these settings should be able to provide the support and resources that caregivers need to be supportive in their relationships (e.g., affective, and responsive) with young people (Silva, Calheiros et al., 2022). In sum, the residential care context (the therapeutic milieu) plays an important role regarding professionals' practices and young people's outcomes. Indeed, we know that young people's perceptions of their relationship with the residential care context are positively associated with their well-being and adjustment (Magalhães & Calheiros, 2015; Magalhães & Calheiros, 2020).

Moreover, our results suggested that it is important to ensure that young people can maintain meaningful and supportive relationships with their families (as they are perceived as emotionally supportive). As such, the relationship between young people and their birth family should be carefully considered in the intervention plan, ensuring that these contacts are purposeful, frequent, and safe, and thus, contributing to the quality of relationships (Sen & Broadhurst, 2011). Families and young people should be supported by staff in residential care so that they can have the opportunity of developing a meaningful relationship, thereby enabling a successful potential family reunification or transition to independent life. As such, young people should be heard on their perspectives about the contact with their birth family to maximize the potential of these contacts (Sen & Broadhurst, 2011) and the emotional support that might be provided by their relatives.

Finally, all these aspects should be ensured bearing in mind that different mental health statuses would be present in this group of adolescents. In fact, there is evidence that resilience and post-traumatic growth could emerge following traumatic experiences, such as violence (Grych et al., 2015; Pinheiro et al., 2021). The literature on youth in care has mainly focused on psychopathology, and consequently, the intervention has been largely dedicated to reducing symptoms and problems, disregarding the promotion of young people's well-being (Magalhães & Calheiros, 2017). Nevertheless, our results show that there is a profile of young people who do not present significant symptoms but also do not present psychological growth or well-being (the Vulnerable group). As such, meaningful, supportive, secure, and warm relationships may be particularly important for this group of adolescents. Interventions based on strengths (and not only on difficulties) should be encouraged in residential care settings to address young people's needs regarding mental health as a holistic state. Similarly, since there are also young people who simultaneously experience difficulties and present high levels of well-being, interventions aimed at reducing symptoms should be combined with the promotion of skills, resilience, and adaptation.

References

Bailey, C., Klas, A., Cox, R., Bergmeier, H., Avery, J., & Skouteris, H. (2018). Systematic review of organisation-wide, trauma-informed care models in out-of-home care (Oo HC) settings. *Health & Social Care in the Community*, *27*(3), e10–e22. https://doi.org/10.1111/hsc.12621

Beeble, M. L., Bybee, D., Sullivan, C. M., & Adams, A. E. (2009). Main, mediating, and moderating effects of social support on the well-being of survivors of intimate partner violence across 2 years. *Journal of Consulting and Clinical Psychology*, *77*(4), 718–729. https://doi.org/10.1037/a0016140

Bravo, A., & Del Valle, J. F. (2003). Las redes de apoyo social de los adolescentes acogidos en residencias de protección. Un análisis comparativo con población normativa [Social support networks for adolescents in residential care. A comparative analysis with normative population]. *Psicothema*, *15*(1), 136–142.

Buhrmester, D. & Furman, W. (2008). *The network of relationships inventory: Relationship qualities version*. Unpublished measure, available from the authors, University of Texas at Dallas.

Calheiros, M., Graça, J., Patrício, J., Morais, I., & Costa, R. (2009). *Programa de Residência e Apoio à Integração de Adolescentes (RAIA)*. [Adolescent Residential and Integration Support Programme] Final Report. Lisbon, CIS-Iscte.

Calheiros, M., & Paulino, A. P. (2007). Construção e determinação das qualidades psicométricas do questionário de suporte social institucional na saúde (QSSIS). *Laboratório de Psicologia*, *5*(1), 17–32. https://doi.org/10.14417/lp.755

Calheiros, M. M., Patrício, J. N., & Graça, J. (2013). Staff and youth views on autonomy and emancipation from residential care: A participatory research study. *Evaluation and Program Planning*, *39*, 57–66. https://doi.org/10.1016/j.evalprogplan.2013.04.003

Calheiros, M. M., Patrício J. N., & Silva, C. (2020). Social support as a moderator of associations between youth's perceptions of their social images and self-representations in residential care. *Children and Youth Services Review*, *119*(105667). https://doi.org/10.1016/j.childyouth.2020.105667

Castro, E., Magalhães, E., & Del Valle, J. F. (2023). A systematic review of non-specific and specific treatment factors associated with lower or greater internalising and externalising symptoms in therapeutic residential care. *Children and Youth Services Review*, *106840*. https://doi.org/10.1016/j.childyouth.2023.106840

Christie, D., & Viner, R. (2005). Adolescent development. *BMJ*, *330*(7486), 301–304. https://doi.org/10.1136/bmj.330.7486.301

Cohen, S., Underwood, L. G., & Gottlieb, B. H. (Eds.). (2000). *Social support measurement and intervention: A guide for health and social scientists*. New York: Oxford University Press.

Ferreira, S., Magalhães, E., & Prioste, A. (2020). Social Support and Mental Health of Young People in Residential Care: A Qualitative Study. *Anuario de Psicologia Juridica*, *11*, 1801–1816. https://doi.org/10.5093/apj2019a12

Furman, W., & Buhrmester, D. (1985). Children's perceptions of the personal relationships in their social networks. *Developmental Psychology*, *21*(6), 1016–1024. https://doi.org/10.1037/0012-1649.21.6.1016

Garcia Quiroga, M., & Hamilton-Giachritsis, C. (2016). Attachment styles in children living in alternative care: A systematic review of the literature. *Child & Youth Care Forum*, *45*, 625–653.

Greenspoon, P. J., & Saklofske, D. H. (2001). Toward an integration of subjective well-being and psychopathology. *Social Indicators Research*, *54*(1), 81–108. https://doi.org/10.1023/A:1007219227883

Grych, J., Hamby, S., & Banyard, V. (2015). The resilience portfolio model: Understanding healthy adaptation in victims of violence. *Psychology of Violence*, *5*(4), 343–354. https://doi.org/10.1037/a0039671

Gunnar, M. R., DePasquale, C. E., Reid, B. M., Donzella, B., & Miller, B. S. (2019). Pubertal stress recalibration reverses the effects of early life stress in postinstitutionalized children. *Proceedings of the National Academy of Sciences*, *116*(48), 23984–23988. https://doi.org/10.1073/pnas.1909699116

Holden, M. J., Anglin, J. P., & Nunno, M. A. (2015). Engaging the total therapeutic residential care program in a process of quality improvement: Learning from the CARE model. In J. K. Whittaker, J. Fernandez Del Valle, & L. Holmes (Eds.), *Therapeutic residential care with children and youth: Developing evidence-based international practice*. Philadelphia, PA: Jessica Kingsley.

Huefner, J., & Ainsworth, F. (2021). Commentary: Recognizing the value of the milieu in therapeutic residential care for children and youth. *Residential Treatment for Children & Youth*, *38*(3), 324–335. https://doi.org/10.1080/0886571X.2021.1915225

ISS (2022). *CASA 2021 – Relatório de Caracterização Anual da Situação de Acolhimento das Crianças e Jovens – Annual Report on Children and Young People in Alternative Care*. Lisboa: Instituto de Segurança Social. Retrieved from https://www.seg-social.pt/documents/10152/13200/Relat%C3%B3rio+CASA_2021/d6eafa7c-5fc7-43fc-bf1d-4afb79ea8f30

Izzo, C. V., Smith, E. G., Sellers, D. E., Holden, M. J., & Nunno, M. A. (2020). Improving relationship quality in group care settings: The impact of implementing the CARE model. *Children and Youth Services Review*, *109*, 104623. https://doi.org/10.1016/j.childyouth.2019

Lakey, B., & Orehek, E. (2011). Relational regulation theory: A new approach to explain the link between perceived social support and mental health. *Psychological Review*, *118*(3), 482–495. https://doi.org/10.1037/a0023477

Law 142/2015 (2015). *The Law for Protection of Children and Youth at Risk. [Lei de Protecção de Crianças e Jovens em Perigo]*. Retrieved from http://www.cnpcjr.pt/preview_documentos.asp?r=5738&m=PDF

Lepore, S. J., Evans, G. W., & Schneider, M. L. (1991). Dynamic role of social support in the link between chronic stress and psychological distress. *Journal of Personality andSocialPsychology*,*61*(6),899–909.https://doi.org/10.1037/0022-3514.61.6.899

Magalhães, E. (2024). Dual-factor models of mental health: A systematic review of empirical evidence. *Psychosocial Intervention*. Ahead of print. https://doi.org/10.5093/pi2024a6

Magalhães, E., & Calheiros, M. M. (2015). Group identification of youth in residential care: Evidences of measurement and dimensionality. *Child Indicators Research*, *8*, 375–388. https://doi.org/10.1007/s12187-014-9257-3

Magalhães, E., & Calheiros, M. M. (2017). A dual-factor model of mental health and social support: Evidence with adolescents in residential care. *Children and Youth Services Review*, *79*, 442–449. https://doi.org/10.1016/j.childyouth.2017.06.041

Magalhães, E., & Calheiros, M. M. (2020). Why place matters in residential care: The mediating role of place attachment in the relation between adolescents' rights and psychological well-being. *Child Indicators Research*, *13*, 1717–1737. https://doi.org/10.1007/s12187-019-09716-5

Magalhães, E., Calheiros, M. M. & Antunes, C. (2018). 'I always say what I think': A rights-based approach of young people's psychosocial functioning in residential care. *Child Indicators Research*, *11*, 1801–1816. https://doi.org/10.1007/s12187-017-9511-6

Magalhães, E., Calheiros, M. M., & Costa, P. (2016). To be or not to be a rights holder: Direct and indirect effects of perceived rights on psychological adjustment through group identification in care. *Children and Youth Services Review*, *71*, 110–118. https://doi.org/10.1016/j.childyouth.2016.10.039

Magalhães, E., Calheiros, M. M., Costa, P. & Ferreira, S. (2021). Youth's rights and mental health: The role of supportive relations in care. *Journal of Social and Personal Relationships*, *38*(3), 848–864. https://doi.org/10.1177/02654075 20975507

Moreira, J. M., Andrez, M., Moleiro, C., Silva, M. F., Aguiar, P., & Bernardes, S. (2002). Questionário de apoio social (versão portuguesa do "social support questionnaire"): Tradução e estudos de validade. *Revista Ibero-Americana de Diagnóstico e Avaliação Psicológica*, *13*(1), 55–70.

Petrie, P., Boddy, J., & Cameron, C. (2006). *Working with children in care: European perspectives*. London: McGraw-Hill Education (UK).

Pinheiro, M., Magalhães, E., & Baptista, J. (2021). Adolescents' resilience in residential care: A systematic review of factors related to healthy adaptation. *Child Indicators Research*, *15*(3), 819–837. https://doi.org/10.1007/s12187-021-09883-4

Pinheiro, M., Magalhães, E., Calheiros, M. M. & Macdonald, D. (2022). Quality of relationships between residential staff and youth: A systematic review. *Child and Adolescent Social Work Journal*, (2022). https://doi.org/10.1007/s10560-022-00909-6

Rodrigues, S., Barbosa-Ducharne, M., & del Valle, J. F. (2013). The quality of residential child care in Portugal and the example of its development in Spain. *Papeles del Psicólogo*, *34*(1), 11–22.

Sarason, I. G., Levine, H. M., Basham, R. B., & Sarason, B. R. (1983). Assessing social support: The social support questionnaire. *Journal of Personality and Social Psychology*, *44*(1), 127–139. https://doi.org/10.1037/0022-3514.44.1.127

Sen, R., & Broadhurst, K. (2011). Contact between children in out-of-home placements and their family and friends networks: A research review. *Child & Family Social Work*, *16*(3), 298–309. https://doi.org/10.1111/j.1365-2206.2010.00741.x

Silva, C., Calheiros, M., Carvalho, H., & Magalhães, E. (2022). Organizational social context and psychopathology of youth in residential care: The intervening role of youth-caregiver relationship quality. *Applied Psychology*, *71*, 564–586. https://doi.org/10.1111/apps.12339

Silva, C., Carvalho, H., Magalhães, E., Attar-Schwartz, S., Ornelas, S. & Calheiros, M. (2022). Organizational social context and academic achievement of youth in residential care: The mediating role of youth-caregiver relationship quality. *Children and Youth Services Review*. https://doi.org/10.1016/j.childyouth.2022.106449

Tarrant, M. (2002). Adolescent peer groups and social identity. *Social Development*, *11*(1), 110–123. https://doi.org/10.1111/1467-9507.00189

Thois, P. (2011). Mechanisms linking social ties and support to physical and mental health. *Journal of Health and Social Behavior*, *52*(2), 145–161. https://doi.org/10.1177/0022146510395592

Wang, X., Zhang, D., & Wang, J. (2011). Dual-factor model of mental health: Surpass the traditional mental health model. *Psychology*, *2*(8), 767–772. https://doi.org/10.4236/psych.2011.28117

Whittaker, J. K., Holmes, L., Del Valle, J. F., Ainsworth, F., Andreassen, T., Anglin, J., … & Zeira, A. (2016). Therapeutic residential care for children and youth: A consensus statement of the international work group on therapeutic residential care. *Residential Treatment for Children & Youth*, *33*(2), 89–106. https://doi.org/10.1080/0886571X.2016.121575

4 Social Support from Nuclear and Extended Family, Peers, and Staff of Youth in Residential Care

Evidence from Israel

Shalhevet Attar-Schwartz, Shulamit Pinchover, Adena Hoffnung-Assouline, Adi Fridman-Teutsch, Netanel Shalem, Yisca Huri and Emmanuel Grupper

Introduction

Social support is closely associated with resilience and coping abilities among adolescents (Berns, 2012; Pinheiro et al., 2024a) and is particularly crucial for vulnerable youth (Demaray & Malecki, 2002; Vanderley et al., 2020). Young people in out-of-home settings, living apart from their biological families, often face a heightened risk of experiencing low social support (e.g., Perry, 2006). However, the existing literature on social support for young people in care is limited and focuses mainly on parental figures, particularly mothers, while often neglecting or downplaying alternative sources of support (see review in Pinchover & Attar-Schwartz, 2018), such as siblings, extended family members, peers, and staff in residential care settings (RCSs).

This chapter presents findings from studies on social support among youth in Israeli RCSs supervised by the Ministries of Education and Social Affairs. The authors conducted research with 1,409 adolescents aged 14–21 in RCSs for underprivileged youth (*Study I*) and 240 youth aged 14–18 in therapeutic RCSs for children at risk (*Study II*). Focusing on the youths' perspectives, the studies examined perceived support from parents, siblings, grandparents, peers, and RCS staff, along with their sense of overall support sufficiency, while considering youth and family characteristics. Furthermore, the chapter reviews findings regarding the relationship between social support and the well-being and functioning of these youths, highlighting different moderating models that explore the conditions under which social support is most beneficial.

Social support is defined as gestures and acts of attention, responsiveness, and assistance that address an individual's emotional and instrumental needs (Cutrona, 1996). Perceived social support refers to individuals' assessments of the extent of support provided by various members of their social

DOI: 10.4324/9781003424468-7

network (Salazar et al., 2011). Research has shown that the perceived availability of social support from diverse sources, along with the overall sufficiency of one's social network, is associated with higher well-being and reduced adjustment difficulties among young people in care (Attar-Schwartz & Fridman-Teutsch, 2018; Attar-Schwartz, 2016; Magalhães & Calheiros, 2017; Perry, 2006). Bronfenbrenner's (1977) socio-ecological model underscores the importance of evaluating influences from various social-ecological circles—such as nuclear and extended family, peers, and educational figures—in the development of young individuals.

Parents are among the most crucial support figures in adolescents' lives (Bokhorst et al., 2010; Helsen et al., 2000; McMahon et al., 2020). Rooted in attachment theory, there is strong agreement among policymakers, practitioners, and researchers that maintaining safe child–parent contact during care is essential for youth well-being (Shalem & Attar-Schwartz, 2022). Despite challenges to sustaining these bonds during placement (Jenson & Whittaker, 1987; Nickerson et al., 2006), research consistently links high-quality parent–child contact with better psychosocial adjustment for youth in care (Attar-Schwartz, 2008, 2009; Attar-Schwartz & Fridman-Teutsch, 2018; Poitras et al., 2022; Small et al., 2015). Yet, studies often focus primarily on mothers or treat parents as a unit, rather than assessing individual parental roles (Attar-Schwartz, 2008, 2009; Delfabbro et al., 2002). Research that does differentiate finds that mothers are generally perceived as more supportive, though fathers remain significant figures, especially for boys (Arteaga & del Valle, 2003; Davidson-Arad & Navaro-Bitton, 2015).

The support of other family members, especially siblings, is essential to consider, as sibling closeness is linked to improved well-being for children in care (Barnea et al., 2023; Davidson-Arad & Klein, 2011; Leichtentritt, 2013). Siblings provide vital social capital within the family microsystem, profoundly influencing youth outcomes. This aligns with attachment theory principles (Bowlby, 1988), emphasizing emotional bonds that foster resilience and stability for young people.

Grandparents also represent a significant source of potential social capital in the lives of adolescents in residential care. Research indicates that they are important figures in the lives of youth within the community and their support has been linked to improved outcomes, particularly during times of adversity (e.g., Attar-Schwartz & Buchanan, 2017; Henderson et al., 2009; Sorek, 2020). However, informal social support from grandparents has been infrequently examined among youth in residential care (see Attar-Schwartz & Huri, 2019, for discussion).

In addition, peers play a crucial role in the perceived social support of youth in the general population, sometimes providing a level of support comparable to that of parents (Helsen et al., 2000; Bokhorst et al., 2010). In the context of residential care, peer relationships are especially vital, as adolescents typically spend most of their time with their peers (see Arteaga &

del Valle, 2003; Emond, 2014; Irvine & Emond, 2023). Additionally, higher levels of support from staff in RCSs are associated with better functioning and lower levels of peer victimization among youth (e.g., Magalhães & Calheiros, 2017; Pinchover & Attar-Schwartz, 2012).

Therefore, it is crucial to map the social support networks of children in residential care and to include various figures in their lives, rather than solely focusing on parents as sources of support. This broader perspective acknowledges the significant roles that siblings, grandparents, peers, and staff members play in the well-being of these youth. By recognizing the diverse sources of social support, we can better understand the complexities of their experiences and improve interventions aimed at enhancing their overall well-being.

The Israeli Context

There are two main types of RCSs for young people in Israel. The first type, supervised by the Ministry of Social Affairs and Services, is treatment-oriented and is designed for children at risk who have been removed from their parents' homes, primarily due to parental maltreatment. Therapeutic RCSs typically include large numbers of youth divided into groups with educational direct caregivers (youth care workers) in rotating shifts. Social workers, psychologists, and psychiatrists are also involved in the life of the therapeutic RCSs (see Attar-Schwartz, 2019). The second type is education-oriented and is overseen by the Ministry of Education, aimed mainly at youth from underprivileged backgrounds. Placement in the educational RCSs is typically initiated by parents seeking to provide their children with better educational opportunities and improve their life prospects. Most of the educational RCS programs include elements of emotional–behavioral treatment by social workers or psychologists (Attar-Schwartz, 2016). A high percentage of youth in educational RCSs come from divorced families and low socioeconomic backgrounds. They also exhibit higher levels of emotional–behavioral difficulties and educational challenges than youth in the general population. Notwithstanding this, they fare significantly better than youth at risk in welfare settings (see Attar-Schwartz, 2016). The current chapter discusses insights from two studies that include samples of youth in both educational RCSs (Assouline & Attar-Schwartz, 2020; Attar-Schwartz, 2019, 2021; Attar-Schwartz & Huri, 2019; Attar-Schwartz & Fridman-Teutsch, 2018; Fridman-Teutsch & Attar-Schwartz, 2019) and therapeutic welfare settings for at-risk children.

Methods

As noted earlier, this chapter presents findings from two distinct studies: the first, the *Social Support Study*, involves youth in Israeli educational RCSs (*Study I*), while the second examines mother–child contact among youth in welfare RCSs (*Study II*).

Study I: The "Social Support Study" Among Youth in Educational RCSs for Youth from Underprivileged Backgrounds

The findings, presented in this section, are part of a comprehensive study conducted in Israel on social support among youth in educational RCSs, exploring various sources of family and extrafamilial support. The study is based on self-reports from 1,409 Israeli middle- and high-school students (Grades 8–12) residing in 16 educational RCSs managed by the Israeli Ministry of Education. Utilizing a random cluster sampling approach, the sampling frame was established from a list provided by the Ministry, which included 42 educational RCSs. From this list, 17 RCSs were randomly selected, with only one opting out of participation, resulting in a response rate of 94.12% for the RCSs. Very few adolescents or their parents/guardians declined to participate in the study, resulting in a response rate of 97.02% among adolescents present at the RCSs during the survey. Additional details about the sample, which varied for different analyses, can be found in Fridman-Teutsch and Attar-Schwartz (2019), Attar-Schwartz (2019), and Pinchover and Attar-Schwartz (2018).

Sample Characteristics

The sample consisted of approximately 53% boys, aged 13 to 20 years (M = 15.99, SD = 1.38). The vast majority of adolescents were between 13 and 18 (99.1%) and the rest were older than 18. About three-quarters of the adolescents (76.8%) were born in Israel and the rest were born in other countries. The adolescents reported an average length of stay of 2.05 (SD = 0.92) in their current RCS on a scale ranging from 1 (*first year*) to 4 (*5 or more years*). A little more than half of the adolescents (55.64%) had biological parents who were married or living together; 44.36% said their parents were divorced or separated. The average score of the parents' education index was 3.65 (SD = 1.23) on a scale ranging from 1 (*no formal education*) to 6 (*undergraduate degree or above*).

Data Collection

Data was collected from the adolescents using an anonymous, structured, and self-report questionnaire, which they completed in the RCS. Letters were sent to the RCS directors requesting their assistance in collecting data. Each director also received an additional letter to send to the children's parents or guardians, outlining the purpose of the study and providing contact information for any inquiries. A slip was also included for parents or guardians to return if they wished to opt out their child's participation in the study. The adolescents were assured that their participation in the survey was voluntary and that they were free to withdraw from the study at any time, for any reason. In the cases where parents or guardians did not permit their child to participate, or the adolescents themselves chose not to take part, the adolescent did not complete the questionnaire. Specially trained research assistants administered the questionnaire to all residents in Grades 8–12 (ages 13 and above) who were present and willing to participate. After completing the questionnaire, adolescents received a resource sheet listing child welfare agencies and services they could contact if they felt distress or required assistance beyond the RCS. All questionnaires, procedures, consent forms, and instructions were reviewed and approved by the Israeli Ministry of Education and the Ethics Committee of the School of Social Work and Social Welfare at the Hebrew University of Jerusalem.

Measures

Background characteristics. Adolescents were asked to provide information on a range of personal characteristics, including age, gender, and length of stay in their current RCS. They were also asked to indicate their birthplace, their parents' marital status, and their father's and mother's education level (for further details, see Pinchover & Attar-Schwartz, 2018).

Perceived availability of family and non-family support. Adolescents were presented with a series of identical questions regarding the perceived support availability from their fathers, mothers, at least one of their siblings, their grandparents, at least one of their peers, and at least one of the members of RCS staff. The scale used is an adaptation of the Social Support Network Questionnaire (SSNQ; Gee & Rhodes, 2008). The adapted seven-item scale, applied to each of the support providers, was designed to measure the provision of basic types of social support, including emotional support, concrete assistance, advice, and social participation (e.g., 'To what extent do you turn to him/her when you want to talk about something that is important to you?'). The questions were on a scale ranging from 1 (*not at all*) to 5 (*always*). The scale's score was based on the items' mean. Regarding grandparents, adolescents were asked about the support of all their living grandparents; here we refer to the support of the "closest grandparent" (see also Griggs et al., 2010) defined as the one with the highest mean score on the emotional support items included in the measure. When identical scores were obtained for more than one living grandparent, one grandparent was selected randomly. Cronbach's alpha coefficients of the measure for the various support providers ranged from 0.89 to 0.95 (Pinchover & Attar-Schwartz, 2018).

Adolescents' adjustment difficulties. Adolescents' adjustment difficulties were assessed using a total difficulties measure derived from the self-report version of the Strengths and Difficulties Questionnaire (SDQ; Goodman, 1997) for 11 to 17 year olds, which was professionally translated into Hebrew and Arabic. The translated questionnaires are available at the official SDQ website (www.sdqinfo.com). The SDQ is a three-point Likert-type scale

(0 = *not true*, 1 = *somewhat true*, and 2 = *certainly true*) measuring four difficulties (hyperactivity, emotional symptoms, conduct problems, and peer problems), as well as prosocial behavior (Goodman, 1997). The total difficulties score (α = .77), ranging from 0 to 40, was calculated by adding the summative scores for the four subscales addressing hyperactivity (e.g., "restless, overactive, cannot stay still for long"), emotional symptoms (e.g., "has many worries, often seems worried"), conduct problems (e.g., "often fights with other children or bullies them"), and peer problems (e.g., "rather solitary, tends to play alone").

Life satisfaction. We used the Student's Life Satisfaction Scale (SLSS) (Huebner, 1991) to measure adolescents' life satisfaction. The SLSS is a widely used, well-validated measure (Huebner et al., 1999) that has been used among children and youth in the general population as well as among children and youth in residential care (Gilman & Handwerk, 2001; Schiff et al., 2006). It is a seven-item measure of global life satisfaction (e.g., "Life is going well," "I wish I had a different life"). Items are rated on a six-point scale, ranging from 1 (*strongly disagree*) to 6 (*strongly agree*). The scale's score was based on the items' mean ranging from 1 (*low life satisfaction*) to 6 (*high life satisfaction*). The Cronbach's alpha coefficient for the sample was 0.87 (Attar-Schwartz & Huri, 2019).

Perceived quality of the relationship between the closest grandparent and the respective parent. Adolescents were asked to assess the bond between their mothers and fathers and each of their living grandparents by responding to the following question: "How well does your parent (mother/father) get along with each of your living grandparents?" (see Attar-Schwartz et al., 2009; Tan et al., 2010), on a scale ranging from 1 (*not getting along well at all*) to 4 (*getting along very well*). In this study, we focused on the adolescent's perception of the quality of the relationship between the closest grandparent and the respective parent (the son or daughter of the closest grandparent) (see also Attar-Schwartz, 2015).

Commitment to school and learning. We used an adaptation of a subscale developed by Hirschi (1969) to assess adolescents' commitment to school and learning, including the level of commitment to beliefs that school and grades are important, and students' investment—that is, their engagement in behaviors necessary for success at school, such as completing homework. The adapted subscale included six items (α = .84), such as: "How important to you is getting good grades?" and "How hard do you work for your studies?" Responses ranged from 1 (*never*) to 5 (*to a large extent*). The measure was based on the average of items, therefore ranging from 1 (*low commitment to school and learning*) to 5 *(high commitment*)

Victimization by peers. Adolescents were asked whether they had ever experienced violence at the hands of their peers (at school, at the RCS, or anywhere else). The answer to that question was dichotomous (yes/no).

Study II: Contact with Mothers in RCSs from a Contextual Perspective

Sample

The study was based on the self-reports of a convenience sample of 240 adolescents aged 14 to 18, about half of whom (48.3%) were aged 14–16 years and half (51.7%) aged 16 to 18, residing in 11 therapeutic RCSs under the responsibility of the Israeli Ministry of Welfare and Social Affairs.

The sample consisted of a similar percentage of girls (49.2%) and boys (50.8%). The percentage of adolescents who had been in their current RCS for more than four years was 44.4%; 18.8% of the adolescents in the sample had been in their RCS for three to four years and 20.1% for two to three years. For 16.7% of the adolescents, this was their first year in the RCS. Most of the adolescents in the sample (69.8%) reported that their parents were divorced or separated. The rest reported that their parents were married/living together (10.6%), their father was deceased (9.8%), their mother was deceased (4.3%), or their mother had never been married (5.5%). In our study, we compared adolescents from families whose parents were married to those from other family structures.

Data Collection

Information was collected from the adolescents through an anonymous, structured, self-report questionnaire. Letters were sent to the RCS directors requesting assistance in collecting data. RCS directors also received letters to send to parents or guardians detailing the purpose of the study and providing the researchers' contact information in case they had any questions. Each parent or guardian was asked to return a slip if they did not want the adolescent to take part in the study. The adolescents were assured that their participation was voluntary. They were made aware that they were free to withdraw from the study at any time for any reason. In those cases, in which parents did not allow their children to participate, or in cases where the adolescent declined to take part in the study, the adolescent did not complete the questionnaire. Of the youth who were approached, only four (1.63% of the sample) did not take part in the study because their parents did not permit their participation.

The adolescents completed the questionnaire online on their mobile phones, while gathered together in one place in the RCS. Given the sensitive nature of the questions, the researchers asked the staff not to be present in the room when the youth were filling out the questionnaires, and they assured the participants that their responses would remain confidential. Upon completing the questionnaire, adolescents received a sheet specifying child welfare agencies and services they could contact if they felt distress or in need of help from outside the RCS. Questionnaires, procedures, consent forms, and instructions were reviewed by the Ethics Committee of the School of Social

Work and Social Welfare at the Hebrew University of Jerusalem and by the Israeli Ministry of Welfare and Social Affairs.

Measures

Background characteristics. Adolescents were asked to report several background characteristics, including their gender, age, and the family status of their biological parents. They also provided information about their length of stay in the current RCS. For additional details, please refer to Shalem and Attar-Schwartz (2022).

Adolescents' adjustment difficulties. The SDQ (Goodman, 1997) described in the Measures section of *Study I* was also utilized in *Study II*. The Cronbach's alpha for total adjustment difficulties in this study was 0.752 (for more details, see Shalem & Attar-Schwartz, 2022).

Attachment to mothers. In this study, child–mother attachment was evaluated using an adjusted version of the Inventory of Parent and Peer Attachment (IPPA; Armsden & Greenberg, 1987). This instrument uses Bowlby's theoretical framework to perform a separate assessment of the adolescents' quality of attachment to each of their parents and their friends, specifying the way in which these figures constitute sources of psychological security for the adolescents. In this study, given the limitations of time and ability to complete a longer questionnaire, we referred to the children's mothers. As noted above, in cases where the child's mother was deceased (4.3%), they were asked to report on their attachment to their father or other significant figures. The adjusted scale consists of 20 items referring to aspects of trust, communication, and alienation in their contact with their mother (e.g., "My mother can tell when I'm upset about something"; "I like to get my mother's point of view on things I'm concerned about"). Participants' responses to the items were on a five-point Likert scale, ranging from 1 (*never or almost never*) to 5 (*always or almost always*). The total attachment measure (α = 0.96) was based on the items' mean (for more details, please see Shalem & Attar-Schwartz, 2022).

Perceived staff attitudes toward mothers. RCS workers' attitudes toward mother involvement in the RCS as perceived by the adolescents were examined through a measure used in Attar-Schwartz's Social Support Study (2016). That study examined, among a large random sample of youth, staff, and directors in RCSs in Israel, eight items (α = 0.88) reflecting youths' perceptions of staff's respectfulness toward the children's mother, the extent to which staff encouraged children's contact with mothers, and children's perceptions of their mother's involvement in the RCS (e.g., "When my mother visits me in the residential care setting, the staff treat her with respect"; "My youth care workers encourage me to be in contact with my mother"; and "When something bothers me, the youth care workers usually share that with my mother"). The items' response scale ranged from 1 (*not true at all*) to 5 (*almost always true*). The summative measure was based on the items' average.

Main Results of Study I: The "Social Support Study" Among Youth in Educational RCSs from Underprivileged Backgrounds

Mapping the Perceived Social Support of Youth in Residential Care

The results show that mothers are perceived as the most significant source of support (*M* = 4.42, *SD* = 0.74, on a scale from 1 = *not supportive at all* to 5 = *highly supportive*), followed by peers (*M* = 4.31, *SD* = 0.81) and siblings (*M* = 4.16, *SD* = 1.08). Fathers were ranked fourth (*M* = 3.94, SD = 1.21), while grandparents (*M* = 3.88, *SD* = 1.19) and RCS staff (*M* = 3.69, *SD* = 1.25) were seen as the least available sources, although both were still rated as providing moderate to high support on average (for full analysis details, see Pinchover & Attar-Schwartz, 2018).

The study revealed that youth characteristics were associated with variations in the hierarchy of social support providers. For example, fathers were perceived as more supportive by boys than by girls, and by adolescents with married parents than by those with divorced/separated parents. Siblings were perceived to provide more support by youth with divorced parents than by youth with married parents. Interestingly, siblings were perceived as most highly supportive by youth born in Ethiopia. Different patterns of support were also found in relation to peer support. Girls perceived significantly more peer support than boys. Peers were also ranked higher by youth from divorced families.

Correlates of Parental Support and Frequency of Contact

The findings (for complete details on analyses conducted and full results, see Attar-Schwartz, 2019) indicate that, on average, both mothers and fathers are highly involved in the lives of adolescents in educational RCSs for youth from underprivileged backgrounds. However, adolescents reported more frequent contact and higher levels of perceived support from mothers than fathers. For example, a large majority of adolescents (90.35%) indicated that their mothers very often or always provided help with necessities like clothing or money, while about two-thirds (66.44%) reported receiving similar support from their fathers. Additionally, 68.71% of adolescents turned to their mothers very often or always for important conversations, compared to just over half (53.47%) who reported doing the same with their fathers.

In terms of contact frequency, adolescents reported more frequent contact with mothers than fathers. On a scale of 1 (*never or almost never*) to 5 (*once a week or more*), measures included visits to the parents' homes, parents' visits to the RCS, and phone conversations. Only 1% of adolescents reported never or almost never visiting their mother's home, and 1.9% visited their mother only once every few months. In contrast, 13.5% of adolescents reported never or almost never visiting their father's home, and 7% visited only once every few months. While 55.3% of adolescents visited their mother's home once a week or more, 42.5% reported the same with their father.

The frequency of parental visits to the RCS also varied. About 18.9% of adolescents said their mothers never or almost never visited them in the RCS, with 28.4% reporting visits every few months. In contrast, 35.2% reported that their fathers never or almost never visited them in the RCS, and 20.9% reported father visits every few months. Roughly one in five adolescents (19.9%) reported that their mothers visited them in the RCS once a week to daily, while 16.2% reported the same frequency for fathers. Finally, phone contact was also more frequent with mothers. Only 1.7% of adolescents reported never or almost never speaking to their mother on the phone, with 1.2% reporting contact only every few months. In comparison, 12.7% of adolescents said they never or almost never spoke to their fathers on the phone, and 4.9% reported phone conversations every few months. While 90.7% of adolescents spoke with their mother on the phone once a week or more, only 67.4% reported the same frequency with their father. Overall, the findings highlight that while both parents maintain regular contact and involvement, mothers were generally perceived as more accessible and supportive in the lives of these adolescents. Fathers, though still significantly present, had comparatively lower reported levels of contact and support.

As for the correlates of child–parent contact, including frequency of contact and parental support, the findings (Attar-Schwartz, 2019) show that adolescents from divorced-parent families reported lower levels of perceived father and mother support, fewer visits to fathers' and mothers' homes, fewer mothers' and fathers' visits to the RCS, and fewer phone conversations with the father. However, the link between parents' divorce and the frequency of phone calls with the mother was statistically insignificant.

In addition, younger adolescents reported higher levels of mother support, more frequent mothers' visits to the RCS, more frequent visits to the mother's home, and more telephone conversations with the mother. They also reported more frequent visits of fathers to the RCS. However, there was a nonsignificant link between age and perceived father support, children's visits to the father's home, and telephone conversations with the father. Boys reported higher levels of perceived availability of support from both fathers and mothers. Nonetheless, gender was insignificantly linked with all measures of frequency of contact with both parents. Having been born in the Former Soviet Union (FSU; vs having been born in Israel) was linked with more mother support but with fewer visits to both mother's and father's home, less frequent phone calls with the father, and fewer father's visits to the RCS. Having been born in Ethiopia (vs Israel) was linked with fewer visits to the father's home and fewer telephone conversations with the father. Adolescents who had been born in other countries reported lower levels of both parents' support, fewer visits to mothers' and fathers' homes, fewer visits of mothers and fathers to the RCS, and fewer telephone conversations with the fathers. There was an insignificant link between phone conversations with mothers and the child having been born in a country other than Israel, Ethiopia, and the FSU.

Adolescents who reported greater geographic distance between their RCS and the home they usually went to on weekends and holidays perceived less availability of both mother and father support and had fewer visits to both father's and mother's homes, fewer visits of fathers and mothers to the RCS, and less frequent telephone conversations with the father. A higher education level of mothers was linked with more frequent visits of the mother to the RCS but with fewer visits of the child to the mother's home. Mother's education level was insignificantly correlated with the perceived levels of mother's support. Father's education level was linked positively with father's support, father's visits to the RCS, and phone conversations with the father. When including all variables in the equation, the link between the number of children in the family was insignificantly correlated with perceived levels of both mother and father support and all types of frequency of contact.

The findings showed a significant moderation effect of parents' divorce on the link between gender and perceived availability of father support and frequency of phone conversations with the father. Specifically, the gap between boys' and girls' reports of father support was significant among youth from divorced-parent families but insignificant among youth from intact families. Girls from divorced-parent families reported the lowest level of father support. The interaction of gender and frequency of phone calls with the father was also significant, showing that among youth from divorced-parent families, being a boy was linked significantly and positively to greater frequency of phone conversations with the father, but among young people from married-parent families, the link between gender and frequency of phone calls with the father was statistically insignificant.

Parental Support and Youth Well-Being

The study (Fridman-Teutsch & Attar-Schwartz, 2019) found that adolescents who reported greater maternal and paternal support reported stronger commitment to school and learning. Notably, the interaction between father support and family status significantly predicted school commitment: for adolescents with married parents, father support was positively and significantly linked to school commitment, while this association was not significant among those with divorced parents. Conversely, maternal support was consistently linked to school commitment regardless of parents' marital status, suggesting that mothers' support remains equally impactful on adolescents' school commitment whether parents are married or divorced.

Our analyses focusing on the fathers (Attar-Schwartz & Fridman-Teutsch, 2018) showed a significant negative association between father support and adjustment difficulties among the total sample. We also explored whether the association between father support and adjustment difficulties is moderated by experiences of peer victimization among boys and among girls. The findings of our study showed no moderating effect of victimization on the relationship between father support and emotional–behavioral difficulties among the sample as a whole. However, when taking gender into account in this moderation analysis, the findings revealed an interesting picture. A three-way interaction was found between peer victimization, father support, and gender in explaining the variance of adjustment difficulties among young people in educational RCSs. Specifically, the findings showed that the moderating role of victimization by peers in the link between father support and adolescent adjustment difficulties is different for boys and girls. As expected for the sample as a whole, among boys who had experienced victimization by peers, there was a significant negative relationship between father support and adjustment difficulties; for boys who had never experienced peer victimization, the relationship between father support and adjustment difficulties was weaker and insignificant. For girls who had experienced victimization by peers, there was no significant link between father support and adjustment difficulties. However, for girls who had never experienced peer victimization, there was a significant negative relationship between father support and emotional–behavioral difficulties.

Sibling Support and Adolescent Well-Being and Functioning

The findings (Attar-Schwartz, 2021) show significant correlations between sibling support and various measures of adolescents' difficulties and positive outcomes. Specifically, significant negative correlations were found between perceived sibling support and reduced adolescent conduct problems, hyperactive symptoms, emotional symptoms, peer problems, and total adjustment difficulties. In addition, perceived sibling support was correlated positively with adolescents' prosocial behavior and life satisfaction.

Grandparental Support and Life Satisfaction of Youth in RCSs

The findings indicate that adolescents who reported higher levels of informal support from grandparents also experienced greater life satisfaction (Attar-Schwartz & Huri, 2019). Additionally, the perceived quality of the relationship between parents and the closest grandparent was positively associated with adolescents' life satisfaction. Notably, the parent–grandparent relationship significantly moderated the link between grandparent support and adolescents' life satisfaction: while grandparent support was positively associated with life satisfaction across all adolescents, this effect was even stronger when the parent–grandparent relationship was positive.

RCS Staff Support and Adolescent Well-Being

The findings show that staff support was significantly and negatively related to adolescents' adjustment difficulties. The study showed that perceiving greater parental support was found to be positively correlated with perceived staff support. A significant interaction was found between the length of stay and staff support in predicting adjustment difficulties. Specifically, among youth residing for longer periods in the RCS, there was a stronger link between staff support and fewer adjustment difficulties. As hypothesized, first, the effect of staff support on adolescents' adjustment difficulties was significant for all adolescents. However, the effect of staff support on adolescent adjustment difficulties was stronger when adolescents stayed for longer periods in the current RCS (Assouline & Attar-Schwartz, 2020).

Main Results of Study II: Child–Mother Contact while in Therapeutic RCSs

Descriptive Statistics

The findings (Shalem & Attar-Schwartz, 2022) show that adolescents reported medium to high frequency of contact with their mothers (or with their father or other significant figure if their mother was deceased). On a scale ranging from 1 (*never or almost never*) to 5 (*every day or almost every day*), the average of frequency of contact was 4.19 (SD = 1.38). About half of the adolescents (53%) reported that they visit their mother's home once every two weeks; 17% reported that they visit their mother's home once a week or more; 18% visited only once a month or every few months; and 12% did not visit their mother's home at all. About half of the adolescents (52.1%) reported that they talk with their mothers on the phone every day or almost every day; 25.2% talked on the phone once a week; 11.9% talked every two weeks or less; and 10.7% never talked to their mothers on the phone. Regarding text, visual, and audio messages, 40.3% of the adolescents reported that they exchanged messages with their mother every day or almost every day; 24.1% once a week or every two weeks; 11.1% once a month or every few months; and 24.6% said they did not exchange messages with their mothers.

The adolescents' self-reports showed a medium level of attachment quality with their mothers (M = 3.55; SD = 1.06; on a scale ranging from 1 = *not true at all to* 5 = *almost always true*). For example, 78.3% reported that it is usually true or almost always true that "My mother accepts me as I am."

The average of perceived staff attitudes toward mother's involvement was medium (M = 3.29; SD = 1.08) on a scale ranging from 1 (*not true at all*) to 5 (*always almost true*). For example, about three-quarters of the youth (75.6%) reported that it is usually or always true that when their mother visits their RCS, she is treated with respect, while 12.1% reported that it is rarely true or not true at all. In addition, while only 32.2% of the adolescents reported that it is usually or always true that the staff calls their mother to share their achievements and successes, only slightly more (38.8%) reported that it is rarely true or not true at all that the staff calls their mother to share the adolescent's problems and difficulties.

Staff Attitudes Toward Mothers' Involvement as a Moderator of the Link Between Child–Mother Attachment Quality and Adolescent Adjustment

The findings show that the background characteristics included in the multivariate regression (gender, age, biological parents' family status, and length of stay in the RCS) were insignificantly linked with adolescents' adjustment difficulties. After controlling for those background characteristics, the regression findings show a significant negative link between child–mother attachment and adolescent emotional–behavioral adjustment difficulties. However, the relationship between perceived staff attitudes toward mothers' involvement and adolescent adjustment difficulties was statistically nonsignificant.

The findings show that adolescents' perception of staff attitudes toward their mothers' involvement moderated the link between child–mother attachment and adolescents' emotional and behavioral adjustment difficulties. Specifically, the findings show that when the staff attitude toward mothers' involvement is not positive (is below average), the negative relationship between child–mother attachment and adolescents' emotional–behavioral adjustment difficulties was nonsignificant. However, when adolescents perceived the staff attitudes toward mothers' involvement as average, the negative relationship between child–mother attachment and adolescents' adjustment difficulties was statistically significant. Finally, when staff attitude toward mothers' involvement was perceived as positive (above average), the negative relationship between child–mother attachment and adjustment difficulties was statistically significant and stronger.

Discussion

Social support is vital for young people's well-being (Magalhães & Calheiros, 2017; Pinheiro et al., 2022). This chapter explores perceived support from familial and nonfamilial figures among youth in educational and welfare RCSs. Using Bronfenbrenner's (1977) socioecological framework, we analyzed support patterns from various sources across the ecological spheres of their lives (Pinchover & Attar-Schwartz, 2018).

The findings indicate that mothers are viewed as the most significant source of support (see also Arteaga and del Valle, 2003). Maternal support is linked to better emotional and behavioral adjustment for youth in welfare and educational RCSs (Assouline & Attar-Schwartz, 2020; Shalem & Attar-Schwartz, 2022) and to stronger commitment to school among those in educational RCSs (Fridman-Teutsch & Attar-Schwartz, 2019). This aligns with other research highlighting the positive relationship between quality parent–child contact in out-of-home placements and youth adjustment (Attar-Schwartz, 2008, 2009; McWey, 2001; Poitras et al., 2022). Grounded in attachment theory (Bowlby, 1988), practitioners and researchers stress the importance of maintaining contact with parents (assuming child safety is not at risk) for the emotional, social, and educational development of children in care (Katsurada et al., 2017; McWey, 2001).

Research on the contextual factors associated with parent–child contact for youth in residential care remains limited. Our study found that positive staff attitudes toward mothers' involvement were linked to more frequent, higher-quality child–mother contact and fewer adjustment difficulties among children in therapeutic RCSs. This finding aligns with foster care research showing that cooperative relationships between foster and biological parents enhance outcomes (Oke et al., 2013; McWey et al., 2023), underscoring the essential role of staff in fostering child–parent connections within RCSs (Chateauneuf et al., 2018; Gillen, 2018; Shalem & Attar-Schwartz, 2022).

Our results also indicated that adolescents who perceived staff as supportive experienced a stronger negative correlation between attachment quality and emotional–behavioral difficulties, suggesting that positive staff attitudes contribute to environments that strengthen parental connections (Shalem & Attar-Schwartz, 2022). Drawing on Winnicott's "holding environment" concept, positive staff attitudes help create stable, respectful spaces that allow adolescents and parents to sustain their bond within a "good enough" care setting (Ainsworth, 1991; Geurts et al., 2012; Grupper & Mero-Jaffe, 2008). Supportive staff may also alleviate loyalty conflicts between parents and care staff, promoting better emotional–behavioral adjustment (Bibi et al., 2016; Dansey et al., 2018). The findings highlight that, beyond parental figures, children and youth in RCSs benefit from other key sources of support. Notably, our study identified peers as the second-most essential source of support (Pinchover & Attar-Schwartz, 2018). Research shows that, particularly during adolescence, peers play a crucial yet often underrecognized role (Bokhorst et al., 2010; Cheng & Chan, 2004). This is consistent with Emond's (2014) study of young people in care in Ireland, which emphasizes the importance of peer support within group settings (see also, Arteaga & Del Valle, 2003).

Siblings emerged as the third most significant source of support for youth in residential care. Notably, sibling support was associated with fewer conduct problems, emotional symptoms, hyperactivity, and adjustment difficulties, along with higher prosocial behavior and life satisfaction (Attar-Schwartz, 2021). These findings align with studies showing that sibling support contributes to well-being in care, regardless of co-residence (James et al., 2008; Barnea et al. 2023), helping youth manage stress and maintain continuity (Caya & Liem, 1998).

Fathers were rated as the fourth most significant source of support, following mothers (see also Arteaga & del Valle, 2003), peers, and siblings (Colarossi & Eccles, 2003). This ranking may be partly due to the high proportion of youth from divorced families, who often report lower levels of support from fathers. Other possible reasons for low levels of paternal support might include family dynamics which might make the father feel excluded and RCS policy and strategies for maintaining relations with parents that tend to focus on mothers (see discussion in Attar-Schwartz, 2019; Attar-Schwartz & Fridman-Teutsch, 2018). Future studies should examine those possible reasons for low father support in RCSs.

Despite ranking fourth as a support source, fathers still provide substantial support to youth in educational RCSs for underprivileged backgrounds (Fridman-Teutsch & Attar-Schwartz, 2019). For example, over three-quarters (78%) of adolescents felt loved and cared for by their fathers, and 71.1% reported feeling close to them most of the time. However, certain groups reported lower father support, particularly youth from divorced or separated families, a trend consistent with general population studies showing reduced contact and support from divorced fathers, especially when parental relationships are strained (Ahrons & Miller, 1993; Booth & Amato, 1994; Kalmijn, & Dronkers, 2015; Shapiro & Lambert, 1999). Additionally, girls reported lower perceived support from fathers than boys, aligning with research indicating that fathers often engage more with sons, leading to stronger father–son closeness (Feldman, 2003; Furman & Buhrmester, 1992). The findings reveal a significant negative association between father support and adjustment difficulties in adolescents, aligning with the main effect model of social support, which posits that support benefits individuals regardless of stress levels (Cohen & Wills, 1985). This pattern holds in both general populations and children in care (e.g., Davidson-Arad & Navaro-Bitton, 2015). These results highlight the valuable role of fathers in out-of-home settings, challenging assumptions about fathers' roles in the lives of these youth.

The study examined father support in relation to peer victimization. Adolescents with victimization histories reported greater emotional and behavioral difficulties, consistent with previous research (Geoffroy et al., 2016). While victimization did not moderate the overall link between father support and adjustment issues, gender differences emerged. For boys who faced victimization, higher father support correlated with fewer adjustment difficulties, supporting the stress-buffering hypothesis (Flouri & Buchanan, 2002). In contrast, father support had less impact on boys without victimization experiences. For girls, the results varied. Those without victimization experienced fewer adjustment issues with high father support, while no significant relationship was found for victimized girls. This may relate to social learning theories, as boys often adopt practical coping strategies from their fathers, whereas girls may benefit more from emotional support, which fathers may provide less frequently (Desjardins & Leadbeater, 2011). Additionally, boys may underreport emotional distress from bullying, perceiving fatherly advice as more supportive. Despite being less effective for victimized girls, father support overall remains important for girls. Further qualitative research could shed light on these gender dynamics in father–adolescent relationships within RCSs.

Grandparents and RCS staff were rated as having the lowest support availability, yet their support was still considered medium to high overall (Attar-Schwartz & Huri, 2019; Pinchover & Attar-Schwartz, 2018). Many adolescents reported their closest grandparents as actively involved, with 70.5% receiving practical support (e.g., clothing, money) and 55.3% seeking them out for important conversations. This aligns with previous research on grandparent involvement in youth living with parents (e.g., Tan et al., 2010). The study found that grandparent support is positively associated with adolescents' life satisfaction (Attar-Schwartz & Huri, 2019), mirroring findings in the general population that link grandparent support to greater well-being and fewer adjustment difficulties (Attar-Schwartz et al., 2009; Griggs et al., 2010). Grandparents play a beneficial role in the well-being of youth in residential care, supporting social capital perspectives that emphasize the importance of family ties.

Additionally, the quality of parent–grandparent relationships was positively and significantly associated with adolescents' life satisfaction. Those with strong connections between parents and grandparents reported higher life satisfaction, suggesting that close multigenerational ties foster a resilient "intergenerational self" linked to better adjustment (Duke et al., 2008). Overall, the study highlights that these adolescents benefit more from grandparent support when parents maintain positive relationships with their own parents, consistent with intergenerational solidarity theory. Strong parent–grandparent bonds enhance grandparent–grandchild connections, serving as a key protective factor in adolescents' lives (Attar-Schwartz, 2015).

With regards to staff support, our study found that about two-thirds of adolescents reported receiving consistent advice and support from staff, aligning with literature identifying staff as attachment figures (Cahill et al., 2016). The perceived availability of parental support was positively correlated with staff support and adolescent well-being, suggesting that strong parent–child relationships enhance connections with adult figures, including RCS staff, reinforcing attachment theory (Bowlby, 1982). However, given the cross-sectional nature of this study, longitudinal research is needed for deeper insights. Additionally, our findings indicate that staff support was significantly associated with reduced adjustment difficulties in adolescents, consistent with previous evidence in other countries (Magalhães & Calheiros, 2017; Magalhães et al., 2021). This underscores the need to acknowledge and support RCS staff in their daily interactions with children, rather than solely focusing on therapeutic interventions (Anglin, 2019).

We also examined whether the duration of stay in the RCS moderated the relationship between staff support and adolescent adjustment. Results showed that among adolescents with longer stays, the relationship between staff support and adolescent adjustment was stronger, likely due to stable relationships formed over time (Pinchover & Attar-Schwartz, 2012), and time is a critical factor in building trust among youth and staff (Cahill et al., 2016; Pinheiro et al., 2024b). While our findings suggest that staff support is particularly beneficial for adolescents who stay longer in care, causal conclusions cannot be drawn. Future studies should employ longitudinal and experimental designs to further explore these relationships.

Study Limitations and Implications for Future Research

The findings in this chapter highlight the complexity of adolescents' perceived social support in RCSs. It is essential to continue exploring social support for youth in residential care and to develop interventions that facilitate access to a network of multiple support providers (Perry, 2006). These studies, however, have limitations: both relied solely on adolescents' self-reports. Future research should triangulate data with input from other sources, such as staff or parents, and investigate differences in support from siblings living in or outside the RCS. Additionally, incorporating other potential support figures—such as teachers, uncles, and aunts—would provide a more complete picture. Longitudinal studies in RCSs are also needed to capture how social support evolves through different stages of adolescence.

Implications for Practice and Policy

Despite the limitations noted above, the findings have important implications for child welfare professionals and policymakers. The study identifies groups at risk for lower social network sufficiency and support availability. It emphasizes the need to devote greater efforts to assess and encourage increased contact with various support sources for various groups of adolescents. For example, programs to enhance parent–child contact in out-of-home care should devote special attention to children from divorced families (Attar-Schwartz & Fridman-Teutsch, 2018; Pinchover & Attar-Schwartz, 2018).

The findings indicate that the role of familial figures beyond mothers, such as fathers, siblings, and grandparents should receive greater attention in future research on the development of children and adolescents in out-of-home settings and policy discussions. The finding regarding the relatively high level of support fathers provide for their adolescent sons and daughters in residential care emphasizes the importance of considering fathers as crucial and influential figures who should be involved in the RCS everyday life as much as possible (Attar-Schwartz & Fridman-Teutsch, 2018). There are several existing programs in Israel and in other countries that are aimed at enhancing the father–child relationship in residential care, such as summer camps for fathers and children (Miro & Grupper, 2006). The effectiveness of such programs should be systematically assessed and should be expanded to include additional residential settings.

In addition, siblings should be prioritized in policies aimed at enhancing social support for youth in residential care. When siblings do not live together, residential social workers should encourage the informal inclusion of siblings in adolescents' activities and promote reliance on their support where beneficial. Interventions designed to enhance the well-being of youth in out-of-home care should actively consider sibling relationships.

Moreover, currently, the potential contributions of grandparents to the well-being of adolescents in residential care are largely overlooked by researchers and practitioners. This study provides a foundation for further exploration of how grandparents and other extended family members can support adolescents in care within the broader context of intergenerational relationships.

The study also highlights the significant involvement of RCS staff in the lives of adolescents in residential care and their crucial role in facilitating adjustment. Childcare policies should prioritize the role of RCS staff by focusing on recruiting and retaining high-quality personnel, along with providing training, consultation, and ongoing supervision (Ellenbogen-Frankovitz, 2018; Magalhães & Cerdeira, 2024). The positive correlation between perceived support from parents and staff underscores the need for therapeutic and policy models that foster healthy parent–child relationships. While many countries, including Israel, aim to limit the length of stay for children in out-of-home care in favor of biological or alternative permanent families (Dozier et al., 2014; Zemach-Marom et al., 2012), residential care professionals and policymakers should recognize the importance of stay duration in placement decisions. Future research should identify specific groups of children who may benefit from longer placements in RCSs.

Acknowledgments

This chapter is dedicated to our dear colleague and friend, Prof. Emmanuel Grupper, who passed away in April 2024. Prof. Grupper made invaluable contributions to this chapter and was a pioneer in the field of residential care and aftercare for children and youth in Israel. May his memory be a blessing.

References

Ahrons, C. R., & Miller, R. B. (1993). The effect of the postdivorce relationship on paternal involvement: A longitudinal analysis. *American Journal of Orthopsychiatry*, *63*, 441– 450. https://doi.org/10.1037/h0079446

Ainsworth, F. (1991, October). A "no blame" approach to work with families of children and adolescents in residential care. *Child and Youth Care Forum*, *20*(5), 301–311.

Anglin, J. (2019). The legacy of *the other 23 hours* and the future of child and youth care. *Residential Treatment for Children & Youth*, *36*(1), 27–34.

Armsden, G. C., & Greenberg, M. T. (1987). The inventory of parent and peer attachment: Individual differences and their relationship to psychological well-being in adolescence. *Journal of Youth and Adolescence*, *16*(5), 427–454.

Arteaga, A. B., & del Valle, J. F. (2003). Social support networks of adolescents in residential child care: A comparative analysis with normative population. *Psicothema*, *15*(1), 136–142.

Assouline, A. A. H., & Attar-Schwartz, S. (2020). Staff support and adolescent adjustment difficulties: The moderating role of length of stay in the residential care setting. *Children and Youth Services Review*, *110*, 104761.

Attar-Schwartz, S. (2008). Emotional, behavioral and social problems among Israeli children in residential care: A multi-level analysis. *Children and Youth Services Review*, *30*(2), 229–248. https://doi.org/10.1016/j.childyouth.2007.09.009

Attar-Schwartz, S. (2009). School functioning of children in residential care: The contributions of multilevel correlates. *Child Abuse & Neglect*, *33*(7), 429–440. https://doi.org/10.1016/j.chiabu.2008.12.010

Attar-Schwartz, S. (2015). Emotional closeness to parents and grandparents: A moderated-mediation model predicting adolescent adjustment. *American Journal of Orthopsychiatry*, *85*, 495–503. https://doi.org/10.1037/ort0000082

Attar-Schwartz, S. (2016). *Social support by family, peers and the residential care setting staff. A summary report submitted to the Ministry of Education*. Jerusalem: The Hebrew University (Hebrew).

Attar-Schwartz, S. (2019). Parental availability of support and frequency of contact: The reports of youth in educational residential care. *Children and Youth Services Review*, *101*, 317–328. https://doi.org/10.1016/j.childyouth.2019.04.016

Attar-Schwartz, S. (2021). Sibling support: The reports of Israeli adolescents in residential care. In A. Buchanan, & A. Rotkirch (Eds.), *Brothers and sisters: Global perspectives on the longest enduring relation* (pp 141–152). London: Palgrave Macmillan, Cham. https://doi.org/10.1007/978-3-030-55985-4_8

Attar-Schwartz, S., & Buchanan, A. (2017). Grandparent-adolescent relationships. In R. J. R. Levesque (Ed.), *Encyclopedia of adolescence* (pp. 1–16). New York: Springer.

Attar-Schwartz, S., & Fridman-Teutsch, A. (2018). Father support and adjustment difficulties among youth in residential care: The moderating role of peer victimization and gender. *American Journal of Orthopsychiatry*, *88*(6), 701–711. https://doi.org/10.1037/ort0000287

Attar-Schwartz, S., & Huri, Y. (2019). Grandparental support and life satisfaction among adolescents in residential care. *Children and Youth Services Review*, *96*, 70–78. https://doi.org/10.1016/j.childyouth.2018.11.033

Attar-Schwartz, S., Tan, J. P., & Buchanan, A. (2009). Adolescents' perspectives on relationships with grandparents: The contribution of adolescent, grandparent, and parent-grandparent relationship variables. *Children & Youth Services Review*, *31*, 1057–1066. https://doi.org/10.1016/j.childyouth.2009.05.007

Barnea, O., Cohen, N., Hindi, I., & Katz, C. (2023). Noticing the unutilized resource of siblinghood: Key conclusions from a scoping review about siblings in out-of-home placements. *Child Abuse & Neglect*, *141*, 106192.

Berns, R. M. (2012). *Child, family, school, community: Socialization and support* (10th ed.). Belmont, CA: Wadsworth.

Bibi, V, Oren-Chipman, T, & Blennero-Adiv, R (2016). *A firm but not painful hug: 'Good enough' care of children separated from their home*. Tel-Aviv: Resiling. (in Hebrew).

Bokhorst, C. L., Sumter, S. R., & Westenberg, P. M. (2010). Social support from parents, friends, classmates, and teachers in children and adolescents aged 9 to 18 years: Who is perceived as most supportive? *Social Development*, *19*(2), 417–426.

Booth, A., & Amato, P. R. (1994). Parental marital quality, parental divorce and relations with parents. *Journal of Marriage and Family*, *56*(1), 21–34.

Bowlby, J. (1982). *Attachment and loss. Vol. 1: Attachment* (2nd ed.). New York, NY: Basic Books.

Bowlby, J. (1988). *A secure base. Parent-child attachment and healthy human development*. London: Basic Books.

Bronfenbrenner, U. (1977). Toward an experimental ecology of human development. *American Psychologist*, *32*(7), 513–531.

Cahill, O., Holt, S., & Kirwan, G. (2016). Keyworking in residential child care: Lessons from research. *Children and Youth Services Review*, *65*, 216–223. https://doi.org/10.1016/j.childyouth.2016.04.014

Caya, M. L., & Liem, J. H. (1998). The role of sibling support in high-conflict families. *American Journal of Orthopsychiatry*, *68*(2), 327–333.

Chateauneuf, D., Turcotte, D., & Drapeau, S. (2018). The relationship between foster care families and birth families in a child welfare context: The determining factors. *Child & Family Social Work*, *23*(1), 71–79. https://doi.org/10.1111/cfs.12385

Cheng, S. T., & Chan, A. C. (2004). The multidimensional scale of perceived social support: Dimensionality and age and gender differences in adolescents. *Personality and Individual Differences*, *37*(7), 1359–1369.

Cohen, S., & Wills, T. A. (1985). Stress, social support, and the Buffering hypothesis. *Psychological Bulletin*, *98* (2), 310–357.

Colarossi, L. G., & Eccles, J. S. (2003). Differential effects of support providers on adolescents' mental health. *Social Work Research*, *27*(1), 19–30.

Cutrona, C. E. (1996) *Social support in couples: Marriage as a resource in times of stress* (Vol. 13). Thousand Oaks, CA: Sage.

Dansey, D., John, M., & Shbero, D. (2018). How children in foster care engage with loyalty conflict: Presenting a model of processes informing loyalty. *Adoption & Fostering*, *42*(4), 354–368. https://doi.org/10.1177/0308575918798767

Davidson-Arad, B., & Klein, A. (2011). Comparative wellbeing of Israeli youngsters in residential care with and without siblings. *Children and Youth Services Review*, *33*, 2152–2159. https://doi.org/10.1016/j.childyouth.2011.06.022

Davidson-Arad, B., & Navaro-Bitton, I. (2015). Resilience among adolescents in foster care. *Children and Youth Services Review*, *59*, 63–70. https://doi.org/10.1016/j.childyouth.2015.09.023

Delfabbro, P. H., Barber, J. G., & Cooper, L. (2002). The role of parental contact in substitute care. *Journal of Social Service Research*, *28* (3), 19–39.

Demaray, M. K., & Malecki, C. K. (2002). The relationship between perceived social support and maladjustment for students at risk, *Psychology in the Schools*, *39* (3), 305–316.

Desjardins, T. L., & Leadbeater, B. J. (2011). Relational victimization and depressive symptoms in adolescence: Moderating effects of mother, father, and peer emotional support. *Journal of Youth and Adolescence*, *40*(5), 531–544. https://doi.org/10.1007/s10964-010-9562-1

Dozier, M., Kaufman, J., Kobak, R., O'Connor, T.G., Sagi-Schwartz, A., Scott, S.,… Zeanah, C. H. (2014). Consensus statement on group care for children and adolescents: A statement of policy of the American Orthopsychiatric Association. *American Journal of Orthopsychiatry*, *84*, 219–225.

Ellenbogen-Frankovitz, S. (2018). *Residential care staff for at-risk children in Israel – An update and strategies for coping with the challenges of their work: Research report*. Brookdale Institute: Jerusalem. (In Hebrew).

Emond, R. (2014). Longing to belong: Children in residential care and their experiences of peer relationships at school and in the children's home. *Child & Family Social Work*, *19*(2), 194–202. https://doi.org/10.1111/j.1365-2206.2012.00893.x

Feldman, R. (2003). Infant-mother and infant-father synchrony: The co-regulation of positive arousal. *Infant Mental Health Journal*, 24,1–23.

Flouri, E., & Buchanan, A. (2002). Life satisfaction in teenage boys: The moderating role of father involvement and bullying. *Aggressive Behavior*, *28*(2), 126–133.

Fridman-Teutsch, A., & Attar-Schwartz, S. (2019). Commitment to school and learning among youth in residential care: The role of mother and father support and parents' divorce. *American Journal of Orthopsychiatry*, *89*(2), 201–211. https://doi.org/10.1037/ort0000364

Furman, W., & Buhrmester, D. (1992). Age and sex differences in perceptions of networks of personal relationships. *Child Development*, *63*(1), 103–115.

Gee, C. B., & Rhodes, J. E. (2008). A social support and social strain measure for minority adolescent mothers: A confirmatory factor analytic study. *Child: Care, Health and Development*, *34*, 87–97.

Geoffroy, M. C., Boivin, M., Arseneault, L., Turecki, G., Vitaro, F., Brendgen, M., & Côté, S. M. (2016). Associations between peer victimization and suicidal ideation and suicide attempt during adolescence: Results from a prospective population-based birth cohort. *Journal of the American Academy of Child & Adolescent Psychiatry*, *55*(2), 99–105.

Gillen, P. (2018). Therapeutic residential care: Partnering with families for improved outcomes. *The Brown University Child and Adolescent Behavior Letter*, *34*(9), 1–7.

Gilman, R., & Handwerk, M. L. (2001). Changes in life satisfaction as a function of stay in residential care. *Residential Treatment for Children and Youth*, *18*(4), 47–65.

Goodman, R. (1997). The strengths and difficulties questionnaire: A research note. *Journal of Child Psychology and Psychiatry*, *38*, 581–586.

Griggs, J., Tan, J. P., Buchanan, A., Attar-Schwartz, S., & Flouri, E. (2010). "They've always been there for me": Grandparental involvement and child well-being. *Children & Society*, *24*, 200–214.

Grupper, E., & Mero-Jaffe, I. (2008). Residential staff's changing attitudes toward parents of children in their care: Rationale and healing effects on children, parents, and staff. *Child & Youth Care Forum*, *37*(1), 43–56.

Helsen, M., Vollebergh, W., & Meeus, W. (2000). Social support from parents and friends and emotional problems in adolescence. *Journal of Youth and Adolescence*, *29*(3), 319–335.

Henderson, C. E., Hayslip, B., Jr., Sanders, L. M., & Louden, L. (2009). Grandmother-grandchild relationship quality predicts psychological adjustment among youth from divorced families. *Journal of Family Issues*, *30*(9), 1245–1264.

Hirschi, T. (1969). *Causes of delinquency*. Berkeley, CA: University of California Press.

Huebner, E. S. (1991). Correlates of life satisfaction in children. *School Psychology*, 6, 103–111.

Huebner, E. S., Gilman, R., & Laughlin, J. E. (1999). A multimethod investigation of the multidimensionality of children's well-being reports: Discriminant validity of life satisfaction and self-esteem. *Social Indicators Research*, *46*(1), 1–22.

Irvine, S., & Emond, R. (2023). 'They feel like another child in care has their back': An exploration of peer support between looked after children in Scotland. *Child & Family Social Work*.

James, S., Monn, A. R., Palinkas, L. A., & Leslie, L. K. (2008). Maintaining sibling relationships for children in foster and adoptive placements. *Children and Youth Services Review*, *30*(1), 90–106.

Jenson, J. M., & Whittaker, J. K. (1987). Parental involvement in children's residential treatment: From preplacement to aftercare. *Children and Youth Services Review*, *9*(2), 81–100.

Kalmijn, M., & Dronkers, J. (2015). Lean on me? The influence of parental separation and divorce on children's support networks in four European countries. *Zeitschrift für Familienforschung/Journal of Family Research*, *27*(1), 21–42.

Katsurada, E., Tanimukai, M., & Akazawa, J. (2017). A study of associations among attachment patterns, maltreatment, and behavior problem in institutionalized children in Japan. *Child Abuse & Neglect*, *70*, 274–282. https://doi.org/10.1016/j.chiabu.2017.06.018

Leichtentritt, J. (2013). "It is difficult to be here with my sister but intolerable to be without her": Intact sibling placement in residential care. *Children and Youth Services Review*, *35*(5), 762–770.

Magalhães, E., & Calheiros, M. M. (2017). A dual-factor model of mental health and social support: Evidence with adolescents in residential care. *Children and Youth Services Review*, *79*, 442–449. https://doi.org/10.1016/j.childyouth.2017.06.041

Magalhães, E., Calheiros, M. M., Costa, P., & Ferreira, S. (2021). Youth's rights and mental health: The role of supportive relations in care. *Journal of Social and Personal Relationships*, *38*(3). https://doi.org/10.1177/0265407520975507

Magalhães, E., & Cerdeira, J. (2024). *Professionals' Insights on Supervision in Portuguese Residential Care. Child & Family Social Work*, https://doi.org/10.1111/cfs.13235

McMahon, G., Creaven, A. M., & Gallagher, S. (2020). Stressful life events and adolescent well-being: The role of parent and peer relationships. *Stress and Health*, *36*(3), 299–310.

McWey, L. M., (2001). I promise to act better if you let me see my family: Attachment theory and foster care visitation. *Journal of Family Social Work*, *5*(1), 91–106.

McWey, L. M., Cui, M., & Stevenson Wojciak, A. (2023). Current caregiver involvement and contact with biological parents are associated with lower externalizing symptoms of youth in out-of-home child welfare placements. *Journal of Social Work Practice*, *37*(1), 63–78.

Miro, I., & Grupper, E. (2006). *Conservation and restoration of family relationship in residential care settings in Israel*. Jerusalem, Israel: Department of Social Security. [In Hebrew].

Nickerson, A. B., Brooks, J. L., Colby, S. A., Rickert, J. M., & Salamone, F. J. (2006). Family involvement in residential treatment: Staff, parent, and adolescent perspectives. *Journal of Child and Family Studies*, *15*(6), 681–694. https://doi.org/10.1007/s10826-006-9041-1

Oke, N., Rostill-Brookes, H., & Larkin, M. (2013). Against the odds: Foster carers' perceptions of family, commitment and belonging in successful placements. *Clinical Child Psychology and Psychiatry*, *18*(1), 7–24. https://doi.org/10.1177/1359104511426398

Perry, B. L. (2006). Understanding social network disruption: The case of youth in foster care. *Social Problems*, *53*(3), 371–391.

Pinchover, S., & Attar-Schwartz, S. (2012). Emotional and behavioral functioning of children and youth in residential care: The contribution of personal characteristics, victimization experience and social climate. *Mifgash: Journal of Social-Educational Work*, *36*, 61–90. (In Hebrew).

Pinchover, S., & Attar-Schwartz, S. (2018). Is someone there for you? Social support of youth in educational residential care from family, peers and staff. *The British Journal of Social Work*, *48*(8), 2195–2214. https://doi.org/10.1093/bjsw/bcx164

Pinheiro, M., Magalhães, E., & Baptista, J. (2022). Adolescents' resilience in residential care: A systematic review of factors related to healthy adaptation. *Child Indicators Research*, *15*, 819–837 https://doi.org/10.1007/s12187-021-09883-4

Pinheiro, M., Magalhães, E., & Baptista, J. (2024a). Resilience in residential care: A qualitative study based on the voices of adolescents. *Children and Youth Services Review*, *162*, 107694 https://doi.org/10.1016/j.childyouth.2024.107694

Pinheiro, M., Magalhães, E., Calheiros, M. M., & Macdonald, D. (2024b). Quality of relationships between residential staff and youth: A systematic review. *Child and Adolescent Social Work Journal*, *41*(4), 561–576.

Poitras, K., Porlier, S., & Tarabulsy, G. M. (2022). Child's adjustment and parent-child contact after child placement into foster care: A systematic review. *Journal of Public Child Welfare*, *16*(5), 575–606.

Salazar, A. M., Keller, T. E., & Courtney, M. E. (2011). Understanding social support's role in the relationship between maltreatment and depression in youth with foster care experience. *Child Maltreatment*, *16*(2), 102–113.

Schiff, M., Nebe, S., & Gilman, R. (2006). Life satisfaction among Israeli youth in residential treatment care. *British Journal of Social Work*, *36*, 1325–1343.

Shalem, N., & Attar-Schwartz, S. (2022). Good enough residential care setting: Child-parent contact and youth adjustment in the context of staff attitudes towards parent involvement. *Children and Youth Services Review*, *143*, 106687. https://doi.org/10.1016/j.childyouth.2022.106687

Shapiro, A., & Lambert, J. (1999). Longitudinal effects of divorce on the quality of the father–child relationship and on fathers' psychological well-being. *Journal of Marriage and the Family*, *61*, 397–408. https://doi.org/10.2307/353757

Small, R. W., Bellonci. C., & Ramsey, S. (2015). Creating and maintaining family partnerships in residential treatment programs. In J. K. Whittaker, J. F. del Valle, & L. Holmes (Eds.), *Therapeutic residential care for children and youth: Developing evidence-based international practice* (pp. 156–170). London: Jessica Kingsley.

Sorek, Y. (2020). Grandparental and overall social support as resilience factors in coping with parental conflict among children of divorce. *Children and Youth Services Review*, *118*, 105443.

Tan, Jo-Pei, Buchanan, Ann, Flouri, Eirini, Attar-Schwartz, Shalhevet, & Griggs, Julia. (2010). Filling the parenting gap? Grandparent involvement with UK adolescents. *Journal of Family Issues*, *31*(7), 992–1015.

Vanderley, I. C. S., Vanderley, M. D. A. S., Santana, A. D. D. S., Scorsolini-Comin, F., Brandão Neto, W., & Monteiro, E. M. L. M. (2020). Factors related to the resilience of adolescents in contexts of social vulnerability: Integrative review. *Enfermería Global*, *19*(3), 612–625.

Zemach-Marom, T., Halaban-Eilat, H., & Szabo-Lael, R. (2012). The number of children in residential care settings and their characteristics: Trends in the 2000–2010 calendar years. *Mifgash: Journal of Social-Educational Work*, *20*, 17–38. (In Hebrew).

5 "Somewhere You Can Grow"

Young People and Workers' Views on Residential Care Settings and the Value of Relationships and Social Support

Tim Moore, Anne Graham and Antonia Canosa

This chapter draws from the 'Beyond Safety: Ethical Practice Involving Children' research project which was funded by the Australian Research Council. The research team included the authors who worked in collaboration with Professor Sally Robinson, Dr Donnah Anderson, Associate Professor Nicola Taylor, Emeritus Professor Patrick Thomas, Dr Mary Ann Powell, Dr Tess Boyle, Dr Paola Castillo, Dr Jenna Meiksans, and Dr Meaghan Vosz. The authors would like to thank the team for their contributions to this chapter. We would also like to thank the young people, direct care workers, and managers for their openness and their wisdom. We are delighted that their insights are included in a text that aims to reclaim and strengthen effective relational practice by providing guidance to those building social support for young people in residential care.

Introduction

The Context of Residential Care in Australia

In Australia and abroad, children and young people who have been removed from their families due to concerns of abuse or neglect are often removed on statutory orders and placed in out-of-home care. One out-of-home care option is 'residential care' where children and young people are placed in congregate care, often with siblings or peers, in a residential building and supported by paid staff. Residential care is mainly delivered by nongovernment agencies that are contracted to provide assistance on behalf of the government. Of the 46,200 Australian children and young people living in out-of-home care, 7.3% live in residential care with others placed with relatives or kin (54%), with foster carers (36%), or in other types of home-based care (1.3%) (AIHW, 2021). Generally, children and young people who are in residential care in Australia are older (87% of those in residential care are aged over 10), although an increasing number of children are being placed in residential care due to a lack of other options available. Young people in residential care often have significant trauma histories, demonstrate challenging behaviors, and

DOI: 10.4324/9781003424468-8

have special needs that are not easily met in other care arrangements (Kor et al., 2022; Whittaker et al., 2023). At the same time, the dwindling numbers of families able to provide foster or kinship care have meant that the options for children and young people, particularly those who are adolescents, are also reduced with many younger children and others with lower care needs being placed in residential care (Kiraly & Humphreys, 2017). Many Australian residential care units now house only one–two children or young people with modest staff–child ratios (usually one staff for two young people).

In Australia, residential care is often described as the 'option of last resort' with a preference that those placed in congregate placements do so for short periods (i.e., a matter of months) before being placed in more stable and home-like environments such as foster or kinship care (Holmes et al., 2018). This policy position reflects a substantial body of research and inquiry findings that while in residential care many young people experience adverse experiences (such as exposure to peer violence and sexual harassment and exploitation) and have poorer physical, emotional, educational, and employment outcomes than their peers living in other forms of out of home care (see e.g., Gallagher & Green, 2013; Moore et al., 2016; Porter et al., 2021).

In Australia, the length of time a young person spends in residential care varies. The reasons why young people in residential care are moved from one unit to another include: concerns about the young person's safety when placed with peers with harmful behaviors, young people placing others at risk due to their own externalizing behaviors (i.e., physical and sexual violence), young people's access to therapeutic supports, and moves that attempt to build young people's social connectedness and reintegration into their birth families and communities (Farrugia & Joss, 2021). Their move from residential care to foster or kinship care is similarly restricted if young people's support needs are significant and suitably skilled carers are unavailable (Asif et al., 2023).

The Value of Reclaiming Residential Care Work and Building Social and Emotional Support

Notwithstanding the above concerns, there is some evidence that residential care can often be the best placement option for some young people with complex needs, who may benefit from the social and emotional support and stability provided (Porter et al., 2021) and value relationships with workers and peers (Evans et al., 2022; Moore et al., 2016). These positive conditions, however, are not assured. As such, international advocates have stressed the need for child protection systems and agencies to develop and implement practice models that move beyond merely providing supervision to young people to meeting their therapeutic and developmental needs within environments that are conducive to their healing and growth (Porter et al., 2021; Whittaker et al., 2023). In Australia, this has led many state and territory governments to require residential care agencies to articulate their approaches and be more explicit about the ways they will meet young people's therapeutic needs (McLean, 2018).

As these policy and practice reforms are still in their infancy, it is difficult to ascertain whether they are impacting the quality of life experienced by children and young people in residential care, strengthening their safety, and improving their time in care. One concern that has been highlighted within sectors outside of Australia is that such policy and practice reforms can unintentionally cast suspicion on, rather than strengthen, good relational residential care practice (Smith, 2009; Warwick, 2021). Further, as welfare systems become increasingly concerned about the threats of sexual abuse in institutions, for example, workers have reported anxieties related to their ability to develop strong relationships with young people and 'cultures of fear' that problematize and diminish the perceived value of their roles (Brown et al., 2018). Residential care workers report a reluctance to engage in practices that are seen as essential for children's growth and healing. Staff have reported a fear that their interactions with young people might be misinterpreted, such as touch associated with developmentally appropriate expressions of care, emotional support, and concern (Warwick, 2021).

Recognizing this current state of play, residential care advocates have stressed the need to reclaim the value of relational residential care work and to identify practices and approaches that meet young people's needs for safety, stability, and a positive sense of well-being. Residential care workers have, at the same time, sought more guidance about what they *can and should* do in a climate focused on what they *cannot* do. Among the suite of assistance that might, in this context, be better understood are social support and the set of practices that culminate in 'relationship-based practice'.

The Current Study

This chapter draws on findings from interviews with young people and workers engaged in a study titled, *Beyond Safety: Ethical Practice Involving Children* (EPIC) which was funded by the Australian Research Council. The EPIC study was informed by previous research conducted by members of the research team, including for the Royal Commission into Institutional Responses to Child Sexual Abuse (Moore et al., 2015; Robinson, 2016), which also involved a nested study focusing on the experiences of young people in residential care (Moore et al., 2016). The EPIC research recognizes that policy and practice guidance, such as the National Principles, necessarily focus primarily on what organizations need to do to comply with standards, rather than what ethical practices foster children and young people's safety and well-being. The study aims to address this gap by identifying these day-to-day practices in residential care, as well as within schools and disability services.

In the EPIC study, we considered the ethical dimensions of practice, viewing ethical practices as those that advance positive consequences or outcomes, adhere to obligations required of those providing services to young people, and acknowledge the virtue of work (Graham et al., 2023). Importantly, we were particularly interested in the value of 'relational ethics', which centers upon moral purpose and the quality of relationships, rather than upon individuals. From a relational ethics perspective 'relationships are built upon the principles of engagement, embodiment, mutual respect and environment' (Cloutier et al., 2015, p. 768).

The EPIC study included four phases: (1) the analysis of relevant policies to understand how safety and ethics are conceptualized (see: Powell et al., 2020a; Powell et al., 2020b); (2) qualitative interviews with young people and staff within different sector contexts to map practices that support young people's well-being and safety and to explore the ethical dimensions of these; (3) quantitative surveys with young people and staff to identify the elements of ethical practice that influence young people's well-being and safety, and (4) a research translation component that aims to further strengthen ethical relationship-based practice in child safe organizations (Graham et al., 2022; Graham et al., 2023; Robinson et al., 2022).

This chapter presents findings from interviews with young people (n = 13) living in residential care and direct care workers and managers (n = 9) as part of Phase 2, which aimed to identify key components of practice that facilitate safety and well-being. Interviews addressed the question: how do young people understand and experience 'ethical' practices that foster their safety and well-being and what do they perceive to be the enablers and barriers? In the following sections, we introduce the theoretical framework informing the study and outline the methodology for Phase 2. We then consider the practices (including those associated with social and emotional support) that foster safety and well-being and, in the discussion section, focus on the factors that enable and constrain these practices. Findings from interviews and focus groups with children and young people in schools and disability services are reported elsewhere (Graham et al., 2022; Graham et al., 2023; Robinson et al., 2022).

Theoretical Framework

Recognizing the centrality of relationships in residential care work, this study adopted a theoretical framework, informed by relational ethics and the three interconnected elements of children's rights, recognition theory, and the theory of practice architectures (TPA). The children's rights perspective acknowledges children and young people's rights to dignity, protection, and voice and the responsibility of agencies to meet their physical, emotional, and developmental needs (McCarthy, 2016; Ten Brummelaar et al., 2018). Recognition theory draws attention to the interpersonal relations in individual and group identity formation via Honneth's (1995) three modes of recognition, namely love, rights, and solidarity, translated into practice settings as being cared for, being respected, and being valued (Graham et al., 2017). This chapter builds on previous research that identifies the ways that social and emotional supports that foster recognition, respect, and reciprocity can be integrated into residential care work (Marshall et al., 2020; Turney, 2012) and how the absence of recognition (or presence of *misrecognition)* is experienced by at-risk youth (Korkiamäki & Gilligan, 2020).

Finally, the study employs TPA to understand practices in residential care as well as the ways in which these are prefigured by arrangements (conditions) found at or introduced to the site (Kemmis et al., 2014). Practices are defined as '*socially established cooperative human activity*' in which characteristic arrangements of actions and activities (*doings*) are comprehensible in terms of arrangements of relevant ideas in characteristic discourses (*sayings*), and when the people and objects involved are distributed in characteristic arrangements of relationships (*relatings*) which 'hang together' in a place, time, and setting (Kemmis et al., 2014, p. 31). This site-ontological approach guided by TPA (Kemmis et al., 2014) was essential in uncovering how the cultural-discursive, material-economic, and sociopolitical conditions enabled and constrained ethical practices at each site. During analysis, we considered the environments within which practices occurred and how organizational cultures and policies, departmental processes, and other external influences enabled and/or constrained residential care work. This is critical given a central tenet of TPA is that transformative change to practices within institutional settings is reliant on close attention to the conditions and arrangements that hold these in place (Nicolini, 2012).

For the purposes of this chapter, we consider the implications for the provision of social support in residential care. We adopt a definition of social support that includes 'the perceived or received assistance that an individual has from other people' (Evans et al., 2022, p. 2). Support might include providing young people with information and opportunities to learn, meet their emotional needs, and strengthen their connections within and outside of care (Hoagwood et al., 2010). Although this type of assistance has been demonstrated to be invaluable, the nature of their practical application and the interpersonal, organizational, and systemic factors that enable or constrain their use is limited (Kor et al., 2022). This chapter endeavors to address this gap, drawing on the lived experiences of young people and staff.

Method

Participants

A total of 13 young people aged 12 to 18 (10 young men and 3 young women) and nine residential care staff (including direct care youth workers (six) and managers(three)) from three organizations providing residential care participated in the study (alongside young people and staff from disability services and schools). Although young men are more likely to live in residential care than young women, we are aware that our sample is skewed, and that young women's perspectives need further exploration in future work.

Interviews with Young People and Workers

The interviews with young people were semi-structured and ranged in length from 20 minutes to one hour. Young people were given the option of completing interviews one-on-one, in small groups, face-to-face or online, and with or without a 'support person' present. Interviewers used a range of activities to engage young people in age-appropriate ways and were offered the choice to stop interviews and continue later if needed. Direct-care youth workers and residential care managers were also interviewed, mostly one-to-one and in person (one worker and a manager chose to be interviewed together). Interviews with workers were between 60 and 90 minutes in length. As the project was conducted during an international pandemic, delays were encountered in recruiting and conducting interviews which led to fewer participants than planned, and some interviews being conducted online rather than face-to-face.

Reflecting the project's overarching theoretical framework, participants were asked about the day-to-day 'happenings' (*sayings, doings, and relatings)* that led young people to feel happy, safe, and well. They explored the residential care contexts, the nature of congregate care, and the influences inside and outside of residential care that helped or constrained workers' engagement with children and young people. Young people were asked to reflect on what workers 'do' and 'say' and how they 'relate' to children and young people who help them feel safe and well. This data on actual day-to-day practices that workers engage in to support children's safety and well-being is consistent with TPA interests.

Worker participants were also invited to consider what ethical practice means within their work environments and how workers make ethical decisions in the residential care context. Given the exploratory and somewhat sensitive nature of the research, interviews were semi-structured and conducted in such a way that enabled participants the opportunity to choose what practices, risks, and constraints they wished to share.

Procedure of Data Collection and Analysis

This study was conducted with the approval of the Southern Cross University's Ethics Committee. The broad ethical approach taken with the research is described more fully elsewhere (see: Graham et al., 2023); however, a number of strategies were put in place to ensure that young people and workers' engagement was safe and ethical, including for example, the use of tools to help young people determine whether they were in a good 'headspace' to participate in the study, 'check-ins' to assess whether participants felt comfortable and to pre-empt any distress, and post-interview debriefs where researchers spent time with participants determining whether supports might be required as a result of their engagement.

Young people and direct residential care workers and managers were recruited through three partner agencies providing residential care in Australia. As young people were under the care of State child protection departments, permission for their involvement was sought and provided. Staff from the partner agencies approached young people, provided them with a short animation about the project, and explained the focus and approach that the researchers would take in engaging them in interviews. If young people expressed an interest, a member of the research team contacted them, answered any remaining questions, and organized a time to meet.

The data was transcribed and coded using a qualitative data management and analysis software, QSR NVivo 12 (Jackson & Bazeley, 2019). The data was analyzed purposively to develop initial themes from the research questions that guided the interviews. More in-depth manual coding was then conducted in four steps: 1) deductive coding to TPA categories (sayings, doings, and relatings); 2) inductive coding to identify which practices in Step 1 had an 'ethical dimension'; and inductive coding to identify which practices in Step 1 related to the modes of recognition (i.e., being cared for (love), being respected (rights), and being valued (solidarity); and 3) coding of enabling and constraining conditions that facilitate or hinder ethical practices that support young people's safety, happiness, and well-being.

Throughout this chapter, we provide quotes that illustrate the findings. For the purposes of the chapter, we indicate whether adults are residential care managers (Mgr), or direct care youth workers (DCYW), and which residential care agency they represented (i.e., RC-1). Quotes from young people include their age and in which service they were living (i.e., YP1, 13–15yo, RC-C). As the number of young people from specific services was small, we do not provide a specific age or gender to protect their anonymity.

Results

Practices that Foster a Sense of Being Loved and Cared for

When asked what they need to feel safe, happy, and well, many of the young people spoke about the importance of workers that they could trust, who were kind and caring, and who kept them safe. They shared that when they had at least one worker they could trust, they experienced understanding and warmth and were protected from harm, they could relax, stay calm, and have a positive experience. Similarly, when asked to consider the key elements of their role, many workers stressed the importance of fostering a relationship that enabled young people to feel loved and cared for.

> Someone that actually cares about you. Someone that actually cares about your wellbeing pretty much.
>
> (YP4, 13–15yo, RC-C)

> When a young person grows up, I want them to look back and think of me and just... know that I cared. That's my ultimate goal[that] each young person can look back, and think, you know what, she actually cared about me.
>
> (Mgr1, RC-C)

Central to this was fostering a sense of stability and reliability within the relationship. Some workers highlighted that this was important because many of the young people in care did not have stable relationships and had been let down before.

> I would make the placement feel more secure and permanent. Make them feel safe. Limit the amount of people that come and go in their life.
>
> (YP2, 16–18yo, RC-A)

Similarly, stability was seen as vital in environments that were often chaotic, marked by turnover of staff and young people, and a lack of predictability. Young people often valued knowing that workers were 'hanging in' and 'coming back' while workers felt that a key role was to foster a sense in young people that they know what is going to happen next.

> [My worker has] been with me since I've been in this placement. And we had ups and downs, when I first came here. And I wasn't well behaved. But then we ended up getting along, because I knew [she] wasn't going to go. And I knew that whatever I did she wasn't going to leave, because she knew that she needed to be here to help me. And then I ended up respecting her, because she respects me.
>
> (YP2, 16–18yo, RC-A)

> I've been working with a young person lately who even has two security guards with him, and his whole system can totally relax while I'm there because he's learned that I'm not a threat.... It's that whole, I'm familiar, I'm safe.
>
> (DCYW1, RC-A)

Participants talked about ways that workers demonstrated that they were 'hanging in'. One young woman, for example, recalled that workers often intentionally left personal items such as clothing at her unit so that she knew that they would be back to retrieve them. Workers talked about making a point of saying 'see you next week' or booking in appointments for a future time.

Managers and workers also spoke about other practices they used to help young people feel cared for and emotionally supported (including small caring gestures, paying special attention to young people when they were going through difficult times, and helping them to overcome a problem they were facing). Young people sometimes talked about workers who 'checked in' with them, asked them whether they were okay, and if they needed any help. They valued this believing that adults were inquiring because they wanted to make sure that they were safe and happy.

Workers stressed the importance of gestures that demonstrated their care for young people, which they believed could counteract some of the trauma and rejection that young people had experienced in the past. Demonstrating care was also about acting in ways that showed young people that workers had their safety and interests at heart: that they were intervening because they worried for a young person and were committed to ensuring that they were not harmed.

> Relationships are at the core of everything we do. The first thing you do when you come into a house is to try and build connection points with each young person and it might look different for one staff member. Unless you['ve] got those connections, you're not going to be able to help them in a crisis if they can't trust you and what we do.
>
> (DCYW1, RC-C)

> I think it's ... expressing that [we're] concerned for their safety and wellbeing and acting on that. Yes, they're not going to want police and ambulance called, but if they've self-harmed, I'm sorry mate, I care about you so much, I'm not going to let something bad happen to you. This is what I need to do.
>
> (Mgr1, RC-B)

Some participants noted, however, that relationship-building was sometimes difficult in the residential care setting. Workers, and some young people, talked about how young people's past trauma and previous experiences of being let down or hurt by adults led them to be resistant to forming relationships. Workers also noted how notions of 'professionalism' could impede the nature of relationships they had with young people. Some, for example, noted that there was a need for boundary-setting which sometimes restricted their ability to demonstrate their care for children. Some talked, for example, about not being able to use touch (i.e., hugging a child, physically comforting a young person) for fear that it might be deemed inappropriate or to mirror young people's language (i.e., when responding to a young person who says 'I love you') for fear that their words might be misinterpreted.

However, some workers and some services were taking steps to be clearer with young people – to help them feel 'loved' but within professional relationships:

> I remember [a] young person turned around to me and said I love you... and internally I went, how do I solve this? I'm like I love her too, but I don't want her to receive that in a different way to how I mean it. So, I

> said…I love you too, I said. Let's look at this word love. I was like, there's so many different levels of what love is in this world. You have the love of your parents, possibly, you have love of siblings, you have love of aunties, uncles, grandmas, friends. You have love of your pet. And I'm not your friend, I'm your house leader. We work together. We have a professional relationship…
>
> (Mgr1, RC-A)

Finally, participants noted that high staff turnover and decisions to move young people from one unit (where they felt settled) to another affected their ability to forge and sustain stable relationships.

Practices that Foster a Sense of Having Rights and Being Respected

When asked what they would change about residential care and what they didn't like about some units, young people often expressed frustration about feeling 'controlled' and having a lack of freedom. They mainly interpreted this control as workers or organizations not trusting them or not respecting that they had rights: to freedom, privacy, and independence. They conceded that sometimes young people in care had demonstrated that they could not be trusted (by lashing out, causing damage, or making poor decisions) but felt that these types of behaviors might have been avoided if young people were given more freedom and choices. Young people also stressed the importance of having some control over their lives and valued opportunities for self-expression:

> [What do young people want?] Freedom of choice. Let them pick most things that happen in their life. More choices mean more happier decisions, more likely to be more thoughtful and more obedient and more friendly… The friendlier the house, the friendlier the people.
>
> (YP3, 12–15yo, RC-C)

> Giving them their space. Letting them do stuff on their own. Letting them express themselves. I've had carers that would not let me wear certain clothes because they wouldn't let me express myself.
>
> (YP4, 16–18yo, RC-A)

Young people also valued having choices about what happens in their units and talked positively when workers took on board their needs and wishes. In some units, young people got to negotiate with their peers and workers about the meals they ate, the activities they shared, and how issues were being managed. However, young people also expressed significant frustration when adults failed to 'listen', particularly when discussing important things like the contact they have with families, whether they can attend extracurricular activities at school or go unaccompanied to meet friends, or their ongoing placements. In some instances, they interpreted this as adults not really valuing their views or failing to appreciate how important these things are to them.

Coupled with the desire for some freedom was a wish to be more independent. Young people often reflected that in contrast to time spent in their birth families or foster care, when they were permitted to do almost anything and, in many cases, were required to be independent, residential care was restrictive and promoted a sense of dependence and learned helplessness. Young people talked about their peers who they believed not only became reliant but were also demanding: expecting workers to do everything from mundane tasks like cleaning to making decisions on behalf of youth. This, they believed, was unhelpful, particularly as young people prepared to move out of care.

> You just sit back, and the workers do everything. But me realizing now, once you get older and you move out of the resi care system into your own house, you're going to... expect it for you... And then you [leave care and] realize that's not how life is. And then you've got to learn it by yourself, basically. That's what I had to do.
>
> (YP4, 16–18yo, RC-A)

A number of workers recognized that this was not satisfactory and expressed a desire to empower young people to take more responsibility and to build their confidence whilst in care.

> I really hope that they become empowered within themselves, to know that they can create the life that they truly want. And that they have the strength and other people to do courage and resilience, I guess, to overcome anything that's thrown at them with the tools and the skills that they've learned [while in our care].
>
> (Mgr1, RC-A)

Participants highlighted a number of practices that they felt helped young people develop their skills and confidence and build their ability to make decisions. This included providing young people with choices in day-to-day matters (such as preparing weekly menus, deciding what social activities they might enjoy), deciding how issues arising in houses might be managed (i.e., addressing peer conflict at weekly resident meetings), and actively engaging in case management meetings.

> Let them pick most things that happen in their life. More choices mean more happier decisions, more likely to be more thoughtful and more obedient and more friendly... The friendlier the house, the friendlier the people.
>
> (YP3, -15yo, RC-C)

> I try to give them a bit of leeway within the guidelines, if you know what I mean. Do you want to do this first or this first? The outcome's not going to make a difference much to me. I'm not giving it an open slather, breaking all the rules and all of that. But I think they do still need to feel like they've got a little bit of control about their life because they haven't had any control over what's happened to them, where they get put, all of that sort of stuff.
>
> (Staff 2, RC-C)

Practices that Foster a Sense of Solidarity and Being Valued

Participants often talked about young people's need to feel valued and for workers to see the best in them. Workers often felt that this was vital: that many young people in care were seen in relation to their past or their behaviors rather than their strengths and values.

Key to this was workers taking time to get to know a young person: their own goals and dreams, their ways of understanding the world, and their aspirations for the future. One worker argued that this required deep listening to truly understand young people.

> And really listening, listening I think is the key because you can hear so much in listening. You can hear so much in a silence, and I think that's... We can get so caught up in being fast in trying to work things out, but actually, if you can slow yourself down, you can read so much of the situation a lot better. And always, you never assume. If you're unsure, just ask.
>
> (DCYW1, RC-A)

Workers gave examples of things that they did, through their words and actions, to demonstrate they saw the best in a young person and valued who they are, what they had overcome in their lives, and the relationship that the worker had with them.

> [In response to a young person who had attachment issues, I needed to formulate a relationship built on a 'heartfelt, genuine connection' and I told her]: 'I have so much deep respect and admiration for you, the strength and courage that you have shown, you make my heart fuzzy. And I enjoy spending time with you, and I feel blessed that we get to work so closely together. I feel honored, thank you and I want you to know that I really do care deeply about you and your path lying ahead of you, the choices that you've made, and I think you're an amazing person.
>
> (Mgr1, RC-A)

Participants also talked about valuing opportunities for staff to 'walk alongside' young people. As discussed above, young people valued a sense of independence but also expressed a need to be able to rely on workers. It appeared that solidarity was often expressed in terms of interdependence and empowerment.

> I really hope that they become empowered within themselves, to know that they can create the life that they truly want. And that they have the strength and courage and resilience, I guess, to overcome anything that's thrown at them with the tools and the skills that they've learned [while in our care].
>
> (Mgr1, RC-A)

Although young people appreciated workers who were with them and supported them, they did voice great frustration when workers were 'too close', 'overbearing', or didn't respect their personal space.

> Being there for them, but not be so in their space. Definitely just make sure they're okay, but not hang around them 24/7. Make sure they're okay. Ask them if they need anything. If they don't, just let them be for the moment.
>
> (Young person 4, 16–18yo, RC-A)

Staff reflected that a key role was to support young people to self-regulate, manage their emotions, and make sense of their behaviors, particularly after a critical incident. Workers recognized that young people often lashed out or hurt themselves or others due to their past trauma and because they had not developed prosocial ways of dealing with stress. A key role, therefore, was to help young people make sense of their behaviors and develop their skills. Rather than just punishing young people, they helped young people reflect, learn, and develop.

> Yes, definitely, all of that really because you're thinking well, what is the young person feeling and how can we integrate them back into the residential care setting once there has been say, an explosive reaction?
>
> (DCYW1, RC-A)

Participants also reported that workers' ability to support young people's freedoms was sometimes restricted by external factors. Many bemoaned the fact that young people's wishes to spend time with friends, attend camps, or engage with family were often dismissed by departmental staff, and that lags in getting permission for young people to do the things they wanted restricted workers' ability to meet their requests. As such, some young people talked about workers playing an important role as advocates: liaising with managers, departmental case workers, and schools to advocate for young people when decisions were being made. Young people often valued this persistence and believed that it showed that workers were there to champion their cause.

Discussion

What Helps or Hinders Good, Relationship-Based, Social Support?

Similar to previous research, young people, managers, and staff reported that social support and relationships were central to the residential care experience. Participants also gave examples of practices that recognition theory would characterize as improving young people's sense of being loved and cared for, of feeling respected and having rights, and being valued and working in solidarity (Hoagwood et al., 2010; Kor et al., 2022). In considering the contexts within which residential care work was practiced, managers and staff recognized that their ability to work in such ways was often enabled and constrained by influencers within and outside of individual units. They pointed to ways in which organizational cultures and leadership strengthened social support and the value of working reflexively to understand and meet young people's needs. In the following section, we provide an overview of these factors. Illuminating these enablers and barriers is important because efforts to change or improve the kind of relational practices identified above need to recognize and consider the arrangements and conditions that hold such practices in place.

Organizational Cultures, Leadership, and Stability in Staff Teams

Adopting the TPA, we invited staff to consider the contexts within which practice was enabled or constrained. Workers and managers believe that when organizational cultures place children and young people's needs at the center of the work and provide support to workers to assist them in their roles, positive outcomes are experienced by all. Echoing the findings of other empirical research (Dalton, 2014; Holden et al., 2010), participants believed that in organizations with child-centered cultures, there was a lower turnover of staff, less altercations between young people and staff and residents, and a greater authorization of staff to respond to children and young people's need.

When asked, workers described a positive organizational culture as one that prioritized the needs of young people as a group, and as individuals, and acted in ways to keep them safe and respond to their wishes. This, some believed, contrasted with a broader view of young people in care and external practices that perceived young people as a file or as a problem that needed to be sorted. Strong leadership was also highly valued, and leaders played a key role in enabling workers to engage in positive, relational work (Bradshaw, 2007). Effective leaders were empathetic to the needs of children and young people (whom they often had a close personal relationship with) and not only set an example for others to follow but also fostered a culture of learning and empowered teams to engage in collective decision-making.

Managers and staff also valued having practice frameworks, that were codified in organizational policies, that clearly articulated what the organization was hoping to achieve, and provided staff with the scaffolding to do good work. Although having clear policies and 'rules' was appreciated by workers, young people were sometimes less positive about how they were implemented. Some, for example, believed that workers were not empowered to make decisions, to have the types of relationships that young people wanted, or to give them the freedom they sought because of the ways that 'rules' were enforced. These contrasting views are replicated in existing research that demonstrates that frameworks are valuable when they promote consistency but promote worker discretion in meeting the needs of young people (Connolly, 2007; Finan et al., 2018). When frameworks primarily focus on compliance and are rigidly applied, they can erode quality practice.

Staff turnover was a problem for many of the services who recognized that residential care work was difficult and often undervalued and that staff did not always stay for extended periods of time. This was viewed as constraining the unit's capacity to do good relational work. Similar to findings from wider research conducted in residential care in Australia and abroad (Curry, 2019; Moore et al., 2018; Skoog et al., 2015; Strolin-Goltzman et al., 2010), participants observed that young people were less willing to form connections with staff when they are aware that they may not be available for long periods. Managers also reflected that their capacity to build teams who could 'live' their organization's mission and strengthen child-centered organizational cultures was constrained when there was a churn in staff.

Reflexive Staff Supported in Care Teams and through Supervision

Worker participants often stressed the value of being reflexive (Formenti & Rigamonti, 2020): taking time to reflect on what young people most need and to look past some of their behaviors and challenges to understand them in the context of previous trauma. Through individual supervision, some staff were encouraged to consider ways of managing ethical issues that routinely emerge, particularly the tensions that often arise between what they *have* to do and what they feel they *ought* to do. Examples of these issues and tensions included balancing young people's safety needs and their rights to autonomy and independence, meeting the often-competing needs of the different young people in care, and establishing boundaries while demonstrating care and support.

Residential care practice has been described as chaotic and constantly changing (Cahill et al., 2016; Jakobsen, 2010). Workers valued efforts to work alongside and have conversations with colleagues to learn new ways of engaging with young people, responding to conflict and crisis, and coming up with different strategies for meeting their needs. In some settings, these discussions were formal and systematized: weekly consultations with clinical staff, team meetings where the needs of individual children were discussed, and routine debriefs after critical incidents, all of which were highly valued.

Staff were also encouraged to challenge themselves and their teams through such reflexive practice. In many instances, managers and staff talked about the need to be reflexive when 'working in the grey' – these being times when established policies and procedures did not provide sufficient guidance on what to do or seemed antithetical to good relationship-based practice. They spoke about the need to step back from a situation, to consider what was going on for each of the players (including what they needed, what was in their best interests, and what they wanted to occur), and to be aware of their own personal needs, values, and biases. To enable these reflexive activities, adult participants perceived that organizations needed to foster a culture of openness and learning, provide time and space, and ensure that staff have trust in the process. As argued elsewhere (Formenti & Rigamonti, 2020), leadership was seen as central in creating the conditions for such mutual trust.

Managers and staff felt that sometimes their own lived experiences, beliefs, and attitudes could thwart their relational practice. Several, for example, talked about how workers' own experiences of childhood trauma, their roles as parents, and their work with children and young people in other settings, all played a part in how they thought about, and acted within, the residential care setting. They viewed these experiences as shaping their judgments and potentially influencing (positively or negatively) the decisions they made. Being aware of and ensuring that one's own experiences enhance (rather than restrict) good practice has been seen as essential in residential care practice (Steckley & Smith, 2011).

While staff described opportunities to reflect on practice with their peers and supervisors, they also highlighted the benefits of having pre-emptive and post-incident discussions with young people. They spoke about the value of debriefing with young people and giving them opportunities to reflect not only on what was going on for them during a critical incident but also on which practices they believed did, or did not, meet their needs. Such co-reflexive activities also have the potential to help young people better understand their traumas and for both workers and youth to build their resilience (Winkler, 2014). In some organizations, this co-reflexivity was enhanced using tools such as Life Space Interviews which encouraged both young people and workers to have an open discussion about what was happening for all stakeholders during a critical incident, what the young person wanted and needed during this experience, and what they and their workers might have done differently to achieve their goals without conflict (Soenen et al., 2013). These co-reflexive activities were often established and reinforced by practice frameworks introduced to the sites.

Compliance with External Policies and Guidelines

When considering what helped or hindered their relational practice, many workers raised compliance issues: particularly compliance with departmental policies or standards that were set by external parties. In both instances, compliance was regarded as simultaneously an enabling and constraining influence. Sometimes, for example, workers reported that they appreciated knowing what was expected of them, what 'rules' they needed to follow, and some guidance about how decisions were made within, and outside of, residential care. 'Compliance' could therefore be helpful when it was instructive and clarifying.

However, both managers and residential care staff reflected that compliance, most often with external expectations, could sometimes be a barrier to relational practice. They spoke about how completing mandatory requirements, such as completing significant paperwork and attending unproductive meetings, could distract them from other practices, such as being with young people and forming relationships. They also reported that, sometimes, these guidelines meant they had less freedom to make certain decisions that they believed to be in the best interests of young people (such as those related to placement, duration of stay, and matching of young people). This made it difficult to do positive relational work with individual children or groups.

As in previous research, young people were often frustrated by the ways in which compliance requirements impeded not only their personal freedoms but also their relationships with workers (McIntosh et al., 2010). They often expressed disappointment when workers were required to implement rules, such as not allowing young people to see friends and families, which they believed were set by decision-makers who did not know them or appreciate their situations. In many cases, young people's trust in workers was fractured for reasons outside of the control of staff.

Limitations and Implications for Practice

This study was conducted during the COVID-19 pandemic which meant that the recruitment of participants was challenging and resulted in fewer young people involved than had been planned. The study was conducted in a small number of Australian agencies and the sample may not be representative of those who live in residential care in other jurisdictions. The qualitative research approach we adopted helped us to explore the contexts and practices within which young people lived and residential care staff practiced their youth work. As the settings within which residential care is provided in Australia and abroad vary considerably, our findings may not be generalized to other contexts.

However, like previous research, the study offers important insights that might be utilized to strengthen residential care practices elsewhere, specifically: a) Promote Child-Centered Organizational Cultures: residential care organizations should prioritize the needs of young people, both as a group and as individuals, placing their safety and well-being at the center of their work. This child-centered approach can lead to lower staff turnover, fewer conflicts, and greater authorization for staff to respond to young people's needs. Current research findings align with this approach; b) Empower

Strong Leadership: effective leadership is crucial in creating an environment that supports good relational work. Leaders should be empathetic to the needs of young people, set an example for others, and foster a culture of learning and collective decision-making; c) Clarify and Implement Practice Frameworks: organizations should provide clear practice frameworks outlined in policies that guide staff in achieving the organization's goals while allowing for flexibility in meeting the needs of young people. The focus needs to be on consistency and empowering workers rather than rigid enforcement of rules, as strict enforcement can erode the quality of practice; d) Address Staff Turnover: staff turnover is a significant challenge in residential care, affecting the ability to build lasting relationships with young people. Strategies to retain staff and create stable teams are essential for improving relational practices; e) Encourage Reflexive Practice: workers should be encouraged to engage in reflective and co-reflexive practices to better understand young people's needs, trauma, and ethical dilemmas. Individual supervision and team discussions can aid in responding to conflicts and crises and in developing strategies for meeting young people's needs. Leadership plays a central role in creating a culture of mutual trust for these activities; and f) Balancing Compliance with External Policies: while compliance with external policies can provide structure and guidance, organizations should strike a balance between compliance and relational work. Excessive paperwork and strict adherence to rules may distract staff from forming relationships with young people and limit their decision-making autonomy. It is important to ensure that young people's trust is not eroded due to inflexible rules.

Concluding Remarks

Young people, staff, and managers all perceived that social support and relationship-based practices are central to safety and well-being in residential care settings and provided rich insight into ways of working that helped young people to feel loved and cared for, that their rights were respected, and that they were valued and working in solidarity. For some time, residential care researchers and practitioners have stressed the importance of providing young people with social support and demonstrated the primacy of relationships in creating conditions within which children and young people are safe and well and can begin to heal and grow (Kor et al., 2021; Moore et al., 2018; Sellers et al., 2020; Warming, 2019; Whittaker et al., 2023). The *Beyond Safety: Ethical Practice Involving Children* built on this work and utilized a methodology that brought together children's rights, recognition theory, and TPA to examine relational practices that support young people's safety and well-being while accounting for the practical, organizational, and systemic factors that enable and constrain this work. We found this approach to be particularly illuminating as it allowed close analysis of the nuanced relational nature of residential care including the tensions and in situ ethical decisions inherent in practice. It also brought into dialogue the views of young people, their workers, and managers about these practices. Importantly, our approach considered the conditions or arrangements that enable or constrain change with the relational practices.

Although the value of relationships and social support have been explored elsewhere (Curry, 2019; Evans et al., 2022; Kor et al., 2022), the EPIC study allowed us to specifically focus on the ways in which residential care practice can meet young people's needs for recognition: to feel loved and cared for, to feel valued as having rights, and to be working in solidarity with others. Our findings amplify those of others (Marshall et al., 2020) and suggest a need to orient social supports to ensure that they engender trust, build connections, and help young people build their confidence in themselves and others. Utilizing TPA allowed us to explore the practical, organizational, and systemic factors that strengthened or constrained the fostering of ethical practices. Our findings emphasize the value of encouraging workers to be reflexive as individuals and in teams. We argue that organizational cultures and child-centered leadership enable good, ethical, and relational work to be conducted. Balancing the need to be compliant with externally driven mandates while enabling relational work is imperative to ensuring that good outcomes are achieved.

References

Asif, N., Breen, C., & Wells, R. (2023). Influence of placement stability on developmental outcomes of children and young people in out-of-home care: Findings from the Pathways of Care Longitudinal Study. *Child Abuse & Neglect*, 106145. https://doi.org/10.1016/j.chiabu.2023.106145

Australian Institute of Health and Welfare. (2021). *Child protection Australia 2019–20* (Child Welfare Series Issue). Canberra: AIHW.

Bradshaw, M. A. (2007). *Organizational leadership and its relationship to outcomes in residential treatment*. Indiana Wesleyan University.

Brown, T., Winter, K., & Carr, N. (2018). Residential child care workers: Relationship based practice in a culture of fear. *Child & Family Social Work*, *23*(4), 657–665. https://doi.org/10.1111/cfs.12461

Cahill, O., Holt, S., & Kirwan, G. (2016). Keyworking in residential child care: Lessons from research. *Children and Youth Services Review*, *65*, 216–223. https://doi.org/10.1016/j.childyouth.2016.04.014

Cloutier, D. S., Martin-Matthews, A., Byrne, K., & Wolse, F. (2015). The space between: Using 'relational ethics' and 'relational space' to explore relationship-building between care providers and care recipients in the home space. *Social & Cultural Geography*, *16*(7), 764–782. https://doi.org/10.1080/14649365.2015.1020336

Connolly, M. (2007). Practice frameworks: Conceptual maps to guide interventions in child welfare. *British Journal of Social Work*, *37*(5), 825–837. https://doi.org/10.1093/bjsw/bcl049

Curry, A. (2019). "If you can't be with this client for some years, don't do it": Exploring the emotional and relational effects of turnover on youth in the child welfare system. *Children and Youth Services Review*, *99*, 374–385. https://doi.org/10.1016/j.childyouth.2019.01.026

Dalton, J. L. (2014). Creating organizational culture change: One agency's transformation towards long-term positive outcomes. In *Residential interventions for children, adolescents, and families* (pp. 170–181). Routledge. https://www.taylorfrancis.com/chapters/edit/10.4324/9780203743492-13/creating-organizational-culture-change-jim-dalton

Evans, R., Katz, C. C., Fulginiti, A., & Taussig, H. (2022). Sources and types of social supports and their association with mental health symptoms and life satisfaction among young adults with a history of out-of-home care. *Children*, *9*(4), 520. https://doi.org/10.3390/children9040520

Farrugia, C., & Joss, N. (2021). *What contributes to placement moves in out-of-home care?* Child Family Community Australia, Australian Institute of Family Studies.

Finan, S., Bromfield, L., Arney, F., & Moore, T. P. (2018). *Assessing the quality and comprehensiveness of child protection practice frameworks.* Adelaide: Australian Centre for Child Protection, University of South Australia.

Formenti, L., & Rigamonti, A. (2020). Systemic reflexivity in residential child care: A pedagogical frame to empower professional competence. *International Journal of Child, Youth and Family Studies*, *11*(4), 115–139. https://doi.org/10.18357/ijcyfs114.2202019991

Gallagher, B. & Green, A. (2013). Outcomes among young adults placed in therapeutic residential care as children. *Journal of Children's Services*, *8*(1), 31–51. https://doi.org/10.1108/17466661311309772

Graham, A., Canosa, A., Boyle, T., Moore, T., Taylor, N., Anderson, D., & Robinson, S. (2022). Promoting students' safety and wellbeing: ethical practice in schools. *The Australian Educational Researcher*, *50*, 1477–1496. https://doi.org/10.1007/s13384-022-00567-8

Graham, A., Canosa, A., Wall, J., & Thomas, P. (2023). Child-safe organizations and the ethics of empowered inclusion. *Children & Society*, *37*, 1719–1736. https://doi.org/10.1111/chso.12732

Graham, A., Powell, M. A., Thomas, N., & Anderson, D. (2017). Reframing 'wellbeing' in schools: The potential of recognition. *Cambridge Journal of Education*, *47*(4), 439–455. https://doi.org/10.1080/0305764X.2016.1192104

Hoagwood, K. E., Cavaleri, M. A., Serene Olin, S., Burns, B. J., Slaton, E., Gruttadaro, D., & Hughes, R. (2010). Family support in children's mental health: A review and synthesis. *Clinical Child and Family Psychology Review*, *13*, 1–45. https://doi.org/10.1007/s10567-009-0060-5

Holden, M. J., Izzo, C., Nunno, M., Smith, E. G., Endres, T., Holden, J. C., & Kuhn, F. (2010). Children and residential experiences: A comprehensive strategy for implementing a research-informed program model for residential care. *Child Welfare*, 131–149. http://www.jstor.org/stable/45400458

Holmes, L., Connolly, C., Mortimer, E., & Hevesi, R. (2018). Residential group care as a last resort: Challenging the rhetoric. *Residential Treatment for Children & Youth*, *35*(3), 209–224. https://doi.org/10.1080/0886571X.2018.1455562

Honneth, A. (1995). The struggle for recognition: The grammar of social conflicts (Cambridge). *Polity*, 163.

Jackson, K., & Bazeley, P. (2019). *Qualitative data analysis with NVivo*. Sage.

Jakobsen, T. B. (2010). 'What troubled children need' constructions of everyday life in residential care. *Children & Society*, *24*(3), 215–226. https://doi.org/10.1111/j.1099-0860.2009.00220.x

Kemmis, S., Wilkinson, J., Edwards-Groves, C., Hardy, I., Grootenboer, P., & Bristol, L. (2014). Praxis, practice and practice architectures. In *Changing practices, changing education* (pp. 25–41). Springer. https://doi.org/10.1007/978-981-4560-47-4_2

Kiraly, M., & Humphreys, C. (2017). The changing face of out-of-home care in Australia–Developing policy and practice for the 21st century. *Children Australia*, *42*(4), 230–232. https://doi.org/10.1017/cha.2017.38

Kor, K., Fernandez, E., & Spangaro, J. (2021). Relationship-based practice in therapeutic residential care: A double-edged sword. *The British Journal of Social Work*, *52*(2), 663–681. https://doi.org/10.1093/bjsw/bcab018

Kor, K., Fernandez, E., & Spangaro, J. (2022). Relationship-based practice in therapeutic residential care: A double-edged sword. *The British Journal of Social Work*, *52*(2), 663–681.

Korkiamäki, R., & Gilligan, R. (2020). Responding to misrecognition – A study with unaccompanied asylum-seeking minors. *Children and Youth Services Review*, *119*, 105687. https://doi.org/10.1016/j.childyouth.2020.105687

Marshall, G., Winter, K., & Turney, D. (2020). Honneth and positive identity formation in residential care. *Child & Family Social Work*, *25*(4), 733–741. https://doi.org/10.1111/cfs.12749

McCarthy, E. (2016). Young people in residential care, their participation and the influencing factors. *Child Care in Practice*, *22*(4), 368–385. https://doi.org/10.1080/13575279.2016.1188763

McIntosh, I., Punch, S., Dorrer, N., & Emond, R. (2010). 'You don't have to be watched to make your toast': Surveillance and food practices within residential care for young people. *Surveillance and Society*, *7*(3/4), 287–300.

McLean, S. (2018). *Therapeutic residential care: An update on current issues in Australia*. Australian Institute of Family Studies Melbourne.

Moore, T., McArthur, M., Death, J., Roche, S., & Tilbury, C. (2016). *Safe and sound: Exploring the safety of young people in residential care*. Australia: Royal Commission into Institutional Responses to Child Sexual Abuse.

Moore, T., McArthur, M., Death, J., Tilbury, C., & Roche, S. (2018). Sticking with us through it all: The importance of trustworthy relationships for children and young people in residential care. *Children and Youth Services Review*, *84*, 68–75. https://doi.org/10.1016/j.childyouth.2017.10.043

Moore, T., McArthur, M., Noble-Carr, D., & Harcourt, D. (2015). *Taking us seriously: Children and young people talk about safety and institutional responses to their safety concerns*. Institute of Child Protection Studies, Australian Catholic University.

Porter, R., Mitchell, F., & Giraldi, M. (2021). *Function, quality and outcomes of residential care: Rapid evidence review*. Glasgow: CELCIS. www.celcis.org

Powell, M. A., Graham, A., Canosa, A., Anderson, D., Moore, T., Robinson, S., Thomas, N. P., & Taylor, N. (2020a). Child safety in policy: Who is being kept safe and from what?. *Social Policy & Administration*, *54*(7), 1160–1178. https://doi.org/10.1111/spol.12591

Powell, M. A., Graham, A., Canosa, A., Anderson, D., Taylor, N., Robinson, S., Moore, T., & Thomas, N. P. (2020b). Children and safety in Australian policy: Implications for organisations and practitioners. *Australian Journal of Social Issues*, *56*(1), 17–41. https://doi.org/10.1002/ajs4.134

Robinson, S. (2016). *Feeling safe, being safe: what is important to children and young people with disability and high support needs about safety in institutional settings?* Centre for Children and Young People, Southern Cross University.

Robinson, S., Graham, A., Canosa, A., Moore, T., Taylor, N., & Boyle, T. (2022). Ethical practice in disability services: Views of young people and staff. *Ethics and Social Welfare*, *16*(4), 412–431. https://doi.org/10.1080/17496535.2022.2072519

Sellers, D. E., Smith, E. G., Izzo, C. V., McCabe, L. A., & Nunno, M. A. (2020). Child feelings of safety in residential care: The supporting role of adult-child relationships. *Residential Treatment for Children & Youth*, *37*(2), 136–155. https://doi.org/10.1080/0886571X.2020.1712576

Skoog, V., Khoo, E., & Nygren, L. (2015). Disconnection and dislocation: Relationships and belonging in unstable foster and institutional care. *The British Journal of Social Work*, *45*(6), 1888–1904. https://doi.org/10.1093/bjsw/bcu033

Smith, M. (2009). *Rethinking residential child care: Positive perspectives*. Policy Press.

Soenen, B., Goethals, I., Spriet, E., D'Oosterlinck, F., & Broekaert, E. (2013). Reflections of caretakers on the process of implementation of life space crisis intervention at a therapeutic centre for youngsters with emotional and behavioural disorders. *Psychiatric Quarterly*, *84*, 239–254. https://doi.org/10.1007/s11126-012-9242-2

Steckley, L., & Smith, M. (2011). Care ethics in residential child care: A different voice. *Ethics and Social Welfare*, *5*(2), 181–195. https://doi.org/10.1080/17496535.2011.571068

Strolin-Goltzman, J., Kollar, S., & Trinkle, J. (2010). Listening to the voices of children in foster care: Youths speak out about child welfare workforce turnover and selection. *Social Work*, *55*(1), 47–53. https://doi.org/10.1093/sw/55.1.47

Ten Brummelaar, M. D., Harder, A. T., Kalverboer, M. E., Post, W. J., & Knorth, E. J. (2018). Participation of youth in decision-making procedures during residential care: A narrative review. *Child & Family Social Work*, *23*(1), 33–44. https://doi.org/10.1111/cfs.12381

Turney, D. (2012). A relationship-based approach to engaging involuntary clients: The contribution of recognition theory. *Child & Family Social Work*, *17*(2), 149–159. https://doi.org/10.1111/j.1365-2206.2012.00830.x

Warming, H. (2019). Messing with the emotions of the other exploring ambiguous youth-adult relations in a residential care institution. *Emotion, Space and Society*, *32*, 100512. https://doi.org/10.1016/j.emospa.2018.05.005

Warwick, L. (2021). "Depends who it is": Towards a relational understanding of the use of adult-child touch in residential child care. *Qualitative Social Work*, *21*(1), 18–36. https://doi.org/10.1177/1473325021990875

Whittaker, J. K., Holmes, L., & del Valle, J. C. F. (2023). *Revitalizing residential care for children and youth: Cross-national trends and challenges*. Oxford University Press. https://doi.org/10.1093/oso/9780197644300.001.0001

Winkler, A. (2014). Resilience as reflexivity: A new understanding for work with looked-after children. *Journal of Social Work Practice*, *28*(4), 461–478.

6 Perceived Social Support in Residential Care

Its Contribution to Adolescents' Mental Health and Quality of Life

Marianne Tevik Singstad

Introduction

Establishing Child Welfare Services in Norway: A Brief History

Norway was the first European country to establish child welfare services (CWS) in 1896, with a dual focus on protecting vulnerable children and preventing juvenile delinquency. Initially, the emphasis was on caring for individual children and providing alternatives to incarceration for delinquents. A significant shift occurred in the mid-1990s with the "best practice for the child" initiative, which led to a more child-centric approach and legislative changes in 1992. This legislation emphasized children's rights and development, recognizing them as dynamic individuals shaped by complex interactions between their individual characteristics, relationships with primary caregivers and family members, connections with their wider social networks and educational institutions, and engagement with their community (Hagen, 2001).

In January 2023, a new legislation was introduced to increase legal certainty for families involved with CWS and ensure a safe childhood for children (Barnevernsloven, 2024). The revised law prioritizes children's needs, emphasizing prevention and early intervention. For Residential Youth Care (RYC) specifically, changes were made to improve legal certainty and institutional quality. For instance, prior to the new legislation, only 50% of institutional staff were required to have higher relevant education. Now, under the new Child Welfare Act §10–16, all staff must hold a relevant bachelor's degree, and institutional leaders must have a master's degree or equivalent (Barnevernsloven, 2024).

Legal certainty is crucial in Norwegian CWS, where authority, openness, and trust are key values. To reduce personal biases in decision-making, the Child Welfare Act includes standards for documentation, time limits, and guidelines to ensure quality and effectiveness (Barnevernsloven, 2024). When a child is at high risk for unhealthy development, the CWS must take action. If home conditions are inadequate, specific measures must be implemented to ensure the best outcomes for the child (Barnevernsloven, 2024). If these

DOI: 10.4324/9781003424468-9

measures are insufficient, out-of-home placements, preferably in foster homes, should be considered (Barne- ungdoms- og familiedirektoratet, 2021). However, for some adolescents, institutional placement may be the best care option. According to the Child Welfare Act (Barnevernsloven, 2024), institutional placement may be considered when:

- The child has exhibited serious behavioral difficulties, such as severe or repeated delinquency or persistent substance abuse (§ 4–4, § 6–1, § 6–2).
- The child is at risk of becoming a victim of human trafficking (§ 4–5).
- The daily care, security, or relationships are seriously deficient and do not meet the child's needs (§ 5–1).
- Primary caregivers are incapable of caring for a child with special needs (§ 5–1).
- The child is maltreated or exposed to severe abuse (§ 5–1).
- The child's health or development is in danger due to parental unresponsiveness (§ 5–1).

Therefore, placements in Norwegian RYC are typically for adolescents in need of extensive supervision, support, and care due to significant challenges. Over time, these institutions have become more specialized, as some focus primarily on caregiving and providing a secure base, while others address adolescent behavior or substance abuse (Barne- ungdoms- og familiedirektoratet, 2021). RYC aims to create environments resembling ordinary homes, offering home-like housing, a caring atmosphere, schooling, and activities. Direct treatment is provided by other agencies, such as primary health care or specialized mental health services. RYC typically employs a milieu-therapeutic model, including substitute parenting, a healthy social climate, and supervision. Institutional staff should meet each adolescent's need for stability, responsiveness, and care (Backe-Hansen et al., 2011). Each adolescent is assigned a primary contact responsible for daily activities, such as schooling, leisure time activities, and participating in meetings with CWS or other services (Barne- ungdoms- og familiedirektoratet, 2010). Typically, each institution accommodates three to five residents, with staff working three daily shifts (daytime, evening, or night) or living with the adolescents for periods ranging from three to seven days before having longer periods off (Barne- ungdoms- og familiedirektoratet, 2010).

Adolescents in Residential Youth Care

Adolescents receiving interventions from CWS often have backgrounds marked by adversity and adverse childhood experiences (ACEs, such as abuse, neglect, household dysfunction, or numerous disrupted attachments) (Clemens et al., 2020; Greger et al., 2015). Exposure to ACEs increases the risk of negative developmental outcomes across emotional, behavioral, and social domains (Brannstrom et al., 2017; Villodas et al., 2015). Exposure to various forms of abuse, parental physical or emotional absence, rejection, and substance abuse significantly impact social development (Berens et al., 2017). However, long-term effects depend on individual differences, including personal vulnerability and the presence of individual or environmental risk and protective factors (Belsky et al., 2007). Therefore, environmental changes that provide stability, care, and professional monitoring can positively alter the developmental trajectory of high-risk adolescents, fostering resilience (Backe-Hansen et al., 2011; Leipoldt et al., 2019). Despite facing numerous adversities, social support, positive feedback, and guidance can act as protective buffers against these adversities (Murberg & Bru, 2004). Consequently, some individuals, despite their troubled backgrounds, may cope better with adversities and attain positive adaptation (Hygen et al., 2015).

Social Relationships, Mental Health, and Quality of Life

Social relationships are fundamental to human well-being. From birth, we rely on social connections for survival, as seen in an infant's search for attachment (Ainsworth et al., 2015). Early relationships shape how we perceive and interpret social interactions, making social support crucial (Sarason et al., 1990). Healthy social relationships fulfill needs for belonging, self-worth, and value (Baumeister & Leary, 1995), promoting better adjustment (Hoffnung Assouline & Attar-Schwartz, 2020) and enhancing mental health (Rueger et al., 2016). Additionally, social support has a stress-reducing function and can buffer against the negative effects of stressful situations, thereby facilitating successful adaptation to new circumstances (Cohen & Wills, 1985; Sciaraffa et al., 2018). Conversely, diminished support increases risks of reduced well-being (Chu et al., 2010), lower self-esteem (Rueger et al., 2010), and mental health problems (Clemens et al., 2020).

For vulnerable adolescents, particularly those with a high number of ACEs and troubled home conditions, establishing and maintaining social relationships can be challenging (Bowlby, 1982; Lum et al., 2018). Adolescents in Norwegian RYC report a high prevalence of ACEs (Greger et al., 2015) and multiple placements (Kayed et al., 2015), putting them at significant risk for negative developmental outcomes, including challenges in social relationships.

Adolescence, as a developmental period marked by high stress and emotional intensity, can further strain mental health, especially in those with disrupted care and over-activated stress systems (Blakemore, 2019; Clemens et al., 2020). While psychiatric disorders affect less than 10% of Norwegian adolescents (Reneflot et al., 2018), they range from 10% to 20% in other countries (Kieling et al., 2011; Polanczyk et al., 2015). Alarmingly, adolescents in out-of-home care have a much higher prevalence of mental disorders, ranging from 20% to 61% across countries (Bronsard et al., 2016; González-García et al., 2017). Among Norwegian RYC adolescents, 76% qualify for at least one psychiatric disorder, with high rates (Jozefiak et al., 2016). The most prevalent diagnoses included depressive disorders (37.0%), anxiety disorders (34.0%), and attention deficit hyperactivity disorder (ADHD) (32.3%). Girls report a higher prevalence of emotional disorders, while boys report a higher prevalence of behavioral disorders (Jozefiak et al., 2016).

Given the strong link between social support and psychiatric disorders (Essau et al., 2011; Rueger et al., 2016), it is crucial to investigate perceived social support as a protective factor. Adolescents in Norwegian RYC also report lower quality of life (QoL) scores compared to the general population, particularly in physical well-being (PWB; M = RYC 58.0/GP 71.4), emotional well-being (EWB; M = RYC 65.9/GP 75.6), self-esteem (M = RYC 50.0/GP 55.6), and friendship (M = RYC 69.4/GP 75.0) (Jozefiak & Kayed, 2015). A clear dose–response relationship exists between the number of ACEs and QoL, with more ACEs correlating with lower QoL scores (Greger et al., 2016). Given the lower QoL reported by RYC adolescents and the potential positive effects of inclusion in social networks on adolescents' QoL (Costa et al., 2020; Swerts et al., 2019), investigating the associations between perceived social support and QoL is pertinent.

Therefore, understanding how RYC adolescents perceive social support, compared to their peers, is essential. RYC staff play a critical role in offering support, yet information on adolescents' perception of this support and its impact on mental health and QoL is lacking. This study aims to address this gap, potentially guiding strategies to enhance social relationships and overall well-being for these vulnerable adolescents.

Methodology

Sample Characteristics

RYC Sample

This chapter presents the findings from a Norwegian national cross-sectional study conducted from 2010 to 2014, approved by The Norwegian Regional Committee for Medical and Health Research Ethics (Project 2014/1516). The study investigated care history, mental health, the need for and utilization of mental health services, perceived social support, QoL, and several other variables among 400 adolescents (girls: n = 230, M_{age} = 16.5 years; boys: n = 170, M_{age} = 16.9 years) living in RYCs (Kayed et al., 2015). All Norwegian RYC institutions that met the inclusion criteria (taking care of adolescents aged 12–20, not living in acute institutions, not unaccompanied minors, and not having participated in the pilot study) were invited to participate, totaling 98 institutions, whereas 12 institutions declined participation. After applying individual exclusion criteria, such as acute crisis placements, insufficient proficiency in Norwegian, unsatisfactory health conditions, or being unaccompanied minors without asylum in Norway, 400 eligible adolescents aged 12–20 agreed to participate in the study, yielding a response rate of 67%.

For the current sample, the main reasons for initial placement were problems between the adolescents and their parents (e.g., constant arguing, disagreements, or violence; 43.4%), individual adolescent issues (e.g., significant problems with anger, violence, substance use, or mental health problems; 30.6%), and parental issues (represented by the same characteristics as described for adolescents; 25.6%). While living in RYC, over 90% of the adolescents maintained contact with their biological parents or previous caregivers (such as foster parents), and nearly 70% reported attending school or participating in other daytime activities (Kayed et al., 2015).

General Population Sample

For the overall investigation of perceived social support, presented first in the results section, a reference sample was drawn from the Young in Norway (YiN) study. This study included all junior and senior high schools in Norway (ages 12–19) from which the schools were selected using cluster sampling. The sampling was then stratified according to geographical region, school size, and school type. The second national round of the YiN study was used for comparison in our study (N = 10 839), with the Social Support Questionnaire (SSQ) (Sarason et al., 1983; Wichstrøm & Hegna, 2003) completed by 8,769 adolescents. After applying the age criteria and removing missing reports of age and sex, a response of n = 7,095 adolescents was available. For further details about the YiN project, please see Wichstrøm (1999).

Data Collection Procedure

All adolescent participants were approached individually and recruited using approved procedures and informed consent. For those under the age of 16, consent was also obtained from a significant caregiver. Data were collected at the RYC institutions by trained research assistants, each holding a bachelor's or master's degree and extensive experience working with children and families. The adolescents completed a series of questionnaires, including those on childhood experiences, perceived social support (SSQ) (Sarason et al., 1983), QoL (KINDL-R) (Ravens-Sieberer & Bullinger, 2000), and the community-oriented programs environment scale (COPES) (Moos, 2009), which took approximately 30 minutes. A psychiatric interview (CAPA) (Angold & Costello, 2000) was also conducted. The research assistants provided assistance and allowed breaks as needed during data collection. However, since this was a comprehensive data collection effort, not all participants completed every questionnaire. Therefore, only 304 adolescents completed the SSQ, representing the current sample.

Measures

Social Support Questionnaire (SSQ)

For the purpose of this study, the SSQ was used in a shortened and adapted version, consisting of five items (Wichstrøm & Hegna, 2003) modeled after the full 27-item version, as constructed by Sarason et al. (1983). The SSQ measures perceived social support by asking the adolescents to whom they could turn, in four hypothetical situations (e.g., "If you had done something illegal," "If you had to take a difficult choice related to school/ work,"), in addition to the question "who accepts you for who you are?" These situations include both informational and emotional support, as well as crisis intervention. A range of potential support persons were listed, including mother, father, boyfriend/girlfriend, sibling(s), friend(s), relative(s), neighbor(s), institutional staff, others, and the option of *none*. Additionally, the adolescents rated their satisfaction with the perceived social support in each of the five main questions, on a scale ranging from very poorly satisfied (1) to very satisfied (4), with higher scores indicating higher satisfaction. A total satisfaction score, with a maximum of 20, could then be calculated by summing the satisfaction ratings across all situations. This information provides insights into three aspects of perceived social support: 1) the variety of support groups listed (e.g., mother, father, friend(s), and institutional staff), 2) satisfaction with the perceived support, and 3) the sources from whom the adolescents perceive support. However, the actual number of supportive individuals, or network size, is not measured, as the adolescents did not report the quantities for each category. Therefore, the term "*number of different types of support persons*" is used.

The Child and Adolescent Psychiatric Assessment (CAPA)

A structured, psychiatric interview, The Child and Adolescent Psychiatric Assessment (CAPA), was used to measure psychiatric disorders (Angold & Costello, 2000). This instrument not only includes information on the presence of symptoms but also includes information on the onset and duration of symptoms, providing a wide-ranging investigation of psychiatric symptoms and diagnoses. For the current sample, prevalent symptoms over the past three months were measured and diagnoses were set. To investigate the associations between social support and mental health, the symptom loads of the most prevalent diagnostic categories were used, including anxiety (total symptom load of agoraphobia, generalized anxiety disorder, social phobia, specific phobia, and panic attacks) and depression (total symptom load of major depressive disorder and dysthymia), as well as conduct disorder (CD) and ADHD diagnoses. For more information about the methods used, please refer to Singstad et al. (2022).

Quality of Life: The Kinder Lebensqualität Fragebogen (KINDL-R)

To measure QoL, a Norwegian translation of the Kinder Lebensqualität Fragebogen revised version (KINDL-R) was used (Ravens-Sieberer & Bullinger, 2000). The questionnaire comprises 24 items divided into six subscales: Physical Well-Being, Emotional Well-Being, Self-esteem, Family, Friends, and School. Respondents rated their experiences over the past week on a five-point scale, with one indicating "never" and five indicating "always." A sum score was calculated for each subscale and for an overall score, with higher scores indicating better QoL. For our study, we excluded the Family, Friends, and School subscales, as they were not relevant to the adolescent's current situation. The Family subscale was excluded because the adolescents were not living at home during data collection, with RYCs providing substitute parenting, and many adolescents did not have daily interactions with their families. The Friend subscale was excluded due to conceptual overlap with the SSQ. The School subscale was excluded because few adolescents were attending school at the time of data collection, and there were several conflicts in the reports of school participation among the adolescents, their primary RYC contacts, and their teachers. For further information and methodology, please refer to Singstad et al. (2021).

Childhood Adversity

Childhood adversity was measured through selected questions from the CAPA, which included four items on witnessing violence, being a victim of physical violence, family violence, or sexual abuse. Additionally, household dysfunction was assessed, including parental history of mental health or psychiatric problems, frequent alcohol or drug abuse, and parental involvement in crime. A childhood adversity scale was constructed based on a number of types of adversities, ranging from 0 to 4 (Greger et al., 2015).

Results

Perceived Social Support among Adolescents Living in Norwegian Residential Youth Care

Adolescents living in Norwegian RYC perceive social support from fewer types of support persons compared to a general population sample of Norwegian adolescents (N = 7,095, aged 12–19) (Singstad et al., 2020; Wichstrøm, 2002). The development of perceived social support also differed across ages between the two populations. Both girls and boys from the RYC sample reported perceiving support from fewer different support persons than adolescents in the general population at age 14, with girls in RYC reporting the fewest support persons. However, by age 18, no difference in the number of available support persons was observed between the two populations (Singstad et al., 2020).

Table 6.1 Comparison of support persons reported by adolescents in residential youth care and the general population

Support person	*RYC (N = 304)*		*General population (N = 7,095)*		
	n	%	*n*	%	p*
None	45	14.8	1,115	15.7	.668
Mother	208	**68.4**	6,578	**92.7**	**<.001**
Father	144	**47.4**	6,050	**85.3**	**<.001**
Boyfriend/girlfriend	155	51.0	3,394	47.8	.282
Sibling(s)	159	**52.3**	4,340	**61.2**	**.002**
Friend(s)	273	89.8	6,260	88.2	.404
Relative(s)	137	**45.1**	2,614	**36.8**	**.004**
Neighbor(s)	22	7.2	1,022	**14.4**	**<.001**
Institutional staff	196	64.5	—	—	—
Others	82	27.0	2,095	29.5	.339

Note: For each of the five questions, respondents could identify their available support persons from eight alternatives listed (in addition to the alternative none). For the sum scores, each support person was counted only once, even if mentioned in multiple scenarios. **Bold** indicates significant differences between the groups. The category "institutional staff" is only available for adolescents in RYC.

* Asymptotic Pearson chi-squared test.

Despite reporting a lower number of different support persons, most RYC adolescents expressed satisfaction with their available support when calculating the total satisfaction score (M = 16.07, SD = 4.123) (Singstad et al., 2020). Additionally, we examined the individual sources of perceived support for adolescents in both populations.

As shown in Table 6.1, adolescents in RYCs less frequently reported their immediate family members as support persons compared to those in the general population. Instead, they relied on additional sources of support, such as other relatives and institutional staff. Consistent with most research, friends are crucial during adolescence, including for those living in care.

Associations between Perceived Social Support and Symptom Loads of Psychiatric Disorders

Linear regression analyses revealed that a higher number of social support persons was associated with lower symptoms of anxiety for both girls ($\beta = -.318$, $p = .011$) and boys ($\beta = -.214$, $p = .031$) in RYC, as well as a lower number of depressive symptoms for girls ($\beta = -.364$, $p = .043$). While support from immediate family members is not associated with lower symptom loads (ranging from $p = .21$ to $p = .93$), associations were found between perceiving social support from other sources and reduced symptom loads. For girls, lower emotional symptoms were associated with perceiving social support from friends (depression (2.153 [0.59, 3.72], $p = .007$; anxiety (2.007 [0.92, 3.09], $p = <.001$) and institutional staff (depression 1.075 [0.14, 2.01], $p = .024$), and lower ADHD symptoms were associated with support from institutional staff (1.502 [0.06, 2.95], p = .042). For boys, perceiving social support from institutional staff was associated with lower symptoms of CD (0.720 [0.10, 1.34], p = .023). For further details, please see Singstad et al. (2022).

Associations between Perceived Social Support and Quality of Life

Linear regression analyses revealed that increased perceived social support was associated with a higher QoL. However, differences exist between boys and girls. For girls, a higher number of different types of support persons was associated with higher scores on the self-esteem subscale (β = 3.62, p = .014). For boys, significant associations were found across several domains, including overall QoL (β = 3.31, p = .005), emotional well-being (β = 3.11, p = .020), and self-esteem (β = 5.46, p = .001). When examining individual support providers, girls who perceived social support from institutional staff reported higher scores on the self-esteem subscale compared to those in lack of such support (−8.210 [−15.96, −.46], p = .038). Additionally, girls who perceived social support from friends reported higher scores on overall QoL (−17.362 [−28.17, −6.56], p = .002), physical well-being (−16.419 [−29.13, −3.71], p = .012), emotional well-being (−16.521 [−28.97, −4.07], p = .010), and self-esteem (−19.146 [−31.77, −6.52], p = .003). For boys, no significant associations were found between individual support persons and QoL. For further information, please see Singstad et al. (2021). Moreover, findings from multiple analyses in this study indicate that boys benefit more from having a larger social network with different support persons available, whereas girls show better outcomes when they receive support from individual persons.

Table 6.2 Potential moderation by social support in the relationship between childhood adversity and overall QoL

	Overall QoL							
	Girls (N = 148)				*Boys (N = 112)*			
	b	*95% CI*		p	*b*	*95% CI*		p
		Lower	*Upper*			*Lower*	*Upper*	
CAS	−4.37	−7.34	−1.40	.004	−2.76	−6.13	.618	.11
SSQ-N*CAS	−1.28	−3.47	.92	.25	−.97	−3.34	1.41	.42
Mother supp.*CAS	−3.12	−9.41	3.17	.33	−2.56	−9.68	4.57	.48
Father supp. * CAS	−2.63	−8.63	3.37	.39	−4.81	−11.65	2.03	.17
Staff supp. * CAS	−2.07	−8.66	4.53	.54	.09	−6.88	7.06	.98
Friend supp. * CAS	3.81	−4.64	12.27	.37	−3.65	−15.57	8.28	.55

Note: QoL = Quality of Life; SSQ-N = total number of different types of support persons; CAS = Childhood Adversity Scale. The first line shows the regression coefficient for the CAS as the independent variable. The rest of the table shows the coefficient for the interaction between a social support variable and the CAS, in an analysis including these variables and their interaction. All analyses are adjusted for age. **Bold:** $p < 0.05$.

The dose–response relationship between ACEs and subsequent QoL led us to test whether perceived social support might moderate the negative effects of prior polyvictimization. However, linear regression analysis found no significant moderation, as shown in Table 6.2.

Discussion

Social support, relational capacities, and a sense of belonging are crucial for individual development (Bowlby, 1973; Ditzen & Heinrichs, 2014). Adolescents with troubled backgrounds, such as those experiencing ACEs and instability in care, face a higher risk of negative development due to often diminished social networks (Zimmer-Gembeck & Collins, 2006). This highlights the importance of optimizing RYC facilities to ensure high-quality social support and foster healthier development for these adolescents.

Research shows that adolescents in RYC report fewer support figures compared to the general population, with girls showing the lowest numbers. This discrepancy can be attributed to high numbers of ACEs (Greger et al., 2015) and frequent placements outside their birth homes (Kayed et al., 2015), leading to hesitancy in forming new social relations. Additionally, girls may be more cautious in entering new relationships following negative life events (Piko, 2001), and are more likely to exhibit symptoms of emotional disorders and withdrawal compared to boys (Jozefiak et al., 2016). Unlike their peers, RYC adolescents' perceived number of supportive individuals remains stable throughout adolescence, while the general population experiences a larger social network in early adolescence that decreases with age, reflecting broader trends in autonomy development (Zimmer-Gembeck & Collins, 2006).

Despite reporting fewer support figures, RYC adolescents generally report satisfaction with their perceived support. The adequacy of support is influenced by individual needs, personality, and prior social experiences (Sarason et al., 1983). RYC adolescents, accustomed to lower-quality parental support due to unstable home environments, may adjust their expectations and be satisfied with fewer support figures (Bowlby, 1982). The quality of support often outweighs the quantity; high-quality support from one individual can be more valuable than low-quality support from many. Both RYC and general population adolescents reported higher satisfaction with an increasing number of support persons.

Adolescents in RYC report less support from immediate family compared to peers living at home, which is expected due to their removal from challenging home conditions. However, they often receive support from institutional staff, who offer professional parenting and compensate for the lack of parental support (Harder et al., 2013). Friends also emerge as important support sources, reflecting the shift from parental to peer support during adolescence, in their seeking toward autonomy and increased independence (Bokhorst et al., 2010).

The associations between a larger number of diverse support figures and lower emotional symptoms can be attributed to the enhanced sense of support and belonging from multiple sources. For girls, it is encouraging that institutional staff members serve as important sources of support, as they often require emotional closeness and one-to-one interactions (Costa et al., 2020). For boys, perceived staff support was associated with fewer CD symptoms, highlighting the importance of a structured and caring environment for their mental health.

However, it's crucial to consider the possibility of a reverse relationship: increased social support may not necessarily lead to lower symptomatology. Adolescents may struggle to recognize or acknowledge available support due to past negative relational experiences, leading to underreporting of supportive individuals and a distorted perception of their actual support network.

Finally, we found associations between perceived social support and QoL. For boys, a variety of support figures increases happiness and serves as a protective factor against loneliness. For girls, social network size was linked with self-esteem, likely due to the acceptance and value provided by supportive relationships (Zimmer-Gembeck & Collins, 2006). Individual support from friends and institutional staff was significantly associated with enhanced QoL for girls, as they benefit from emotional closeness and one-on-one interactions (Costa et al., 2020; Lanctôt et al., 2016). Notably, girls who perceived support from friends reported higher QoL scores across all subscales. Furthermore, perceived support from institutional staff was significantly associated with girls' self-esteem, underscoring the importance of daily presence and consistent, high-quality support. However, perceived social support does not moderate the negative effects of adverse life experiences on later QoL. This underscores the critical and long-lasting consequences of growing up under highly vulnerable home conditions, suggesting that more complex and comprehensive approaches are needed to address the multifaceted developmental challenges faced by high-risk adolescents.

Limitations of the Study

This study is among the first to examine perceived social support within a high-risk Norwegian population, with robust and extensive data collection as a significant strength. However, several limitations must be acknowledged. The cross-sectional design limits the ability to draw causal inferences (Bryman, 2016). We cannot definitively identify the underlying reasons for low perceived social support or specific risk factors. The absence of prior mental health information for adolescents prevents us from asserting potential mitigating effects on symptomatology. The SSQ has constraints as it cannot provide insights into the actual number of individuals in an individual's social network. Additionally, relying solely on adolescents' self-reports leaves uncertainty about potential social support providers who may not have been mentioned. Organizational variations in CWSs and RYC institutions across countries (Berrick et al., 2017) may limit the generalizability of our findings.

Implications for Future Research

To enhance the assessment of perceived social support, expanding the SSQ to evaluate satisfaction with support from each source of support is recommended. Including diverse support persons, such as grandparents and teachers, would provide a more holistic view. Additionally, allowing respondents to list persons as alternative sources of support could offer valuable insights. Incorporating additional factors like attachment structures, prior mental health history, delinquent behavior, and past social networks would yield valuable insights. Delving deeper into social support structures and identifying specific initiatives or actions that contribute to a sense of support could pinpoint what precisely fosters a feeling of care and belonging. In this regard, comparisons of RYC adolescents and the general population's perceptions of supportive behavior can offer profound insights into how previous caregiving conditions influence subsequent perceptions of social support. Longitudinal studies are imperative to understand the effects of supportive structures over time and identify risk and protective factors. Key areas of investigation include the development of social support providers over time, the impact of the duration of institutional stays on social relationships, and the efficacy of social skill training. Additionally, exploring how adolescents define social networks and social support over time, and whether these definitions evolve with the availability of new, stable support structures is crucial.

Implications for Practice and Policy

Despite limitations, our findings establish perceived social support as crucial for high-risk adolescents' mental health and QoL. Adolescents in RYC typically have limited social networks, necessitating initiatives to provide supportive networks. Younger girls, in particular, are vulnerable and should be targeted for intervention. Ensuring supportive individuals for adolescents, especially girls who prefer one-to-one support, is essential. Institutional staff, friends, and other family members are key support providers, concluding that a collective supportive environment is important for reducing emotional symptoms and fostering a sense of belonging. Gender differences in social support suggest the need for sex-differentiated adjustments in interventions.

High-quality caring environments in RYC should be a priority, with educated and competent institutional staff providing consistent and genuine caregiving. Institutional routines and structures promoting ongoing training and development of, for example, relational competence or other relevant theory and research are recommended. Furthermore, institutional leaders should ensure an adequate number of staff members have the time and resources to be actively present in adolescents' everyday lives. Work shifts should be structured to ensure stability and continuity, minimizing the number of adolescents interacting within a day. Creating an inclusive, developmental, and motivating collegial fellowship among staff members can also provide stability and predictability, counteracting turnover.

Matching institutional staff with individual adolescents based on trust and mutual respect is crucial when allocating primary contacts. Ensuring individual diversity among the staff will therefore increase the possibility for all adolescents to find a trusted person. Facilitating opportunities for adolescents to maintain preexisting social networks and form new relationships, especially in socialization arenas, is essential. Furthermore, institutional staff should identify changes in mental health symptoms and have expertise in psychiatric disorders and interventions. Finally, supportive and flexible aftercare is crucial as adolescents transition to adulthood, with primary contacts providing stability and security during the transition.

References

Ainsworth, M. D. S., Blehar, M. C., Waters, E., & Wall, S. N. (2015). *Patterns of attachment: A psychological study of the strange situation*. Psychology Press.

Angold, A., & Costello, E. J. (2000). The child and adolescent psychiatric assessment (CAPA). *Journal of the American Academy of Child and Adolescent Psychiatry*, *39*(1), 39–48. https://doi.org/10.1097/00004583-200001000-00015

Backe-Hansen, E., Bakketeig, E., Gautun, H., & Grønningsæter, A. B. (2011). *Institusjonsplassering – siste utvei?: betydningen av barnevernsreformen fra 2004 for institusjonstilbudet. (Placement in institutions – the last opportunity. The importance of the child welfare reform in 2004 for placement policy in institutions)* (Vol. 21/2011). Norsk institutt for forskning om oppvekst, velferd og aldring.

Barne- ungdoms- og familiedirektoratet. (2010). *Kvalitet i barneverninstitusjoner (Quality in child welfare institutions)*. https://bibliotek.bufdir.no/BUF/101/Kvalitet_i_barneverninstitusjoner.pdf

Barne- ungdoms- og familiedirektoratet. (2021). *Barn og unge i institusjon (Children and youths in institutions)*. https://bufdir.no/Statistikk_og_analyse/Barnevern/Barn_og_unge_med_tiltak_fra_barnevernet/barn_i_institusjon

Barnevernslovenbarneverntjenester (*The Child Welfare Act*) (2024). *Lov om barneverntjenester* (LOV-2024-12-13-78). Lovdata. https://lovdata.no/dokument/NL/lov/2021-06-18-97?q=barnevernloven

Baumeister, R. F., & Leary, M. R. (1995). The need to belong: Desire for interpersonal attachments as a fundamental human motivation. *Psychological Bulletin*, *117*(3), 497–529. https://doi.org/10.1037/0033-2909.117.3.497

Belsky, J., Bakermans-Kranenburg, M. J., & van IJzendoorn, M. H. (2007). For better and for worse: Differential susceptibility to environmental influences. *Current Directions in Psychological Science*, *16*(6), 300–304. https://doi.org/10.1111/j.1467-8721.2007.00525.x

Berens, A. E., Jensen, S. K. G., & Nelson, C. A. (2017). Biological embedding of childhood adversity: From physiological mechanisms to clinical implications. *BMC Medicine*, *15*(1), 135. https://doi.org/10.1186/s12916-017-0895-4

Berrick, J., Dickens, J., Pösö, T., & Skivenes, M. (2017). A cross-country comparison of child welfare systems and workers' responses to children appearing to be at risk or in need of help. *Child Abuse Review*, *26*(4), 305–319. https://doi.org/10.1002/car.2485

Blakemore, S.-J. (2019). Adolescence and mental health. *The Lancet*, *393*(10185), 2030–2031. https://doi.org/10.1016/S0140-6736(19)31013-X

Bokhorst, C. L., Sumter, S. R., & Westenberg, P. M. (2010). Social support from parents, friends, classmates, and teachers in children and adolescents aged 9 to 18 years: Who is perceived as most supportive? *Social Development*, *19*(2), 417–426. https://doi.org/10.1111/j.1467-9507.2009.00540.x

Bowlby, J. (1973). *Attachment and loss: Volume II: Separation, anxiety and anger*. Hogarth Press.

Bowlby, J. (1982). *Attachment and loss: Vol 1: Attachment* (2nd ed., Vol. 1). Basic Books.

Brannstrom, L., Forsman, H., Vinnerljung, B., & Almquist, Y. B. (2017). The truly disadvantaged? Midlife outcome dynamics of individuals with experiences of out-of-home care. *Child Abuse and Neglect*, *67*, 408–418. https://doi.org/10.1016/j.chiabu.2016.11.009

Bronsard, G., Alessandrini, M., Fond, G., Loundou, A., Auquier, P., Tordjman, S., & Boyer, L. (2016). The prevalence of mental disorders among children and adolescents in the child welfare system: A systematic review and meta-analysis. *Medicine*, *95*(7). https://doi.org/10.1097/MD.0000000000002622

Bryman, A. (2016). *Social research methods* (4th ed.). Oxford University Press.

Chu, P. S., Saucier, D. A., & Hafner, E. (2010). Meta-analysis of the relationships between social support and well-being in children and adolescents. *Journal of Social and Clinical Psychology*, *29*(6), 624. https://doi.org/10.1521/jscp.2010.29.6.624

Clemens, V., Bürgin, D., Eckert, A., Kind, N., Dölitzsch, C., Fegert, J. M., & Schmid, M. (2020). Hypothalamic-pituitary-adrenal axis activation in a high-risk sample of children, adolescents and young adults in residential youth care – Associations with adverse childhood experiences and mental health problems. *Psychiatry Research*, *284*. https://doi.org/10.1016/j.psychres.2020.112778

Cohen, S., & Wills, T. A. (1985). Stress, social support, and the buffering hypothesis. *Psychological Bulletin*, *98*(2), 310–357. https://doi.org/10.1037/0033-2909.98.2.310

Costa, M., Melim, B., Tagliabue, S., Mota, C. P., & Matos, P. M. (2020). Predictors of the quality of the relationship with caregivers in residential care. *Children and Youth Services Review*, *108*. https://doi.org/10.1016/j.childyouth.2019.104579

Ditzen, B., & Heinrichs, M. (2014). Psychobiology of social support: The social dimension of stress buffering. *Restorative Neurology and Neuroscience*, *32*(1), 149–162. https://doi.org/10.3233/RNN-139008

Essau, C. A., Ishikawa, S.-I., Sasagawa, S., Sato, H., Okajima, I., Otsui, K., Georgiou, G. A., O'Callaghan, J., & Michie, F. (2011). Anxiety symptoms among adolescents in Japan and England: Their relationship with self-construals and social support. *Depression and Anxiety*, *28*(6), 509–518. https://doi.org/10.1002/da.20819

González-García, C., Bravo, A., Arruabarrena, I., Martín, E., Santos, I., & Del Valle, J. F. (2017). Emotional and behavioral problems of children in residential care: Screening detection and referrals to mental health services. *Children and Youth Services Review*, *73*, 100–106. https://doi.org/10.1016/j.childyouth.2016.12.011

Greger, H. K., Myhre, A. K., Lydersen, S., & Jozefiak, T. (2015). Previous maltreatment and present mental health in a high-risk adolescent population. *Child Abuse and Neglect*, *45*, 122–134. https://doi.org/10.1016/j.chiabu.2015.05.003

Greger, H. K., Myhre, A. K., Lydersen, S., & Jozefiak, T. (2016). Child maltreatment and quality of life: A study of adolescents in residential care. *Health and Quality of Life Outcomes*, *14*(1), 1–17. https://doi.org/10.1186/s12955-016-0479-6

Hagen, G. (2001). *Barnevernets historie: om makt og avmakt i det 20. århundret (The history of child welfare: power and powerlessness in the 20th century)*. Akribe.

Harder, A. T., Knorth, E. J., & Kalverboer, M. E. (2013). A secure base? The adolescent–staff relationship in secure residential youth care. *Child & Family Social Work*, *18*(3), 305–317. https://doi.org/10.1111/j.1365-2206.2012.00846.x

Hoffnung Assouline, A. A., & Attar-Schwartz, S. (2020). Staff support and adolescent adjustment difficulties: The moderating role of length of stay in the residential care setting. *Children and Youth Services Review*, *110*. https://doi.org/10.1016/j.childyouth.2020.104761

Hygen, B. W., Belsky, J., Stenseng, F., Lydersen, S., Guzey, I. C., & Wichstrøm, L. (2015). Child exposure to serious life events, COMT, and aggression: Testing differential susceptibility theory. *Developmental Psychology*, *51*(8), 1098–1104. https://doi.org/10.1037/dev0000020

Jozefiak, T., Kayed, N., Rimehaug, T., Wormdal, A., Brubakk, A., & Wichstrøm, L. (2016). Prevalence and comorbidity of mental disorders among adolescents living in residential youth care. *European Child and Adolescent Psychiatry*, *25*(1), 33–47. https://doi.org/10.1007/s00787-015-0700-x

Jozefiak, T., & Kayed, N. S. (2015). Self- and proxy reports of quality of life among adolescents living in residential youth care compared to adolescents in the general population and mental health services. *Health & Quality of Life Outcomes*, *13*(1), 104. https://doi.org/10.1186/s12955-015-0280-y

Kayed, N. S., Jozefiak, T., Rimehaug, T., Tjelflaat, T., Brubakk, A. M., & Wichstrøm, L. (2015). *Resultater fra forskningsprosjektet psykisk helse hos barn og unge i barneverninstitusjoner (Results from the research project "Mental Health of Children and Adolescents in Child Welfare Institutions")*. NTNU, Bufdir, & Helsedirektoratet. https://www.ntnu.no/trykk/publikasjoner/Barnevernrapport_RKBU/

Kieling, C., Baker-Henningham, H., Belfer, M., Conti, G., Ertem, I., Omigbodun, O., Rohde, L. A., Srinath, S., Ulkuer, N., & Rahman, A. (2011). Child and adolescent mental health worldwide: evidence for action. *The Lancet*, *378*(9801), 1515–1525. https://doi.org/10.1016/S0140-6736(11)60827-1

Lanctôt, N., Lemieux, A., & Mathys, C. (2016). The value of a safe, connected social climate for adolescent girls in residential care. *Residential Treatment for Children & Youth*, *33*(3–4), 247–269. https://doi.org/10.1080/0886571X.2016.1207218

Leipoldt, J. D., Harder, A. T., Kayed, N. S., Grietens, H., & Rimehaug, T. (2019). Determinants and outcomes of social climate in therapeutic residential youth care: A systematic review. *Children and Youth Services Review*, *99*, 429–440. https://doi.org/10.1016/j.childyouth.2019.02.010

Lum, J. A. G., Powell, M., & Snow, P. C. (2018). The influence of maltreatment history and out-of-home-care on children's language and social skills. *Child Abuse and Neglect*, *76*, 65–74. https://doi.org/10.1016/j.chiabu.2017.10.008

Moos, R. H. (2009). *Community oriented programs environment scale manual* (4th ed.). Mind Garden.

Murberg, T., & Bru, E. (2004). Social support, negative life events and emotional problems among Norwegian adolescents. *School Psychology International*, *25*(4), 387–403. https://doi.org/10.1177/0143034304048775

Piko, B. (2001). Gender differences and similarities in adolescents' ways of coping. *The Psychological Record*, *51*(2), 223. https://doi.org/10.1007/BF03395396

Polanczyk, G. V., Salum, G. A., Sugaya, L. S., Caye, A., & Rohde, L. A. (2015). Annual research review: A meta-analysis of the worldwide prevalence of mental disorders in children and adolescents. *Journal of Child Psychology and Psychiatry*, *56*(3), 345–365. https://doi.org/10.1111/jcpp.12381

Ravens-Sieberer, U., & Bullinger, M. (2000). *KINDL-R. Questionnaire for measuring health-related quality of life in children and adolescents – Revised version 2000*. https://www.kindl.org/english/manual/

Reneflot, A., Aarø, L. E., Aase, H., Reichborn-Kjennerud, T., Tambs, K., & Øverland, S. (2018). *Psykisk helse i Norge (Mental Health in Norway)*. Norwegian Institute of Public Health. https://www.fhi.no/globalassets/dokumenterfiler/rapporter/2018/psykisk_helse_i_norge2018.pdf

Rueger, S. Y., Malecki, C. K., & Demaray, M. K. (2010). Relationship between multiple sources of perceived social support and psychological and academic adjustment in early adolescence: Comparisons across gender. *Journal of Youth and Adolescence*, *39*(1), 47–61. https://doi.org/10.1007/s10964-008-9368-6

Rueger, S. Y., Malecki, C. K., Pyun, Y., Aycock, C., & Coyle, S. (2016). A meta-analytic review of the association between perceived social support and depression in childhood and adolescence. *Psychological Bulletin*, *142*(10), 1017–1067. https://doi.org/10.1037/bul0000058

Sarason, B. R., Pierce, G. R., & Sarason, I. G. (1990). Social support: The sense of acceptance and the role of relationships. In B. R. Sarason, I. G. Sarason, & G. R. Pierce (Eds.), *Social support: An interactional view* (pp. 97–128). John Wiley & Sons, Inc.

Sarason, I. G., Levine, H. M., Basham, R. B., & Sarason, B. R. (1983). Assessing social support: The social support questionnaire. *Journal of Personality and Social Psychology*, *44*(1), 127–139. https://doi.org/10.1037/0022-3514.44.1.127

Sciaraffa, M. A., Zeanah, P. D., & Zeanah, C. H. (2018). Understanding and promoting resilience in the context of adverse childhood experiences. *Early Childhood Education Journal*, *46*(3), 343–353. https://doi.org/10.1007/s10643-017-0869-3

Singstad, M. T., Wallander, J. L., Greger, H. K., Lydersen, S., & Kayed, N. S. (2021). Perceived social support and quality of life among adolescents in residential youth care: A cross-sectional study. *Health and Quality of Life Outcomes*, *19*(1), 29. https://doi.org/10.1186/s12955-021-01676-1

Singstad, M. T., Wallander, J. L., Lydersen, S., & Kayed, N. S. (2022). Perceived social support and symptom loads of psychiatric disorders among adolescents in residential youth care. *Social Work Research*, *46*(1), 30–43. https://doi.org/10.1093/swr/svab031

Singstad, M. T., Wallander, J. L., Lydersen, S., Wichstrøm, L., & Kayed, N. S. (2020). Perceived social support among adolescents in residential youth care. *Child & Family Social Work*, *25*(2), 384–393. https://doi.org/10.1111/cfs.12694

Swerts, C., De Maeyer, J., Lombardi, M., Waterschoot, I., Vanderplasschen, W., & Claes, C. (2019). "You shouldn't look at us strangely": An exploratory study on personal perspectives on quality of life of adolescents with emotional and behavioral disorders in residential youth care. *Applied Research in Quality of Life*, *14*(4), 867–889. https://doi.org/10.1007/s11482-017-9534-7

Villodas, M. T., Litrownik, A. J., Newton, R. R., & Davis, I. P. (2015). Long-term placement trajectories of children who were maltreated and entered the child welfare system at an early age: Consequences for physical and behavioral well-being. *Journal of Pediatric Psychology*, *41*(1), 46–54. https://doi.org/10.1093/jpepsy/jsv031

Wichstrøm, L. (1999). The emergence of gender difference in depressed mood during adolescence: The role of intensified gender socialization. *Developmental Psychology*, *35*(1), 232–245. https://doi.org/10.1037/0012-1649.35.1.232

Wichstrøm, L. (2002). Ung i Norge (Young in Norway). *Norsk epidemiologi*, *12*(3), 231–237. https://doi.org/10.5324/nje.v12i3.371

Wichstrøm, L., & Hegna, K. (2003). Sexual orientation and suicide attempt: A longitudinal study of the general Norwegian adolescent population. *Journal of Abnormal Psychology*, *112*(1), 144. https://doi.org/10.1037/0021-843X.112.1.144

Zimmer-Gembeck, M. J., & Collins, A. W. (2006). Autonomy development during adolescence. In M. D. Berzonsky & G. R. Adams (Eds.), *Blackwell handbook of adolescence* (pp. 174–204). Blackwell Publishing.

7 Social Support and Well-being among Canadian Young People in Family Foster Care, Kinship Care, or Group Care

Elena Gallitto and Robert J. Flynn

Introduction

Malecki and Demaray (2003) defined social support as "an individual's perceptions of general support or specific supportive behaviors (available or acted on) from people in their social network, which enhances their functioning or may buffer them from adverse outcomes (p. 232)." These authors adopted a conceptualization developed by House (1991) more than four decades ago, in which social support was seen as consisting of four main types: *emotional support*, communicating feelings of trust and love to another person; *informational support*, furnishing information or advice to the other person; *instrumental support*: providing resources to the other person, such as shared time, materials, or money; and, *appraisal support*: giving evaluative feedback to the other person. The first three types of social support are encountered most frequently in research on young people in care (Evans et al., 2022) and are employed in this chapter.

It is commonplace that young people in care face greater threats to their well-being than their age peers in the general population. For example, Long et al. (2017) analysed data from a large cross-sectional sample of 28,838 secondary school students aged 11–16 who had participated in a School Health Research Network survey in Wales (U.K.) in 2015–2016. The sample included 295 young people (1%) who resided in foster care. Long et al. (2017) compared the outcomes of substance use, well-being, and interpersonal relationships among those in foster care and those in private homes. The youth in foster care had higher rates of adverse outcomes across all those studied: higher rates of mephedrone use and multiple substance misuse, poorer relationships with peers and teachers, more frequent experiences of being bullied and dating violence, and lower well-being. It was noteworthy, however, that the association between being in foster care and poorer well-being was no longer statistically significant once the relationship variables had been considered. Long et al. (2017) hypothesized that the more negative outcomes experienced by young people in foster care may be explainable by the influence of several pre-care and in-care risk factors on their subsequent social relationships, namely, more frequent substance use and poorer life

DOI: 10.4324/9781003424468-10

satisfaction, and that interventions aimed at nurturing healthy social relationships may improve both their substance use and well-being.

Evans et al. (2022) conducted a recent study in the United States on the association between the sources and types of social support and mental health symptoms and life satisfaction in a cross-sectional sectional sample of 215 young people aged 18–22 years with a history of out-of-home care. Regarding the sources and types of social support experienced by the young people, almost all said they had family-based support in the form of a family member to whom they could turn. A third mentioned a birth parent, a third indicated an extended family member, and smaller proportions named an adult sibling, adoptive family, foster family, legal guardian, or others. Two-thirds stated they could always count on the family member in question and a third said they could count on them most of the time (Evans et al., 2022).

Three-quarters of the young adults also reported having friendship-based social support in the person of a good friend whose help they could rely on; three-quarters said they had one to four friends, and a fifth reported five to nine friends. About half felt they could always count on their friends, and 40% said most of the time. In addition, over half of the sample said they had a non-family adult to turn to when needed, with a quarter naming a family friend or neighbour, a fifth a work colleague, and smaller proportions indicating a teacher or coach, a non-relative mentor, an adult from a faith-based community, a caseworker or staff person from a residential facility or group home, a lawyer, or other adults. Half of the young adults stated they could always count on the non-family adult, and a third said most of the time. Regarding the types of support they had, 73% of the young adults reported having enough people to provide informational support (e.g., advice), and 48% stated that they had enough people to provide material support, such as money (Evans et al., 2022). On the other hand, in another U.S. sample, one drawn from the California Youth Transitions to Adulthood Study (CalYOUTH; Okpych et al., 2018), young adults who were 19 years of age and in care reported relatively low levels of support: 40% said they did not have enough people to turn to for emotional support and nearly half reported not having enough people to provide material support. More than 30% said they had too few people to give them advice and guidance.

Regarding the relationship between the sources and types of social support, Evans et al. (2022) noted that social support is a well-established protective factor for mental health and life satisfaction, such that adolescents and young adults with higher levels of perceived social support tend to have lower levels of depression and anxiety than their peers (Rueger et al., 2016; Scardera et al., 2020). Multiple regression analyses also indicated that significant predictors of lower mental health symptoms included having enough people to provide informational support and material support, respectively. Also, there was a trend in which support from a family member was associated with fewer mental health symptoms, and having a family member for support and enough people to turn to for material support were significant predictors of greater life satisfaction.

Aim of the Present Study

The findings from the studies mentioned above indicate the critical role of social support in promoting the well-being of child welfare-involved youth. However, the links between specific forms of social support and youth well-being are still unclear (Evans et al., 2022). Moreover, besides addressing this latter question, the present study is also one of the first to examine the link between different types of social support and mental health outcomes in a representative sample of Canadian young people in care. Our research had three main purposes. First, we evaluated the factor structure of a new tripartite social support measure created from 19 items from the Canadian Casey Life Skills Assessment (CCLSA; Flynn et al., 2023, chapter 9). This is a measure incorporated into a structured interview schedule used with a large number of young people each year in Ontario. It thus has considerable potential to be employed regularly in social-support research and applications in the province. Second, we used structural equation modelling (SEM) to compare the new CCLSA support measure with two proxy measures of emotional support furnished by the young person's family of origin and his or her current caregivers. Third, we used these proxy measures and the CCLSA social support factors and SEM to predict three specific mental health outcomes among young people aged 16 or 17 and residing in out-of-home care in Ontario, Canada: well-being (a synonym here for positive mental health), negative mental health, and placement satisfaction.

Method

Research Context

We drew upon the database of the Ontario Looking After Children (OnLAC) project (Flynn et al., 2006; Flynn et al., 2023) as the source of our sample in the present study. Initiated at the University of Ottawa in 2000 with a strategic research grant from the Social Sciences and Humanities Research Council of Canada (SSHRC), the project has given rise to numerous peer-reviewed journal articles, chapters, conference presentations, and PhD theses (Miller et al., 2023). From the beginning, the project has been conducted in partnership with the Ontario Association of Children's Aid Societies (OACAS), with the participation of many local Children's Aid Societies (hereafter, Societies) across the province. Moreover, after completion of the SSHRC grant, the Ontario Social Services Ministry (the current name of which is the Ministry of Children, Community, and Social Services [MCCSS]) began to fund the OnLAC project in 2004 on a year-to-year basis, with funds allocated through OACAS in the form of annual contracts and has continued to do so ever since. In 2007, the ministry mandated that the main OnLAC assessment instrument, the Assessment and Action Record (AAR), be used in local Societies across Ontario to assess the service needs and monitor the service outcomes and well-being (Biglan, 2014, 2015) of children or youths who have been in out-of-home care in the province for one year or more.

Currently, the project completes some 3,000 individual assessments of children and youth aged 0–18+ years each year. Since 2000, we have gathered needs assessment and outcome monitoring data on more than 35,000 young people in out-of-home care who have figured in more than 80,000 annual AAR interviews. These interviews are conducted with the young person (if ten years or older), their caregivers (e.g., foster parents in foster families and youth care workers in residential care settings), and their child welfare worker. The latter is responsible for conducting the annual interviews and submitting the AAR data to the OnLAC project at the University of Ottawa.

The AAR is also used as the data source for three standardized well-being performance indicators (P.I.s) for Ontario Societies, which MCCSS makes available to the public annually. The P.I.s are measures of the young person's educational success, the quality of their relationships (as perceived by the young person) with their caregivers, and the number of their developmental assets. These well-being P.I.s, in combination with other AAR data on outcomes, are intended by MCCSS to increase the accountability of child welfare services in Ontario at the level of individual youths in care, local Societies, and the provincial government.

Data Source

The data used in this chapter was gathered with the current standardized version of the AAR since 2016 (i.e., the AAR-C2-2016). As mentioned, the AAR is a structured conversational interview where the young person in care (if ten years or older), the caregiver (e.g., foster parent; child welfare workers in residential care settings), and the child welfare worker participate. Relevant for present purposes is that the AAR includes specific variables intended for older adolescents and young adults aged 16–17 or 18+ (as well as for younger age groups, from newborns to 15 year olds). The older young people may be preparing to leave care for independent living or already attending college or university while still in care. The AAR for youths in care aged 16 and over includes the CCLSA (see Flynn et al., 2023), a Canadianized version of the US Ansell-Casey Life Skills Assessment (Nollan et al., 2000). Like the Ansell-Casey Life Skills Assessment, the CCLSA includes the following eight psychometric scales: permanency, daily living, self-care, relationships and communication, housing and money management, work and study life, career, and education planning, and looking forward.

Participants

The sample of 486 participants was drawn from 2016 to 2020 in the AAR database and consisted of young people in care with AAR data on the variables of interest at two time points (time-1 and time-2), approximately one year apart. The youths were about 16 years of age at time-1 and 17 at time-2 and resided in Ontario in kinship care homes, foster family homes, or group homes. Youths residing in independent living placements were excluded because of the absence of adult caregivers in such settings. The mean age of the sample at time-1 was 16.02 years ($SD = 0.14$), with more males ($n = 256$; 52.7%) than females ($n = 230$; 47.3%). Regarding the youths' placement settings, 239 (49.2%) were living at time-1 in foster family homes operated by local non-profit Societies, 102 (21.0%) were in foster homes run by for-profit organizations, 48 (9.9%) were in non-profit kinship care homes supervised by local Societies, 88 (18.1%) were in group homes operated by for-profit organizations, and 9 (1.9%) were in group homes administered by non-profit Societies. Paired sample t-tests revealed that two statistically significant changes took place in the sample on two outcome variables between time-1 and time-2: negative mental health increased ($t = 4.05$; $p < .001$), and placement satisfaction declined ($t = -3.08$; $p = .002$).

Measures

Emotional, Informational, and Instrumental Social Support

The CCLSA instrument (Flynn et al., 2023) is a self-report instrument that measures youths' behaviours and skills relevant to achieving a positive transition to adulthood. It comprises eight scales: daily living, self-care, relationships and communications, housing and money management, work and study life, career and education planning, and looking forward. We examined the 112 CCLSA items regarding their conceptual relevance to the central construct of social support. We then used exploratory factor analysis (EFA) and confirmatory factor analysis (CFA) procedures to derive a new, 19-item CCLSA measure of social support, composed of three sub-scales: *emotional support* (12 items; $\alpha = .87$; I know at least one adult I can depend on when I exit care), *informational support* (four items; $\alpha = .69$; I have an adult in my life who cares about how I am doing at school or work), and *instrumental support* (three items; $\alpha = .69$; I know how to get emergency help to pay for water, electricity, and gas bills), in answering each item on the Canadian Casey, the young person in care had rated its perceived applicability to their life situation on a five-point scale, with "Yes" = 5, "Mostly Yes" = 4, "Somewhat" = 3, "Mostly No" = 2, and "No" = 1. A higher score on each subscale indicated that the youth in care perceived receiving a higher level of social support.

Proxy Measures of Emotional Support

We also used two proxy measures of emotional support taken from the AAR, as we wanted to compare them with the new CCLSA social support measures in terms of their respective abilities to predict mental health outcomes. The first proxy measure was the Quality of Relationships with the Youth's Family of Origin scale, which consisted of four AAR items that we had originally taken from the National Longitudinal Survey of Children and Youth (NLSCY; Statistics Canada, 1999). The four items assessed the quality of the young person's relationship (as perceived and rated by the young person) with a member of his or her family of origin, as follows: "How well do you feel he/she understands you?" "How much fairness do you receive from him/her?" "How much affection do you receive from him/her?" and "Overall, how would you describe your relationship with him/her?" The first three items were answered on a three-point scale: 2 = "A great deal," 1 = "Some," and 0 = "Very little." The fourth item was also rated on a three-point scale: 2 = "Very close," 1 = "Somewhat close," and 0 = "Not very close." The four-item scale was used separately for two members of the young person's family of origin, A and B. The total scores for family members A and B were correlated significantly with one another ($r = .55$, $p < .001$), such that we combined the two scales into a single eight-item scale that had excellent internal consistency ($\alpha = .91$).

The second proxy measure of emotional support was the Quality of Relationships with the Youth's Out-of-Home Caregivers. The same items and scoring as in the first proxy measure were used to assess the quality of relationships with two caregivers, A and B, from the young person's foster, kinship care, or group home. In this case, young people were asked to relate to two caregivers that are closest to them. Again, the total scores for the two caregivers were correlated significantly with one another ($r = 51$, $p < .001$), such that again, we combined the two measures into a single eight-item scale ($\alpha = .87$).

Placement type

A single item assessed the type of placement in which the young person resided and had three categories: a *foster home* ($n = 341$), operated either by a non-profit Society or by a for-profit organization; a *kinship care home* ($n = 48$), supervised by a non-profit Society; or a *group home* ($n = 98$), operated by a for-profit organization or a non-profit Society.

Well-Being/Positive Mental Health

We had already incorporated into the AAR Keyes's (2006) 14-item short-form measure of well-being, which has been used internationally for a number of years to measure adolescent well-being (which we take here as a synonym for *positive mental health*). The first three items assess *emotional well-being* (e.g., interested in life, happy), items 4–8 assess *social well-being* (e.g., belonged to a community), and items 9–14 assess *psychological well-being* (e.g., thinking that life has a sense of direction). The young person rates each item on a six-point scale, ranging from 0 = "Never" to 5 = "Every day." The total score on the scale ranges from 0 to 70, with higher scores indicating higher levels of well-being or positive mental health. Previous research (Flynn et al., 2023) demonstrated that Keyes' 14-item measure is a consistently good predictor of four positive and four negative AAR measures of mental health. The internal consistency of the well-being scale in the current sample was excellent ($\alpha = .93$).

Negative Mental Health

The 20-item Total Adjustment Difficulties scale of the Strengths and Difficulties Questionnaire (Goodman, 1997) was used to measure negative mental health. The scale consists of four five-item subscales: emotional problems, conduct problems, hyperactivity and inattention, and peer problems. These items were rated by the young person's caregiver on a three-point scale, ranging from 0 = "Not True" to 2 = "True" (or the reverse, depending on the positive or negative wording of the item). The total score ranged from 0 to 40, with higher scores indicating poorer mental health. The scale's internal consistency in the current sample was good ($\alpha = .81$).

Data Analysis

Social Support Measures: Exploratory and Confirmatory Factor Analyses

The factorial validity of the new social support scale was assessed in an EFA that was followed by a CFA (Fabrigar et al., 1999). We randomly split the sample into halves, with the EFA carried out on one half ($n = 243$) and the CFA on the other ($n = 243$). The maximum number of factors extracted in the EFA was determined based on the scree test (Cattell, 1966). It was assumed that the identified factors would be intercorrelated because we were measuring different types of a common construct, social support. Thus, an oblique rotation (Geomin) was applied (Preacher & MacCallum, 2003). To decide which items to retain from the CFA analysis, we used the .40 –.30 –.20 rule suggested by Howard (2016): items should (1) load onto their primary factor above .40, (2) load onto other factors below 0.30, and (3) exhibit a difference of at least .20 between the cross-loadings on the primary and other factors.

The final version of the social-support measurement model, as confirmed via CFA, was based on several fit indices: the Tucker–Lewis Index (TLI; Tucker & Lewis, 1973), the Comparative Fit Index (CFI; Bentler, 1990), and the Root Mean Square Error (RMSEA; Steiger & Lind, 1980). Criterion values for these fit statistics were based on Hu and Bentler's (1999) recommendations for determining a close fit of a model, namely, RMSEA ≤ 0.06 and CFI and TLI ≥ 0.95. The diagonally weighted least squares (WLSMV) statistic was used as the estimation method as it is robust against violations of multivariate normality (Li, 2016). Mplus Version 8.1 (Muthén & Muthén, 2007) was employed for the EFA, CFA, and SEM.

Comparison of Placement-Type Means

Several one-way analyses of variances (ANOVAs) were conducted, with placement type (i.e., foster home, kinship care, or group home) as the independent variable and the other study variables (i.e., emotional, informational, and instrumental support) as the dependent variables. Because of the unequal placement-type group sizes, we applied Levene's test for homogeneity of variances. The significant results indicated that the variances were unequal across the three placement types. Thus, we used the Brown–Forsythe (1974) F-test, which is robust to violations of the assumption of equal variances, as well as the Games–Howell's adjustment in our post hoc testing for differences in means, as it assumes neither homogeneity of variances nor equal sample sizes.

Structural Equation Modelling

After establishing the social-support measurement model, we used SEM (Cole & Preacher, 2014; Hayduk, 1987) to test the hypothesized associations of our five social support variables with the youths' positive well-being/positive mental health, negative mental health, and placement satisfaction. Finally, we evaluated the fit of the model using the cutoff criteria: for a good fit, RMSEA $\leq .06$, CFI $\geq .95$, and TLI $\geq .95$; for an acceptable fit, RMSEA $\leq .10$, CFI $\geq .90$, and TLI $\geq .90$ (Weston & Gore, 2006).

Results

Preliminary Analysis

In the preliminary analyses, we examined missing data rates, univariate and multivariate normality, and outliers (Kline, 2005). The sample of young people in care comprised 486 participants, in which missing data rates were very low (2–4%). The results from simulation studies have indicated that with a low rate of missing data (i.e., below 5%), virtually all imputation methods are equally valid (Olinsky et al., 2003). In the present sample, we imputed missing data with the Expectation Maximization (E.M.) method, which produces unbiased estimates with a missing data rate of less than 5% compared to other imputation methods (Rubin et al., 2007). Skewness and kurtosis indices were inspected to evaluate univariate and multivariate normalities. Nine of the 48 items had skewness values ≥ 2 and 12 had kurtosis > 7. Non-normality is expected in data based on self-ratings, such that we applied WLSMV as the robust estimator for non-normally distributed data (Li, 2016).

Exploratory and Confirmatory Factor Analysis Results

The EFA was conducted with a randomly generated half of the sample (n = 243). The scree plot obtained from a principal components analysis was used to decide the maximum number of factors to be extracted. The scree plot

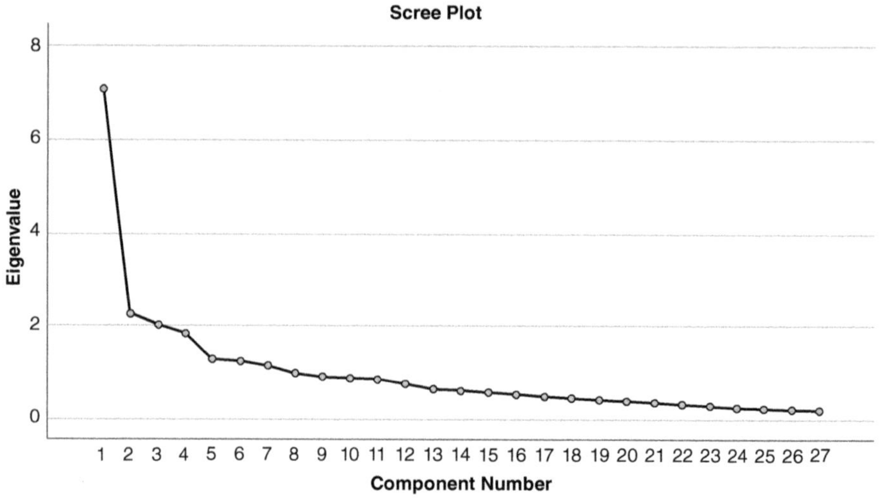

Figure 7.1 Principal component analysis scree plot.

displayed four eigenvalues (7.09, 2.25, 2.02, and 1.82) above the scree line, with the fifth eigenvalue on the scree line and substantially smaller (1.28; see Figure 7.1). Based on these results, a maximum of four factors were selected for the EFA.

Table 7.1 presents the fit indices for the EFA models, from one- to four-factor solutions. Overall, the four-factor model indicated the best fit regarding our goodness-of-fit indices. However, this model was problematic because nine items had unacceptable cross-loadings (i.e., the same item had loadings greater than .30 on two or more factors, with differences of less than .20; Howard, 2016). On the other hand, the three-factor EFA model exhibited a satisfactory to good fit and had a lower number of cross-loadings, indicating a better overall fit. Table 7.2 presents the factor loadings for the final set of 19 items.

A CFA conducted on the second random subsample of adolescents (n = 243) indicated that the three-factor model had an acceptable fit (CFI =0.987; TLI = 0.989; and RMSEA = 0.032). In addition, the three social support factors were positively and moderately intercorrelated (r = .45 to .66), adding to the picture of a good fit for the social support model (see Figure 7.2).

Factor 1, which we labelled *emotional support*, included 12 items related to receiving affection, reassurance, and encouragement from the young person in care. This factor had good reliability (α = .87). Factor 2, *informational support*, comprised four items tapping the young persons' receiving help from an adult regarding future educational and career training. This factor had acceptable reliability (α = .70). Finally, factor 3, *instrumental support*, included three items regarding the young persons' obtaining information and help with activities necessary for a successful transition from care, such as paying bills or completing income taxes. This factor also demonstrated an acceptable reliability (α = .71).

Table 7.1 Model fit indices for the exploratory factor analysis (n = 243)

	CFI	*TLI*	*RMSEA*	*SMR*
Four-factor Model	0.964	0.948	0.055	0.057
Three-factor Model	0.953	0.940	0.056	0.068
Two-factor Model	0.880	0.913	0.066	0.083
One-factor Model	0.834	0.820	0.099	0.126

Comparison of Predictor and Outcome Variable Means across Placement Types

As mentioned previously, before carrying out post hoc tests to discover whether there were significant differences among the placement-type means on our eight predictor or outcome variables, we found that Levine's test had shown the variances to be unequal ($p <.001$). Thus, we employed the Brown–Forsythe *F*-test and the Games–Howell's adjustment for the post hoc tests of differences in means. As shown in Table 7.3, there were significant differences among the placement-type means on seven of the eight predictors or outcomes. The sole exception was the quality of the young person's self-perceived relationship with their caregivers, a measure that, given its content, we considered a proxy for caregiver emotional support.

The young persons experienced greater emotional support, as assessed by the Canadian Casey, in kinship care than in either foster care (mean difference = 3.36; $p < .001$) or group care (mean difference = 6.88, $p < .001$). Similarly, youth in foster care reported higher emotional support than youth in group care (mean difference = 3.52, $p < .001$). Also, placement type explained a moderate proportion of the variance in youth's emotional support (effect size [E.S.]: $h^2 = .074$). The same pattern of significant mean differences was also found for informational support, albeit the E.S. due to placement type was smaller ($h^2 = .032$). Regarding instrumental support, youths residing in kinship and foster care reported higher levels of instrumental support than those in group care (mean differences = 1.56, $p < .001$ and 0.94, $p < .011$, respectively), but there was no difference between the means of the youths in kinship and foster care. Regarding the first proxy variable for emotional support, namely, the quality of the youth's relationships with their family of origin, the youths in kinship care perceived their relationships to be better than those of youths in either foster care (mean difference = 2.37, $p < .001$) or group care (mean difference = 2.52, $p < .001$), with no difference between the kinship care and foster care means and a small placement-type E.S. ($h^2 = .026$). Interestingly, on the second emotional-support proxy variable, the youth's perceived relationship with their caregivers, there were no statistically significant mean differences among the three placement types (all p-levels > .05).

Table 7.2 Exploratory factor analysis of the social support scale (n = 243)

	Factor 1	*Factor 2*	*Factor 3*
SS1: I know at least one adult, other than my worker, who would take my call in the middle of the night if I had an emergency	0.834[a]	0.079	−0.168
SS2: An adult I trust, other than my worker, checks in with me regularly	**0.832**	0.051	−0.036
SS3: I have at least one trusted adult who would visit me if I were in the hospital	**0.887**	0.060	0.034
SS5: I am part of a family, and we care about each other	**0.699**	0.008	0.026
SS6: I can get in touch with at least one family member when I want to	**0.869**	−0.133	−0.027
SS7: I have friends or family to spend time with on holidays and special occasions	**0.757**	0.036	0.007
SS8: I know at least one adult I can depend on when I exit care	**0.850**	−0.079	0.038
SS9: I know an adult who could be a grandparent, aunt, or uncle to my children now or my future children	**0.833**	−0.034	0.003
SS12: I know an adult who would help me if I had a financial emergency	**0.593**	−0.033	−0.018
SS13: I know an adult I could live with for a few days or weeks if I needed to	**0.829**	0.204	−0.015
SS14: There is at least one adult that I have regular contact with, other than my child welfare worker who lives in stable and safe housing	**0.882**	0.151	−0.211
SS16: I know an adult who will go with me if I need to change schools	0.083	**0.752**	0.012
SS17: I have an adult in my life who cares about how I am doing at school or work	0.229	**0.716**	−0.066
SS19: I have talked about my education plans with an adult who cares about me	0.004	**0.598**	0.165
SS20: I know an adult who will help me apply for training or education after high school	−0.029	**0.716**	0.232
SS56: I have friends I like to be with who help me feel valued and worthwhile	**0.632**	0.013	0.139
SS72: I know how to get emergency help to pay for water, electricity, and gas bills	0.092	0.126	**0.532**
SS92: I know where I can get help with an income tax form	−0.031	0.320	**0.795**
SS100: I know where to find information about job training	0.109	−0.009	**0.806**

[a] items bolded black indicate significant loadings.

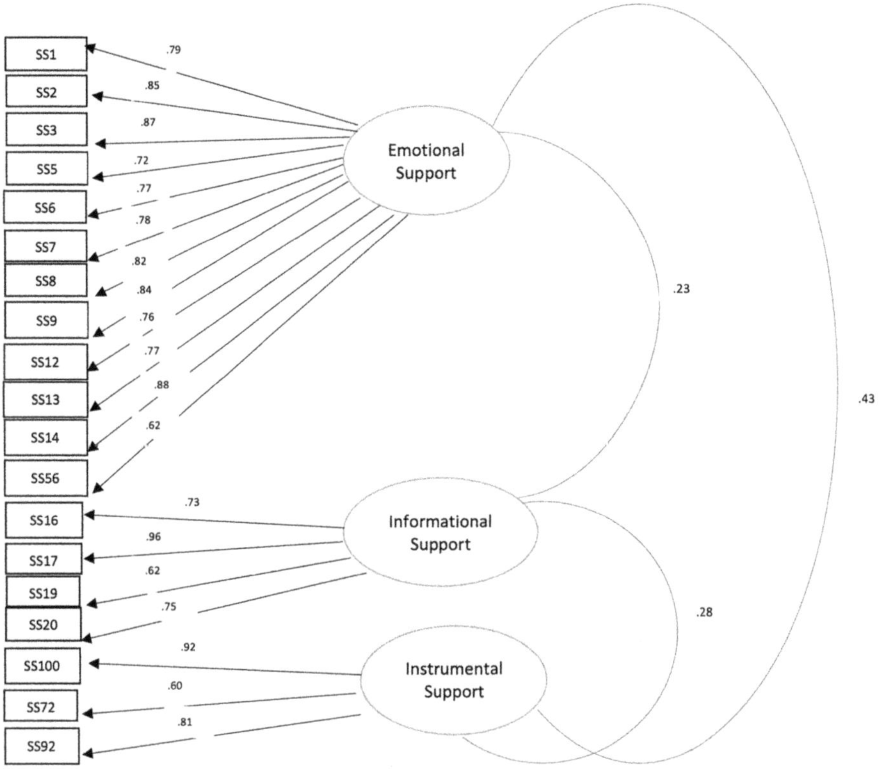

Figure 7.2 Confirmatory factor analysis model for social support (n = 243).

On the first mental-health outcome variable, well-being (a synonym herein for positive mental health), the young people in foster care had significantly better outcomes than those in group care (mean difference = 5.20, $p = .005$), although the overall E.S. was small. Concerning total behavioural difficulties, the kinship care and foster care youths reported lower total behavioural difficulties than those in group care (mean differences = -5.60 and -1.94, $p < .001$, respectively). There was a sizable E.S. ($h^2 = .064$). Finally, the young people in kinship care had greater placement satisfaction, on average, than those in group care (mean difference = 2.14, $p < .001$), as did those in foster care (mean difference = 1.74, $p < .001$), and the placement-type E.S. was moderately large.

Social Support Variables as Predictors of Mental Health Outcomes: SEM Results

We used SEM to estimate the predictive models, based on the total sample of 486 youths in care. As a first step, the measurement model's fit was assessed and found to be satisfactory (CFI = 0.94, TLI = 0.94, RMSEA = 0.05). We present a correlation matrix of the latent factors in Table 7.4.

Table 7.3 Means, standard deviations, and F-tests from eight one-way ANOVAs: Three placement types, by the five social support predictors and three mental health outcomes (N = 486)

Variable	*Family foster home* (n = *341)*M *(S.D.)*	*Kinship care* (n = *48)*M *(S.D.)*	*Group care* (n = *97)*M *(S.D.)*	*Brown-Forsythe* F-*test*	p	*Effect size* ($h^{2)}$
Canadian Casey Social Support Predictors						
Emotional Support	47.74 (6.22)	51.10 (1.66)	44.22 (9.01)	18.87	.001	.074
Informational Support	6.94 (3.68)	8.09 (3.15)	5.66 (3.84)	7.09	.001	.032
Instrumental Support	14.92 (2.11)	15.54 (1.03)	13.98 (3.07)	9.63	.001	.037
Proxy Emotional Support Predictors						
Relationship Quality with Family of Origin	10.44 (4.56)	12.81 (3.43)	10.29 (4.67)	4.56	.001	.026
Relationship Quality with Caregivers	12.39 (3.41)	12.60 (3.16)	11.84 (3.52)	1.26	.286	.006
Mental Health Outcomes						
Well-Being/Positive Mental Health	55.76 (11.99)	55.95 (14.05)	50.75 (14.16)	6.12	.002	.025
Negative Mental Health	19.59 (6.26)	17.65 (7.14)	23.25 (6.51)	16.26	.001	.064
Placement Satisfaction	10.41 (2.42)	10.81 (1.91)	8.67 (3.37)	18.60	.001	.073

Table 7.4 Correlations among latent social support predictor and mental health outcome variables (N = 486)

Variable	*1*	*2*	*3*	*4*	*5*	*6*	*7*	*8*
1. Casey's Emotional Support	—							
2. Casey's Informational Support	.43***	—						
3. Casey's Instrumental Support	.23***	.28***	—					
4. Emotional Support Proxy: Relationship Quality with Family of Origin	.29***	.06	.02	—				
5. Emotional Support Proxy: Relationship Quality with Caregivers	.24***	.22***	.05	.31***	—			
6. Well-Being/ Positive Mental Health	.23***	.24***	.13**	.12**	.37***	—		
7. Negative Mental Health (Total Behavioural Difficulties)	-.12**	.13**	–.10*	–.01	–.15***	–.38***	—	
8. Placement Satisfaction	.16***	.16***	.09*	.17***	.42***	.35***	–.26***	—

*** $p < .001$ ** $p < .01$ * $p < .05$.

Intercorrelations among the Latent Variables

As Table 7.4 shows, higher Casey *emotional support* was significantly associated in the sample of youths in care with greater Casey informational and instrumental support, as well as with greater youth-reported relationship quality with both members of the family of origin (a proxy for emotional support) and out-of-home placement caregivers (also a proxy for emotional support). Casey's emotional support was also significantly correlated with higher well-being (i.e., positive mental health), lower negative mental health (SDQ Total Behavioural Problems), and greater placement satisfaction.

Higher Casey *informational support* was significantly associated with higher Casey instrumental support, better relationship quality with out-of-home caregivers, greater well-being/positive mental health, lower negative mental health, and greater placement satisfaction. Higher Casey *instrumental support* was also significantly—albeit weakly—associated with greater well-being, lower negative mental health, and greater placement satisfaction. Finally, well-being was related to lower negative mental health and higher placement satisfaction, with higher placement satisfaction also significantly associated with lower negative mental health.

Structural Equation Modelling

In the SEM analysis, we tested the model's ability to predict the following endogenous variables: well-being (positive mental health), total behavioural difficulties (negative mental health), and placement satisfaction. As exogenous predictor variables, we used the three Casey measures of emotional, informational, and instrumental social support and the two emotional support proxies of the quality of the youth's perceived relationships with members of the family of origin and with their out-of-home caregivers. We entered gender (coded 1 = female, 0 = male) as a covariate.

The SEM model predicting *negative mental health* demonstrated an adequate fit (RMSEA = .050; CFI = 0.92; TLI = 0.93). In this predictive model, both informational support (b = -0.276; p = .025) and the quality of relationship with out-of-home caregivers (b = -0.215; p < .001) were statistically significant predictors of lower negative mental health scores. The SEM model predicting *well-being* also demonstrated an adequate fit (RMSEA = .050; CFI = 0.94; TLI = 0.93). The quality of the youth's relationship with the out-of-home caregivers was the only significant predictor of well-being, over and above the effect of the other predictors (b = 0.385; p < .001). Finally, the model predicting *placement satisfaction* demonstrated a satisfactory fit (RMSEA = .050; CFI = 0.94; TLI = 0.93). Again, the quality of the youth's relationship with the out-of-home caregivers was the only significant predictor of placement satisfaction, above and beyond the effect of the other predictors (b = 0.558; p < .001).

Discussion

We had three interrelated objectives in conducting the present study. First, in a sample of young people aged 16–17 and residing in out-of-home care in Ontario, Canada, we examined the psychometric characteristics and predictive validity of a new multidimensional measure of social support that we had derived from the CCLSA instrument (Flynn et al., 2023). Second, we compared the new Casey instrument with two proxies for emotional support that are part of the AAR instrument from the OnLAC project by examining how the three social support and two proxy variables varied across different placement types (i.e., kinship care, family foster care, and group homes). Third, we used SEM to map how these predictors influenced the positive and negative mental health and placement satisfaction of the youths in care. We conducted secondary analyses of data from the OnLAC project (Flynn et al., 2023), a data set widely used to investigate the development of children and youths in care in Ontario, Canada.

We factor-analysed a selected set of items from the CCLA, using both exploratory and confirmatory approaches, to obtain a new multidimensional measure of social support for youth in out-of-home care. These analyses suggested that social support in youths in care has a three-dimensional nature, consisting of emotional, informational, and instrumental support, which corroborated the results of prior research by Evans et al. (2022). Moreover, we also found that the quality of the young person's relationship with their caregiver is a critical protective factor that has been shown to contribute to resilience among care-involved children and youth (Evans et al., 2022).

We discovered that the amount of social support received by our sample of youths in care depended on their type of placement. Among the three placement settings considered, the youths in kinship care reported relatively high levels of emotional, informational, and instrumental support and better mental health and placement satisfaction. In contrast, the youths in group care obtained relatively low scores on the same outcome measures, with those in non-kinship family foster care scoring at intermediate levels on the Casey outcome measures but similarly to those in kinship care on the three mental-health outcomes.

We then used SEM to examine the predictive role of the social support and proxy emotional-support variables on mental health outcomes and placement satisfaction. We found that a higher level of relationship quality with foster caregivers or youth caseworkers in residential care was related to higher well-being and placement satisfaction and lower negative mental health one year later. Moreover, informational support, assessed when the youth was approximately 16 years of age, was particularly important in predicting decreased problem behaviour a year later. This latter finding aligns with what Evans et al. (2022) previously reported in a sample of U.S. young people in out-of-home care. In that research, support targeting educational activities and career development was influential in promoting the well-being of youth transitioning out of services.

Findings from this study help advance our understanding of the unique social support needs of young people in residential care. These results will also inform the future work of researchers, child welfare practitioners, and other stakeholders in implementing interventions and policies to improve the outcomes of young people in care by providing additional resources to foster multiple forms of social support made available to youth in care.

Limitations of this study should be noted for purposes of future research. Most important, perhaps, is that the AAR data relied almost exclusively on self-reports by youth, which increased the likelihood of method bias (Campbell & Fiske, 1959). We mitigated this risk, however, by using SEM, which allows for correlations among error terms and minimizes the risk of shared method variance (Cole, 2006). Future research, including any based on the OnLAC data set, should strive as much as possible to use data from multiple informants rather than restrict the data to those derived mainly from the youths.

References

Bentler, P. M. (1990). Comparative fit indexes in structural models. *Psychological Bulletin*, *107*(2), 238–246. https://doi.org/10.1037/0033-2909.107.2.238

Biglan, A. (2014). *A comprehensive framework for nurturing the well-being of children and adolescents*. Integrating safety, permanency and well-being series. Washington, DC: Administration for Children and Families, U.S. Department of Health and Human Services.

Biglan, A. (2015). *The nurture effect: How the science of human behavior can improve our lives & our world*. Oakland, CA: New Harbinger Publications.

Brown, M. B., & Forsythe, A. B. (1974). The small sample behavior of some statistics which test the equality of several means. *Technometrics*, *16*, 129–132. https://doi.org/10.1080/00401706.1974.10489158

Campbell, D. T., & Fiske, D. W. (1959). Convergent and discriminant validation by the multitrait-multimethod matrix. *Psychological Bulletin*, *56(*2), 81–105. https://doi.org/10.1037/h0046016

Cattell, R. B. (1966). The Scree test for the number of factors. *Multivariate Behavioral Research*, *1*(2), 245–276. https://doi.org/10.1207/s15327906mbr0102_10

Cole, D. A. (2006). Coping with longitudinal data in research on developmental psychopathology. *International Journal of Behavioral Development*, *30*, 20–25. https://doi.org/10.1177/0165025406059969

Cole, D. A., & Preacher, K. J. (2014). Manifest variable path analysis: Potentially serious and misleading consequences due to uncorrected measurement error. *Psychological Methods*, *19*(2), 300. https://doi.org/10.1037/a0033805

Evans, R., Katz, C. C., Fulginiti, A., & Taussig, H. (2022). Sources and types of social supports and their association with mental health symptoms and life satisfaction among young adults with a history of out-of-home care. *Children*, *9*, 520. https://doi.org/10.3390/children9040520

Fabrigar, L. R., Wegener, D. T., MacCallum, R. C., & Strahan, E. J. (1999). Evaluating the use of exploratory factor analysis in psychological research. *Psychological Methods*, *4*(3), 272–299. https://doi.org/10.1037/1082-989X.4.3.272

Flynn, R. J., Dudding, P. M., & Barber, J. G. (Eds.). (2006). *Promoting resilience in child welfare*. Ottawa, ON: University of Ottawa Press.

Flynn, R. J., Miller, M., Bell, T., Greenberg, B., & Vincent, C. (2023). *Young people in care: Findings from the Ontario Looking After Children project*. Ottawa, ON: University of Ottawa Press.

Goodman, R. (1997). The strengths and difficulties questionnaire: A research note. *Journal of Child Psychology and Psychiatry*, *38*(5), 581–586. https://doi.org/10.1111/j.14697610.1997.tb01545.x

Hayduk, L. A. (1987). *Structural equation modeling with LISREL: Essentials and advances*. Baltimore, MD: Johns Hopkins University Press.

House, J. (1991). *Work stress and social support*. Reading, MA: Addison-Wesley.

Howard, M. C. (2016) A review of exploratory factor analysis decisions and overview of current practices: What we are doing and how can we improve? *International Journal of Human-Computer Interaction*, *32*(1), 51–62. https://doi.org/10.1080/10447318.2015.1087664

Hu, L., & Bentler, P. M. (1999). Cutoff criteria for fit indexes in covariance structure analysis: Conventional criteria versus new alternatives. *Structural Equation Modeling*, 6,1–55. https://doi.org/10.1080/10705519909540118

Keyes, C. L. M. (2006). Mental health in adolescence: Is America's youth flourishing?. *American Journal of Orthopsychiatry*, 76, 395–402. https://doi.org/10.1037/0002-9432.76.3.395

Kline, R. B. (2005). *Principles and practice of structural equation modeling*. New York, NY: The Guilford Press.

Li, C-H. (2016) Confirmatory factor analysis with ordinal data: Comparing robust maximum likelihood and diagonally weighted least squares. *Behavior Research Methods*, *48*, 936–949. https://doi.org/10.3758/s13428-015-0619-7

Long, S. J., Evans, R. E., Fletcher, A., Hewitt, G., Murphy, S., Young, Y., & Moore, G. F. (2017). Comparison of substance use, subjective well-being and interpersonal relationships among young people in foster care and private households: A cross sectional analysis of the School Health Research Network survey in Wales. *BMJ Open*, 7, e014198. https://doi.org/10.1136/bmjopen-2016-014198

Malecki, C. K., & Demaray, M. K. (2003). What type of support do they need? Investigating student adjustment as related to emotional, informational, appraisal, and instrumental support. *School Psychology Quarterly*, *18*(3), 231–252. https://psycnet.apa.org/buy/2003-08719-001

Miller, M., Vincent, C., & Flynn, R. (2023). *Bibliography of papers, chapters, and conference presentations from the Ontario Looking After Children (OnLAC) Project*. Ottawa, ON: Centre for Research on Educational and Community Services, University of Ottawa

Muthén, L. K., & Muthén, B. O. (2007). *Mplus user's guide*. Los Angeles, CA: Muthén & Muthén.

Nollan K. A., Wolf, M., Ansell, D., Burns, J., Barr, L., Copeland, W., & Paddock, G. (2000). Ready or not: Assessing youths' preparedness for independent living. *Child Welfare*, *79*(2), 159–176. https://www.jstor.org/stable/45400210

Okpych, N. J., Park, K., Torres-Garcia, A., & Courtney, M. E. (2018). *Memo from CalYOUTH: Differences in social support at age 19 by extended foster care status and placement type*. Chicago, IL, USA: Chapin Hall at the University of Chicago.

Olinsky, A., Chen, S., & Harlow, L. (2003). The comparative efficacy of imputation methods for missing data in structural equation modelling. *European Journal of Operational Research*, *151*(1), 53–79. https://doi.org/10.1016/S0377-2217(02)00578-7

Preacher, K. J., & MacCallum, R. C. (2003). Repairing Tom Swift's electric factor analysis machine. *Understanding Statistics*, 2, 13–43. https://doi.org/10.1207/S15328031US0201_02

Rubin, L. H., Witkiewitz, K., Andre, J. S., & Reilly, S. (2007). Methods for handling missing data in the behavioral neurosciences: Don't throw the baby rat out with the bath water. *Journal of Undergraduate Neuroscience Education*, *5*(2), A71. http://www.ncbi.nlm.nih.gov/pmc/articles/pmc3592650/

Rueger, S. Y., Malecki, C. K., Pyun, Y., Aycock, C., & Coyle, S. (2016). A meta-analytic review of the association between perceived social support and depression in childhood and adolescence. *Psychological bulletin*, *142*(10), 1017. https://doi.org/10.1037/bul0000058

Scardera, S., Perret, L. C., Ouellet-Morin, I., Gariépy, G., Juster, R. P., Boivin, M., Turecki, G., Tremblay, R. E., Côté, S., & Geoffroy, M. C. (2020). Association of social support during adolescence with depression, anxiety, and suicidal ideation in young adults. *JAMA Netw Open*, *3*(12), e2027491. https://doi.org/10.1001/jamanetworkopen.2020.27491

Statistics Canada. (1999). *National longitudinal survey of children and youth*. Ottawa, ON: Author.

Steiger, J. H., & Lind, J. C. (1980). *Statistically based tests for numbers of common factors*. Paper presented at the annual meeting of the Psychometric Society, Iowa City, IA.
Tucker, L. R., & Lewis, C. (1973). A reliability coefficient for maximum likelihood factor analysis. *Psychometrika*, *38*(1), 1–10. https://doi.org/10.1007/BF02291170
Weston, R., & Gore Jr, P. A. (2006). A brief guide to structural equation modeling. *The Counseling Psychologist*, *34*(5), 719–751. https://doi.org/10.1177/0011000006286345

Part 3

Care Leavers and Transition from Residential Care

8 Trends in Social Support During the Transition to Adulthood for Youths who Spent Time in Congregate Care in California

Keunhye Park, Nathanael J. Okpych and Mark E. Courtney

Introduction

Social support is an important contributor to the successful transition for young people entering adulthood. Having a strong social support network can enhance the likelihood of positive outcomes during adulthood (Mendes et al., 2012). This is particularly true for youth who have encountered hardship early in life such as child maltreatment and environmental instability and those who undergo accelerated or challenging transitions to adulthood (Courtney et al., 2012; Osgood et al., 2010). International research, however, shows that many youths with foster care backgrounds often experience disconnection or social marginalization as they transition to adulthood (Courtney & Heuring, 2005; Mendes et al., 2012; Wade, 2008). This is, in part, because youth transitioning from foster care have often experienced disruptions in their social support networks (e.g., placement moves, school changes) and the loss of access to practical services and resources after they are discharged from care (Courtney & Dworsky, 2006; Perry, 2006; Rosenberg, 2019; Stott & Gustavsson, 2010). Furthermore, research suggests that these youth may lack certain sources and types of social support or may feel uncertain about how to effectively maintain and utilize the support they have, leading to a sense that support is either inadequate or unavailable (Okpych et al., 2018; Rosenberg, 2019).

However, this may not be universally the case as youth differ in the characteristics of their supportive networks. Some of the differences could be explained by placement type, since support networks of youth in foster care are shaped, at least in part, by the living arrangement that the youth reside in (Okpych et al., 2018). In particular, youth in congregate care settings have received special consideration (e.g., Whittaker et al., 2016), both because they tend to have elevated rates of behavioral health problems and there may be less opportunity to develop lasting connections than in family-like placements. For example, youth living in foster homes or kinship care spend a good deal of time with their caregivers, and this may lend itself to forming supportive relationships. In contrast, congregate care is a more restrictive

DOI: 10.4324/9781003424468-12

environment that is staffed by rotating shift workers with high turnover. There may be additional obstacles to building and sustaining supportive relationships in these settings, which can in turn make the transition to adulthood more challenging (Field et al., 2021; Okpych et al., 2018; Stott & Gustavsson, 2010).

To date, there has been little research that examines different characteristics of social support networks and changes over time as youth transition to adulthood, particularly among youth in congregate care settings. In this chapter, we address this understudied area by comparing trends in social support characteristics between youth with and without congregate care histories.

Background

Context of Congregate Care Placements in the US Child Welfare System

When a child is removed from their family due to concerns about maltreatment, child welfare agencies must place children in the least restrictive and most family-like setting possible (Capacity Building Center for States, 2020; Covington et al., 2022). The first priority is to consider foster homes with kin, which includes close relatives (e.g., grandparents or aunts/uncles) or extended family or friends. The next priority is placement in nonrelative foster homes. In some cases, children with intensive mental health or behavior needs are placed in therapeutic foster homes, in which the foster parents undergo specialized training and receive more therapeutic support from the child welfare agency when caring for the child. In the United States, congregate care placements are used when family-like placements are not a viable option. Congregate care in the United States includes several types of placements such as group homes, residential treatment centers, short-term psychiatric hospitals, shelters, and other child-caring institutions.

Statistics show that between 2000 and 2019, there was a substantial decline in the use of congregate care in the United States (Covington et al., 2022). A Chronicle of Social Change report (2019) shows that between 2011 and 2017, the overall percentage of youth placed in congregate care dropped by about 12% nationwide, although the rate rose by 20% in more than 10 states. The most recently available national data tells us that on 30 September 2021, about 9% of the 391,098 children and young adults in U.S. foster care were placed in a congregate care setting, while most young people were placed in family-like settings with kin (35%) or non-kin (44%) (Children's Bureau, 2022).[1] Similarly, a study by Covington et al. (2022) shows that nationally 10% of youth in out-of-home care lived in congregate care settings as of 2019.

Rates of congregate care use vary by state. Covington et al. (2022) reported that while the majority of states had rates ranging from 10% to 20%, five states (Massachusetts, New Hampshire, New York, South Carolina, and

South Dakota) with the highest cumulative rates of children and adolescents entering congregate care ranged from 23% to 34%, while the three states (Connecticut, Maine, and Oklahoma) with the lowest rates ranged from 5% to 6%. California had a rate (9.4%) similar to the national average. Research also shows that congregate care placement rates are higher for older youth (aged 13–17) than for younger children and that Black youth and Native American/Alaskan Native youth experience a disproportionately higher rate of congregate care placement than other racial/ethnic groups (Covington et al., 2022). The extent to which racial disproportionality exists in congregate care placements also varies across states, but there is no state in which White youth are overrepresented in these settings (Covington et al., 2022).

Building on the downward trend in congregate care placement rates between the 2000s and 2010s, the federal 2018 Family First Prevention Services Act (Family First) ushered in sweeping changes to child welfare funding and service requirements that had a pronounced effect on the use of congregate care. The law redirects federal funding away from congregate care and toward services intended to prevent children from being removed from their homes in the first place. Family First also established a set of requirements that must be met in order for states to receive federal reimbursement when children are placed in congregate care. If a child remains in congregate care for more than 14 days, the placement must be a licensed Qualified Residential Treatment Program (QRTP). QRTPs use a trauma-informed treatment model, have 24–7 onsite nursing and clinical staff, outreach to families and engage them in treatment as appropriate, and provide six months of post-discharge family aftercare services (Children's Bureau, 2018). A functional assessment must also be conducted by a qualified professional within 30 days of a child being admitted to the QRTP, and the assessment must conclude that continued placement in the QRTP is in the best interest of the child. Additionally, a court hearing must take place within 60 days after admission to approve the placement, and a high-level review is required for longer stays (e.g., children over the age of 13 must have a higher-level review after 12 months of consecutive care in the QRTP). The intent of the law is to restrict the use of QRTPs only when necessary to treat serious emotional or behavioral issues (Children's Bureau, 2018).

In addition to federal legislation, some states in the United States have also enacted policies that shape the funding and utilization of congregate care. For example, in 2015 California passed the Continuum of Care Reform (CCR, Assembly Bill 403), which placed an emphasis on tailoring services so that stable, permanent family connections can be maintained. CCR views congregate placement as one option on a continuum of care available to support children and families. Similar to Family First, CCR limits the use of congregate care as a time-limited therapeutic intervention to meet youths' complex behavioral health needs by Short-Term Residential Therapeutic Centers (STRTC) that must be licensed and nationally accredited (California Department of Social Services, 2023). As a result of CCR, there has been a

Table 8.1 Number and percentage of children in congregate care in California on a given day by age and year (2010 and 2020)

	In out-of-home Care	*In Congregate Care*					
	All ages	*All ages*	*1–5*	*6–10*	*11–15*	*16–17*	*18–21*
10/1/2010	57.043	3.739 (6.6%)	M	357 (3.1%)	1.745 (11.7%)	1.368 (15.7%)	241 (9.9%)
10/1/2020	59.935	2.300 (3.8%)	M	M	1.051 (8.2%)	891 (14.6%)	184 (2.2%)

Note: M = masked due to too few observations. For this analysis, congregate care included group homes and Short-Term Residential Therapeutic Centers (STRTCs).

reduction in the use of congregate care placements in California, particularly among certain age groups. Table 8.1 displays the numbers and percentages of children in California foster care who were placed in a congregate care setting in 2010 and 2020. Across all ages, the overall percentage of children who were placed in congregate care decreased by about 42% across the decade, from 6.6% in 2010 to 3.8% in 2020 (Webster et al., 2022). The largest percentage-point decreases from 2010 to 2020 were observed among younger children between ages 6 and 10 (from 3.1% to a percentage too small to report) and among young adults between ages 18 and 21 (from 9.9% to 2.2%). Decreases were also observed among adolescents, although the declines were not as large as those of other age groups.

The move to reduce the utilization of congregate care across the United States has been buoyed by a few initiatives. First, as referenced above, since 2017 the Chronicle of Social Change (renamed The Imprint) launched the *Who Cares: A National Count of Foster Homes and Families* website, which is a publicly available data resource that tracks the number of children in foster care and the types of placements they reside in. *Who Cares* has drawn attention to trends in congregate care placements and differences that exist between states. Second, *Ending the Need for Group Placements* is a collaboration between two large foundations that focus on the child welfare system—the Annie E. Casey Foundation and the Casey Families Foundation—as well as other community partners (Casey Family Programs, 2023). This initiative collects and assembles research and resources to inform child welfare policy, administration, and practice around reducing the use of congregate care. Finally, in 2021 an advocacy organization, Think of Us, released a report entitled, *Away From Home: Youth Experiences of Institutional Placements in Foster Care* (Fathallah & Sullivan, 2021), which has gained national attention and is featured in the U.S. Children's Bureau webpage (Children's Bureau, 2023). The report shares the firsthand experience of young people who had lived in congregate care settings and draws attention to the overrepresentation of racial minority children in congregate care settings.

Changes in Social Support Characteristics Over Time as Youth Become Young Adults

Acknowledging the evolving and malleable nature of social networks in emerging adulthood, it is important to assess differences in social support characteristics (e.g., adequacy, type, size, and source of social support) at multiple timepoints. Youth navigate many transitional tasks that may require functionally distinct types of support such as tangible support (e.g., tuition, housing), informational support (e.g., advice/guidance on job and college applications), and emotional support (e.g., comfort, encouragement). Moreover, youth may derive support from different sources, including formal sources (e.g., caseworkers, teachers, therapists) and informal sources (e.g., birth family, friends). Additionally, youth may vary in the number of people they can turn to for various support (i.e., size of support network) and their own perceptions of whether they have enough support in different areas (i.e., support adequacy).

In reviewing studies on changes in social support over time, most research has mainly focused on the size of youths' social support networks. Prior findings from international research have consistently found that young people generally report a decrease in the size of their support networks as they transition from care (e.g., Greeson et al., 2015a, 2015b; Muir et al., 2019; Okpych et al., 2018; Sulimani-Aidan, 2014; Sulimani-Aidan & Melkman, 2018). Few studies to date have employed a longitudinal method to closely examine changes in other dimensions of social support (e.g., adequacy, type).

Looking at the dimensions of social support, prior studies have primarily focused on sources of support, predominantly support from youths' biological relatives. Some studies show that youth tend to rely on or reconnect with their biological families after leaving foster care (e.g., siblings, mothers) (Curry & Abrams, 2015; Mendes et al., 2012), while other studies suggest that as young adults, some care leavers have ambivalent feelings toward birth families (Samuels, 2009; Samuels & Pryce, 2008; Unrau et al., 2008) including stress or anxiety due to unreconciled family issues or youth-family conflicts (Geenen & Powers, 2006; Iglehart & Becerra, 2002). Other research also suggests that birth families are often limited in the types of support they can provide youth as they transition to adulthood (Sulimani-Aidan & Melkman, 2018). Even when youth maintain contact with their family as they transition out of foster care, this contact often decreases over time (Wade, 2008). Similarly, one study conducted in Australia found that while most youth maintained some form of family contact within four to five years after leaving care, the quality and regularity of contact varied widely (Mendes et al., 2012).

Less research has examined other sources of support, such as peers and professionals (e.g., child welfare workers). One study (Okpych et al., 2018) conducted in the United States found that "peer" support increased as youth transitioned to adulthood between ages 17 and 19. Regarding professionals, Okpych et al. (2018) also found that "professionals" were the least commonly reported source of social support, although other research claims that child welfare professionals are an important source of support for some youth (Campos et al., 2020; Curry & Abrams, 2015; Sulimani-Aidan & Melkman, 2018). Additionally, a few studies suggest that youth who remain in contact with their child welfare professionals are those who may have weak family bonds and that those youth can make the successful transition from care with support from child welfare workers (Mendes et al., 2012; Wade, 2008).

Regarding other dimensions of social support, there are few studies that examine how social support types and adequacy change over time as youth enter adulthood. One exception is a study by Okpych et al. (2018), showing that types of social support were steady between ages 17 and 19 and that most youth reported feeling they had enough people to turn to for informational support (e.g., advice/guidance).

Differences in Social Support by Congregate Care Histories

There is very limited research that has examined how the development of social support networks is influenced by histories of congregate care placement. One study by Okpych et al. (2018) found that youth living in congregate care at age 17 were less likely to report having support from peers than youth living in other foster homes; youth in congregate care were also less likely to report having enough emotional support. Additionally, a study by Rosenberg (2019) conducted in a Southeastern state in the United States on young people between the ages of 18 and 25 who had aged out of care or were in extended foster care reported descriptive findings, showing that youth living in group homes were more likely than those living in other foster homes to have formal support in their social networks.

Present Study

This chapter seeks to increase our understanding of the evolving nature of social support networks among young people transitioning from foster care to adulthood, particularly those who have spent time in congregate care. We will analyze data collected from the California Youth Transitions to Adulthood Study (CalYOUTH), one of the most extensive studies of care leavers in the United States that followed several hundred young people from late adolescence to early adulthood. This chapter has two aims:

1. To examine changes in different social support characteristics (adequacy, type, size, and source) over time at ages 17, 19, 21, and 23 CalYOUTH participants.

2. To compare changes in different social support characteristics over time between CalYOUTH participants with a congregate care history and CalYOUTH participants who had never spent time in congregate care.

Methods

Study Context

Of all 50 states in the United States, California is the most populous state that has the largest share of the foster care population (Kids Count Data Center, 2022). California has a decentralized child welfare system, meaning that while the state agency allocates federal and state resources and establishes program policy requirements based on federal and state regulation, county child welfare departments have local discretion in how child welfare services are administered within their counties. Through state Assembly Bill 12 (AB12), California elected to extend the foster care age limit from 18 to 21 beginning on 1 January 2012. The AB12 law also called for an evaluation of the impact of the extended foster care policy, which was fulfilled by the CalYOUTH Study. CalYOUTH was funded by several foundations and was conducted in collaboration with the California Child Welfare Co-investment Partnership (https://co-invest.org), including the California Department of Social Services (CDSS), the County Welfare Directors Association of California, the Judicial Council of California, and a group of philanthropic funders with longstanding interests in improving child welfare services.

Data and Sample

Our analyses below draw on data collected by CalYOUTH, a longitudinal study of care leavers in California that took place between 2012 and 2020 (Courtney et al., 2014). Young people were eligible to participate in CalYOUTH if they had been in California foster care for at least six months and were between the ages of 16.75 and 17.75 in December 2012. We worked with CDSS to generate a list of the entire population of youth meeting these criteria ($n = 2.583$) and used a stratified random sampling procedure to generate a sample of 880 youths. During the field period that spanned from April to October 2013 when in-person baseline interviews were conducted, 117 young people were found to be ineligible for various reasons (e.g., youth had been on runaway status for more than two months, returned home, and were physically or mentally incapable of participating). Of the remaining 763 eligible youths, interviews were completed with 727 young people when the youth were 17.5 years old on average. Three follow-up interviews were conducted at age 19 ($n = 611$), age 21 ($n = 616$), and age 23 ($n = 620$). The surveys were administered by trained interviewers, took approximately 75–90 minutes to complete, and collected information on a wide range of key life domains (e.g., experience in care, social support, education and employment, romantic relationships and parenting, and behavioral health). For more information on the study procedures, readers can refer to the study report (Courtney et al., 2014).

In our analyses in this chapter, we first used CDSS's administrative child welfare records to identify which of the CalYOUTH participants had ever spent time in congregate care before the age of 18. Because 15 participants either did not consent to CalYOUTH researchers accessing their administrative data or were missing administrative data, we used their responses from survey questions to obtain information about their past involvement in congregate care.

Measures

The CalYOUTH survey used the Social Support Network Questionnaire (SSNQ; Gee & Rhodes, 2007) to capture information about specific people the youth could rely on for different dimensions of social support. During the interview, youth were first asked to name up to three people they could turn to for emotional support, tangible support, and advice/guidance. It is important to note that each nominated person had to be a salient presence in the youth's life, enough so for the youth to think of them and include them on their shortlist. This generated a roster of support figures, and the youth were then asked specific questions about their relationship to each nominated person. While the original SSNQ instrument (Gee & Rhodes, 2007) allows individuals to name more than three people and asks about three additional types of support (i.e., positive feedback, social participation, and support with pregnancy/parenting), CalYOUTH used a modified version focusing on three support types (emotional support, tangible support, and advice/guidance) due to time constraints. In addition to the SSNQ items, youth were also asked to rate their overall adequacy of emotional support, tangible support, and advice/guidance, as described in detail below. Drawing on these social support data, we created two main sets of social support measures: (1) adequacy of social support and (2) size of support networks.

Adequacy of Social Support

The first set pertains to youths' perceptions of whether they have enough support. In the original survey questions, the youth were asked about the amount of support they had for the three support types: emotional support, tangible support, and advice/guidance. For each support type, the youth could choose from three response options: "enough," "too little," or "none." For this chapter, we used youths' original responses to create simplified binary versions of support adequacy. For instance, if a youth originally answered that they had "enough" emotional support, they were marked "yes" on the binary variable for emotional support adequacy. If they originally answered "too little" or "none," they were marked "no" on the binary variable for emotional support adequacy. A similar approach was used to create binary measures for tangible support adequacy and advice/guidance adequacy. Lastly, we wanted to identify youth who had enough support in all three areas versus youth who were lacking in one or more support areas. The former youth were marked "yes" in our overall support adequacy measure, while the latter youth were marked "no" in our overall support adequacy measure.

Size of Support Networks

The second set of measures counts how many family members and relatives, peers, and institutional agents the youth nominated. Family and relatives include people the youth were biologically related to, such as birth parents, grandparents, aunts/uncles, siblings, cousins, or other relatives. Peers include people the youth nominated as their friends, romantic partners, classmates, or coworkers. Institutional agents/professionals include foster parents, caseworkers, teachers, school counselors, mentors, therapists/counselors, and other professionals. These are individuals who assumed a position of institutional authority and could potentially act on the youths' behalf (e.g., advocate, connect to resources, and vouch for them) (Stanton-Salazar, 2011). Lastly, we created a measure of the total number of people the youth nominated as supports (ranging from 0 to 9 people).

Analyses

In our results below, we first present the percentages of youth who had adequate emotional, tangible, and advice/guidance support and the average number of nominated family/relatives, peers, institutional agents, and total supports. We then report these statistics separately for youth who did and did not have a history of congregate care. We test for statistically significant differences using Chi-square tests (for categorical measures of social support) and t-tests (for continuous measures of social support). We present survey-weighted means and percentages to account for the stratified sampling design used in CalYOUTH.

Results

Sample Description

Table 8.2 describes the characteristics of CalYOUTH participants during the baseline interview when youth were 17.5 years old on average. Less than two-thirds of youth were female and about a half identified as Hispanic. Regarding race, nearly half of respondents identified as multiracial, followed by White (24%), Black (18%), Native American or Alaskan Native (4%),

Table 8.2 Sample description at age 17 (unweighted n; weighted %; weighted mean/SD)

Age 17 (n = 727)	n	% *Mean (SD)*
History of Congregate Care Placement (%)		
Ever in congregate care before 18	386	54.0
Demographic Characteristics		
Age at the interview (Mean/SD)	727	17.50 (0.30)
Gender (%)		
Female	429	59.4
Male	298	40.6
Race (%)		
White	231	24.2
Black	112	18.0
Native American/Alaskan Native	26	3.6
Asian/Pacific Islander	18	2.2
Multiracial	336	48.7
Hispanic (%)	323	47.4

Table 8.3 Sample description by congregate care history (weighted %; weighted mean)

Congregate Care History	*Age 17* (n = 727)		*p*
	Yes	*No*	
Age at the interview (Mean)	17.51	17.48	0.168
Gender (%)			0.012
Male	60.3	39.7	
Female	49.7	50.3	
Race (%)			0.044
Black	66.9	33.1	
Multiracial	52.4	47.6	
White	50.6	49.4	
Native American/Alaskan native	50.1	49.9	
Asian/Pacific Islander	37.0	63.0	
Ethnicity (%)			0.059
Hispanic	49.9	50.1	
Non-Hispanic	57.7	42.3	

and Asian or Pacific Islander (2%). Although not displayed in the table, the average ages of participants in the follow-up interviews were 19.5 at Wave 2, 21.6 at Wave 3, and 23.6 at Wave 4.

About half of CalYOUTH participants (54%) had ever lived in a congregate care setting before age 18. Table 8.3 displays the rates of congregate care histories by gender, race, and ethnicity. There was a statistically significant ($p < .05$) difference by gender, with males being more likely than females to have ever lived in a congregate care setting (60% vs. 50%). Youths' race and congregate care history were also significantly associated, with Black youth (67%) being more likely than multiracial youth (52%), White youth (51%), and Asian/Pacific Islander youth (37%) to have ever been in congregate care settings before the age of 18.

Dimensions and Changes in Social Support Networks Over Time (Ages 17–23)

Table 8.4 displays our findings on social support for the entire sample across ages. When looking at the adequacy of social support (top of Table 8.4), in most cases, a majority of youth felt they had enough people to turn to for emotional, tangible, and informational support. However, some types of support were more common than others; across ages, the largest percentages of youth felt they had enough advice/guidance. For all ages except age 23 (53%), less than half felt like they had enough people to turn to for all three types of support. When looking at the different people youth named (bottom of Table 8.4), family or relatives were the most commonly reported sources of social support (on average 1.05–1.47 nominated individuals per youth), while professionals were the least commonly named sources of support (on average 0.18–0.45 nominated individuals per youth). On average, youth nominated about 3.7 distinct people as supports at age 17, and this fell to 3.2 at age 19 and 2.8 at ages 21 and 23.

When looking at changes in social support over time, as youth became older both their perception of having adequate support and the size of their support networks generally decreased. For example, support adequacy was highest at age 17 when most youth were in care and generally decreased at older ages. One exception was the combined adequacy measure (i.e., having "enough" people to turn to for all three support types), which increased from age 19 (42%) to age 23 (53%). Similarly, tangible support adequacy was lowest at age 19 (47% of youth felt they had "enough") and increased at ages 21 and 23 to 55% or higher when youth were out of care. The total number of people youth nominated as supportive figures was highest at age 17 and tended to decrease over time. When looking at support from specific types of people, this downward trend was true for family/relatives and institutional agents. Peers remained a fairly consistent source of support; across ages, youth nominated about 1.0 to 1.2 peers.

Differences in Social Support Networks by Congregate Care History

Next, we look at the differences in social support between youth with and without a congregate care history. In terms of support adequacy (top rows of Table 8.5), compared to youth who had never been in congregate care, youth with congregate care histories were more likely to feel that they did not have enough support for almost all types of support at all ages. This was especially true for emotional support, where there were up to 17-percentage point

Table 8.4 Dimensions and changes in social support networks (unweighted n; weighted %; weighted mean/SD)

	Age 17 (N = 727)		*Age 19 (N = 611)*		*Age 21 (N = 616)*		*Age 23 (N = 622)*	
	n	% *Mean (SD)*	n	% *Mean (SD)*	n	% *Mean (SD)*	n	% *Mean (SD)*
Perceived Adequacy of Social Support (% Enough)								
Advice/guidance support (%)	542	71.8	416	65.1	419	66.5	419	66.5
Emotional support (%)	429	65.3	366	58.4	398	62.4	374	56.9
Tangible support (%)	443	59.5	342	46.7	353	55.4	374	57.7
All three support types above (%)	351	44.6	267	41.5	305	47.9	312	53.1
Size of Social Support (Count Nominated)								
Family/relatives (Mean/SD)	720	1.47 (1.23)	611	1.21 (1.08)	615	1.08 (1.23)	620	1.05 (1.02)
Peers (Mean/SD)	720	0.99 (1.10)	611	1.13 (1.10)	615	1.08 (1.10)	620	1.21 (1.10)
Institutional agents (Mean/SD)	720	0.45 (0.81)	611	0.39 (1.10)	615	0.25 (0.81)	620	0.18 (0.50)
Total support (Mean/SD)	720	3.72 (1.38)	611	3.16 (1.40)	615	2.79 (1.38)	621	2.80 (1.38)

Table 8.5 Differences in social support networks by congregate care history status (unweighted n; weighted %; weighted mean/SD)

History of Congregate Care Placement Before Age 18	*Age 17* (N = 727)			*Age 19* (N = 611)			*Age 21* (N = 616)			*Age 23* (N = 622)		
	Yes	*No*	*p*	*Yes*	*No*	*p*	*Yes*	*No*	*p*	*Yes*	*No*	*p*
Perceived Adequacy of Social Support (% Enough)												
Emotional support (%)	60.2	71.2	0.007	50.5	67.4	<0.001	55.0	70.7	<0.001	49.2	65.0	<0.001
Tangible support (%)	55.9	63.6	0.064	45.6	62.1	<0.001	49.8	61.7	0.009	53.0	62.6	0.035
Advice/guidance (%)	67.4	76.9	0.015	60.7	70.1	0.036	64.9	68.4	0.426	59.1	74.3	<0.001
All three types above (%)	40.3	49.8	0.022	34.7	49.4	0.001	41.3	55.3	0.003	39.1	55.0	<0.001
Size of Social Support (Count Nominated)												
Relatives (Mean)	1.47	1.47	0.958	1.15	1.29	0.154	0.99	1.18	0.055	0.96	1.15	0.039
Peers (Mean)	0.89	1.11	0.021	1.01	1.27	0.012	0.99	1.17	0.031	1.15	1.27	0.232
Institutional agents (Mean)	0.48	0.40	0.234	0.44	0.34	0.109	0.30	0.20	0.081	0.23	0.13	0.032
Total support (Mean)	3.67	3.77	0.405	2.97	3.36	0.003	2.65	2.95	0.013	2.70	2.91	0.101

differences in support adequacy. For example, compared to peers who had never been in congregate care, significantly more youth with congregate care histories felt that they did not have enough emotional support at age 17 (60% vs. 71%). Fairly consistently, differences in perceived adequacy persisted even after youth had been out of foster care for years (e.g., emotional support differences were 49% vs. 65% at age 23).

Looking at the sizes of youths' support networks (bottom rows of Table 8.5), youth with congregate care histories tended to name fewer people than their peers with no history of congregate care, but this was not universally the case. For example, when looking at the total number of people youth nominated, significant differences were found at ages 19 and 21 but not at ages 17 and 23. The number of peers nominated as support was the most consistent difference. For example, compared to those who had never been in congregate care, youth with congregate care histories nominated significantly fewer peers at age 17 (0.89 vs. 1.11), age 19 (1.01 vs. 1.27), and age 21 (0.99 vs. 1.17). In comparison, few significant differences were found by congregate care status in terms of the number of relatives/family members and institutional agents, except at age 23. At age 23, youth with congregate care histories named significantly fewer relatives (0.96 vs. 1.15) and significantly more institutional agents (0.23 vs. 0.13) than their peers without congregate care histories.

Although space prohibits us from presenting the full results, further cross-tabulation analyses showed some demographic characteristics (i.e., gender and race) associated with their congregate care status. In terms of the combined measure of perceived adequacy of support (having enough support in all three types), females in congregate care tended to be the least likely to say they had enough social support. Although rates were not entirely consistent across ages, Black youth in congregate care and Native American/Alaskan Native youth in congregate care tended to have the lowest rates of perceived adequacy of support for the combined measure. Readers interested in the full results may contact the lead author.

Discussion and Conclusion

While at any point in time relatively few older adolescents are placed in congregate care settings, our findings show that among youth transitioning to adulthood from the foster care system in California, over half (54%) had been in congregate care at some point before their 18th birthday. Given the concern expressed by critics of congregate care, particularly their perception that it leads to disruption in positive social connections for youth, our findings on the associations between a history of congregate care and social support during the transition to adulthood provide much food for thought. At 17, 19, 21, and 23 years of age, we find that from one-third to over half of the youths in our study reported not having enough of one or more of the kinds of social support they were asked about and that the adequacy of some forms of support declined over time, indicating that there is a reason for continuing concern about their well-being. Consistent with trends for the general population of young adults, over time their social support networks became populated less by family members than by peers.

We also find that a history of congregate care placement is associated with differences in the perceived adequacy of and makeup of youths' social support networks. Youth with congregate care histories were more likely than their peers to report not having enough support and fewer people to turn to for almost all types and sources of social support. One notable exception was that youths with congregate care experience were more likely than those without to report having institutional agents as members of their support network, raising the possibility that a congregate care history serves as a proxy for needing the help of professionals in early adulthood.

Some limitations of the current study should be noted. First, the characteristics of social support networks measured in this chapter may not capture the full picture of youths' social supports (e.g., the number of nominees was limited to three; only three types of social support were investigated). Second, it is important to recognize that while our analyses draw attention to differences in social support by youths' congregate care history status, we cannot conclude that being in congregate care is causing those differences. Our analyses do not account for differences between youths who experienced congregate care and those who did not in their characteristics and experiences that might account for the kinds of social support they reported. Third, we estimated a large number of between-group comparisons raising the likelihood that some of what we report as significant findings may be due to chance alone. Lastly, our findings from the study conducted in California may not be generalizable to the experiences of youth transitioning to adulthood in other states in the United States or in counties abroad where care leaving policies and contexts vary.

Implications for Practice and Policy

Despite those limitations, the findings have clear implications for child welfare practice and policy. These findings call for greater attention to providing youths in congregate care settings with normative experiences that help them engage with their peers and master interpersonal skills that foster social connections. Efforts should also be redoubled to help youth develop and maintain connections with potentially supportive members of their extended family that they can rely on for support during the transition to adulthood.

Declarations of Interest

None.

Disclaimer

The findings reported herein were performed with the permission of the CDSS. The opinions and conclusions expressed herein are solely those of the author and should not be considered as representing the policy of the collaborating agency or any agency of the California government.

Acknowledgment

The authors would like to thank partners at the CDSS and CalYOUTH Study project funders—the Conrad N. Hilton Foundation, the Reissa Foundation, the Walter S. Johnson Foundation, the Zellerbach Family Foundation, the William T. Grant Foundation, and the California Wellness Foundation—for the support for administrative data used in this study and the commitment to policy evaluation and program development for youth.

Note

1 The remaining youth in care on 30 September 2021 were placed in a pre-adoptive home (4%), a trial home visit (4%), a Supervised Independent Living Placement (2%), or were on runaway status (1%).

References

California Department of Social Services. (2023). *Continuum of care reform*. https://www.cdss.ca.gov/Portals/9/CCR/CDSS_CCR_Issue_Brief_APU.pdf

Campos, G., Goig, R., & Cuenca, E. (2020). Relevance of the social support network for the emancipation of young adults leaving residential care. *Electronic Journal of Research in Educational Psychology*, *18*(1). https://doi.org/10.25115/ejrep.v18i50.2599

Capacity Building Center for States. (2020). *Congregate care in the age of family first: Overview*. Children's Bureau, Administration for Children and Families, U.S. Department of Health and Human Services.

Casey Family Programs. (2023). *Ending the need for group placements*. https://www.casey.org/ending-need-for-group-placements/#:~:text=Ending%20the%20Need%20for%20Group,in%20a%20safe%2C%20supportive%20home

Children's Bureau. (2018). *Information memorandum 18-02. New Legislation – Public Law 115-123, the Family First Prevention Services Act within Division E, Title VII of the Bipartisan Budget Act of 2018*. U.S. Department of Health and Human Services, Administration on Children, Youth, and Families. https://www.acf.hhs.gov/cb/policy-guidance/im-18-02

Children's Bureau. (2022). *The AFCARS report: Preliminary FY[1] 2021 estimates as of June 28, 2022 – No. 29*. U.S. Department of Health and Human Services, Administration on Children, Youth, and Families. https://www.acf.hhs.gov/cb/report/afcars-report-29

Children's Bureau. (2023). *Group and residential care*. https://www.childwelfare.gov/topics/outofhome/group-residential-care/

Chronicle of Social Change. (2019). Who cares: A national count of foster homes and families. https://www.fostercarecapacity.com/

Courtney, M. E., Charles, P., Okpych, N. J., Napolitano, L., & Halsted, K., (2014). *Findings from the California Youth Transitions to Adulthood Study (CalYOUTH): Conditions of foster youth at age 17*. Chapin Hall Center for Children at the University of Chicago. https://www.chapinhall.org/research/calyouth/

Courtney, M. E., & Dworsky, A. (2006). Early outcomes for young adults transitioning from out of-home care in the USA. *Child & Family Social Work*, *11*(3), 209–219. https://doi.org/10.1111/j.1365-2206.2006.00433.x

Courtney, M. E., & Heuring, D. H. (2005). The transition to adulthood for youth "aging out" of the foster care system. In D. W. Osgood, E. M. Foster, C. Flanagan, & G. R. Ruth (Eds.), *On your own without a net: The transition to adulthood for vulnerable populations* (pp. 27–67). The University of Chicago Press.

Courtney, M. E., Hook, J. L., & Lee, J. S. (2012). Distinct subgroups of former foster youth during young adulthood: Implications for policy and practice. *Child Care in Practice*, *18*(4), 409–418. https://doi.org/10.1080/13575279.2012.718196

Covington, C. C., Sernaker, S., & Wildeman, C. (2022). The cumulative prevalence of congregate care placement for U.S. children by race/ethnicity, 2019. *Child Maltreatment*. https://doi.org/10.1177/10775595221125456

Curry, S. R., & Abrams, L. S. (2015). Housing and social support for youth aging out of foster care: State of the research literature and directions for future inquiry. *Child and Adolescent Social Work Journal*, *32*(2), 143–153. https://doi.org/10.1007/s10560-014-0346-4

Fathallah, S. & Sullivan, S. (2021). *Away from home: Youth experiences of institutional placements in foster care*. https://www.thinkof-us.org/case-studies/away-from-home

Field, A., Sen, R., Johnston, C., & Ellis, K. (2021). Turning 18 in specialised residential therapeutic care: Independence or a cliff edge? *Children & Society*, *35*(5), 633–834. https://doi.org/10.1111/chso.12450

Gee, C. B., & Rhodes, J. E. (2007). A social support and social strain measure for minority adolescent mothers: A confirmatory factor analytic study. *Child: Care, Health and Development*, *34*(1), 87–97. https://doi.org/10.1111/j.1365-2214.2007.00754.x

Geenen, S. J., & Powers, L. E. (2006). Transition planning for foster youth. *Journal for Vocational Special Needs Education*, *28*(2), 4–15.

Greeson, J. K. P., Garcia, A. R., Kim, M., & Courtney, M. E. (2015a). Foster youth and social support: The first RCT of independent living services. *Research on Social Work Practice*, *25*(3), 305–397. https://doi.org/10.1177/1049731514534900

Greeson, J. K. P., Garcia, A. R., Kim, M., Thompson, A. E., & Courtney, M. E. (2015b). Development & maintenance of social support among aged out foster youth who received independent living services: Results from the multi-site evaluation of foster youth programs. *Children and Youth Services Review*, *53*, 1–9. https://doi.org/10.1016/j.childyouth.2015.03.016

Iglehart, A. P., & Becerra, R. M. (2002). Hispanic and African American youth: Life after foster care emancipation. *Journal of Ethnic and Cultural Diversity in Social Work*, *11*(1–2), 79–107. https://doi.org/10.1300/J051v11n01_04

Kids Count Data Center. (2022). *Children in foster care in the United States*. Annie E. Casey Foundation. https://datacenter.kidscount.org/data/tables/6243-children-in-foster-care#detailed/1/any/false/574,1729,37,871,870,573,869,36,868,867/any/12987

Mendes, P., Johnson, G., & Moslehudden, B. (2012). Young people transitioning from out-of-home care and relationships with family of origin: An examination of three recent Australian studies. *Child Care in Practice*, *18*(4), 357–370. https://doi.org/10.1080/13575279.2012.713849

Muir, S., Purtell, J., Hand, K., & Carroll, M. (2019). *Beyond 18: The longitudinal study of leaving care wave 3 research report: Outcomes for young people leaving care in Victoria*. Australian Institute of Family Studies.

Okpych, N., Feng, H., Park, K., Torres-García, A., & Courrtney, M. E. (2018). Living situations and social support in the era of extended foster care: A view from the U.S. *Longitudinal and Life Course Studies*, *9*(1), 6–29. https://doi.org/10.14301/llcs.v9i1.449

Osgood, D. W., Foster, E. M., & Courtney, M. E. (2010). Vulnerable populations and the transition to adulthood. *The Future of Children*, *20*(1), 209–229. http://www.jstor.org/stable/27795066

Perry, B. (2006). Understanding social network disruption: The case of youth in foster care. *Social Problems*, *53*(3), 371–391. https://doi.org/10.1525/sp.2006.53.3.371

Rosenberg, R. (2019). Social networks of youth transitioning from foster care to adulthood. *Children and Youth Services Review*, *107*. https://doi.org/10.1016/j.childyouth.2019.104520

Samuels, G. M. (2009). Ambiguous loss of home: The experience of familial (im) permanence among young adults with foster care backgrounds. *Children and Youth Services Review*, *31*(12), 1229–1239. https://doi.org/10.1016/j.childyouth.2009.05.008

Samuels, G. M., & Pryce, J. M. (2008). "What doesn't kill you makes you stronger": Survivalist self-reliance as resilience and risk among young adults aging out of foster care. *Children and Youth Services Review*, *30*, 1198–1210. https://doi.org/10.1016/j.childyouth.2008.03.005

Stanton-Salazar, R. D. (2011). A social capital framework for the study of institutional agents and their role in the empowerment of low-status students and youth. *Youth and Society*, *43*(3), 1066–1109. https://doi.org/10.1177/0044118X10382877

Stott, T., & Gustavsson, N. (2010). Balancing permanency and stability for youth in foster care. *Children and Youth Services Review*, *32*(4), 619–625. https://doi.org/10.1016/j.childyouth.2009.12.009

Sulimani-Aidan, Y. (2014). Care leavers' challenges in transition to independent living. *Children and Youth Services Review*, 46, 38–46. https://doi.org/10.1016/j.childyouth.2014.07.022

Sulimani-Aidan, Y. & Melkman, E. (2018). Risk and resilience in the transition to adulthood from the point of view of care leavers and caseworkers. *Children and Youth Services Review*, *88*, 135–140. https://doi.org/10.1016/j.childyouth.2018.03.012

Unrau, Y., Seita, J., & Putney, K. (2008). Former foster youth remember multiple placement moves: A journey of loss and hope. *Children and Youth Services Review*, *30*, 1256–1266. https://doi.org/10.1016/j.childyouth.2008.03.010

Wade, J. (2008). The ties that bind: Support from birth families and substitute families for young people leaving care. *British Journal of Social Work*, *38*, 39–54. https://doi.org/10.1093/bjsw/bc1342

Webster, D., Lee, S., Dawson, W., Magruder, J., Exel, M., Cuccaro-Alamin, S., Putnam-Hornstein, E., Wiegmann, W., Saika, G., Courtney, M., Eastman, A. L., Hammond, I., Gomez, A., Prakash, A., Sunaryo, E., Guo, S., Berwick, H., Hoerl, C., Yee, H., Flamson, T., Gonzalez, A., Ensele, P., Nevin, J., & Guinan, B. (2022). *CCWIP reports*. Retrieved Mar 3, 2023, from University of California at Berkeley California Child Welfare Indicators Project website. URL: https://ccwip.berkeley.edu

Whittaker, J. K., Holmes, L., del Valle, J. F., Ainsworth, F., Andreassen, T., Anglin, J., … & Zeira, A. (2016). Therapeutic residential care for children and youth: A consensus statement of the international work group on therapeutic residential care. *Residential Treatment for Children & Youth*, *33*(2), 89–106. https://doi.org/10.1080/0886571X.2016.1215755

9 Formal and Informal Social Networks of Israeli Care Leavers during the Transition to Adulthood

Yafit Sulimani-Aidan

Introduction

When young people leave residential care, they begin their journey into emerging adulthood, a life stage during which they – like their same-aged counterparts – must make important decisions about housing, employment, career, marriage, and other areas of adult life (Arnett, 2000). The lack of personal and social assets they have, as well as the lack of family backing, limits their future options and has a major impact on their perceptions of themselves and on the way they may fare in the future (Courtney et al., 2011; Stein & Munro, 2008; Sulimani-Aidan et al., 2013).

Research on the factors that enable residential care leavers to achieve favorable outcomes despite past and present stressors show that social support networks play an important role during their transition to adulthood (Collins et al., 2010; Geenen & Powers, 2007; Wade, 2008). Social networks include formal and informal relational aspects and are crucial for gaining access to a desired career, housing, and/or social life. They also play an essential role in a person's ability to survive difficult and transitional periods (Hiles et al., 2013; Melkman, 2017) and promote social integration and connectedness. Indeed, studies have shown that young people who have better post-leaving-care outcomes are those who are more likely to have at least one stable relationship, maintain ongoing contact with former caregivers, and are better able to make the most of the support that is offered to them (Stein, 2006). Higher levels of social support have also been found to correlate with improved well-being after transitioning from care (Cashmore & Paxman, 2006; Daining & DePanfilis, 2007; Pinkerton & Dolan, 2007), higher academic achievements, better social adjustment (Cashmore & Paxman, 2006), better financial status, and greater stability in living accommodations (Sulimani-Aidan et al., 2013). For care leavers with less relational capital, familial relationships that have ruptured, and who are separated from friends and staff, social networks are particularly important, especially during the transition from care to independent living. Nevertheless, many earlier studies have shown that care leavers receive little support from their social networks (e.g., Goodkind et al., 2011; Rutman & Hubberstey, 2016; Sulimani-Aidan,

DOI: 10.4324/9781003424468-13

2018; Sulimani-Aidan et al., 2017). The emphasis of most of these studies has been on the complexity and problematic nature of care leavers' social networks; namely, they have been characterized as smaller than the social networks of young people in the community, unstable, unavailable, untrustworthy, or fragmented.

The goal of this chapter is to review and discuss the current literature on care leavers' social networks, internationally and especially in Israel, specifically in relation to their role in care leavers' developmental tasks during the transition to adulthood and their potential impact on care leavers' outcomes as adults. The main objectives of the chapter are to: a) define and describe the formal and informal social figures in the lives of care leavers; b) describe the characteristics, roles, and nature of care leavers' social networks during the transition to adulthood; and c) review and discuss the ways in which social networks contribute to care leavers' status and outcomes in various areas of adult life. Based on the review presented in the chapter, implications for practice and policy will be presented.

Social Support Network: Definition and Theory

Social support comprises the psychological and material resources provided by people's social networks intended to benefit their ability to cope with stress (Cohen, 2004). Social support can manifest in a variety of forms such as emotional support (e.g., love and empathy), instrumental support (e.g., money and time), informal support (e.g., guidance and advice), and appraisal (e.g., feedback used for self-evaluation) (Pinkerton & Dolan, 2007). It has been shown in various studies that the tangible and intangible resources that come from social support can help individuals cope with stress. Indeed, social support plays a key role in promoting physical, mental, and material well-being (Newsom et al., 2005; Uchino, 2009). It is therefore generally agreed upon that social networks are essential to an individual's personal well-being and social and professional integration (Blakeslee, 2015).

Two main sources of support have been widely examined in the literature: informal and formal. Informal support is provided by the young adults' social environment, mainly family members and friends. Formal support, for its part, is provided by professional figures and formal services such as extended care programs or various social services (e.g., housing, education, counseling) as part of aftercare policy (Refaeli et al., 2019). The literature indicates that as opposed to their peers, who can rely on social support from parents and peers, care leavers may experience a significant lack of such support (Hiles et al., 2013).

In addition to distinguishing between formal and informal types of social support, researchers often distinguish between its structural and qualitative aspects. The structural/quantitative aspects of social support, such as network size or strength of ties with members (measured by frequency of contact), are thought to determine the social network's capacity to link the person in question with various resources (Marsden, 1990). The qualitative aspects, by contrast, refer to the perceived subjective quality of these resources (e.g., satisfaction with support); they thus reflect people's inclination to make use of their social ties as well as the extent to which the network adequately addresses their needs (i.e., network adequacy). Involvement in multiple networks (e.g., birth family, foster family, peer networks) is considered to be important and to serve as a protective factor (Perry, 2006). In terms of network adequacy, there is great variability in the social support that is available to youth who leave care. It has been found in qualitative studies that whereas some care leavers report sufficient support, many feel either completely unsupported or lacking in specific types of support (Geenen & Powers, 2007; Mulkerns & Owen, 2008; Samuels & Pryce, 2008).

The emphasis of some studies about youth in care and youth who have aged out of care is on the importance of network size, whereas in other studies the emphasis is on network quality. For example, some researchers argue that having a close and caring relationship with any one adult is the single most important protective factor for at-risk youth (Melaville et al., 1993; Vaillant 1993). Other researchers have found that individuals receive more support when they have larger and more accessible networks (Wellman & Gulia, 1999). Perry (2006) suggested that youth with only one strong network domain are missing out on network resources that are critical in terms of protecting one from psychological distress. However, most scholars in the field of marginalized groups of young people, including care leavers, claim that both the structural aspects (i.e., network size and frequency of contact) and the qualitative attributes (i.e., satisfaction with support or network adequacy) predict concrete and intangible outcomes (Calsyn & Winter, 2002; Degli Antoni, 2009; Liu et al., 2013; Yakubovich, 2005).

With regards to context, care leavers in Israel graduate from three main types of out-of-home settings, including welfare settings supervised by the Ministry of Welfare and Social Services, and educational settings overseen by the Ministry of Education. Young people are placed in welfare settings based on professional discretion and/or court decisions due to a range of family and child problems. Of the children and youth removed annually from home by the welfare system, about 80% are placed in residential settings, and only about 20% are placed with foster families (National Council for the Child, 2011). It is likely that the type of setting, the youths' family, and their own history and characteristics may impact their social networks after emancipation. However, there is not a study that has explored these aspects comparatively between settings. In his study on care leavers that included graduates from three types of out-of-home settings in Israel, Melkman (2017) found that while two-thirds of the participants indicated having enough people supporting them across support types, the smallest proportion reported having adequate support in the practical domain. In addition, females scored lower on all other measures of support, though these differences reached significance only for the practical and information and guidance support network adequacy.

It is likely that the type of setting, the youths' family and own history, and characteristics may impact their social networks after emancipation. However, there is not a study that explored these aspects comparatively between settings. In his study on care leavers that included graduates from three types of out-of-home settings in Israel, Melkman (2017) found that while two-thirds of the participants indicated having enough people supporting them across support types, the smallest proportion reported having adequate support in the practical domain. In addition, females scored lower on all other measures of support, though these differences reached significance only for the practical and information and guidance support network adequacy.

What Do We Know about the Social Support Networks of Care Leavers?

The transition to adulthood has been found to be one of the most challenging life tasks in modern society (Arnett, 2000). For young at-risk individuals who leave care, this transition is even more challenging, as they must move from a protective and supportive environment to a situation of independent living while being unable to depend economically and emotionally on their parents' support. At the same time, studies have shown that during this period their social networks do not change or expand. This finding is troubling given that, formally, the care system is no longer responsible for them, and the support they are able to receive from the professional figures they knew in the care system is quite limited (Hiles et al., 2013; Stein, 2019).

Earlier studies in which the transition to adulthood of care leavers was explored emphasized the care leavers' feelings of isolation and loneliness upon leaving care (Morgan, 2012; Munro et al., 2011; Sulimani-Aidan, 2016a). Indeed, from the perspective of care leavers, the need for continued emotional and social support and guidance during emerging adulthood is one of the most important aspects. At the same time, receiving such support/guidance is one of their greatest challenges (Geenen & Powers, 2007; Goodkind et al., 2011). At least three distinct network domains of social support of youth in care and care leavers have been outlined in various studies, including biological families, care settings and aftercare services, and peers, from which they can obtain health-protective resources such as instrumental and emotional support. The role of these support figures when youth are in care has been well documented (Jones, 2014; Sulimani-Aidan, 2016a; Sulimani-Aidan, 2017a). However, less is known about who these support figures are, and the nature of care leavers' relationships with them, during the transition to adulthood. In earlier studies, former social workers, counselors, and foster parents have been identified by care leavers as sources of support (Lemon et al., 2005). For example, in one study, the majority of care leavers reported they had contacted former in-care staff for support for up to six years after leaving care (Sulimani-Aidan, 2016a). It is understandable why these young people, who spent years in care and formed close relationships with professional figures, would turn to them for support and guidance after they leave. However, it is likely that the kind of support needed by these young adults after leaving care differs from the kind of support they needed during care.

In addition to a loosening of ties with former staff, many care leavers have distant, problematic, or unsupportive relationships with their families (Biehal & Wade, 1996; Sinclair et al., 2005). Although some care leavers get support from their extended families, many report lacking a "safety net" (Hiles et al., 2013) and discuss their families' inability to provide economic and/or emotional support or advice regarding instrumental and developmental tasks during the transition to adulthood (Sulimani-Aidan & Melkman, 2018). They are thus confronted with concrete and financial barriers that force them to concentrate on their daily needs instead of planning and working toward achieving future goals that can lead to social mobility (Sulimani-Aidan, 2017a).

Although when at-risk youth are in care, they are away from their parents, they are also surrounded by their peer group, and they establish close relationships with same-age friends. However, the transition out of care often brings to an end many of these relationships, leaving these young people even lonelier. Also, in some cases, the presence of these peers in their lives increases their vulnerability, especially when these peers are struggling themselves and tend to lean on, rather than offer, their support (Sulimani-Aidan, 2017b). Care leavers, leaving a familiar and protective environment, thus struggle to create new social networks that would support them in their journey to adulthood.

A further examination of the nature of care leavers' social support networks reveals a complex picture (Sulimani-Aidan, 2019). As mentioned, compared with their non-care leaver peers, care leavers' social networks are characterized as unstable, fragmented, and unreliable. One of the main aspects that colors this complex picture is their sense of certainty versus uncertainty. For example, the descriptions care leavers provided of their relationships with support figures were typified by a great sense of ambivalence and insecurity regarding the support figures' ability or willingness to support them. In addition, compared with young adults who lived with their families and perceived their support network as holistic – that is, offering various types of support during emerging adulthood, including emotional support, financial assistance, and counseling – care leavers described how they ended up needing to receive different types of support from different support figures. In other words, in most cases, there is not a sole figure that can provide all the types of support that care leavers need, and each support figure provides a specific type of support according to their ability.

The Contribution of Social Support Networks to the Care Leavers' Lives as Emerging Adults

In accordance with resilience theory, resilient care leavers are those who see adversity as inevitable, believe in their ability to contend with difficulties, and strive to cope with their challenges with the help of social ties (Masten &

Powell, 2003). Expanding our understanding of care leavers' social networks might allow us to enhance their resilience during the challenging transition to adulthood. Indeed, in resilience studies, the specific contribution to the instrumental and emotional adjustment of at-risk young adults (and care leavers in particular) of social support networks, as well as access to their associated resources, has long been recognized as important during the transition to adulthood (e.g., Guttyee, 2019; Sulimani-Aidan, 2020).

The importance of both informal and formal social support for care leavers' adjustment and outcomes during their transition to adulthood has been duly noted in the literature (e.g., Achdut et al., 2022; Guttyee, 2019; Lee et al., 2014; Mendes & Snow, 2016; Sulimani-Aidan, 2018). For example, in two studies among care leavers in Israel, support from peers and former staff was found to be linked with higher life satisfaction and lower psychological distress (Dinisman, 2014; Sulimani-Aidan et al., 2022). Also, formal support was found to contribute to care leavers' integration into the labor market (Arnau-Sabatés & Gilligan, 2015). Higher levels of social support were also correlated with better emotional, educational, social, and financial outcomes in adulthood (Cashmore & Paxman, 2006; Pinkerton & Dolan, 2007; Sulimani-Aidan et al., 2013). In addition, compared with their peers who did not have strong social networks, care leavers who had a strong support network were more likely to obtain a higher education, be employed, and have a stable housing situation (Jones, 2012).

Although the contribution of social networks to care leavers' lives in various areas is well documented, less is known about the processes and mechanisms that lead to better outcomes. A series of studies focusing on the role of social networks in the lives of Israeli care leavers from the perspectives of young adults and their case workers revealed the ways in which social support figures contributed to care leavers' outcomes and personal development. In these studies, most of the care leavers said that relationships with professional figures such as social workers, mentors, and therapists were a main source of support for their abilities, skills, motivation, and self-competence in achieving their goals and following their expectations. In terms of motivation and the actual process of pursuing higher goals, former and current professional figures were mentioned as role models and supportive figures who encouraged them and pushed them to believe in themselves and their aspirations (Sulimani-Aidan, 2020; Sulimani-Aidan & Melkman, 2018).

A main way in which formal social support contributes to care leavers' lives is via the provision of practical guidance and support as well as access to needed resources. Formal support sources can act as mediators between care leavers and various institutions or authority figures and help them realize their rights by communicating on their behalf. This type of tangible and moral support pertains to different life areas including education and work opportunities and coping with the demands of balancing work, study, and other parts of life (Arnau-Sabatés & Gilligan, 2015; Sulimani-Aidan & Melkman, 2022).

Another way in which formal support figures contribute to care leavers is by supporting them in adopting new coping strategies and perspectives, including promoting a positive future outlook and providing a place and time for self-reflection (Sulimani-Aidan & Melkman, 2022). For example, formal support figures were perceived as encouraging care leavers to have higher aspirations for themselves and to believe in their abilities to achieve goals. In addition, they offered the young adults a safe, nonjudgmental space that allowed for self-reflection and the exploration of current and future possibilities. This setting encouraged the young adults to adopt a new perspective on life events and more adaptive coping skills/behaviors in the present, as well as promoting future aspirations and higher ambitions and expectations. This quote by an Israeli 22-year-old care leaver describing her social worker demonstrates many of these aspects:

> She believes in me, didn't judge me, accepted me as I am, and listened...she lifted me up, helped me to find a scholarship to pay for my studies...came to visit me after I was admitted for cutting myself...like a mother.

Informal social support figures, including parents, siblings, and friends (in some cases intimate partners), are also key figures in the lives of care leavers during emerging adulthood. However, their contribution is more limited. Studies have shown that these relationships offer young adults a sense of belonging, which they need for their sense of stability, and that they provide a feeling of empathy, belonging, and shared experiences. A sense of belonging is a fundamental human need defined by lasting, stable, and positive interpersonal relationships. At the core of this sense is the belief that one is valued and cared for by others on a regular basis. As such, at times of change and/or instability, as in the case of emerging adulthood, this type of support is critical (Lambert et al., 2013).

Most studies in the field have highlighted the importance of care leavers' families' concrete and emotional support in terms of care leavers' outcomes and adjustment after transitioning to independent living (Collins et al., 2008; Sulimani-Aidan, 2015; Sulimani-Aidan et al., 2013; Wade, 2008). New evidence, however, has revealed another aspect during the transition from care to independent living that might lead to such outcomes, whereby the young adults' motivation and goals are in fact driven by their parents' struggles, difficulties, and painful histories (Sulimani-Aidan, 2018). Namely, parents play a significant role in the care leavers' expectations and pursuit of goals, not by providing support but by serving as a "mirror": It is their life narrative and painful history that seems to drive the care leavers to achieve more in life in order to avoid their parents' fate. In this way, parents represent a mirror to the possible future of young adults, in which they would like to see a different reflection of themselves.

Leveraging Social Networks' Support during Emerging Adulthood: Practical Considerations

According to the theory of emerging adulthood, the transition to adulthood is one during which one accepts responsibility for one's self, makes independent decisions, and becomes financially independent (Arnett, 2000). In addition, exploration of future possibilities is a dominant feature of this period (Arnett, 2007). If becoming an adult means learning to stand on one's own two feet as a self-sufficient person, then the support that care leavers receive can be a powerful asset during this challenging period and help them gradually become independent. There is no doubt that building resources of formal and informal social support is critical for care leavers (Collins et al., 2010; Courtney & Heuring, 2005). Therefore, one of the implications for policy is to acknowledge this cohort's need for further support, through their 20s, and extend the state's responsibility for their well-being even after they are officially considered adults. Indeed, many countries have developed formal service systems for care leavers, and some countries have anchored these services in legislation (Mendes & Snow, 2016). Currently, in Israel, there is no legislation regarding support for care leavers. Young people aging out of care can partake of services that are available to all needy young people in the general population (e.g., the national program for at-risk young adults supervised by the Ministry of Welfare and Social Affairs). They can also make use of the few services provided to them by privately funded NGOs via follow-up frameworks and transitional housing that allow care leavers the time and psychological space they need to make this transition. That said, there is no specific system that addresses all of the specific needs of care leavers. However, in 2018, an innovative program was developed for graduates of youth villages under the leadership of the Ministry of Education and Israel–Ashalim Joint, called "You Have an Address." The main goal of the program is to accompany young people in the process of leaving the framework and subsequently help them integrate optimally into the community and society. This includes acquiring education and/or professional training and leading an independent, mature life while achieving occupational and financial stability. As part of the program, a new role of care leavers' facilitator (mentor) was developed and implemented in each youth village. The purpose of this role is to professionally accompany the graduates by providing long-term support and guidance. This involves establishing contact with community professionals and facilitating access to rights, resources, and services in areas significant to adult life, in accordance with the needs and abilities of young people. The mission of these facilitators is to maintain an educational continuum for young people from the age of 16 to 26. This continuity spans from the phase of separation from the care system, before military/national service, and during and after the end of service, through the beginning of civilian life. Throughout the period of accompaniment, the coordinators serve as anchors, assisting young people in facing challenges and working to reduce barriers in their lives. This is achieved through building personalized accompaniment plans and organizing group activities. In a following longitudinal intervention study of the program (Sulimani-Aidan & Paldi, 2022), which included 683 care leavers, it was found that the status of those who were accompanied by the program and maintained contact with the facilitator and care staff was better than that of graduates who were not in contact after leaving care. This improvement was observed in key areas of life, including military service, independent life skills, and their perception of the future. These findings demonstrate the necessity of such a program in the first years after leaving care and beyond.

As has been stated herein, the majority of care leavers perceive their social networks as unstable and have a great deal of uncertainty regarding their support figures' ability to support them in the future. Thus, there is a need to design programs that will continue to provide support to these young adults over a longer period, so as to enhance their connections with more stable support figures in their communities. Care leavers must, at the very least, be offered the opportunity to receive the continuing support of professionals who are familiar to them, during the transition from care to independent living and throughout the early years of emerging adulthood. Professionals from former care, such as youth care workers and social workers, as well as foster parents, are described in the literature as "bridge relationships" for care leavers, as they continue to play an important support role while care leavers simultaneously establish other supportive relationships (Antle et al., 2009). Therefore, residential care leaders should design programs in which specific professional figures are assigned – while the youth are still in care – to support them after they leave care, specifically to help them adjust to new frameworks, realize their rights, and offer emotional support.

In addition, given that this period includes both concrete tasks (e.g., further studies and financial independence) and emotional-cognitive developmental tasks (e.g., identity exploration) (Arnett, 2007), it is also important that care leavers be supported by professional figures previously not known to them. Social workers who have the knowledge and skills in working with at-risk young adults, and especially young adults with a history of care, can act as "active agents" and provide both emotional and concrete support, offer new connections and opportunities, and boost care leavers' motivation to pursue higher future goals, as well as help them with the actual process of pursuing them.

Investing in the formal figures themselves is also important in order to promote care leavers' status during the transition to adulthood. Service entities should invest more resources in designing programs based on long-term meaningful mentoring as well as in helping caseworkers improve their skills in meeting these young people's complex needs. In addition, support must be provided for caseworkers' emotional needs in dealing with the young adults' harsh life circumstances; they will also need ongoing resources to help them support the young adults' various concrete needs.

Care leavers struggle to build new support networks after leaving care. Therefore, it is essential to proactively connect them to new support figures such as professionals or mentors via mentoring programs or via transitional housing. In this way, they will be introduced to supportive figures who are available to them and knowledgeable about the instrumental and developmental tasks of emerging adulthood. Indeed, it should be noted that mentoring (both natural and assigned) is one of the most evidence-based practices for good outcomes for care leavers (Ahrens et al., 2008; Greeson & Bowen, 2008; Sulimani-Aidan, 2016c, 2016d). Counseling and information provided by the mentor are crucial during this time period, as are support and interventions that increase competence, abilities, and self-confidence. In addition, programs targeting care leavers should integrate more components that connect care leavers with other young adults while strengthening their existing friendships. These steps will support their ability to explore their options and utilize this period to the fullest.

The literature indicates that although care leavers have complex, ambivalent, and limited relationships with their informal social networks (Blakeslee & Best, 2019; Sulimani-Aidan, 2017b; Sulimani-Aidan & Melkman, 2018), these relationships are still significant and provide them with a sense of belonging and connection, as well as a feeling of stability and a sense of "home" and family. Such contributions are very valuable during emerging adulthood, a period typified by instability, anxiety, and change. As such, in terms of practice, it is important that professionals acknowledge these aspects as resources that can be used to promote care leavers' well-being and sense of "normalcy." In fact, they should be considered a therapeutic tool in professionals' work with this population. Specifically, a family-focused approach upon leaving care should be implemented. Residential care placements should aim to integrate the families in the youths' discharge plans, assessing the parents' ability to support the young adults after their return home, and assisting in making connections with other family members, services, and programs that might compensate for the limited support they are able to provide.

In sum, in the model for positive change during emerging adulthood developed by Masten et al. (2006), the authors claimed that positive adaptation/resilience during this developmental window involves the capacity to change, adult support, and opportunities. Indeed, the literature demonstrates the importance of social support not only in terms of buffering the negative effects that take place during the transition from care to emerging adulthood but also as a promoter of the pursuit of future goals. Both formal and informal figures have the potential to provide care leavers with more opportunities to realize their plans for the future and develop personally by increasing their access to services and programs, helping them claim their rights, strengthening their social ties, and encouraging them to lean on these ties: extended family, close friends, peers, and communities.

References

Achdut, N., Sulimani-Aidan, Y., Benbenishty, R., & Zeira, A. (2022). Life satisfaction among alumni of youth villages in Israel: A life course perspective. *American Journal of Orthopsychiatry*, *92*(4), 483–496. https://doi.org/10.1037/ort0000622

Ahrens, K. R., DuBois, D. L., Richardson, L. P., Fan, M. Y., & Lozano, P. (2008). Youth in foster care with adult mentors during adolescence have improved adult outcomes. *Pediatrics*, *121*(2), 246–252. https://doi.org/10.1542/peds.2007-0508

Antle, B. F., Johnson, L., Barbee, A., & Sullivan, D. (2009). Fostering interdependent versus independent living in youth aging out of care through healthy relationships. *Families in Society*, *90*(3), 309–315. https://doi.org/10.1606/1044-3894.3890

Arnau-Sabatés, L., & Gilligan, R. (2015). What helps young care leavers to enter the world of work? Possible lessons learned from an exploratory study in Ireland and Catalonia. *Children and Youth Services Review*, *53*, 185–191. https://doi.org/10.1016/j.childyouth.2015.03.027

Arnett, J. J. (2000). Emerging adulthood: A theory of development from the late teens through the twenties. *American Psychologist*, *55*(5), 469–480. https://doi.org/10.1037/0003-066X.55.5.469

Arnett, J. J. (2007). Afterword: Aging out of care—Toward realizing the possibilities of emerging adulthood. *New Directions for Youth Development*, *2007*(113), 151–161. https://doi.org/10.1002/yd.207

Biehal, N., & Wade, J. (1996). Looking back, looking forward: Care leavers, families and change. *Children and Youth Services Review*, *18*(4–5), 425–445. https://doi.org/10.1016/0190-7409(96)00013-8

Blakeslee, J. E. (2015). Measuring the support networks of transition-age foster youth: Preliminary validation of a social network assessment for research and practice. *Children and Youth Services Review*, *52*, 123–134. https://doi.org/10.1016/j.childyouth.2015.03.014

Blakeslee, J. E., & Best, J. I. (2019). Understanding support network capacity during the transition from foster care: Youth-identified barriers, facilitators, and enhancement strategies. *Children and Youth Services Review*, *96*, 220–230. https://doi.org/10.1016/j.childyouth.2018.11.049

Calsyn, R. J., & Winter, J. P. (2002). Social support, psychiatric symptoms, and housing: A causal analysis. *Journal of Community Psychology*, *30*(3), 247–259. https://doi.org/10.1002/jcop.10004

Cashmore, J., & Paxman, M. (2006). Wards leaving care: Follow up five years on. *Children Australia*, *31*(3), 18–25. https://doi.org/10.1017/S1035077200011196

Cohen, S. (2004). Social relationships and health. *American Psychologist*, *59*(8), 676–684. https://doi.org/10.1037/0003-066X.59.8.676

Collins, M. E., Paris, R., & Ward, R. L. (2008). The permanence of family ties: Implications for youth transitioning from foster care. *American Journal of Orthopsychiatry*, *78*(1), 54–62. https://doi.org/10.1037/0002-9432.78.1.54

Collins, M. E., Spencer, R., & Ward, R. (2010). Supporting youth in the transition from foster care: Formal and informal connections. *Child Welfare*, *89*(1), 125–143. http://www.jstor.org/stable/45400625

Courtney, M., Dworsky, A., Brown, A., Cary, C., Love, K., & Vorhies, V. (2011). *Midwest evaluation of the adult functioning of former foster youth: Outcomes at age 26*. Chapin Hall at the University of Chicago.

Courtney, M. E., & Heuring, D. H. (2005). The transition to adulthood for youth "aging out" of the foster care system. In D. W. Osgood, E. M. Foster, C. Flanagan, & G. R. Ruth (Eds.), *On your own without a net: The transition to adulthood for vulnerable populations* (pp. 27–67). The University of Chicago Press.

Daining, C., & DePanfilis, D. (2007). Resilience of youth in transition from out-of-home care to adulthood. *Children and Youth Services Review*, *29*(9), 1158–1178. https://doi.org/10.1016/j.childyouth.2007.04.006

Degli Antoni, G. (2009). Does satisfaction matter? A microeconomic empirical analysis of the effect of social relations on economic welfare. *The Journal of Socio-Economics*, *38*(2), 301–309. https://doi.org/10.1016/j.socec.2008.07.001

Dinisman, T. (2014). Life satisfaction in the transition from care to adulthood: The contribution of readiness to leave care and social support. *Child & Family Social Work*, *21*(4), 401–411. https://doi.org/10.1111/cfs.12156

Geenen, S., & Powers, L. E. (2007). "Tomorrow is another problem": The experiences of youth in foster care during their transition into adulthood. *Children and Youth Services Review*, *29*(8), 1085–1101. https://doi.org/10.1016/j.childyouth.2007.04.008

Goodkind, S., Schelbe, L. A., & Shook, J. J. (2011). Why youth leave care: Understandings of adulthood and transition successes and challenges among youth aging out of child welfare. *Children and Youth Services Review*, *33*(6), 1039–1048. https://doi.org/10.1016/j.childyouth.2011.01.010

Greeson, J. K., & Bowen, N. K. (2008). "She holds my hand" the experiences of foster youth with their natural mentors. *Children and Youth Services Review*, *30*(10), 1178–1188. https://doi.org/10.1016/j.childyouth.2008.03.003

Guttyee, M. (2019). Social networks and social support in the transition to adulthood. In M. Goyette & V. R. Mann-Feder (Eds.), *Leaving care and the transition to adulthood: International contributions to theory, research, and practice* (pp. 31–50). Oxford University Press.

Hiles, D., Moss, D., Wright, J., & Dallos, R. (2013). Young people's experience of social support during the process of leaving care: A review of the literature. *Children and Youth Services Review*, *35*(12), 2059–2071. https://doi.org/10.1016/j.childyouth.2013.10.008

Jones, L. P. (2012). Predictors of success in a residential education placement for foster youths. *Children & Schools*, *34*(2), 103–113. https://doi.org/10.1093/cs/cds024

Jones, L. P. (2014). The role of social support in the transition from foster care to emerging adulthood. *Journal of Family Social Work*, *17*(1), 81–96. https://doi.org/10.1080/10522158.2013.865287

Lambert, N. M., Stillman, T. F., Hicks, J. A., Kamble, S., Baumeister, R. F., & Fincham, F. D. (2013). To belong is to matter: Sense of belonging enhances meaning in life. *Personality and Social Psychology Bulletin*, *39*(11), 1418–1427. https://doi.org/10.1177/0146167213499186

Lee, J. S., Courtney, M. E., & Tajima, E. (2014). Extended foster care support during the transition to adulthood: Effect on the risk of arrest. *Children and Youth Services Review*, *42*, 34–42. https://doi.org/10.1016/j.childyouth.2014.03.018

Lemon, K., Hines, A. M., & Merdinger, J. (2005). From foster care to young adulthood: The role of independent living programs in supporting successful transitions. *Children and Youth Services Review*, *27*(3), 251–270. https://doi.org/10.1016/j.childyouth.2004.09.005

Liu, Y., Croft, J. B., Chapman, D. P., Perry, G. S., Greenlund, K. J., Zhao, G., & Edwards, V. J. (2013). Relationship between adverse childhood experiences and unemployment among adults from five US states. *Social Psychiatry and Psychiatric Epidemiology*, *48*(3), 357–369. https://doi.org/10.1007/s00127-012-0554-1

Marsden, P. V. (1990). Network data and measurement. *Annual Review of Sociology*, *16*(1), 435–463. https://doi.org/10.1146/annurev.so.16.080190.002251

Masten, A. S., Obradović, J., & Burt, K. B. (2006). Resilience in emerging adulthood: Developmental perspectives on continuity and transformation. In J. J. Arnett & J. L. Tanner (Eds.), *Emerging adults in America: Coming of age in the 21st century* (pp. 173–190). American Psychological Association. https://doi.org/10.1037/11381-007

Masten, A. S. & Powell, J. L. (2003). A resilience framework for research, policy, and practice. In S. S. Luthar (Ed.), *Resilience and vulnerability: Adaptation in the context of childhood adversities* (pp. 1–25). Cambridge University Press.

Melaville, A. I., Asayesh, G., & Blank, M. J. (1993). *Together we can: A guide for crafting a profamily system of education and human services*. Diane Publishing.

Melkman, E. P. (2017). Childhood adversity, social support networks and well-being among youth aging out of care: An exploratory study of mediation. *Child Abuse & Neglect*, 72, 85–97. https://doi.org/10.1016/j.chiabu.2017.07.020

Mendes, P., & Snow, P. (Eds.). (2016). *Young people transitioning from out-of-home care: International research, policy and practice*. Springer.

Morgan, R. (2012). *After care: Young people's views on leaving care*. Office for Standards in Education, Children's Services and Skills (Ofsted).

Mulkerns, H., & Owen, C. (2008). Identity development in emancipated young adults following foster care. *Smith College Studies in Social Work*, *78*(4), 427–449. https://doi.org/10.1080/00377310802378594

Munro, E. R., Pinkerton, J., Mendes, P., Hyde-Dryden, G., Herczog, M., & Benbenishty, R. (2011). The contribution of the United Nations Convention on the Rights of the Child to understanding and promoting the interests of young people making the transition from care to adulthood. *Children and Youth Services Review*, *33*(12), 2417–2423. https://doi.org/10.1016/j.childyouth.2011.08.025

National Council for the Child. (2011). *Children in Israel: Statistical abstract*. National Council for the Child.

Newsom, J. T., Rook, K. S., Nishishiba, M., Sorkin, D. H., & Mahan, T. L. (2005). Understanding the relative importance of positive and negative social exchanges: Examining specific domains and appraisals. *The Journals of Gerontology Series B: Psychological Sciences and Social Sciences*, *60*(6), 304–312. https://doi.org/10.1093/geronb/60.6.P304

Perry, B. L. (2006). Understanding social network disruption: The case of youth in foster care. *Social Problems*, *53*(3), 371–391. https://doi.org/10.1525/sp.2006.53.3.371

Pinkerton, J., & Dolan, P. (2007). Family support, social capital, resilience and adolescent coping. *Child & Family Social Work*, *12*(3), 219–228. https://doi.org/10.1111/j.1365-2206.2007.00497.x

Refaeli, T., Benbenishty, R., & Zeira, A. (2019). Predictors of life satisfaction among care leavers: A mixed-method longitudinal study. *Children and Youth Services Review*, *99*, 146–155. https://doi.org/10.1016/j.childyouth.2019.01.044

Rutman, D., & Hubberstey, C. (2016). Is anybody there? Informal supports accessed and sought by youth from foster care. *Children and Youth Services Review*, *63*, 21–27. https://doi.org/10.1016/j.childyouth.2016.02.007

Samuels, G. M., & Pryce, J. M. (2008). "What doesn't kill you makes you stronger": Survivalist self-reliance as resilience and risk among young adults aging out of foster care. *Children and Youth Services Review*, *30*(10), 1198–1210. https://doi.org/10.1016/j.childyouth.2008.03.005

Sinclair, I., Baker, C., Wilson, K., & Gibbs, I. (2005). *Foster children, where they go and how they get on*. Jessica Kingsley.

Stein, M. (2006). Young people aging out of care: The poverty of theory. *Children and Youth Services Review*, *28*(4), 422–434. https://doi.org/10.1016/j.childyouth.2005.05.005

Stein, M. (2019). Supporting young people from care to adulthood: International practice. *Child & Family Social Work*, *24*(3), 400–405. https://doi.org/10.1111/cfs.12473

Stein, M., & Munro, E. R. (2008). *Young people leaving care: Supporting pathways to adulthood*. Kingsley Publishers.

Sulimani-Aidan, Y. (2015). Do they get what they expect?: The connection between young adults' future expectations before leaving care and outcomes after leaving care. *Children and Youth Services Review*, *55*, 193–200. https://doi.org/10.1016/j.childyouth.2015.06.006

Sulimani-Aidan, Y. (2016a). In between formal and informal: Staff and youth relationships in care and after leaving care. *Children and Youth Services Review*, *67*, 43–49. https://doi.org/10.1016/j.childyouth.2016.05.025

Sulimani-Aidan, Y. (2016c). Future expectations as a source of resilience among young people leaving care. *British Journal of Social Work*, *47*(4), 1111–1127. https://doi.org/10.1093/bjsw/bcw077

Sulimani-Aidan, Y. (2016d). Present, protective, and promotive: Mentors' roles in the lives of young adults in residential care. *American Journal of Orthopsychiatry*, *88*(1), 69–77. https://doi.org/10.1037/ort0000235

Sulimani-Aidan, Y. (2017a). Barriers and resources in transition to adulthood among at-risk young adults. *Children and Youth Services Review*, *77*, 147–152. https://doi.org/10.1016/j.childyouth.2017.04.015

Sulimani-Aidan, Y. (2017b). To dream the impossible dream: Care leavers' challenges and barriers in pursuing their future expectations and goals. *Children and Youth Services Review*, *81*, 332–339. https://doi.org/10.1016/j.childyouth.2017.08.025

Sulimani-Aidan, Y. (2018). Assets and pathways in achieving future goals of residential care alumni. *Children and Youth Services Review*, *89*, 71–76. https://doi.org/10.1016/j.childyouth.2018.04.023

Sulimani-Aidan, Y. (2019). Qualitative exploration of supporting figures in the lives of emerging adults who left care compared with their noncare-leaving peers. *Child & Family Social Work*, *24*(2), 247–255. https://doi.org/10.1111/cfs.12609

Sulimani-Aidan, Y. (2020). Social networks during the transition to adulthood from the perspective of Israeli care leavers and their social workers. *Children and Youth Services Review*, *115*, 1–8. https://doi.org/10.1016/j.childyouth.2020.105075

Sulimani-Aidan, Y., Achdut, N., Zeira, A., & Benbenishty, R. (2022). Psychological distress among care leavers during the transition to adulthood: Risk and protective factors throughout their life course. *Child & Family Social Work*, *27*(2), 324–339. https://doi.org/10.1111/cfs.12887

Sulimani-Aidan, Y., Benbenishty, R., Dinisman, T., & Zeira, A. (2013). Care leavers in Israel: What contributes to better adjustment to life after care?. *Journal of Social Service Research*, *39*(5), 704–718. https://doi.org/10.1080/01488376.2013.834283

Sulimani-Aidan, Y., & Melkman, E. (2018). Risk and resilience in the transition to adulthood from the point of view of care leavers and caseworkers. *Children and Youth Services Review*, *88*, 135–140. https://doi.org/10.1016/j.childyouth.2018.03.012

Sulimani-Aidan, Y., & Melkman, E. (2022). School belonging and hope among at-risk youth: The contribution of academic support provided by youths' social support networks. *Child & Family Social Work*, *27*(4), 700–710. https://doi.org/10.1111/cfs.12918

Sulimani-Aidan, Y., & Paldi, Y. (2022). *"You have an address" – Program for youth villages care leavers: Findings from a longitudinal intervention study*. Tel Aviv University, School of Social Work. (Hebrew)

Sulimani-Aidan, Y., Sivan, Y., & Davidson-Arad, B. (2017). Comparison of hope and the child-parent relationship of at-risk adolescents at home and in residential care. *Children and Youth Services Review*, *76*, 125–132. https://doi.org/10.1016/j.childyouth.2017.03.005

Uchino, B. N. (2009). Understanding the links between social support and physical health: A life-span perspective with emphasis on the separability of perceived and received support. *Perspectives on Psychological Science*, *4*(3), 236–255. https://doi.org/10.1111/j.1745-6924.2009.01122.x
Vaillant, G. E. (1993). 11 Avoiding negative life outcomes: Evidence from a forty-five year study. In P. B. Baltes & M. M. Baltes (Eds.), *Successful aging: Perspectives from the behavioral sciences* (pp. 332–358). Cambridge University Press.
Wade, J. (2008). The ties that bind: Support from birth families and substitute families for young people leaving care. *British Journal of Social Work*, *38*(1), 39–54. https://doi.org/10.1093/bjsw/bcl342
Wellman, B., & Gulia, M. (1999). Virtual communities as communities. In M. A. Smith & P. Kollock (Eds.), *Communities in cyberspace* (pp. 167–194). Routledge.
Yakubovich, V. (2005). Weak ties, information, and influence: How workers find jobs in a local Russian labor market. *American Sociological Review*, *70*(3), 408–421. https://doi.org/10.1177/000312240507000303

10 Social Support for Residential Care Leavers in Ghana

The Perspectives and Experiences of Social Workers and Residential Care Youth Workers

Kwabena Frimpong-Manso

Introduction

In Africa, the number of young people transitioning from alternative care into adulthood is increasing (van Breda & Frimpong-Manso, 2020). This situation has arisen because, in addition to HIV/AIDS and the recent COVID-19 pandemic, poverty, conflicts, and harmful cultural traditions have contributed to many African children becoming orphaned, abandoned, maltreated, and deprived of proper parental care (Hillis et al., 2021; Petrowski et al., 2017). Most African children without parental supervision are cared for by extended families, but a growing number of these children are in residential care, such as orphanages and children's homes (Islam & Fulcher, 2016; Martin & Zulaika, 2016). As deinstitutionalization efforts sweep across the continent in countries such as Ghana, Sierra Leone, Egypt, and Rwanda, many institutionalized children are reuniting with their families or being adopted (Abdel Aziz, 2021; Frimpong-Manso et al., 2024; Horvath et al., 2019; Kanyamanza & Nsabimana, 2023). However, others remain in residential care until they reach the majority, usually 18 years old, at which point they are no longer eligible for child welfare support (van Breda & Frimpong-Manso, 2020).

Researchers have investigated the experiences of young people who have left residential care in several African countries in recent years (Bodiroa & Ross, 2022; Frimpong-Manso, 2018; Pryce et al., 2015; Uwitonze & Mhando, 2023). These studies show that care leavers in Africa have poor adult outcomes, which include unemployment, poverty, homelessness, and social isolation. A key reason noted in these studies for poor outcomes is the limited social support available to young people during and after they leave care.

In most African countries, there is hardly any formal support for care leavers (Bond, 2018). The absence of post-care support significantly impacts care leavers' independence and future outcomes, particularly during the critical first few years after leaving care (Van Breda, 2018). Care leavers also often lack parental support because they are unavailable or incapable, mainly

DOI: 10.4324/9781003424468-14

because of death or poverty (Amissah, 2021). Additionally, residential care facilities attempt to offer support to care leavers, but they lack established policies and programs, as well as funding (Pote et al., 2022). Few nongovernmental organizations are beginning to offer transitional services for care leavers in some countries, such as South Africa and Zimbabwe (Dadirai Gwenzi, 2023; Tanur, 2012).

Research involving care leavers in Africa shows that most rely on informal networks for social support (Moodley et al., 2020; Pouw et al., 2017). These networks are often composed of former carers, care peers, volunteers, and other relationships developed during their stay in care, providing both emotional and practical support. Additionally, care leavers find support from social networks developed after leaving care, such as church communities (Frimpong-Manso, 2017). However, they face challenges in building supportive relationships and developing rich social networks because of difficulties with social skills, experiences of stigma and prejudice, and the distance between their care placements and home communities (Diraditsile & Nyadza, 2018; Dadirai Gwenzi & Ringson, 2023).

While studies have examined care leavers' perspectives on social support (Adley & Jupp Kina, 2014; Melkman & Benbenishty, 2018), there is still a need for research investigating the viewpoints of support providers, such as social workers and other practitioners, in residential care facilities (Sulimani-Aidan, 2020). Such research could help identify effective approaches to support care leavers and improve collaboration among different support providers. To fill this gap in the current literature, this chapter explores the perspectives of practitioners—social workers and residential care youth workers—within Ghana's residential care system on social support for care leavers. The chapter's specific objectives are to understand (1) the social support needs of residential care leavers, (2) the strategies employed by stakeholders in residential care to support care leavers, and (3) the challenges that prevent these residential care stakeholders from providing adequate social support for care leavers.

Literature Review

Collins et al. (2010) define social support as help, whether perceived or real, provided by others. Social support can take various forms, including emotional support (such as empathy, comfort, and reassurance), instrumental support (e.g., transportation), informational support (e.g., advice and guidance), and appraisal support (e.g., feedback). Social support plays a crucial role in improving well-being and life satisfaction during the transition from care to adulthood (Dinisman, 2014). It helps improve their mental health by boosting their self-esteem, fostering a sense of security, and decreasing feelings of isolation and loneliness (Evans et al., 2022; Törrönen, 2021). Additionally, care leavers who receive social support experience have improved academic success, better employment prospects, and greater economic stability through social support while also having lower rates of homelessness (Katz & Geiger, 2020; Melkman & Benbenishty, 2018; Packard & Benuto, 2020; Refaeli, 2020). Having supportive connections, including positive role models, such as mentors or supportive adults, can also help care leavers develop resilience, positive self-esteem, and a sense of purpose (Arnau-Sabatés & Gilligan, 2020; Rutman & Hubberstey, 2016; van Breda, 2022).

Care leavers use both formal and informal relationships as sources of social support, with each type offering unique benefits (e.g., Collins et al., 2010; Ibrahim, 2019; Zinn et al., 2017). In countries lacking formal post-care support, informal social networks are especially crucial for providing practical and emotional support to care leavers (Stubbs et al., 2023; Teer, 2021). The role of the family as a source of support is mixed. Some studies indicate that family members, such as siblings, grandparents, and aunts, are important for providing practical and emotional support and helping care leavers maintain a sense of identity (Jones, 2014). However, other research suggest that care leavers often receive minimal support from their families and can sometimes feel overwhelmed by the demands placed on them by their social networks (Berejena Mhongera & Lombard, 2017; Dima & Pinkerton, 2016). Outside of family, many care leavers rely on friends for social support, especially in countries without formal post-care support (e.g., Dima & Pinkerton, 2016; Ibrahim, 2019). Friends can provide practical, emotional, and financial assistance and peers who have experienced care can offer a sense of belonging and a safe space for sharing experiences. Additionally, supportive relationships with former carers, coworkers, romantic partners, and mentors are significant sources of social support for care leavers (Arnau-Sabatés & Gilligan, 2020; Stubbs et al., 2023; Teer, 2021).

In addition to the often-limited support from informal sources, care leavers need support from child welfare workers and other practitioners. According to Paulsen and Berg (2016), support from formal sources differs from that obtained from informal networks. For example, in Ghana, care leavers often rely on informal sources for practical and emotional support while turning to formal sources for financial and informational support (Frimpong-Manso, 2020). Practitioners offer various forms of social support, including identifying the needs of care leavers, guiding them through complex procedures, such as welfare applications, and coordinating services (Paulsen & Berg, 2016; Sulimani-Aidan, 2020). However, formal support for care leavers typically decreases or ceases during their early adult years, regardless of existing policies and legislative frameworks (Katz & Geiger, 2020). Owing to the importance of social support for care leavers during their transition to adulthood, child welfare services in different countries have developed interventions to enhance supportive networks. These interventions include mentoring, network facilitation, and self-help groups, as noted in a recent scoping review (Okland & Oterholm, 2022). However, most of the studies reviewed were small in scale and did not assess the effectiveness of these interventions, highlighting the need for further research to identify the most effective ways to provide social support to care leavers (Häggman-Laitila et al., 2020).

Compared with their non-care peers (Melkman & Benbenishty, 2018; Sulimani-Aidan, 2019), care leavers have smaller social networks (Blakeslee, 2015; Rosenberg, 2019) and experience a decline in social support as they age (Zinn et al., 2017). Research has indicated that both personal and systemic factors contribute to challenges in providing social support to care leavers. For example, Zinn et al. (2017) reported that delinquency and attachment problems can negatively impact care leavers' social support by hindering their community engagement. Many care leavers lack the relational skills necessary to form informal relationships, making it difficult for them to build supportive connections (Teer, 2021). Additionally, care leavers often experience trauma before they enter care and may go through multiple placements during their time in the system. This instability can interfere with their capacity to develop trusting relationships with friends and practitioners (Packard & Benuto, 2020).

Even when help is available, care leavers do not always make use of it because they feel it might indicate that they are not managing well in adulthood (Frimpong-Manso, 2017). Some academics argue that this reluctance stems from an emphasis on self-sufficiency during their preparation for adulthood (Paulsen & Berg, 2016). Tanur (2012) claimed that focusing on interdependent living would shift the focus from care leavers feeling pressured to be completely self-reliant to developing supportive social networks to meet their needs. The literature on social support highlights that emotional support is a primary need for most care leavers, especially those from residential care as many experience loneliness, isolation, and vulnerability after leaving care (Packard & Benuto, 2020; Okpych et al., 2018; Refaeli, 2020). However, their preparation for adulthood often focuses on providing financial and practical support rather than building social networks or offering emotional support (Adley & Jupp Kina, 2014; Dinisman, 2014).

Residential Care Leavers in Ghana

Most children in alternative care in Ghana stay in residential care facilities funded and managed by the state (children's homes) or a privately run organization (orphanages), such as faith-based agencies.

Children's homes, which accept vulnerable children from diverse backgrounds—including abandoned children—are mostly dormitory-style structures that house approximately 100 children and young people. In contrast, private facilities accept only orphans and have between 20 and 50 children and young people. State-owned facilities receive government funding, whereas private residential facilities rely on donations from individuals and organizations and income-generating activities (Frimpong-Manso, 2021). Child sponsorship programs, which allow donors to provide monthly or annual support for a child, a group of children, or the entire institution, are frequently used in these residential facilities. These sponsorship programs are often advertised on "orphanage" websites and are open to both international and local donors. Recent evaluations indicate that many residential facilities in Ghana are poorly managed, with inadequate infrastructure and funding systems; only a third of them have licenses to operate (Petrowski et al., 2022).

A survey of Ghanaian children's residential facilities revealed that 3,530 children were housed in 139 homes (Ghana Department of Social Welfare & UNICEF, 2021). In contrast, the Lancet Global Study reported 39,233 children in residential care, including those in unregulated and unregistered facilities (Desmond et al., 2020). Most children in residential care (65%) were aged 10–17 years, with 24% aged 15–17 years. Children enter care for various reasons, including familial poverty, abandonment, orphanhood, and disability. Most children (87%) had entered care before the age of five years and had been in care for three to ten years. Adolescents and older children are overrepresented, with 64% of children aged 10–17 (Ghana Department of Social Welfare & UNICEF, 2021). Although exact statistics are not available, some young people leave care when they are 18 years old. Overall, policy and practice often ignore care leavers and their needs. Few residential care facilities focus on leaving care to prepare young people for leaving care (Frimpong-Manso, 2012; Manful et al., 2015). In addition, there are no transition policies or programs to help young people integrate into society. However, Standard 7 of the National Standards for Residential Homes for Children mandates that residential facilities provide young people with "assistance to find appropriate and affordable accommodation and basic equipment to start an independent life" (Ghana Department of Social Welfare & UNICEF, 2018, p. 18).

A study on care leavers in Ghana highlighted that many people, particularly pregnant women and those with disabilities, face significant challenges in securing employment, housing, and other essentials (Amissah, 2021). A variety of variables contribute to these unsatisfactory results. Many young people leave care underprepared for life, lack social and cultural skills, and lack the capacity to manage finances and housing (Frimpong-Manso, 2012). Although care leavers may receive some support from previous carers, non-governmental organizations, and churches, after leaving care at 18, they often face challenges accessing formal and informal support. These challenges include the lack of standardized criteria in residential care facilities, leading to discretionary and potentially discriminatory support provisions; the incorrect assumption by family members that they do not need assistance since they are cared for by staff and professionals; and the stigma associated with their care or orphan background (Kelly et al., 2024). Despite these obstacles, some care leavers demonstrate resilience in their journey toward independent living. A study involving young people who had left private residential care facilities in Ghana, for example, reported that those who had strong social support from churches and other social networks, supportive relationships with at least one adult, and personal perseverance were more successful in their transition to adulthood (Frimpong-Manso, 2020).

Methods

The current chapter focuses on participants' perspectives on providing social support for care leavers. A qualitative design was chosen to capture these insights. The study included ten social workers and two residential care youth workers who were selected through purposeful sampling. The inclusion criteria required participants to have worked in residential care settings for at least one year, ensuring that they could provide relevant information concerning the support provided to care leavers. Additionally, participants needed to be able to communicate in English. The recruitment of participants began in November 2022. The researcher approached managers of 20 residential facilities in Greater Accra to identify potential participants. The managers of the selected residential facilities were provided with information about the study and the sampling criteria to assist in the recruitment process. Facility managers then approached staff members who met the inclusion criteria and were willing to participate. Those who consented to participate were given permission to contact the researcher directly.

Twenty staff members agreed to be contacted by the researcher, who then called them to set up a suitable time and location for the interviews. Four of the contacted staff members declined to participate for personal reasons, such as time constraints, and four did not meet the qualifications for being social workers or residential care youth workers. Ultimately, 12 participants, comprising nine women and three men, participated in the study, which was conducted on the basis of data saturation. Eight of the participants were from privately funded facilities. The participants were aged between 26 and 45 years, with their experience in residential care ranging from 1.5 to 11 years. Among them were ten social workers and two youth residential care workers. The participants' experience in residential care settings ranged from 1.5 to 11 years.

Instruments and Procedures

Semi-structured interviews were used to collect data on the social support of young people transitioning from residential care to independent living. The interview guide was developed using the study's objectives and current literature. It included questions about young people's social needs, professional practices for providing social support, and the challenges encountered in providing such support. The interviews took place at various locations as requested by the participants. Each interview, conducted in English, lasted between 25 minutes and one hour and was audio-recorded. The recordings were transcribed verbatim, and the transcripts were then reviewed and cleaned for errors and identifying information.

The researcher used the framework approach to analyze the transcripts (Ritchie & Spencer, 1994). This process began with familiarization with the data to identify recurring concepts and themes. A thematic framework was then developed, categorizing the data into primary and sub-themes, each assigned a numerical value for indexing. The framework was manually applied to code all transcripts. The data were further refined through comparative analysis and theme-based matrix charts were created to uncover relationships and explain the findings. Ethical approval for the study was obtained from the University of Ghana. The participants provided informed consent, having been informed of their right to decline participation or withdraw at any time, as well as issues related to confidentiality and privacy. As a token of appreciation for their time and effort, the participants received a gift voucher.

Results

The analysis of the interview data revealed three main themes and four subthemes. The first theme focused on current assistance and unmet support needs. The second theme addressed strategies used by practitioners to increase social support for care leavers, such as sponsoring programs and connections to "family" and community networks. The final theme explored challenges associated with providing social support, including resource constraints and the inherent difficulties care leavers face in accessing support.

Provided Support and Unaddressed Needs

Most participants stated that they supported young people in becoming self-sufficient by offering them different forms of support, although this support was not always formalized. The assistance provided was often instrumental and informational, including help with room rental and basic household supplies. Doris, a social worker, shared,

> We find a place for them [care leavers] to stay or else they will end up on the streets. We usually make rent payments for 2 years in the hope that they have a job, so that they can renew their lease.

Similarly, Margaret, another social worker, described her approach: "As they transition to independence, we provide them with basic items such as cooking utensils, bedsheets, and buckets, along with a three-month allowance and a maximum three-year lease for their accommodation."

The participants also reported providing employment support given Ghana's high unemployment rates and the care leavers' limited social networks. They offered job information, career guidance, connections with employers, and financial assistance for small business start-ups. Mildred, a residential care youth worker, described this support:

> We offer help for our young people to gain employment before they leave us. We have links with the Army, Police, and other security services as well as some government and private institutions. We help young people gain employment behind the scenes.

Some social workers in privately funded residential facilities mentioned having a formal counseling process for young people transitioning out of care. This process, which begins a year before a young person leaves care, provides guidance on future prospects, the realities of the outside world, and psychological support for emotions such as anger, anxiety, and desperation that could arise during the transition. As Margaret, a social worker, explained,

> When they are leaving, we call them and talk to them about the future, what is about happening, and how to prepare their minds. We don't just let them go into the world without preparing them for what lies ahead.

In addition to counseling, these private facilities offer transitional accommodations, or youth homes, for young adults aged 18 and above who are pursuing education or vocational training. In these homes, young people receive financial support and guidance from a residential care youth worker, helping them develop essential living skills and fostering interdependent living.

When young people left care, the social workers reported staying in touch and following up with them. However, this support was provided for a brief period because of the social workers' hectic work schedules and limited resources. Much of the post-care support was provided at the care leaver's request. Most of their requests for support were centered around food, housing, and employment. As Agnes, a social worker, explained:

> The basic things they often need are food and work. They will call that they have lost their job and have nothing done. They will come, those who don't have a place to stay. Three basic things are food, money, and work, and some also want to further their education.

The participants noted that, in addition to formal support, several staff members, particularly primary carers, offered informal assistance to young people after they transitioned into the community. This support often includes instrumental, emotional, and cognitive support, such as babysitting, advice, guidance, or calls to check-up on care leavers. Brian, a social worker, explained the support the carers provided to care leavers:

> Most of them [carers] play an active role in young people's lives because they want to follow up on their progress. They have direct contact with them. Most house mothers had phone numbers. They give extra

> support and financial assistance to resettled youth [care leavers] who are not doing well.

One of the social workers shared an instance of how some retired carers supported a care leaver:

> One of our young people [care leavers], who gave birth, needed assistance in caring for her child. The former caregiver, who had retired, went to stay with her for some time to assist her. This is just one example of how mothers [carers] continue to support children who leave their care.
> (Agnes, social worker)

Strategies to Enhance Care Leavers' Social Support

Interview analysis revealed that the social support provided by practitioners included securing sponsors and fostering connections with family and the community.

Sponsors

Several practitioners interviewed stated that their residential facilities supported care leavers through a sponsorship program. While donors' assistance was primarily intended for use while young people were still in care, social workers used some of the resources to help young people during their transition out of care. They saved some of the donations in bank accounts that the care leavers could access upon leaving care, ensuring that the funds were used for positive purposes. As stated by Vida, a social worker:

> The money gift [donations] is checked before a young person leaves the home [residential facility]. We [staff] thrash out with the young person what they want to do with the money. Some care leavers use it to buy laptops for further study or to buy machines for their businesses. Then, we monitor that they use it as discussed.

Even though the primary purpose of sponsors is to provide financial assistance, the social workers noted that they often encouraged and facilitated other forms of support as well. While this was not always desirable, some sponsors, particularly local ones, maintained ongoing relationships with young people. These relationships included letter exchanges, sharing life experiences, and providing guidance and encouragement, especially concerning education. Social workers observed that active communication between young people and sponsors sometimes led to lasting connections, which are especially beneficial for orphaned and abandoned youths who lack known relatives. These relationships help bridge relational gaps and provide a supportive network. As Nancy, a social worker, explains:

> Some sponsors continue to support a young person after they have been weaned off [leave care]. We [social workers] allow them to have direct contact with out our supervision because at that stage, they [young people] are by then adults, and they have attained independence. These sponsors continue to give the children money to help with their education and give them advice and guidance with life.

Fostering Connections with Family and Community Social Networks

The participants shared several strategies they utilized to cultivate supportive relationships with young people before they left care. Some social workers use the "holiday visit program" to reconnect or strengthen ties between young people and their families (including parents and extended family members). During school vacations or holidays, this program allows young people in residential care to visit and stay with family members. These visits aim to help young people develop a sense of belonging and supportive relationships within a family setting. As stated by Mildred, a residential care youth worker:

> We send them on holidays with their families to develop links with them. For abandoned children, we [social workers] find mentors in the community for them. The mentors have direct involvement in their upbringing, as the children can visit them during the school vacation or even over the weekend.

The participants stated that they helped young people while they were in care to build and expand their supportive networks within their communities by encouraging their participation in various activities and community groups, such as churches. Brian, a social worker, stated, "We connect them to church activities and other social events, which we think will help them build their social network." In addition to helping young people establish positive relationships with peers and adults who could provide support after they leave care, these initiatives also aimed to reduce the stigma and discrimination that they frequently faced. By addressing these issues, the initiatives sought to increase the overall level of social support available to them. The assistance in establishing family connections was not limited to young people's biological families but also included the establishment of family-like networks between young people and their carers and peers in residential facilities. Several participants noted that these connections often led carers to continue offering informal support to care leavers even after retirement.

Challenges in Delivering Social Support

Two main themes emerged regarding the challenges participants faced in providing social support for care leavers: resource constraints and lack of engagement with support.

Resource Constraints

Data from the participants revealed that the support provided to care leavers was not tailored to individual needs. Instead, transitional support was uniformly applied to all young people. In addition, post-care support for care leavers was not always aligned with the specific requests of the care leavers but was instead based on the capabilities of the residential facility. As Theresa, a social worker, explains:

> We [staff] try to support them with food, further counselling, and supervision while they are out there. Young people have different requests as well. However, it is sometimes difficult to do these things, especially if they are financially related, because we do not have the means. We give them what we have.

The researcher's comments indicate that she often struggled to provide the support young people needed. The participants discussed the challenges that hindered their ability to support care leavers effectively, with the primary barrier being inadequate funding and office equipment, such as functional telephones and reliable internet access. These limitations made it difficult for them to perform their duties, including addressing practical needs requests for educational support. Joan, a social worker, highlighted the specific difficulties her residential facility faced in providing support to care leavers:

> There are times that we are unable to help because we are also faced with financial challenges. In recent times, this has been a challenge because the support we used to have financially is going down, so the organization has not received enough support from care leavers.

In addition, the social workers interviewed also indicated that their heavy workloads made it challenging to maintain contact and follow up with care leavers, as noted by Doris, a social worker in residential care:

> Social workers monitor youth. Owing to the enormous workload in villages [residential facilities], they usually prevent us from undertaking this task. There are supposedly seven children on our caseload, but the lowest caseload is 19, and the highest is 25. The number is not reduced. I sometimes want to do more to support care leavers, but my workload is too much.

Care Leavers' Challenges in Requesting and Receiving Support

Another key challenge highlighted by the participants was the lack of engagement from care leavers, who often struggled to ask for support or use support when it was available. Nancy, a social worker, explained that:

> Many of them [care leavers] don't open up. When you speak to them, you can see they are not okay. You ask what is happening; they tell you nothing is wrong. It is difficult to offer help. Our young people act strangely.

While Nancy seemed uncertain as to why care leavers failed to engage in supportive relationships and take advantage of social support, others expressed an understanding of the challenges care leavers experienced in seeking and receiving help. For instance, Arnold, a residential care youth worker, noted that the difficulties they experienced in engaging care leavers often arose because of a breakdown in their relationship, especially during their transition out of care:

> Getting the young person to understand that it is time to leave the [name of facility] is sometimes a challenge because they perceive us as bad people who want them out, although we know that [name of facility] is not meant for adults. It becomes a battle, and they don't want to relate to you again.

Several participants also highlighted the impact of stigma on care leavers' ability to develop supportive relationships in the community. As Sarah, a social worker, stated:

> The community looks at care leavers differently. As soon as they hear the young person from [name of facility], they look at them negatively. This leads to our young people feeling frustrated and not interacting with people in the community.

In addition to the stigma experienced by care leavers, which hampers their efforts to access social support within the community, this stigma also creates difficulties for social workers in offering support. Some care leavers intentionally broke off contact with practitioners from residential care to avoid the negative attention and discrimination associated with their experience in care. As highlighted by Theresa, a residential care youth worker:

> Even when you rent accommodations for them, they should not be identified as coming from [name of institution]. When you visit them and go by official bus, they say no, they do not want you. They keep to themselves and make it difficult for people to help them.

Discussion and Implications for Practice

The current study examined the perceptions of social workers and residential care youth workers of social support for young people transitioning from residential care to independent living in Ghana. The findings revealed that housing and employment-related instrumental and informational assistance are key components of the transitional support provided by most residential settings. This aligns with findings from other developing countries (Collins & Tuyền, 2016; Wilson & Mokgoko, 2024). Notably, this support reflects a proactive approach to helping care leavers secure housing and employment, aiming to prevent homelessness and unemployment.

Given that there is no clear formal policy to support young people leaving care and given the limited social welfare provisions in Ghana, securing stable employment and housing is crucial for their successful integration into society and self-sufficiency (Frimpong-Manso, 2018). Thus, initiatives involving residential care facilities to support care leavers are vital, especially because care leavers in Ghana and other African countries face significant challenges in finding employment and accessing suitable housing (e.g., Frimpong-Manso, 2018; Pryce et al., 2015).

Another key finding from the study is that, apart from a few private facilities with a structured counseling process to address the emotional support needs of young people transitioning out of care, most other facilities did not report providing this form of social support. However, existing studies highlight the importance of emotional support for care leavers, as it helps build resilience, coping skills, and a sense of self during the transition to adulthood (Adley & Jupp Kina, 2014; Packard & Benuto, 2020; Refaeli, 2020). While participants' narratives suggest some informal support through network-building, care, and encouragement provided by carers, there is no unambiguous evidence that practitioners offer formal emotional support or assistance in identifying gaps in emotional networks, which is a critical area that needs to be addressed.

An interesting finding from this study is that the social support provided to care leavers was uniform and not individualized. Care leavers are often treated as a homogeneous group rather than as individuals with unique needs and abilities who require personally tailored assistance. Research shows that social support is most effective when individual care leavers' perceived needs are met (Packard & Benuto, 2020). It is possible that the resource constraints, including limitations in funding and personnel highlighted by the participants, may have prevented the provision of such tailored support. Despite these challenges, social workers still assess each care leaver's needs, abilities, and difficulties in determining the most beneficial type of support. They can also engage in active communication with care leavers to design a support plan tailored to their specific needs and goals. This finding suggests that practitioners need to be provided with appropriate resources to provide adequate support for care leavers. Therefore, the Department of Social Welfare (DSW) in Ghana, which oversees social welfare for vulnerable populations, should allocate resources to district social workers to enhance their ability to address the needs of care leavers in each residential care setting.

Most of the social support provided to care leavers by residential facilities was provided primarily during their transition out of care, with post-care support being offered only on an ad-hoc basis. This lack of formal and consistent post-care contact is concerning. Research from African countries with poor social and economic conditions, such as high unemployment rates and limited social welfare systems, highlights that insufficient post-care support significantly impairs care leavers' ability to manage independent living (Bond, 2018; Tanur, 2012). Longitudinal studies from South Africa further emphasize that intensive support for care leavers should take place for at least the first 12 months after leaving care, as this period sets the tone for outcomes that care leavers achieve over the following two years (van Breda, 2018).

Several factors may contribute to the inadequate support provided to young people leaving residential care facilities. First, current regulations in Ghana, including the National Standards for Residential Homes for Children 2018 and the 1998 Children's Act (Act 560), do not mandate post-care support. As a result, many facilities may not view it as part of their responsibilities. Additionally, given that most residential facilities experience financial constraints due to inadequate or lack of state funding and high dependency on irregular donations from private individuals (Frimpong-Manso, 2021), it could be challenging for them to offer comprehensive post-care assistance, including financial aid, employment opportunities, housing, or access to higher education. To address these challenges, implementing a policy that ensures statutory post-care support for at least two years would be both beneficial and sustainable. Such a policy would ensure that the government, through DSW, allocates the necessary financial and human resources to residential care settings for post-care support. By establishing a structured and coordinated approach, this policy can help mitigate the risk of inadequate or nonexistent support for care leavers. A key challenge to social support identified in this study was young people's difficulty seeking help and their resistance to offers of support, which are issues that align with findings from other studies (Adley & Jupp Kina, 2014; Packard & Benuto, 2020). While some participants provided reasons for care leavers' reluctance and challenges in engaging with support, others found these behaviors incomprehensible or unexplained. Care leavers often struggle to seek or accept support for various reasons, including a lack of trust stemming from past experiences of abandonment and trauma, an idealized view of independent living, attachment insecurity, and the stigma associated with requesting help (Packard & Benuto, 2020).

Adley and Jupp Kina (2014) suggest that social workers and other practitioners should destigmatize support, persist in offering help over time to ensure effectiveness, establish trusting relationships with care leavers, and recognize the appropriate timing for support. Additionally, it would be helpful for practitioners in Ghana to receive training in trauma-informed practice to better understand how care leavers' past experiences influence their behavior.

This study suggests that reconnecting with biological families is a crucial strategy for young people in residential care to establish long-term relationships and secure social support. Re-establishing these connections can help young people develop meaningful relationships with adults who provide an informal social safety net, offering diverse forms of support during their transition out of care. This finding is consistent with previous research indicating the value of such familial ties in offering ongoing support (Okland & Oterholm, 2022).

This study aimed to examine the effects of social workers and residential care youth workers on the support provided to young people transitioning from residential care and its impact on their ability to independently live in Ghana. This highlights the importance of housing and employment-related assistance in transitional support provided by practitioners (Dadirai Gwenzi, 2023). However, this study also reveals a significant gap in the provision of emotional support, which is essential for developing resilience during the transition to adulthood. The findings emphasize the need for personalized, tailored social support for care leavers, particularly given the current resource constraints and the lack of formal post-care support. Recommendations include destigmatizing support, establishing trust, and employing trauma-informed practices. Additionally, reconnecting with biological families is suggested as a strategy for fostering long-term relationships and providing ongoing support. A comprehensive policy framework and tailored support strategies are crucial for addressing these needs effectively.

References

Abdel Aziz, A. (2021). Deinstitutionalization and alternative care systems: A case study of children without parental care in Egypt. In H. Ali & S. Bhuiyan (Eds.), *Institutional reforms in governance and services delivery in the global south* (1st ed., pp. 75–99). Palgrave Macmillan.

Adley, N., & Jupp Kina, V. (2014). Getting behind the closed door of care leavers: Understanding the role of emotional support for young people leaving care. *Child & Family Social Work*, *22*(1), 97–105. https://doi.org/10.1111/cfs.12203

Amissah, F. G. (2021). *Transitioning from care to adulthood: Reintegration experiences of young people leaving residential care in Ghana* (Master's dissertation). University of Gothenburg.

Arnau-Sabatés, L., & Gilligan, R. (2020). Support in the workplace: How relationships with bosses and coworkers may benefit care leavers and young people in care. *Children and Youth Services Review*, *111*, 104833. https://doi.org/10.1016/j.childyouth.2020.104833

Berejena Mhongera, P., & Lombard, A. (2017). Who is there for me? Evaluating the social support received by adolescent girls transitioning from institutional care in Zimbabwe. *Practice*, *29*(1), 19–35. https://doi.org/10.1080/09503153.2016.1185515

Blakeslee, J. E. (2015). Measuring the support networks of transition-age foster youth: Preliminary validation of a social network assessment for research and practice. *Children and Youth Services Review*, *52*, 123–134. https://doi.org/10.1016/j.childyouth.2015.03.014

Bodiroa, A., & Ross, E. (2022). Challenges, agency, and ecology in the transition of youth from state residential care to independent living in Johannesburg, South Africa. *Child & Youth Services*, 1–27. https://doi.org/10.1080/0145935x.2022.2113871

Bond, S. (2018). Care-leaving in South Africa: An international and social justice perspective. *Journal of International and Comparative Social Policy*, *34*(1), 76–90. https://doi.org/10.1080/21699763.2017.1413994

Collins, M., & Tuyền, B. (2016). Youth leaving care in developing countries: Observations from Vietnam. In P. Mendes & P. Snow (Eds.), *Young people transitioning from out-of-home care: International research, policy, and practice* (1st ed., pp. 329–348). Palgrave Macmillan.

Collins M. E., Spencer R., Ward R. (2010). Supporting youth in the transition from foster care: Formal and informal connections. *Child Welfare*, *89*, 125–143. http://www.jstor.org/stable/45400625

Dadirai Gwenzi, G. (2023). Provision of transitional housing: A socially sustainable solution for care leavers in Zimbabwe. *Practice*, *35*(2), 103–120. https://doi.org/10.1080/09503153.2022.2083100

Dadirai Gwenzi, G., & Ringson, J. (2023). "Why would they call me an orphan when I have parents": Care leavers' experiences of labeling and stereotyping while living in residential care facilities in Zimbabwe. *New Ideas in Psychology*, *68*. https://doi.org/10.1016/j.newideapsych.2022.100968

Desmond, C., Watt, K., Saha, A., Huang, J., & Lu, C. (2020). Prevalence and number of children living in institutional care: Global, regional, and country estimates. *The Lancet Child & Adolescent Health*, *4*(5), 370–377. https://doi.org/10.1016/S2352-4642(20)30022-5

Dima, G. & Pinkerton, J. (2016). The role of informal leaving care support networks in Romania. In P. Mendes & P. Snow (Eds.), *Young people transitioning from out-of-home care* (pp. 409–426). Palgrave Macmillan.

Dinisman, T. (2014). Life satisfaction in the transition from care to adulthood: The contribution of readiness to leave care and social support. *Child & Family Social Work*, *21*(4), 401–411. https://doi.org/10.1111/cfs.12156

Diraditsile, K., & Nyadza, M. (2018). Life after institutional care: Implications for research and practice. *Child & Family Social Work*, *23*(3), 451–457. https://doi.org/10.1111/cfs.12436

Evans, R., Katz, C. C., Fulginiti, A., & Taussig, H. (2022). Sources and types of social supports and their association with mental health symptoms and life satisfaction among young adults with a history of out-of-home care. *Children*, *9*(4), 520. https://doi.org/10.3390/children9040520

Frimpong Manso, K. A. (2012). Preparation for young people leaving care: The case of SOS Children's Village, Ghana. *Child Care in Practice*, *18*(4), 341–356. https://doi.org/10.1080/13575279.2012.713850

Frimpong-Manso, K. (2017). The social support networks of care leavers from a children's village in Ghana: Formal and informal supports. *Child & Family Social Work*, *22*(1), 195–202. https://doi.org/10.1111/cfs.12218

Frimpong-Manso, K. (2018). Building and utilizing resilience: The challenges and coping mechanisms of care leavers in Ghana. *Children and Youth Services Review*, *87*, 52–59. https://doi.org/10.1016/j.childyouth.2018.02.016

Frimpong-Manso, K. (2020). Stories of care leaving: The experiences of a group of resilient young adults on their journey to interdependent living in Ghana. *Emerging Adulthood*, *8*(1), 16–25. https://doi.org/10.1177/2167696818807114

Frimpong-Manso, K. (2021). Funding orphanages on donations and gifts: Implications for orphans in Ghana. *New Ideas in Psychology*, *60*. https://doi.org/10.1016/j.newideapsych.2020.100835

Frimpong-Manso, K., Cudjoe, E., Agbadi, P., Abdullah, A., Deliege, A., & Bansal, A. (2024). Deinstitutionalization of children in residential care facilities: Experiences and perceptions of professionals in Ghana. *Child & Family Social Work*, *29*(2), 306–315. https://doi.org/10.1111/cfs.13081

Ghana Department of Social Welfare, & UNICEF Ghana. (2018). *National standards for residential homes for children in Ghana* (Report). Department of Social Welfare. https://www.unicef.org/ghana/reports/national-standards-residential-homes-children-ghana

Ghana Department of Social Welfare & United Nations Children's Fund. (2021). *Children living in residential care in Ghana: Findings from a survey of wellbeing*. UNICEF.

Gwenzi, G. D. (2022). Provision of transitional housing: A socially sustainable solution for care leavers in Zimbabwe. *Practice*, 1–18. https://doi.org/10.1080/09503153.2022.2083100

Häggman-Laitila, A., Salokekkilä, P., & Karki, S. (2020). Integrative review of the evaluation of additional support programs for care leavers making the transition to adulthood. *Journal of Pediatric Nursing*, *54*, 63–77. https://doi.org/10.1016/j.pedn.2020.05.009

Hiles, D., Moss, D., Wright, J., & Dallos, R. (2013). Young people's experience of social support during the process of leaving care: A review of the literature. *Children & Youth Services Review*, *35*(12), 2059–2071. https://doi.org/10.1016/j.childyouth.2013.10.008

Hillis, S. D., Unwin, H. J. T., Chen, Y., Cluver, L., Sherr, L., Goldman, P. S., Ratmann, O., Donnelly, C. A., Bhatt, S., Villaveces, A., Butchart, A., Bachman, G., Rawlings, L., Green, P., Nelson, C. A., & Flaxman, S. (2021). Global minimum estimates of children affected by COVID-19-associated orphanhood and deaths of caregivers: A modeling study. *The Lancet*, *398*(10298), 391–402. https://doi.org/10.1016/s0140-6736(21)01253-8

Horvath, L., Nabieu, M., & Curtiss, M. (2019). Why we decided to transition from residential to family-based care. *Scottish Journal of Residential Child Care*, *18*(2), 1–10.

Ibrahim, R. W. (2019). The longer-term contributions of formal and informal support: Experiences of Jordanian care leavers. In V. R. Mann-Feder & M. Goyette (Eds.), *Leaving care and the transition to adulthood: International contributions to theory, research, and practice* (pp. 221–240). Oxford Academic. https://doi.org/10.1093/oso/9780190630485.003.0012

Islam, T., & Fulcher, L. C. (Eds.). (2016). *Residential child and youth care in a developing world: Global perspectives*. CYC-Net Press.

Jones, L. P. (2014). The role of social support in the transition from foster care to emerging adulthood. *Journal of Family Social Work*, *17*(1), 81–96. https://doi.org/10.1080/10522158.2013.865287

Kanyamanza, C., & Nsabimana, E. (2023). Childcare reform strategy in Rwanda: A cornerstone of child protection system. In T. Gatwa & D. Mbonyinkebe (Eds.), *Home grown initiatives and nation building in Africa: The dynamic of social and cultural heritage in Rwanda* (pp. 251–269). LIT Verlag Münster.

Katz, C. C., & Geiger, J. M. (2020). 'We need that person who doesn't give up on us'. *Child Welfare*, *97*(6), 145–164. https://www.jstor.org/stable/48626320

Kelly, B., van Breda, A. D., Pinkerton, J., Frimpong-Manso, K., Chereni, A., & Bukuluki, P. (2024). Youth in Transition: Exploring a Life Course Perspective on Leaving care in Africa. *Youth & Society*, *56*(5), 926–945. https://doi.org/10.1177/0044118X231193708

Manful, E., Takyi, H., & Gambrah, E. (2015). Admission to exit: Acquiring life skills while in residential care in Ghana. *Social Work and Society*, *13*(2), 1–13.

Martin, F. S., & Zulaika, G. (2016). Who cares for children? A descriptive study of care-related data available through global household surveys and how these could be better mined to inform policies and services to strengthen family care. *Global Social Welfare*, *3*(2), 51–74. https://doi.org/10.1007/s40609-016-0060-6

Melkman, E. P., & Benbenishty, R. (2018). Social support networks of care leavers: Mediating between childhood adversity and adult functioning. *Children & Youth Services Review*, 86, 176–187. https://doi.org/10.1016/j.childyouth.2018.01.040

Moodley, R., Raniga, T., & Sewpaul, V. (2020). Youth transitioning out of residential care in South Africa: Toward Ubuntu and interdependent living. *Emerging Adulthood*, *8*(1), 45–53. https://doi.org/10.1177/2167696818812603

Okland, I., & Oterholm, I. (2022). Strengthening supportive networks for care leavers: A scoping review of social support interventions in child welfare services. *Children & Youth Services Review*, *138*, 106502. https://doi.org/10.1016/j.childyouth.2022.106502

Okpych, N., Feng, H., Park, K., Torres-García, A., & Courtney, M. (2018). Living situations and social support in the era of extended foster care: A view from the U.S. *Longitudinal and Life Course Studies*, 9(1). https://doi.org/10.14301/llcs.v9i1.449

Packard, F. E., & Benuto, L. T. (2020). Examining social support needs of emerging adults transitioning out of foster care. *Child Welfare*, *98*(1), 51–72. https://www.jstor.org/stable/48623679

Paulsen, V., & Berg, B. (2016). Social support and interdependency in transition to adulthood from child welfare services. *Children & Youth Services Review*, *68*, 125–131. https://doi.org/10.1016/j.childyouth.2016.07.006

Petrowski, N., Cappa, C., Deliege, A., & Khan, M. R. (2022). Residential homes for children in Ghana: Compliance with standards, quality of care, and case management. *Global Studies of Childhood*, *12*(1), 40–55. https://doi.org/10.1177/20436106221075636

Petrowski, N., Cappa, C., & Gross, P. (2017). Estimating the number of children in formal alternative care: Challenges and results. *Child Abuse & Neglect*, *70*, 388–398. https://doi.org/10.1016/j.chiabu.2016.11.026

Pote, C., Carelse, S., & Dykes, G. (2022). Social support networks for youths aging out of residential care to promote positive transition outcomes – A scoping review. *Social Work*, *58*(1). https://doi.org/10.15270/58-1-992

Pouw, N., Hodgkinson, K., Le Mat, M., & van Dam, K. (2017). *The social exclusion of vulnerable youth: Synthesis report: Côte d'Ivoire, Guatemala, Indonesia, Kenya, Malawi, and the Netherlands*. University of Amsterdam, Amsterdam Institute for Social Science Research.

Pryce, J., Jones, S., Wildman, A., Thomas, A., Okrzesik, K., & Kaufka-Walts, K. (2015). Aging out of care in Ethiopia: Challenges and implications facing orphans and vulnerable youth. *Emerging Adulthood*, *4*(2), 119–130. https://doi.org/10.1177/2167696815599095

Refaeli, T. (2020). Needs and availability of support among care-leavers: A mixed-methods study. *Child & Family Social Work*, *25*(2), 412–420. https://doi.org/10.1111/cfs.12697

Ritchie, J., & Spencer, L. (1994). Qualitative data analysis for applied policy research. In A. Bryman & R. Burgess (Eds.), *Analyzing qualitative data* (pp. 305–329). Routledge.

Rosenberg, R. (2019). Social networks of youth transitioning from foster care to adulthood. *Children and Youth Services Review*, *107*. https://doi.org/10.1016/j.childyouth.2019.104520

Rutman, D., & Hubberstey, C. (2016). Is anybody there? Informal supports accessed and sought by youth from foster care. *Children and Youth Services Review*, *63*, 21–27. https://doi.org/10.1016/j.childyouth.2016.02.007

Stubbs, A., Baidawi, S., & Mendes, P. (2023). Young people transitioning from out-of-home care: Their experience of informal support: A scoping review. *Children & Youth Services Review*, *144*, 106735. https://doi.org/10.1016/j.childyouth.2022.106735

Sulimani-Aidan, Y. (2019). Qualitative exploration of supporting figures in the lives of emerging adults who left care compared with their noncare-leaving peers. *Child & Family Social Work*, *24*(2), 247–255. https://doi.org/10.1111/cfs.12609

Sulimani-Aidan, Y. (2020). Social networks during the transition to adulthood from the perspective of Israeli care leavers and their social workers. *Children & Youth Services Review*, 115, 105075. https://doi.org/10.1016/j.childyouth.2020.105075

Tanur, C. (2012). Project Lungisela: Supporting young people leaving state care in South Africa. *Child Care in Practice*, *18*(4), 325–340. https://doi.org/10.1080/13575279.2012.713851

Teer, P. (2021). The role of informal networks in the lives of young people transitioning from care: A review of the literature. *Scottish Journal of Residential Child Care*, *20*(1), 7–28. https://doi.org/10.17868/strath.00084171

Törrönen, M. (2021). Social relationships and their connection to mental health for young people who have been in the care system. *The British Journal of Social Work*, *51*(3), 927–944. https://doi.org/10.1093/bjsw/bcab028

Uwitonze, F., & Mhando, N. E. (2023). Challenges facing former street youth graduating from rehabilitation centers in Rwanda. *Tanzania Journal of Development Studies*, 21 (1), 38–59.

Van Breda, A. (2018). The first two years out of residential care in South Africa: A critical period for care-leaving services. *Child Welfare*, *95*(6), 63–82. https://www.jstor.org/stable/48623607

Van Breda, A. D. (2022). The contribution of supportive relationships to care-leaving outcomes: A longitudinal resilience study in South Africa. *Child Care in Practice*, 1–16. https://doi.org/10.1080/13575279.2022.2037516

Van Breda, A. D. P., & Frimpong-Manso, K. (2020). Leaving care in Africa. *Emerging Adulthood*, *8*(1), 3–5. https://doi.org/10.1177/2167696819895398

Wilson, L., & Mokgoko, L. (2024). Social support provided to care leavers by residential care facilities in Gauteng Province, South Africa, during their transition to independent living. *Social Work and Social Sciences Review*, *24*(2), 1–24. https://doi.org/10.1921/swssr.v24i2.1997

Zinn, A., Palmer, A. N., & Nam, E. (2017). The predictors of perceived social support among former foster youth. *Child Abuse & Neglect*, *72*, 172–183. https://doi.org/10.1016/j.chiabu.2017.07.015

11 Is Someone There for Them?

Care Leavers' Experiences, Challenges, and Support During and After Residential Care

Kiran Modi, Gurneet Kaur Kalra and Leena Prasad

Introduction

Children placed in alternative care represent a vulnerable population, often facing severe adversities, such as orphanhood, broken families, poverty, abuse, and neglect (Nnama-Okechukwu et al., 2018). Research indicates that exposure to such difficult circumstances can negatively impact their physical and mental health, while also hindering the development of positive social relationships and healthy attachments (Belsey & Sherr, 2011). In a historic move, for the first time, the United Nations General Assembly included, for the first time, a resolution on "Children without Parental Care" in its agenda. This resolution urges states to ensure that Children and Young People (CYP) leaving alternative care receive proper support, whether they are returning to families or transitioning to independent living (UNGA Advocacy Working Group, 2019). The 2021 Day of General Discussion (DGD) focused on "Children's Rights and Alternative Care" aiming to create meaningful engagement for CYP, allowing them to voice their opinions on what constitutes quality care and advocate for care reforms. Key points emerging from the DGD discussion include the importance of listening to CYP, giving special attention to young people who have been affected by the COVID-19 pandemic, and ensuring psychological and practical support for young people transitioning from alternative care to adulthood so that they can lead fulfilling lives (United Nations Convention on the Rights of Child (UNCRC), 2021; DGD, 2021).

Emerging adulthood is a complex period, especially for young care leavers (CLs), as they make significant life decisions and often struggle with issues of identity exploration and instability (Belsey & Sherr, 2011). For these youth who have experienced disrupted relationships and trauma, social relations and social support networks become even more crucial during and after the transition to adulthood. Yet several studies have found that they often receive minimal support from their social networks (Goodkind et al., 2011; Rutman & Hubberstey, 2016; Sulimani-Aidan, 2018a; Sulimani-Aidan et al., 2017). At both the community and individual levels, social networks and supportive

DOI: 10.4324/9781003424468-15

relationships are considered crucial resources for social inclusion (Korkiamäki & Kallio, 2018), especially for young CLs (Collins et al., 2010). Social supportive relationships and strong social networks provide CLs with significant resources to deal with new challenges and opportunities embedded in the emerging adulthood phase in their lives (Zorn, 2017). Indeed, CLs with increased social support tend to show greater resilience and are often better able to adapt to their challenging circumstances, despite having faced significant adversity (Jones, 2014; Melkman, 2017). Social relationships are recognized as a protective factor that is beneficial for CLs' emotional and mental health (Rahamim & Mendes, 2016). Research also indicates that CLs who have long-term adult support through friendship or mentoring have better outcomes than those without such social support (Ahmann, 2017; Gypen et al., 2017). Additionally, informational, practical, and emotional support from social networks have been shown to positively impact the economic well-being of CLs and improve their educational opportunities (Melkman & Benbenishty, 2018).

The strength and weakness of any relationship are often determined by its duration, the depth of emotional intimacy, and the resources shared. However, in order to cope with challenging experiences such as abuse, disrupted relationships, and maltreatment, CLs may develop protective mechanisms, like emotional distancing and mistrust, which in turn might lead to compromising their ability to form long-lasting, healthy relationships (Goodkind et al., 2011; Hiles et al., 2013; Hebert et al., 2016).

Alternative Care and Aftercare in India

India, with a population of 1.43 billion—the largest in the world—includes approximately 40% children. The country is home to 23.6 million orphaned and abandoned children (MOSPI, 2018), of which nearly 470,000 reside in Child Care Institutions (CCIs), registered under the Juvenile Justice Act, or in other forms of residential care that may or may not be registered and often focus on specific needs like education and health (MWCD, 2018). Around 2.1 million orphaned children fall within the 15–17 age group (World Bank Group and World Health Organization, 2021).

The Constitution of India mandates the state to implement policies to protect children from exploitation, material, and moral abandonment (Constitution of India, 1950, under Article 39(f)). The National Youth Policy 2021 (2022) aims to promote youth development across five priority areas: employment and entrepreneurship; youth leadership and development; health, fitness, and sports; and social justice. This policy encourages inclusive social and economic growth and specifically addresses the requirement of additional support for orphaned youth as a distinct category.

In India, legal acts and schemes such as the Juvenile Justice (Care and Protection of Children) Act, 2015 (JJ Act), its Model Rules 2016, and the "Mission Vatsalya" scheme provide aftercare services to support youth leaving the care system. Aftercare is defined as "making provision of support, financial or otherwise, to persons who have completed the age of eighteen years but have not completed the age of twenty-one years, and have left any institutional care to join the mainstream of the society" (Section 2(5), JJ Act, 2015). Although these schemes and acts clearly articulate the need to reintegrate CLs into mainstream society and outline the responsibilities of authorities in meeting their needs, on-ground implementation remains largely inadequate. There is an urgent need to establish a far more comprehensive aftercare program, informed by a deeper understanding of the current situation of this population and the challenges they face at various stages of their transition.

At the age of 18, the transition of youth from living in a protective care facility of a CCI to independent living often brings a cloud of difficulties. This difficult transition is exacerbated by the absence of a supportive family-like ecosystem, marginal community integration, inadequate access to essential resources in the care setting, and multiple placements. Additionally, despite being mandated by law, the lack of participatory transition planning, preparedness, and aftercare support further compounded these difficulties. Studies in India reveal that most Indian young people transitioning from CCIs feel unprepared to leave their care settings, leading to struggles in various domains of independent living (Modi et al., 2020). They face numerous challenges and instability, such as inadequate life skills, physical and mental health issues, lack of education and vocational training, high risk of unemployment, lack of economic independence, and homelessness (Beyond 18, 2019; Modi et al., 2016).

Research Context

The study titled "Beyond 18: Leaving Child Care Institutions—Supporting Youth Leaving Care" published in 2019, by Udayan Care, an NGO in India, with support from UNICEF India and Tata Trusts, captured the voices of 435 CLs and over 100 child protection professionals. These professionals included representatives from various CCIs, aftercare providers, program managers, social workers, practitioners, policymakers in child protection, and other state officials across the states of Delhi, Gujarat, Karnataka, Maharashtra, and Rajasthan. The study revealed the significant struggles faced by youth growing up in CCIs and then transitioning out at 18 without adequate preparation or planning. This lack of preparation negatively impacted their education and social stability and left them with insufficient skills for a smooth transition into adulthood. In addition, it appeared that more than 59% of CLs were unaware of the available aftercare provisions in the country, 44% of them were not able to pursue higher education, and about 50% of them failed to secure employment opportunities. Most of them also struggled to arrange safe, secure, and adequate living conditions. Beyond these practical challenges, many CLs experienced a profound lack of trust and emotional trauma.

To address these issues comprehensively, this study developed the "Sphere of aftercare", which outlines eight distinct, yet interdependent, domains essential for the success of CLs. These domains include independent living skills, housing, physical health, emotional well-being, social support and interpersonal skills, educational and vocational skills, financial independence, and career, identity, and legal awareness (Beyond 18, 2019) (Figure 11.1).

This study offers important recommendations for policy and practice, such as introducing an Individual Aftercare Plan (IAP); increased investment in aftercare alongside enhanced financial support to CLs; and the provision of comprehensive support through the integration of various schemes. It also suggests revising budgetary norms, expanding linkages, and empowering CLs by creating spaces and platforms where they can build peer networks and mentoring relationships, such as CL networks. Additionally, the study emphasizes the importance of capacity building and sensitizing the various

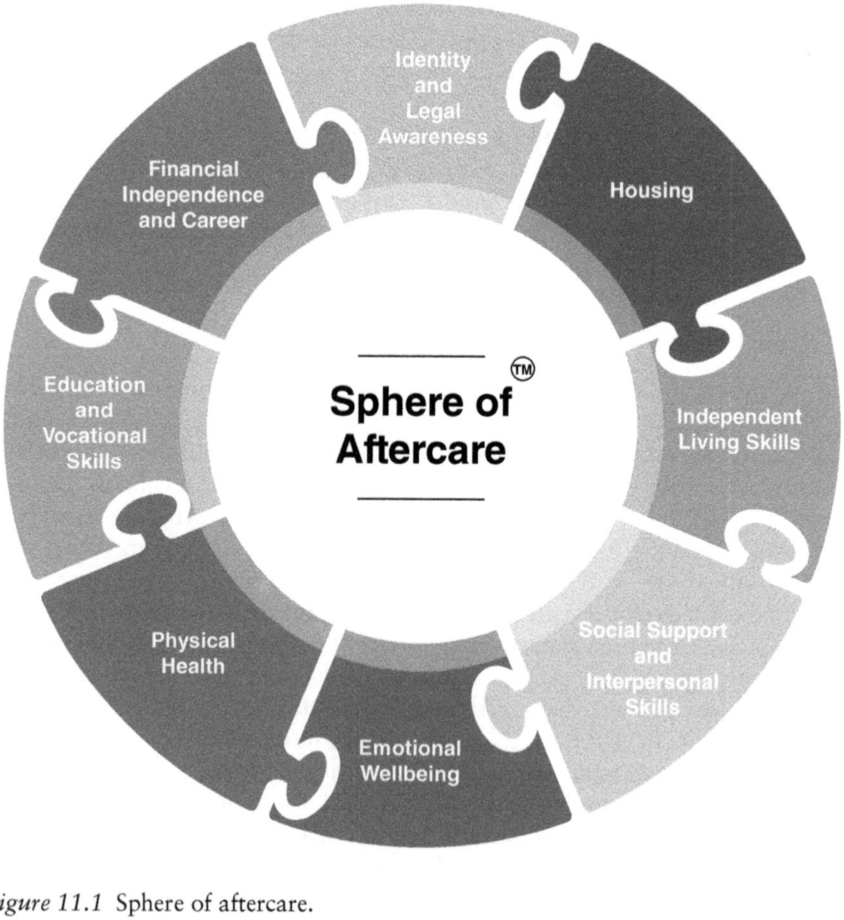

Figure 11.1 Sphere of aftercare.

stakeholders involved with children and youth without parental care. In this chapter, we focus on the social relationship domain—one of the eight key domains—and examine the challenges identified within this domain, its implications, and its interrelatedness to other domains within the sphere of aftercare.

Since the publication of the "Beyond 18" study in 2019, there has been a tremendous development in policies, schemes, and on-the-ground practices for aftercare support of CLs. Notably, the Mission Vatsalya Policy, introduced in 2022, marks the first time the term 'alternative care' has been included in an Indian government policy document. This policy addresses transition planning for children in care homes starting at the age of 16, focusing on areas such as housing, education, employable skills, industry apprenticeship, and loan support. Thereafter, the introduction of the IAP in Mission Vatsalya in 2022 represents a pivotal step forward. Financial support for CLs has also increased, with state governments in India showing greater commitment to their welfare. Many states have issued State Guidelines, and young people have begun forming formal and informal networks (Kalra & Prasad, 2022). In light of these recent developments, there is a growing recognition of the evolving trends across several domains of aftercare, particularly in relation to the "Beyond 18" study. There has also been recognition of the need to further address the changing needs and challenges brought about by the COVID-19 pandemic, especially in terms of the social relationships of CLs in India. This study, conducted at the beginning of 2023, addresses the overall well-being of CLs, examining the formal and informal support they received, the challenges they faced, and their support needs. It also deliberates on the struggles they experience during their transition to an independent life and the consequences of these struggles. In addition, the study assesses additional challenges faced by CLs against the backdrop of COVID-19 and the quality of aftercare services provided to them. By capturing the direct voices of care-experienced youths, this study offers recommendations for improving their situation and addressing policy gaps in India.

Using a mixed-method approach, this study employed a cross-sectional research design to collect data from CLs and stakeholders involved in alternative care and aftercare, including representatives of childcare institutions, social workers, practitioners, and some state child protection professionals across various states of India. This chapter especially focuses on the social relationship domain and analyses its interconnections with the other domains of the Sphere of Aftercare.

Method

Sample and Data Collection

The findings of this study are based on data collected from two groups of respondents: (a) 164 CLs who grew up in care homes across India and (b) interviews with 30 child protection professionals working in alternative care, representing both the government and private sectors. The second group included representatives from various childcare institutions, aftercare providers, social workers, practitioners, child protection experts, and state officials. All stakeholders included in the present study were seasoned professionals, with experience ranging from 5 to over 30 years in child protection and aftercare, and were drawn from across the country, including Delhi, Madhya Pradesh, Bihar, Jammu and Kashmir, Telangana, and Karnataka. The majority of these stakeholders (69%) were women, and 31% were men.

We employed a non-random purposive sampling technique, based on availability, to select professionals, while a snowball sampling technique was utilized to recruit CLs for this study. The respondents were chosen based on their willingness and availability to participate in the survey. Our outreach efforts targeted practitioners and CLs with whom we established connections through our extensive experience in child welfare. Initially, we aimed to reach 200 CLs and 50 stakeholders. After considering respondent availability and conducting data cleaning, the final sample included 164 CLs and 30 stakeholders.

The study included CLs who had exited the care system and were living independently at the time of the survey. Of the 200 CLs contacted, 164 (82%) agreed to participate. The age distribution among these respondents was as follows: 37% were between 19 and 21 years, 24% were 18 and 19 years, 23% were 21 and 23 years, and 16% were over 23 years old. More than half of the CLs (55%) were female, the majority were single (91%), 7% were married, 1% were living with a partner, and 1% were widowed.

Regarding living arrangements, 20% of CLs were living with their immediate families, having been restored to their families upon turning 18; 8% were living with their spouses or partners; 5% were with extended families, and 4% were living only with their siblings. Additionally, 31% of CLs resided in aftercare homes, 21% lived alone, 8% lived with friends, and 3% lived with other youth from childcare institutions.

In terms of financial independence, approximately one-third (32%) of CLs had their own sources of income. Among the 68% without independent income, 27% were supported by their families, 31% by aftercare homes, 9% by extended families and siblings, and 2% by scholarship. When looking at gender differences, 26% of female CLs did not have any source of income compared to 39% of male CLs. Conversely, 74% of females and 61% of males had their own source of income.

In the housing domain, 26% of CLs were restored to and living with their families, with a gender distribution of 63% males and 37% females. Another 23% were staying in aftercare homes, of which the vast majority were female (95%) and 5% were male. A total of 18% of CLs stayed in hostels, comprising 26% males and 74% females. Additionally, 12% were living independently and paid rent from their own income, with 80% of these being male and 20% female. A small percentage (2 %) was provided accommodation through their workplace, all of whom were male. Only 1% of CLs had managers purchase or build their own homes. The study also revealed that another 4% of CLs, all of whom were female, were living in shelters for the homeless.

Instruments

Self-Report Questionnaire for CLs

Following an extensive literature review and collaborative discussions with CLs and practitioners, a self-reported assessment survey questionnaire was meticulously developed for CL completion. The survey was administered online using Google Forms. A pilot study involving 15 CLs was carried out to refine and validate the content of the assessment tools. The final version was reviewed and validated by a team of researchers, analysts, statisticians, and experts in alternative care and aftercare.

A comprehensive demographic profile of the respondents was obtained, followed by an analysis of various parameters to assess the overall well-being of CLs. The content validity of the final questionnaires was rigorously evaluated to ensure the clarity, relevance, simplicity, and consistency of each question. The questionnaire addressed multiple aspects, including socio-demographic background characteristics, overall well-being, social support received and social support needs and challenges, areas of struggle during the transition to independent life, and the impact of the COVID-19 pandemic. A total of 51 questions were included in the instrument in both open-ended and closed-ended formats. The questionnaire also included a five-point Likert scale to assess the "attitude and satisfaction levels of CLs regarding their experiences in CCI and the Aftercare services they received." Key indicators covered in the questionnaire included demographic information (including, e.g., gender, educational qualification, marital status, accommodation status, and financial status) and 12 questions covering their experiences in and after being in CCIs. These questions addressed their satisfaction levels, preparation to leave care, guidance and monitoring, availability of support and resources, and legal information.

Additionally, CLs were asked about their education, vocational training, and career development during and after leaving the care system (i.e., career aspirations, support received, and current employment status), their emotional well-being status (including questions directed toward the education level at the time of leaving care home, at the time of leaving aftercare home, and their current education status; reasons for discontinuing education, if any; and sources of support if any for education; career aspirations; career guidance; motivating factors toward continuing education; and challenges faced"), and their housing status and financial stability. Three questions focused on the impact of COVID-19 on CLs' lives. The questionnaire had three questions on social support and relationships (immediate support system, association with networks, and satisfaction level), and another two questions on their suggestions for improvement required in the aftercare support system and their recommendations.

Interview Guide for Stakeholders

An interview guide was developed for stakeholders to capture their views and experiences in various settings. The interview guide addressed the following issues regarding the stakeholders' insights on their work with CLs: their awareness of the existing laws and policies on child protection in India, their understanding of the importance of rehabilitation and social integration, information about training imparted to them, their challenges and experiences of handling CLs, sharing of interventions and good practices on care leaving, and their recommendations and suggestions. The content validity of the final version of the interview guide was determined to consider the clarity, relevance, simplicity, and consistency of each question within the question set.

Data Analysis

The data was cleaned by the researchers for inaccuracies, inconsistencies, and omissions. For the analysis of data, the "Sphere of aftercare" framework was used, and the quantitative data was processed with the help of Statistical Package for Social Sciences (SPSS). Descriptive statistics, frequencies, cross-tabulations, and indexing were used to analyze the data. Thereafter, tables, charts, and graphs were created.

Results

Support Received during Stay in CCIs

The majority of respondents (80%) grew up in NGO-run CCIs, and the remaining 20% grew up in government CCIs. According to the findings of this study, 45% of the CLs shared that they had received one-on-one *mentoring and support* from an adult during their stay at the CCIs, regarding their interests, hobbies, and academic aspirations to a great extent during their stay in the CCI; 30% of the CLs had received mentoring support to some extent, followed by only 8% of the CLs receiving very little mentoring support, and 9% not receiving any kind of mentoring support. The remaining 8% of CLs responded "not sure." The data reflected the importance of mentoring support, a social support to CLs on an individual basis, as also highlighted by one of the CLs from Delhi:

> This year, I returned after completing my higher education from a reputed international university. My dream of attaining higher education from abroad could have been possible with the help of the organisation in whose care home I lived in. I am grateful to my mentor, who

> guided and supported me in making career choices, taking into consideration my choices and abilities, which helped me prepare for higher education since the beginning.

Approximately 38% of CLs shared that while they were in CCI, they had received guidance to a great extent on *how to manage finances* to lead an independent adult life. This was followed by 27% of the CLs receiving this guidance to some extent, 15% of them not receiving any guidance, and 7% of them receiving very little guidance on managing household finances to lead an independent adult life. The remaining 13% of CLs responded "not sure" to that question. This is reflected in what a stakeholder stated:

> The majority of young adults transitioning from childcare do not have access to financial means to plan for independent living, and there is a dearth of social networks or guidance to counsel/help them with progression outside childcare institutions.

Nearly half of the respondents (48%) received *emotional support and counseling services* during their stay at CCIs to a great extent, followed by 29% to some extent; 12% did not receive any kind of support, 4% received very little support, and the remaining 7% responded "not sure." The findings suggest that CLs who received emotional support and guidance during their stay at care homes were able to connect better with others, whereas a CL from Delhi who did not receive adequate support said:

> The lack of social connections for CLs can have a significant impact on their lives. This may lead to feelings of isolation, mental health challenges, limited support networks, difficulties in finding employment or stable housing, and overall hindered personal development and well-being. Social connections are vital for emotional support, opportunities, and sense of belonging, which are crucial for transitioning into independent adulthood.

With regard to *legal rights and obligations*, around 40% of the CLs received relevant information to a great extent from their CCIs, followed by 30% of them to some extent, 13% did not receive any kind of information and guidance, and another 8% received very little information, while the remaining 9% of the CLs responded as "not sure."

Regarding *preparation to leave care homes*, 38% of the CLs felt that they were prepared to some extent to leave the CCIs, followed by preparation to a great extent by 26%, little preparation by 8%, and another 15% were not at all prepared to leave the CCIs. The remaining 13% of CLs responded "not sure." The study identified gender differences in the level of preparation of CLs leaving CCIs at the age of 18 years. As stated by 15% of female CLs, they were prepared to a great extent to leave CCI, whereas 21% of them were prepared to some extent to leave CCI. While only 11% of male CLs were prepared to a great extent to move out of the CCI, another 17% were prepared to some extent.

One of the CLs from Assam stressed the importance of social support and social relations during and after the transition from care homes:

> It is believed that the foundations of human beings are based on the evolving nature of social relations, and if a CL does not have a social connection, it is unlikely to obtain any form of social support. Therefore, in the scenario of not having a social connection, a CL as an individual unit of society would remain in isolation, which is against the basic fundamentals of society. This peculiarity to a CL means to be beneficial in a short distance of life; however, in the long run, it will indeed have an adverse effect on the holistic growth of an individual.

Aftercare Support Experiences as perceived by CLs

In this study, only 57% of the CLs were aware of the provisions of aftercare, while the remaining 43% were unaware of this term and its provisions for youth without parental care exiting CCI. As stated in Figure 11.2, the study findings also indicated that 35% of the CLs did not receive aftercare support from their

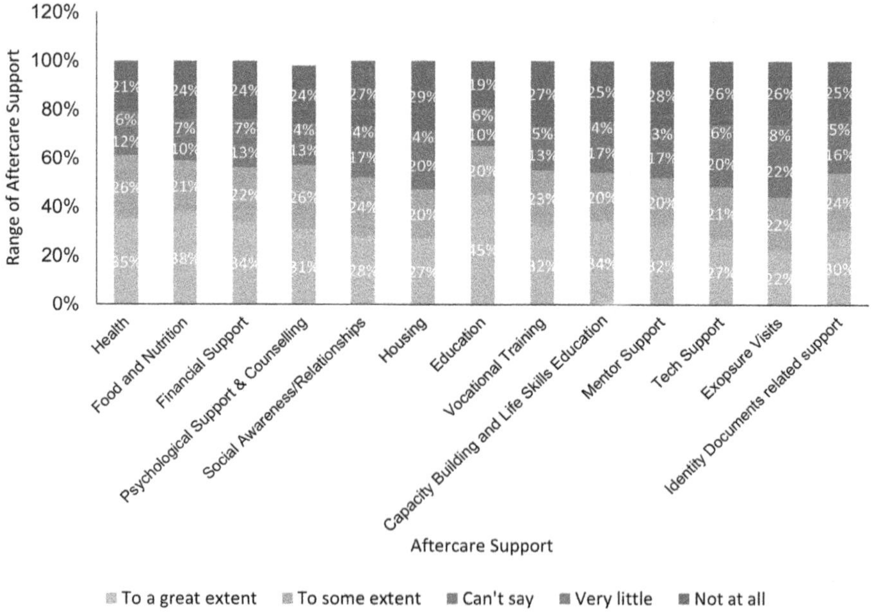

Figure 11.2 Details of aftercare support received.

CCIs, while 19% received it partially, and another 46% received aftercare support from their CCI during their transition after turning 18. The challenges at the stakeholder level were captured by a statement by one of the stakeholders:

> The staff at CCIs, especially in Govt. homes is often not oriented toward transitional preparedness and aftercare. A strict focus on the preparation of an exhaustive individual care plan is lacking; hence, holistic planning of children and their transition to independent life suffers. Furthermore, due to a lack of staff, special difficulties are observed when placing female CLs. While there has definitely been growth in learning, aftercare remains a novel concept.

All stakeholders unanimously recognized the essential role of ongoing aftercare support in facilitating the effective rehabilitation and social integration of CLs. They emphasized that such support can significantly address the challenges faced by CLs and assist caregivers in managing numerous aspects of their transition to independent living.

They shared that financial security is essential for the successful transition of CLs and independent living, along with support for other domains, especially strengthening their social network, inclusion and social protection, and the presence of platforms such as CL networks. This is captured by the stakeholder statement:

> The delicate minds of young people in care are affected by a sense of rejection, loss of love and affection, insecurity about their future, and general hatred towards life itself. Many of them fail in their endeavours when sent out for educational purposes or to pursue jobs. Most times, they unconsciously end up misbehaving with people because of their circumstances and mindset. Social networks and connections help young people understand that they are loved and valued, and that they have a place in society. It helps them understand the nuances of dealing with people both socially and productively and the value of inculcating good habits and building character while focusing on being educated and building skills.

This study addressed various indicators across which aftercare support was received by CLs. It examined 13 indicators of aftercare support, including health, food and nutrition, financial support, psychological support and counseling, social awareness/relationships, housing, education, vocational training, capacity building and life skill education, mentor support, tech support, exposure visits, and identity documents related to support. CLs reported receiving substantial support to a "great extent" in areas such as education, food and nutrition, health, financial support, capacity building, vocational training, and mentoring support, and least in areas of social awareness/relationship building, tech support, and exposure visits.

Current Emotional Well-being and Support

As per the study findings, 65% of the CL respondents shared facing different kinds of difficulties or worries that made them sad and worried and impacted their health, and further examined the *emotional issues* faced by these CLs, such as sleep disturbances, disturbances in food intake, mood dysregulation, getting tired easily, affecting day-to-day and work-related functioning, need to push themselves for all engagements, feel worthless, helpless, not interested in things that gave them pleasure, having violent thoughts of harming oneself or another, violent action based on the above thoughts, etc. (Figure 11.3).

The results highlight that a deficiency in social support has a notable effect on the emotional well-being of CLs, manifesting as feelings of loneliness and challenges related to self-esteem. This is exemplified by a statement from one CL, who expressed "I lost all connections when I exited my care home. I do not have anyone to obtain emotional support whenever I feel low or anxious. I am unable to make many friends because of trust issues". One of the stakeholders highlights the importance of having a transition plan and interpersonal relations by stating that:

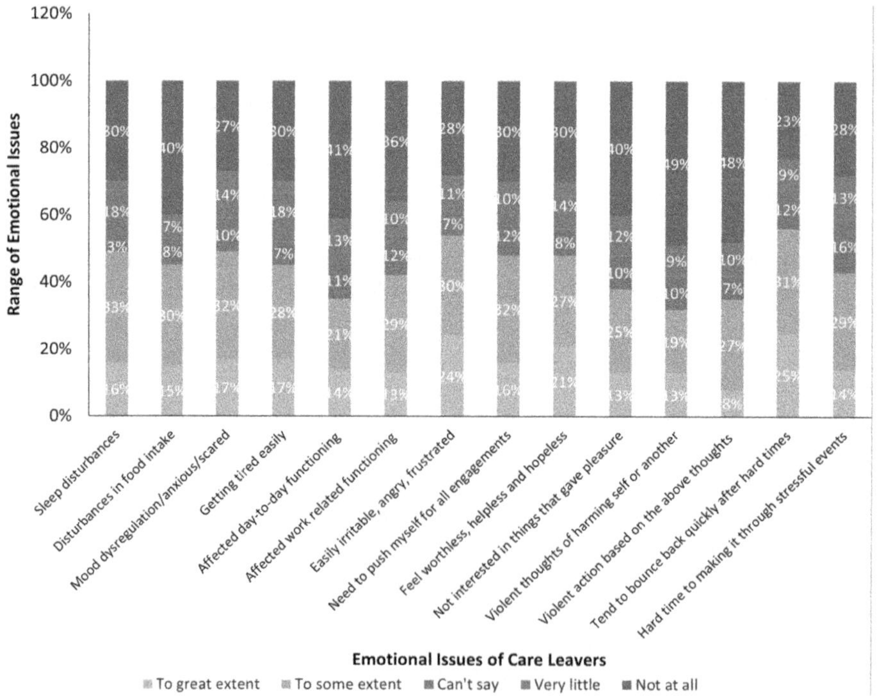

Figure 11.3 Details of emotional issues of care leavers.

> The development of a detailed individual childcare plan is necessary for a child's smooth transition into life after care. It helps explore their interest areas, highlight potential mental and emotional wellbeing related challenges, and help chart a path for their future. Celebrating symbolic days with children, among other things, and consistent life skill training on a plethora of aspects help understand the importance of interpersonal relations and foster a social connection.

Education and Career Development Support

This study examines the *educational status* of CLs at various stages. Around 40% of CLs were graduates, while only 7% could continue their education beyond graduation. Another 7% of the CLs completed diploma courses, whereas 27% of the CLs completed class XII (i.e., senior secondary education) but could not continue their education further. Around 5% of the CLs (all females) could not study beyond class V, that is, primary education, and 14% (76% male, 24% female) of the CLs had studied beyond class V but could not complete class X.

During their stay at CCIs, more than half of the CLs (55%) had opportunities to pursue and continue their education to a great extent; 29% could pursue and continue with their education while being at CCIs to some extent; 4% of them had very few opportunities, and another 6% did not get any such opportunities. The study identified differences in obtaining opportunities to pursue and continue education among male and female CLs, which stated that 32% of the female CLs had opportunities to a great extent to pursue and continue their education during their stay at CCI in comparison to 22% of the male CLs. On the other hand, 16% of males had educational opportunities to some extent compared to 13% of female CLs. The importance of social support for education is captured by a CL from Gujarat:

> I wanted to become an engineer since childhood but had no knowledge of how to pursue that path. As I was constantly shifting from one care home to another, I could not get any guidance or support because of the lack of bonding with the care home and caregivers. I could not continue my education, and still struggled with living expenses.

Most CLs (70%) continued their education as they were supported in aftercare. Additionally, 11% of CLs managed their studies by engaging in part-time jobs, while 5% were supported by their families. Another 6% had received scholarships to continue their education. However, 8% of CLs dropped out of education after moving out of the CCIs as they could not afford it. With regard to career guidance, around 40% of the CLs received it when they were at CCI, 26% received it while being at aftercare, 25%

received guidance on different career paths at individual levels (teachers, mentors, and counselors), while another 9% did not receive any such guidance.

Mentoring and caregiving, as forms of social support, play a crucial role in guiding CLs along educational and career pathways from the point of transition. This assistance aids them in acquiring the necessary skills, consequently enhancing their employment prospects. This sentiment is underscored by a statement from a CL who emphasized the following:

> I stayed in a care home set up with a family like environment, where I was provided with a mentor to guide me in all aspects of my life. He guided me in my career choice and helped me acquire skills based on my area of interest. Today, I am working with a reputed organisation in the field I always wanted to work in.

Social Support, Stigmatization, and Relationships

Social support impacts adult outcomes in pre- and post-CLs' experience of care systems as they can help develop resilience during their stay (Masten, 2004). Social care professionals help young people become resilient by building connections with caring adults. This was captured by a stakeholder, who stated:

> A social connection with CLs is extremely important in their lives, as it provides them with a solution to the problems CLs are facing. Stakeholders must try to develop such a connection, as they must act as a Go-To person when they face problems and want solutions. Such a person or group must have a meaningful and high-quality relationship with the CLs to the extent that such youth must be able to trust them. Considering their often traumatic backgrounds, CLs may often have issues of trust; hence, a sensitive approach is of utmost importance. Anyone working at a superficial or tokenistic level will eventually not be able to develop trust in such youth.

According to the respondents, the significant sources of assistance and support after leaving care homes included parents (21%), friends (21%), mentors (15%), caregivers of previous CCIs (12%), and teachers (4%). Conversely, 16% of CLs did not have any support, while the remaining 11% received assistance from other sources, such as religious organizations and communities. In this study, 69% of the CLs were aware of the existing CLs' *networks* at various state levels, whereas 31% were not aware of any of these networks. Among the CLs, who were connected to some or the other CLs networks, 55% had joined one of their state-specific networks, had contributed in some or the other way to the networks, and also felt that these networks helped them in their lives in many ways. This is well captured by a statement from a CL from Delhi: "The main challenging point was to find connections as I had no family to go to, or to celebrate any festival. Getting associated with a CL network helped me find a family like environment." These CLs' networks provide a sense of stability, belonging, support, and normalcy and serve their need for empathy, guidance, and understanding. These networks are a support system which provide them with access to available opportunities, services, information, and peer support and a safe space where they can collectivize and put forward their shared voice, advocate for their rights, build their leadership capacities, share their challenges, and discuss possible opportunities and good practices.

The findings also indicate that the personal resources of CLs significantly influence their ability to cultivate meaningful and robust relationships. Proficiency in social and communication skills enables CLs to establish strong connections with their peer groups and the broader community. A statement from a CL in Delhi vividly illustrates this point:

> Before entering the childcare institute, I lived with my family. As a child, I was introverted and felt shy when interacting with my close friends. My father's strictness limited my social interaction, leaving a lasting impact. During my childcare time, I was surrounded by a diverse group, but I struggled to connect because of my low confidence. Even at school, I hesitated to leave the classroom for lunch breaks. Despite making friends over time, my poor social skills have hindered me from forming more connections. Throughout higher education, similar challenges persisted, prompting me to recognize the importance of social skills. I've since worked on improving my communication, although further efforts are needed to foster stronger social connections and support.

Finally, the findings indicate that CLs face *stigma or discrimination* at different levels in their lives because of their care experience. As recorded, 28% of the CL experienced discrimination at the CCI itself, 27% faced discrimination at the school and college levels, 24% faced discrimination after leaving the CCI, 29% of the CLs having faced discrimination from their communities, and 15% of the CLs facing discrimination at their jobs.

Satisfaction in Social Relationships

The satisfaction levels of CLs were diverse: 42% expressed satisfaction, 18% reported being very satisfied, 32% indicated a neutral stance (neither satisfied nor dissatisfied), and the remaining 8% revealed dissatisfied (7%) or very dissatisfied (3%) with their current social relationships. A CL from Odisha shared insights into their experience: "I connected with other CLs through my care home in charge, receiving various types of support. The primary support was connecting with individuals from similar backgrounds, receiving financial assistance during difficult times, and constant motivation, crucial in every aspect."

Furthermore, a stakeholder emphasized the significance of a CL network, stating the following:

> The importance of a social group or network is crucial, especially for CLs. A CL mentioned in a recent YSS members' meeting that a network can provide a home away from home—a family of one's own. At CCI, we strive to instill the concepts of society, independent life, and interpersonal skills through support from training partners. These life skills are essential for a smooth transition from care to aftercare, although there is a need for more awareness and capacity building.

Social Relationships during COVID times

Due to pandemic-related restrictions, CLs found themselves in a challenging situation, lacking resources, and virtually devoid of social connections, leading to a range of psychological issues. These challenges included sleep disturbances, disruptions in food intake, mood dysregulation (manifesting as anxiety and fear), increased fatigue, impaired day-to-day and work-related functioning, heightened irritability, anger, frustration, and the constant need to push themselves for various engagements. The absence of access to their social circle, friends, and mentors left them feeling worthless, helpless, and hopeless. They lost interest in activities that once brought pleasure and grappled with violent thoughts of self-harm or harm to others, occasionally translating into actual violent actions. A stakeholder emphasized these challenges, noting that "the pandemic induced fear and anxiety among CLs, significantly impacting their psycho-social well-being, a consequence that persisted even in the post-pandemic period."

Conclusions

As is evident from the existing literature (e.g., Modi et al., 2020), CLs frequently express a sense of exclusion from the development of their transition plans, leading to the neglect of their unique needs. This study further substantiates the prevailing evidence underscoring the pivotal role of aftercare in the concluding phase of ongoing support for children and youth in care. This emphasizes the imperative for comprehensive support across various domains within the sphere of aftercare. Facilitating CLs in building their own networks and support systems is crucial.

This research echoes a common challenge faced by many CLs in terms of social support: a decline in their ability to form social relationships as they transition into adulthood. Stakeholders emphasized the multifaceted issues encountered by children with a history of institutional care during their transition phase. It is important to recognize the uncertainty prevalent among children in CCIs about their future, a lack of occupational skills for decent employment, anxiety about losing existing support systems provided by carers and fellow residents, and uncertainties related to reconnecting with birth or extended families due to severed bonds.

The current findings indicate that CLs face severe trust issues in forming new relationships. Moreover, many reported disrupted relationships with family members. Establishing a social support network poses a challenge for most CLs (Sulimani-Aidan, 2018b; Zinn et al., 2017). Upon becoming part of these social support networks, CLs undergo a transformative process that influences their attitudes and behaviors while also enhancing their access to various social resources (Tindall & Wellman, 2001). To foster the social construction and mainstream integration of CLs, it is crucial to discern the conditions within the relationships they uphold, both with themselves and others. This involves the implementation of supportive measures aimed at cultivating positive relationships. As underscored in this study, these conditions frequently correlate with heightened vulnerability during the transition of CLs to adulthood (Goyette et al., 2011). Any intervention related to social relationships and support should strive to establish a robust connection with CLs, maintain consistency, and evolve into a significant resource and guiding pillar for CLs and their networks.

The social support and social connection levels of care-experienced individuals can vary based on their current condition, past experiences, relationships, and duration of their stay in the facility. For instance, individuals who have been isolated for an extended period and are then relocated to a care shelter with a suitable environment may still exhibit a tendency to isolate themselves despite having good social surroundings because their minds have learned and retained their initial observations and evolved accordingly. After being restored, a person may take longer to socialize with people outside the care institute to seek social support and connections, whether for basic needs or career-related reasons.

Children who spend a long time caring for themselves tend to develop a strong sense of self-reliance. They are accustomed to taking care of themselves, from choosing their own meals to deciding what to wear and whether to study. This newfound independence can lead them to make decisions on their own, which can make them feel more confident and able to control their lives. However, it is important to remember that not all children can use their decision-making skills wisely, which can lead to negative consequences. Additionally, some children may lack social skills because of their tendency to make independent decisions without seeking advice from their elders or peers.

CLs can benefit from real-life experiences while in care, with a focus on interventions aimed at fostering friendship development (Mann-Feder, 2018). It is crucial to acknowledge the fundamental need for CLs for continuous emotional support, especially for those lacking familial resources. Ensuring that CLs have a voice in all stages of program development is imperative, and there is a significant journey ahead for aftercare reform in India. Despite the recent policy changes in 2022, a more robust push is required for effective implementation. Priority should be given to participatory approaches in evaluating the status of care and other support systems, addressing the challenges faced by children during their stay in CCIs throughout and after the transition. Moreover, the involvement of young people who leave care is central to this process.

Individuals leaving the care system require personalized support. Practitioners must engage in dialogue with CLs to ensure that there is a designated support figure in various scenarios, thereby strengthening the overall support system. This tailored approach has the potential to significantly enhance the effectiveness of care for young individuals transitioning from this system. Further research is imperative in the domain of social network interventions for CLs. Studies comparing diverse forms of intervention, such as network facilitation, involvement of natural helpers, skills training, and self-help groups, could offer valuable insights (Mann-Feder, 2018). Such research endeavors could shed light on the effectiveness of different approaches to bolstering social support for CLs. Furthermore, the outcomes of such research hold the potential to influence resource allocation, contribute to practical guidelines, and inform the decision-making processes in this field.

As expressed by CLs themselves, it is imperative to provide them with guidance and support to sustain their sense of hope, tap into their inherent capabilities, fortify their self-assurance, and foster supportive networks. This is vital to equip them with the foundational elements necessary for a secure life, as they navigate the challenges of adulthood. Emphasizing the establishment and maintenance of robust support networks is crucial in this context, as these networks can serve as indispensable pillars of assistance and encouragement for CLs during their transition into adulthood.

References

Ahmann, E. (2017). Supporting youth aging out of foster care. *Pediatric Nursing*, *43*(1), 43.

Belsey, M. A., & Sherr, L. (2011). The definition of true orphan prevalence: Trends, contexts, and implications for policies and programmes. *Vulnerable Children and Youth Studies*, *6*(3), 185–200. https://doi.org/10.1080/17450128.2011.587552

Beyond 18, Leaving Child Care Institutions –A Study of Aftercare Practices in Five States of India (2019). Udayan Care. https://www.udayancare.org/upload/Reports/2019-20/Full%20report_%20Beyond%2018.pdf

Collins, M., Spencer, R., & Ward, R. (2010). Supporting youth in the transition from foster care: Formal and informal connections. *Child Welfare*, 89, 125–143. http://www.jstor.org/stable/45400625

DGD. (2021). Committee on the Rights of the Child 2021 Day of General Discussion. *Children's Rights and Alternative Care Outcome Report*. https://www.ohchr.org/sites/default/files/2022-06/13Jun2022-DGD-Outcome-report-and-Recommendations.pdf

Goodkind, S., Schelbe, L. A., & Shook, J. J. (2011). Why youth leave care: Understandings of adulthood and transition success and challenges among youth aging out of child welfare. *Children and Youth Services Review*, *33*, 1039–1048. https://doi.org/10.1016/j.childyouth.2011.01.010

Goyette, M., Bellot, C., & Pontbriand, A. (2011). *Les transitions à la vie adulte des jeunes en difficulté: Concepts, figures et pratiques* (Vol. 51). PUQ.

Gypen, L., Vanderfaeillie, J., De Maeyer, S., Belenger, L., & Van Holen, F. (2017). Outcomes of children who grew up in foster care: Systematic-review. *Children and Youth Services Review*, *76*, 74–83. https://doi.org/10.1016/j.childyouth.2017.02.035

Hébert, S. T., Lanctôt, N., & Turcotte, M. (2016). "I didn't want to be moved there": Young women remembering their perceived sense of Agency in the Context of placement instability. *Children and Youth Services Review*, 70, 229–237.

Hiles, D., Moss, D., Wright, J., & Dallos, R. (2013). Young people's experience of social support during the process of leaving care: A review of the literature. *Children and Youth Services Review*, *35*(12), 2059–2071.

Jones, L. P. (2014). The role of social support in the transition from foster care to emerging adulthood. *Journal of Family Social Work*, *17*(1), 81–96. https://doi.org/10.1080/10522158.2013.865287

Kalra, G. K., & Prasad, L. (2022). The Evolving Care Leavers Networks in South Asia: An Overview. *Institutionalised Children Explorations and Beyond*, *9*(2), 176–187. https://doi.org/10.1177/23493003221119564

Korkiamäki, R., & Kallio, K. P. (2018). Experiencing and practising inclusion through friendships. *Area*, *50*(1), 74–82. https://doi.org/10.1111/area.12352

Mann-Feder, V. R. (2018). (You gotta have) friends: Care leaving, friendships, and agency intervention. *International Journal of Child, Youth and Family Studies*, *9*(1), 154–167. https://doi.org/10.18357/ijcyfs91201818125

Masten, A. S. (2004). Regulatory processes, risk, and resilience in adolescent development. *Annals of the New York Academy of Sciences*, *1021*(1), 310–319.

Melkman, E. P. (2017). Childhood adversity, social support networks and well-being among youth aging out of care: An exploratory study of mediation. *Child Abuse & Neglect*, 72, 85–97. https://doi.org/10.1016/j.chiabu.2017.07.020

Melkman, E. P., & Benbenishty, R. (2018). Social support networks of care leavers: Mediating between childhood adversity and adult functioning. *Children and Youth Services Review*, *86*, 176–187. https://doi.org/10.1016/j.childyouth.2018.01.040

Ministry of Statistics and Programme Implementation, Government of India. (2018). *Youth in India 2017*.

Ministry of Youth Affairs and Sports, Government of India. (2021). *Draft National Youth Policy 2021*.

Modi, K., Sachdev, H., & Prasad, L. (2016). Udayan Care's (Sunshine Homes) after care program: Successful transitions from children's home to independence. *CYC-Online December*, *214*, 17–28. https://cyc-net.org/CYC-Online/dec2016.pdf#page=18

Modi, K., Wadhwa, A., & Prasad, L. (2020). The development of leaving care law, policy, and practice in India. *Child & Family Social Work*, *26*, 231–239. https://doi.org/10.1111/cfs.12817

MWCD. (2018). Ministry of Women and Child Development Government of India. Government of India: Annual Report.

Nnama-Okechukwu, C. U., Anazonwu, N. P., & Okoye, U. O. (2018). Vulnerable children, alternative care system and placement decision in Nigeria: In who's best interest?. *African Population Studies*, *32*(2), 4215–4227. https://aps.journals.ac.za/pub/article/view/1194

Rahamim, A., & Mendes, P. (2016). Mental health supports and young people transitioning from out-of-home care in Victoria. *Children Australia*, *41*(1), 59–68. https://doi.org/10.1017/cha.2015.35

Rutman, D., & Hubberstey, C. (2016). Is anybody there? Informal supports accessed and sought by youth from foster care. *Children and Youth Services Review*, *63*, 21–27. https://doi.org/10.1016/j.childyouth.2016.02.007

Sulimani-Aidan, Y. (2018a). Assets and pathways in achieving future goals of residential care alumni. *Children and Youth Services Review*, *89*, 71–76. https://doi.org/10.1016/j.childyouth.2018.04.023

Sulimani-Aidan, Y. (2018b). Qualitative exploration of supporting figures in the lives of emerging adults who left care compared with their noncare-leaving peers. *Child & Family Social Work*, *24*(2), 247–255. https://doi.org/10.1111/cfs.12609

Sulimani-Aidan, Y., Sivan, Y., & Davidson-Arad, B. (2017). Comparison of hope and the child-parent relationship of at-risk adolescents at home and in residential care. *Children and Youth Services Review*, *76*, 125–132. https://doi.org/10.1016/j.childyouth.2017.03.005

The Constitution of India. 1950, Art. 39(f). https://cdnbbsr.s3waas.gov.in/s380537a945c7aaa788ccfcdf1b99b5d8f/uploads/2024/07/20240716890312078.pdf

The Juvenile Justice (Care and Protection) of Children Act. (2015). Government of India. https://cara.nic.in/PDF/JJ%20act%202015.pdf

The National Youth Policy 2021. (2022). Ministry of Youth Affairs and Sports. https://static.pib.gov.in/WriteReadData/specificdocs/documents/2022/may/doc20225553401.pdf

The United Nations Convention on the Rights of Child (UNCRC). (1992). https://www.unicef.org/child-rights-convention

Tindall, D., & Wellman, B.. 2001. "Canada as social structure: Social network analysis and Canadian sociology." *The Canadian Journal of Sociology/Cahiers Canadiens De Sociologie*, 26 (3): 265–308. https://doi.org10.2307/3341889

United Nations Committee on the Rights of the Child. (2021). *General Comment No. 25 on children's rights in relation to the digital environment*. United Nations.

United Nations General Assembly. (2018–2019). *Resolutions adopted by the General Assembly at its 73rd session*. United Nations. Retrieved from https://research.un.org/en/docs/ga/quick/regular/73

United Nations General Assembly. (2019). *Report of the Third Committee on Social Development* (A/74/395). United Nations. Retrieved from https://bettercarenetwork.org/sites/default/files/2019-12/Third%20Committee%20Report%20on%20Social%20Development%202019.pdf

World Bank Group and World Health Organization. (2021). Children: The Hidden Pandemic. https://documents1.worldbank.org/curated/en/588071626413800295/pdf/Children-The-Hidden-Pandemic-2022.pdf

Zinn, A., Palmer, A. N., & Nam, E. (2017). The predictors of perceived social support among former foster youth. *Child Abuse & Neglect*, *72*, 172–183. https://doi.org/10.1016/j.chiabu.2017.07.015

Zorn, C. (2017). *Protected*. Sourcebooks, Inc.

Part 4

Young People in and after Residential Care Through an Intersectional Lens

12 LGBTQIA+ Young People Leaving Care

Exploring Social Challenges and Social Support in Three Countries

Mónica López López, Mijntje ten Brummelaar, Gerald P. Mallon and June C. Paul

Introduction

LGBTQIA+ young people who transition from residential foster care systems to adulthood face all of the same issues as other young people who are exiting care including, for example, disruptive events, missing opportunities to build strong support networks, and lack of emotional and financial support. However, some of their challenges are unique to their sexual orientation and/or gender identity/expression. The reality of these challenges is markedly improved when there are opportunities to develop relationships with friends and mentors, particularly those who self-identify as LGBTQIA+ individuals. Additionally, there are challenges that these young people face in developing relationships with child welfare and other professionals who may not have adequate knowledge about their lived experiences as LGBTQIA+ young people who spend time in residential foster care systems.

Grounded in a review of the literature and using data from three studies conducted in the Netherlands, Spain, and the United States, this chapter examines the experiences of LGBTQIA+ young people leaving care by exploring the challenges and sources of social support in their process of transition to independent living. Pseudonyms are used throughout the manuscript to protect the confidentiality of the young people interviewed for all three studies. In the final section of this chapter, we discuss the policy and practice implications for the development of safer and more inclusive care settings, as well as leaving care services better tailored to the particular needs of this group in care.

The Current Study

This chapter is based on data from three studies that examined the experiences of LGBTQIA+ young people in child welfare systems. The study conducted in the Netherlands, the Audre project (López López et al., 2021), explored the experiences of LGBTQIA+ young people and young adults who lived in residential and (professional) foster care in the Netherlands, as well as

DOI: 10.4324/9781003424468-17

the practitioners' perspectives on caring after LGBTQIA+ young people in care. In total, 13 LGBTQIA+ young people (aged 15–28 years), and 29 practitioners participated in the project through in-depth semi-structured interviews.

The study carried out in Spain (in the region of Cantabria), also known as the FIRMUS project (López López et al., 2023a; López López et al., 2024) employed a mixed-methods approach (surveys, interviews, and focus groups) to investigate the experiences and needs of LGBTQIA+ young people living in children's homes, as well as to explore the knowledge, attitudes, and experiences of the professionals working with this group. In total, 15 LGBTQIA+ young people were interviewed and 11 participated in the focus groups (ages 14–21). Moreover, 92 professionals completed the survey and 21 attended the focus groups.

The study conducted in the United States (Paul, 2020) used qualitative interviewing and eco-mapping techniques to explore the experiences and perspectives of 21 LGBTQ (lesbian, gay, bisexual, transgender, and queer/questioning) foster young people, ages 17–21, to identify the social support sources, needs, and challenges they may be experiencing during their transition to adulthood.

Despite important differences in the cultural context, the legal framework, and social welfare distinctions, these three international studies have identified a common set of challenges and opportunities that are discussed in the following section. While the authors wish to be clear that these studies were not multisite in nature but rather three different studies with different measurement and sampling contexts, the core themes that are explored and the methodological approaches (in-depth qualitative interviews) are similar and as such a comparison of these themes are facilitated in the discussion herein. Although the Audre project and the FIRMUS project also include the perspectives of professionals, in this chapter we focus exclusively on the experiences of young people. All quotes used in this chapter are from young people.

Literature Review and Findings: Challenges and Sources of Social Support LGBTQIA+ Young People's Transition to Adulthood from Care

Experiences of Discrimination and Violence in Different Contexts

International research shows that LGBTQIA+ people experience a higher risk of victimization throughout life than cisgender and heterosexual people, including experiences of verbal and physical harassment and sexual abuse (Goldbach & Gibbs, 2017). LGBTQIA+ young people are exposed to these situations in different contexts: their homes, schools, and communities (Meyer, 2003; Testa et al., 2015), as well as the child protection services

(Gallegos et al., 2011; Mallon et al., 2022; Mallon et al., 2022). For example, as revealed in the study by Mallon et al. (2022), LGBTQIA+ young people in the foster care system not only grappled with challenges during their time in care but also faced substantial risks of victimization during their transition to emerging adulthood. This included experiences of verbal and physical harassment, along with instances of sexual abuse. These experiences of victimization, discrimination, and harassment in everyday life may impact a young person's mental health long after they have left care.

Such evidence is in line with the accounts shared by the young people interviewed in the three countries of LGBT-phobia, discrimination, and hate crimes suffered in public spaces: disapproving looks, whistles, inappropriate comments or insults, threats, as well as experiences of physical and/or sexual assault on the street (López López et al., 2021, 2023a, 2023b; Paul, 2020). Moreover, these experiences are intensified for trans and non-binary young people. For instance, this particular group of young people often experience harassment related to the use of public spaces (e.g., restrooms, transportation, schools, and parks) which has been associated with increased risk of depression, suicidal ideation, and suicide attempts (Price-Feeney et al., 2021).

> I did have one occasion, of course, when I was addressed at the toilet, "I don't think you belong here"... before I was in transition, I experienced that both at the men's toilet and the women's toilet... So that drove me absolutely mad....
>
> (Audre, 2021)

> We were holding hands and they asked us if we could stop and kiss in front of them. They began to masturbate on the same street and we had to go to a bar in case something happened to us
>
> (FIRMUS, 2023)

> I don't get on the bus. I mean, if I have to I will but...you know, I'm transgender and just don't want nobody else to come at me wrong...I been shot at a couple of times before. (transgender, straight, age 18, transitional living program) (Paul, 2020)

The three studies provide abundant evidence of the discrimination experiences of LGBTQIA+ children in educational settings. A large majority of the people interviewed have described situations of bullying that they experienced in the first person or have witnessed. The perpetrators in these accounts are generally other students, but sometimes also teaching staff and other members of the school community. Faced with these situations, they denounce the lack of intervention by teachers, as well as the lack of support from some care workers to deal effectively with bullying suffered at school.

> I've been bullied a lot, really, in high school for a stupid reason because I had a purple case from [company] for my phone. But I thought it was a nice case. I thought it was handy. Somehow, they started calling me gay...
>
> (Audre)

> Interviewer: How did the care workers respond? [after describing a situation of bullying at school]. Young woman: They said that I must have done something
>
> (FIRMUS)

> I dropped out of high school because I was molested. I got molested at high school in the locker room.
>
> (Paul, 2020)

After leaving care, LGBTQIA+ young people in our studies report having suffered harassment and discrimination in the workplace due to their sexual orientation and/or gender identity/expression. These situations can result in self-protective responses from young people that may be considered problematic at work, such as resistance and fighting back, as well as dismissal or resignation from the job and reduced opportunities to advance in their professional careers, all of which have been linked in previous studies to the appearance of mental health problems (Badgett, 2020).

> At a job I was harassed by a boy. I told him that I had a partner. I didn't say I liked girls. And, well, there was a problem and I had to leave the job (...). The last day he tried to kiss me. So I said: I won't return there anymore. And the next day I told my boss. Well, I told her and she replied: I don't believe it (...)."
>
> (FIRMUS)

> When I was working for McDonald's, somebody told me they didn't want the food because I made it because I dress like a boy and I'm a girl...so I threw it at them.
>
> (Paul, 2018)

The young people interviewed across the three countries have shared their concern for the increase of LGBT-phobia in their societies. For instance, young people at project FIRMUS recalled different cases of attacks against LGBTQIA+ people in Spain and described the impact of witnessing this violence as one of the worst things that could happen to them due to the insecurity and mistrust that generates. Young people in the US study experienced similar concerns. One young person, for example, talked about having ongoing fears related to their identity being disclosed to others. In this regard, it is important to consider that the awareness of these acts of violence can produce fear in LGBTQIA+ young people, concern for their personal safety and that of their community, anxiety, and severe stress responses (Parra et al., 2022).

> Well, it's the worst thing that can happen to you (…) Being unsafe because of comments and looks, if they're going to do something to you… It's like everything starts to scare you, because you don't know what to trust or who, not even in what moment something can happen to you, or anything. And this is when you start to question yourself and to feel unsafe about everything.
>
> (FIRMUS)

> Basically, I'm trans, I don't want to go through anything in life as far as being killed or practically [being] shot…because of what happened last year, I think it was Orlando…Sometimes I don't tell because I don't feel like it's a need to know basis for everyone because you can never know the outcome of what is going to happen.
>
> (Paul, 2018)

Unmet Needs and Discrimination in Care Settings

Various studies show that LGBTQIA+ young people are overrepresented in the child welfare systems and that their needs are not always adequately addressed in these settings (Baams et al., 2019; Cossar et al., 2017; De Groot et al., 2018; Fish et al., 2019; McCormick et al., 2017). Oftentimes, LGBTQIA+ young people face a lack of understanding, indifference, or even hostility from care workers and other young people in care with regard to the needs related to their sexual orientation and/or gender identity/expression (Paul, 2018; Rosenwald, 2009; Wilson et al., 2014). Transgender young people in care settings have needs that are unique to their gender identity/expression and are in many cases, not at all addressed by the care system or are completely medicalized with a focus on medical transition and not at all focused on social transition factors that are so crucial to trans young people's development (Mallon, 2021). When the needs of LGBTQIA+ young people are not adequately addressed during their time in care and they receive little or no validation of who they are from care professionals and peers, this may force them to leave such a care setting earlier than intended or unprepared for the next steps in life. Lack of knowledge of professionals can even reduce the access to LGBTQIA+ informed and affirming resources and services both pre- and post transition.

The young people interviewed in the three studies in focus refer to very different experiences regarding the acceptance and affirmation of their LGBTQIA+ identity in their care settings. For instance, some young people in Spain, the Netherlands, and the United States highlighted the atmosphere of tolerance and acceptance in their residential homes (Paul, 2020: "She basically said, 'You can tell me anything, I won't judge you. I'm here for you'"), the freedom to talk about their identities (Audre: "She was like 'okay, we have to change your name in the system right now to a woman and to [own name]'"), and the good preparation of the staff (FIRMUS: "In this home they are informed and they help you and ask you questions").

However, throughout the three studies, we have collected many accounts showing the normalization of negative stereotypes and the use of offensive words about the LGBTQIA+ community in care settings. Some young people describe specific instances of persistent name-calling and bullying by other teens in their homes.

> Because here [institution] is not such a good living environment for transgender people and so. Because I get a lot, at least here I was bullied a lot and... discriminated against. And that still happens. And on Monday I had my lowest point, I really did not want to continue. I didn't want to be here anymore.
>
> (Audre, 2021)

> But there were some roommates at my house who didn't like me that much. Well, I don't know, maybe they thought that since I said I liked girls, I would like all the girls, and I would like more the ones who slept with me [in my room]. (...) Well, they would still tell me that I only knew about scissoring. Uneducated people who don't know anything. And things like that.
>
> (FIRMUS, 2023)

> The whole house, the sons, everything, treated me like shit, like I was nothing, like was scum. It was about the way I chose to live my life...I am pansexual and bigender.
>
> (Paul, 2020)

In addition to suffering rejection and violence from other young people in their care settings, the young people interviewed also had to face inappropriate responses from their foster carers or professionals working in their homes. In this sense, young people informed us about the lack of listening and understanding by adults in their lives, the refusal of some care workers to use the appropriate pronouns, the influence of their staff's religious beliefs in the performance of their care work, and the imposition of gender roles in the care settings.

> I was not allowed to talk about being a girl, I was not allowed to dress like that, and otherwise I would have to go back to my parents, where I was abused. [...] I didn't really have a choice, did I? The one was bad, the other even worse [silence]. So I agreed.
>
> (Audre, 2021)

> In some cases, the educators simply do not understand it, or do not want to understand it. They just don't listen. They have an idea and they don't listen to what you tell them. So, there is no point in telling them anything, because they are not listening to you anymore.
>
> (FIRMUS, 2023)

> [The] first time I told her I kissed a girl...she started talking to me about how I need to listen more in church and it's a sin.
>
> (Paul, under review)

One of the most consistent messages shared by the young people throughout the three studies is the need to better educate and train care professionals on LGBTQIA+ issues. The young people interviewed considered that even when the attitudes of the professionals towards the LGBTQIA+ community are positive, there is a lack of understanding of their experiences in the care homes. At the same time, they complain that the responsibility of educating their care workers and other people in the home about their LGBTQIA+ identities often falls on themselves. One US young people put it like this "I just wanted someone I didn't have to train, someone to just help me, you know?" (Paul, 2020).

Unstable and Challenging Living Circumstances in Care and After Leaving Care

LGBTQIA+ young people who are preparing for the transition to adulthood and leaving the care system face many unstable and challenging living circumstances. They often experience multiple placement challenges, such as experiencing more breakdowns and placement changes (Baams et al., 2019; De Groot et al., 2018; Wilson et al., 2014). Although research finds that young people tend to fare better in family foster care settings, LGBTQIA+ young people are more likely to be placed in group or residential homes (Wilson & Kastanis, 2015). These experiences have grave consequences for LGBTQIA+ young people, as they are less likely to achieve placement permanency while in care, which in turn increases the likelihood that they may experience homelessness upon exiting the system. For instance, it is estimated that homelessness among LGBTQIA+ young people in the United States may be as high as 20–40% (Morton et al., 2018; Page, 2017). Studies with LGBTQIA+ young people that have experienced homelessness, often point directly back at a lack of affirmative care practices and insufficient guidance during transitioning from care (de Groot et al., 2018).

This was also the case for many of the young people in our three studies who faced multiple placement breakdowns, resulting in changing primary carers and network "turnovers". Next to these rapidly changing environments, some of the young people also experienced homelessness at some point in their lives (Paul: "I am always on the run...We are all homeless...and we are all LGBTQ..."). Other young people told us how they struggled during this transitioning period, experiencing unstable housing and getting by with little support and financial resources.

> I was able to receive social assistance for a while, I lived on that for a while. And at some point it stopped. I started doing more prostitution ... ehm [silence] yes. But that wasn't easy either. You pay your window rent, sometimes your boyfriend wants something too, you still have to pay normal rent, food and drink...
>
> (Audre, 2021)

> Housing-wise, that's still a challenge, still trying to figure out where I'm gonna go.
>
> (Paul, 2020)

Oftentimes young people do not feel well-prepared or equipped for the next phase of independence. Although one of the primary goals of young people preparing to leave care is to get them ready for this milestone, young people acknowledged that there was a level of stress that professionals or the system puts on them, pressuring them to get ready for leaving care. Many young people experienced this transitioning phase to come "rather sudden", and they would have preferred to receive more support and guidance during this period. During this transitioning phase, some of the young people made use of care services (e.g., independent or assisted living arrangements), while others were supported by their foster carers, extended and nuclear families, or friends. A couple of young people did not find supportive support structures a common phenomenon for young people exiting care and had to rely strongly on themselves to navigate this phase of transition.

> Back then, at the guest house, ehmm [...] I had to do everything myself, so they didn't really help me a lot.
>
> (Audre, 2021)

> Anxiety from the care workers, because they pressure you to... because we really have to become independent at a very young age. So, it's like you have to look for work, yes or yes. You have to work, work, work, make 'your mattress' and go. I appreciate that they are on top of us, because some people, myself included, need them to be on top of things. But in the end it is exhausting.
>
> (FIRMUS, 2023)

> I feel like me being in the system and people telling me how to live my life. I never do anything myself...but now I gotta do it on my own cuz nobody gonna be telling me.
>
> (Paul, 2018)

Health and Mental Health Issues

The minority stress approach contributes to the understanding of the impact of the adverse experiences described by LGBTQIA+ people. Minority stress models maintain that stigma and prejudice toward persons belonging to a sexual or gender minority create a social environment that predisposes them to experience stress (Testa et al., 2015). This stress can come from both interpersonal and institutional factors. Interpersonal stressors include, among others, the use of insults, discrimination, or attacks based on sexual orientation and/or gender identity/expression. On the other hand, institutional stressors refer to discriminatory laws and policies or the normalization of hostile discourses for LGBTQIA+ people. Besides these stressors, LGBTQIA+ children in care have often suffered experiences of rejection by their own families (McGeough & Sterzing, 2018). Exposure to these situations can trigger various mental health difficulties in this group, including anxiety and depressive symptoms, post-traumatic stress disorder (Balsam et al., 2010; Beckerman & Auerbach, 2014), suicidal ideation and behaviors (Fulginiti et al., 2020; Paul & Monahan, 2019), and substance use disorders (Goldbach et al., 2014). These mental health issues resulting from these stressors can affect young people during their time in care and follow them into adulthood when young people are not adequately supported.

Consistent with previous research on this population, throughout the three projects we found numerous explicit references to young people's mental health and health issues (such as chronic pain, eating disorders, anxiety, loneliness, depression, and suicide attempts or ideations), as well as the presence of unhealthy habits (such as tobacco use, substance abuse, or lack of physical exercise).

> I just didn't want to pay any attention to it, and in the end I got into a depression. So to speak, I am still in this. [...] Sometimes, I just really have days when I think I don't want to get out of bed. And so on. That I really don't feel well. My school results, of course, also deteriorated because of that.
>
> (Audre, 2023)

> Basically it started with stigmatization...That's why I tend to sit in my house and eat and sleep my life away because if I take a walk then my brain is gonna be going crazy...
>
> (Paul)

> I had a drinking addiction, like I started at 16. I had a friend who would buy me drinks and we would drink together because he was a depressed person and I was depressed and supported each other's habits.
>
> (Paul, 2018)

Some young people have reflected on the intensification of their mental health symptoms during the preparation process for the transition to independent living. Furthermore, many of the young people in the studies expressed the lack of access to adequate resources and physical and mental health care services both during care and in the transition process. When young people did receive services during their time in care, they were afraid to lose these services when transitioning from care.

> Right now I am managing quite badly. I am in a time in which I have a lot of stress, I have many things to do in front of me. The self-concept I have, the self-image I have, varies a lot. Sometimes it is very 'low'. Being alone doesn't help me much either. Having goals that I don't meet doesn't help me either. So, there is a set of conflicts that I just know I can't manage.
>
> (FIRMUS, 2023)

> I just wish I had resources such as phone numbers, for like trauma or cutting or anything like that.
>
> (Paul, 2020)

> I didn't even know they had LGBT services and I was like this whole time nobody help me! I didn't know about pills and stuff because I would have been doing that, but it's just like nobody ever told me.
>
> (Paul, 2020)

Social Support during the Transition to Adulthood

Social support is a relevant protective factor for young people in care and exiting from care, since it can contribute to overcoming early adversity (Martín & Dávila, 2008). However, it is well known that young people coming into care often suffer disruptions in their social support relationships, as well as estrangement from significant others (Hiles et al., 2013). The lack of acceptance of their sexual orientation and/or gender identity/expression in care contexts can further increase the feelings of isolation and loneliness.

Social support on the other hand can provide young people unique tools to deal with these feelings of isolation and experiences of discrimination. The relationships built with others, friends, family of origin and chosen family, mentors, and former carers can ease the transition and provide necessary social support for young people during times of stress or times of happiness (Courtney et al., 2011; Mallon et al., 2022; Mountz & Capous-Desyllas, 2020). A number of studies have highlighted the importance of care workers for the development of a positive LGBTQIA+ identity for young people growing up in care (Gallegos et al., 2011; Mallon et al., 2002; Robinson, 2018). Moreover, care workers can help young people mitigate their experiences of vulnerability, stigmatization, and rejection in relation to their sexual orientation (Ragg et al., 2006), as well as provide affirmation of their sexual orientation and/or gender identity/expression (Paul, 2020). These caring relationships provide LGBTQIA+ young people with emotional, instrumental, and informational support which can strengthen their resilience resources in, during, and after their transition from care (Samuels & Pryce, 2008).

The evidence collected in our three studies suggest that this group may not have access to the same sources of social support as their cisgender or heterosexual peers (FIRMUS: "I have not had as many people as in a normal life. I've always been alone"). In this vein, a recurring theme in the three studies when analyzing the social networks of LGBTQIA+ young people is the deterioration in their relationships after coming out of the closet. Some young people interviewed have felt abandoned by their friends after coming out to them and sometimes they have made the hard decision to distance themselves from their friends to avoid exposure to LGBTI-phobic comments. Overall, many young people interviewed in the three countries have recognized the difficulties they have had in finding a safe and inclusive circle of friends.

> There were negative ones. But to those people who were negative, I discarded them from my life. Because they didn't do me any good and that's it.
>
> (FIRMUS, 2023)

> Some of my friends they know I go by male pronouns, that I am trans, but they are like 'oh, I have known you for so long, it feels weird to call you that, I'm still going to call you by your regular name', and I'm like 'no, I'm telling you, this is what I go by' and you are like 'no', you know? And it's frustrating cuz these are my friends, and you are supposed to kind of go with it, cuz if you wanted me to call you something I would, but not everyone is the same or understanding about that...some of them at least call me nicknames...but it's still like... hard.
>
> (Paul, 2018)

Young people interviewed in the three countries recognize the importance of maintaining a group of LGBTQIA+ friends. These friends provide a sense of safety and security within the group, as well as unconditional acceptance of who they are. Moreover, these friends can act as models when navigating their identities, offering strategies to face the experiences of LGBT-phobia in their lives.

> Yes and I have a very good relationship with my brother, so that is very nice. It's not officially my official brother [...] Then I got severely ill and he did not let me go home, and then he also came to the hospital. So that was quite a difficult time, but he really dragged me through it. And since then we call each other brothers.
>
> (Audre, 2021)

> I feel support because in this society it is very difficult, with these issues it is very difficult. There are always impertinent people and people who will never understand it, but because they don't want to understand it. So, having people next to you, who are also in the same collective, is quite comforting.
>
> (FIRMUS, 2023)

> One of my friends...she knew I was going through hard times with my adopted family...so she used to let me spend the night over at her house...I could always run there when I was a kid, I would always go there. It's a place to eat or lay at. [She] lived literally next door to me, down the street kind of and when they were being abusive or talking mean to me, I would sneak out and go to her house and spend the night there. After school I would go straight there too.
>
> (Paul, 2018)

Our studies demonstrate that LGBTQIA+ young people need contact with their community in a different way than their peers; they need communities and chosen families that support them and help them navigate the stresses inherent in micro-aggressions and LGBT-phobic violence in their daily lives: "This family I created and that is my best interest that's gonna help me get better personally because it's not easy to find people who accept me for who I am, it's very hard". In addition to the benefits of having friends within the community, the people interviewed have reflected on other forms of social support at the community level related to the possibility of accessing information about their identities, the establishment of support networks, and community resistance against LGBT-phobia (Paul: "I always wanted to help me about my gender and sexuality, somebody to help me find friends that were similar to me, stuff like that").

Another source of social support for some interviewees in the three countries seems to be their participation in activism and social justice movements. This development of ties and participation in the LGBT community has been shown to have clear benefits for the mental health of LGTBIQ+ people of different ages (Kosciw et al., 2015).

> Very nice people, everyone has a story, everyone has an experience, and ehh, it is just nice to exchange everything, to see people who have also experienced the same thing, almost the same things that you can relate to. So, that is very pleasant.
>
> (Audre, 2021)

> You will always have support. There are groups, there are collective associations and wherever you go now, there will always be an LGBT person who will understand you, who will support you. It is like unconditional support that we have (…). It is true that we have quite a feeling of sisterhood, because when they attack one it is as if they were attacking us all. Because we have all experienced the same thing, and we help each other a lot, and defend each other.
>
> (FIRMUS, 2023)

The positive benefits of the relationships with care workers seem evident in the three studies. Young people interviewed are able to identify at least one person in their homes or support networks with whom they have managed to develop a special connection. When talking about the characteristics that make that person special, they repeatedly mention generosity with their time, active listening without judging, unconditional support, or honesty when talking to them about important issues.

> […] from my psychotherapist, I received another show ['serie']. With a movie at the end. He said, and then you have all sorts of characters and people, and situations. Go watch that and see what you think of it. When I was really dealing with that. Therefore, I really had a lot of support from him.
>
> (Audre, 2021)

> They give you a certain margin until you are 21 to be able to develop, to save money; especially, to develop autonomy and independence. So, the care workers make it easy for you. And the work of the case workers is also very important. Everyone's support is needed.
>
> (FIRMUS, 2023)

> We have had nice conversations about romance and she was there to help me out and maneuver being gay. She always just understood, and she let me talk…when I said there was an issue in a foster home, she would check it out and make sure everything was ok. They tried. That goes a long way.
>
> (Paul & Cruys, 2024)

Conclusions and Implications for Policy, Practice, and Future Research

In all three studies (Audre, 2021; FIRMUS, 2023; Paul, 2020) young people experienced multiple forms of oppression in different contexts, such as in schools, in their workplaces, and in public spaces. Furthermore, young people often faced unmet needs in care settings and were confronted with unstable living conditions both in and after their time in care. In nearly all stories, the importance of social support was evident.

These three studies point toward several considerations that may be helpful for working with LGBTQIA+ young people transitioning from care to adulthood. Given the nature of these studies, as well as the paucity of available research in this area, findings are discussed as potential implications to practice, policy, and research.

These studies reiterate evidence indicating that young people in this population are exposed to added risk during this critical time in their lives, and as such, are likely to have a variety of unique needs that may go unmet by 'practice as usual' approaches, especially around issues of safety. Thus, professionals working with this population should be vigilant about LGBTQIA+ young people's pervasive exposure to risks, take the proper steps to protect them from harm, and intervene when they are experiencing discrimination, mistreatment, and/or violence in any context. For example, child welfare professionals could significantly reduce risks of harm by being conscientious about placing young people with safe and supportive caregivers and in residential living placements that are located in safe neighborhoods and communities with staff trained to care for them (López López et al., 2022). In the same vein, findings suggest that professionals may better facilitate healthy developmental functioning among LGBTQIA+ transitioning young people by developing specific skills best obtained by ongoing training and written policies for assisting them.

Albeit preliminary, these studies provide further evidence that supports the implementation of policies that prevent discrimination and promote safe and appropriate care and services for LGBTQIA+ young people in child welfare. Studies investigating administrative strategies that support and protect LGBTQIA+ individuals indicate that at the most basic level, governments and social service agencies should develop written policies that prohibit harassment and victimization based on sexual orientation and gender identity/expression (Mallon, 2019; McCormick et al., 2017). It is also fundamental that services provide structures both during and after transitioning from care to support young people to help them process these negative experiences and protect them from further harm.

Findings from these studies may also have implications for social services agencies and professionals in terms of examining how they care for the LGBTQIA+ young people in their care. Although most young people in these studies were receiving some measure of transitional support provisions, only some had received a form of LGBTQIA+ specific support, and most indicated that they had several unmet needs associated with their sexual and/or gender expression status and mental health. Therefore, child welfare systems should consider delivering a more comprehensive range of resources and services to this group transitioning out of care, particularly in the area of support that is more LGBTQIA+ specific.

Findings may also underscore the importance of ensuring that supports provided to young people in transition are universally safe and affirming of LGBTQIA+ individuals. Child welfare agencies should ensure that employees at all levels within the organization receive guidance and become competent at interacting with LGBTQIA+ young people in order to create positive environments and provide them with access to as many supportive adults as possible. Additionally, once such support systems are in place, it might be beneficial to provide child welfare staff and other service providers with opportunities to receive hands-on guidance (i.e., clinical case consultation) to help problem-solve and implement what they have learned in their practice.

Further research is needed to extend the results of these studies internationally and develop a more robust understanding of the experiences of LGBTQIA+ young people in residential care and family foster care and other distinct subgroups transitioning from care. Specifically, more research is needed to examine issues related to intersectionality and disproportionality among dimensions of race, class, sexual orientation, and gender identity for LGBTQIA+ transitioning young people (López López et al., 2023a, 2023b), as well as studies focused on resilience (González-Álvarez et al., 2021, 2022, 2023; López López et al., 2024). Future research in this area would also benefit from international studies that help to conceptualize how experiences with LGBTQIA+-related stigma, discrimination, and oppression may further complicate young people's abilities to develop supportive relationships with individuals in their networks and function as independent adults. Such scientific efforts will increase our ability to develop policies and programs that better address the developmental needs of this unique population of young people.

References

Baams, L., Wilson, B. D. M., & Russell, S. T. (2019). LGBTQ youth in unstable housing and foster care. *Pediatrics*, *143*(3), e20174211. https://doi.org/10.1542/peds.2017-4211

Badgett, M. L. (2020). *The economic case for LGBT equality: Why fair and equal treatment benefits us all*. Beacon Press.

Balsam, K. F., Lehavot, K., Beadnell, B., & Circo, E. (2010). Childhood abuse and mental health indicators among ethnically diverse lesbian, gay, and bisexual adults. *Journal of Consulting and Clinical Psychology*, *78*(4), 459–468. https://doi.org/10.1037/a0018661

Beckerman, N. L., & Auerbach, C. (2014). PTSD as aftermath for bullied LGBT adolescents: The case for comprehensive assessment. *Social Work in Mental Health*, *12*(3), 195–211. https://doi.org/10.1080/15332985.2014.888026

Cossar, J., Schofield, G., Belderson, P., Ward, E., Keenan, J., Larsson, B., Dodsworth, J., & Cocker, C. (2017). *SpeakOut: A study of the experiences and identity development of lesbian, gay, bisexual, transgender and questioning young people in care – and the support they receive*. Research Briefing. Centre for Research on Children and Families, University of East Anglia.

Courtney, M. E., Dworsky, A., Brown, A., Cary, C., Love, K., & Vorhies, V.. (2011). *Midwest evaluation of the adult functioning of former foster youth: Outcomes at age 26*. Chapin Hall.

de Groot, N., Vijlbrief, A., & Emmen, M. (2018). *Out on the streets. Onderzoek naar de hulp aan Amsterdamse lhbti-jongeren die thuisloos zijn*. Research Briefing. Movisie.

Fish, J. N., Baams, L., Wojciak, A. S., & Russell, S. T. (2019). Are sexual minority youth overrepresented in foster care, child welfare, and out-of-home placement? Findings from nationally representative data. *Child Abuse and Neglect*, *89*, 203–211. https://doi.org/10.1016/j.chiabu.2019.01.005

Fulginiti, A., Goldbach, J. T., Mamey, M. R., Rusow, J., Srivastava, A., Rhoades, H., Schrager, S. M., Bond, D. W., & Marshal, M. P. (2020). Integrating minority stress theory and the interpersonal theory of suicide among sexual minority youth who engage crisis services. *Suicide and Life Threatening Behavior*, *50*(3), 601–616. https://doi.org/10.1111/sltb.12623

Gallegos, A., White, C. R., Ryan, C., O'Brien, K., Pecora, P. J., & Thomas, P. (2011). Exploring the experiences of lesbian, gay, bisexual, and questioning adolescents in foster care. *Journal of Family Social Work*, *14*, 226–236. https://doi.org/10.1080/10522 158.2011.571547

Goldbach, J. T., & Gibbs, J. J. (2017). A developmentally informed adaptation of minority stress for sexual minority adolescents. *Journal of Adolescence*, *55*, 36–50. https://doi.org/10.1016/j.adolescence.2016.12.007

Goldbach, J. T., Tanner-Smith, E. E., Bagwell, M., & Dunlap, S. (2014). Minority stress and substance use in sexual minority adolescents: A meta-analysis. *Prevention Science*, *15*, 350–363. https://doi.org/10.1007/s11121-013-0393-7

González Álvarez, R., ten Brummelaar, M., Orwa, S., & López López, M. (2021). "I actually know that things will get better": The many pathways to resilience of LGBTQIA+ youth in out-out-of-home care. *Children & Society*, *36*(2), 234–248. https://doi.org/10.1111/chso.12464

González-Álvarez, R., Hofman, S., ten Brummelaar, M. D. C., & López López, M. (2023). Care professionals' perspectives and roles on resilience among LGBTQIA+ youth in out-of-home care: A multidimensional perspective. *Children and Youth Services Review*, *150*, 107012. https://doi.org/10.1016/j.childyouth.2023.107012

González-Álvarez, R. Parra, L. A., ten Brummelaar, M., Avraamidou, L., & López López, M. (2022). Resilience among LGBTQIA+ youth in out-of-home care: A scoping review. *Child Abuse and Neglect*, *129*. https://doi.org/10.1016/j.chiabu.2022.105660

Hiles, D., Moss, D., Wright, J., & Dallos, R. (2013). Young people's experience of social support during the process of leaving care: A review of the literature. *Children and Youth Services Review*, *35*(12), 2059–2071. https://doi.org/10.1016/j.childyouth.2013.10.008

Kosciw, J., Palmer, N., & Kull, R. (2015). Reflecting resiliency: Openness about sexual orientation and/or gender identity and its relationship to well-being and educational outcomes for LGBT students. *American Journal of Community Psychology*, *55*(1–2), 167–178. https://doi.org/10.1007/s10464-014-96

López López, M., González-Álvarez, R., ten Brummelaar, M., Van Mierlo, R. O., & Wieldraaijer-Vincent, L. (Eds.) (2021). *Working with LGBTQIA+ youth in the child welfare system. Perspectives from youth, professionals and families*. University of Groningen Press. https://doi.org/10.21827/60e5a36110a93

López López, M., Mallon, G. P., & Wieldraaijer-Vincent, L. (2022). Creating safe and welcoming residential care placements for LGBTQIA+ youth. In J. K. Whittaker, L. Holmes, J. Fernández Del Valle & S. James (Eds.), *Revitalizing residential care for children and youth: Cross-national trends and challenges* (pp. 321–335). Oxford University Press. https://doi.org/10.1093/oso/9780197644300.003.0022

López López, M., Martínez Jothar, G. A., ten Brummelaar, M., Parra, L. A., González-Álvarez, R., San Juan Morán, G., Wieldraaijer-Vincent, L., & Mallon, G. P. (2023a). *Informe FIRMUS. Estudio de la juventud LGTBIQ+ en los centros de acogimiento residencial del sistema de protección a la infancia de Cantabria*. Dirección General de Políticas Sociales – Gobierno de Cantabria.

López López, M., Martínez-Jothar, G., ten Brummelaar, M., Parra, L. A., San Román, B., & Mallon G. P. (2024) "They told me that you can be with whomever you want, be who you are": Perceptions of LGBTQ+ youth in residential care regarding the social support provided by child welfare professionals. *Children and Youth Services Review, 159*. https://doi.org/10.1016/j.childyouth.2024.107498

López López, M., ten Brummelaar, M., & Wieldraaijer-Vincent, L. (2023b). Reimagining Participation of Young People in Decision Making in Contexts of Vulnerability. In B. Taylor, J. D. Fluke, A. Shlonsky, E. Keddell, A. Whittaker and C. Killick (Eds.), *Sage handbook of decision making, assessment and risk in social work*. SAGE.

Mallon, G. Aledort, N., & Ferrera, M. (2002). There's no place like home: Achieving safety, permanency, and well-being for lesbian and gay adolescents in out-of-home care settings. *Child Welfare, 81(*2), 407–439.

Mallon, G. P. (2019). *LGBTQ youth issues. A practical guide for youth workers serving lesbian, gay, bisexual, transgender, & questioning youth*. CWLA Press.

Mallon, G. P. (2021). *Strategies for child welfare professionals working with transgender and gender expansive youth*. Jessica Kingsley.

Mallon, G. P., Paul, J., & López López, M. (2022). Child protection for LGBTQ+ youth. In J. E. Korbin & R. Krugman (Eds.), *Handbook of child maltreatment*, 2nd ed. (pp. 575–591). Springer.

Martín, E., & Dávila, L. M. (2008). Redes de apoyo social y adaptación de los menores en acogimiento residencial. *Psicothema*, *20*(2), 229–235.

McCormick, A., Schmidt, K., & Terrazas, S. (2017). LGBTQ youth in the child welfare system: An overview of research, practice, and policy. *Journal of Public Child Welfare*, *11*(1), 27–39. https://doi.org/10.1080/15548732.2016.1221368

McGeough, B. L., & Sterzing, P. R. (2018). A systematic review of family victimization experiences among sexual minority youth. *The Journal of Primary Prevention*, *39*(5), 491–528. https://doi.org/10.1007/s10935-018-0523-x

Meyer, I. H. (2003). Prejudice, social stress, and mental health in lesbian, gay, and bisexual populations: Conceptual issues and research evidence. *Psychological Bulletin*, *129*, 674–697. https://doi.org/10.1037/0033-2909.129.5.674

Morton, M. H., Samuels, G. M., Dworsky, A., & Patel, S. (2018). *Missed opportunities: LGBTQ young people homelessness in America*. University of Chicago

Mountz, S., & Capous-Desyllas, M. (2020). Exploring the families of origin of LGBTQ former foster youth and their trajectories throughout care. *Children and Youth Services Review*, *109*, 104622. https://doi.org/10.1016/j.childyouth.2019.104622

Page, M. (2017). Forgotten youth: Homeless LGBT youth of color and the Runaway and Homeless Youth Act. *Northwestern Journal of Law & Social Policy*, *12*(2), 17.

Parra, L. A., Helm, J. L., & Hastings, P. D. (2022). Adrenocortical responses of emerging adults in California in the two months following the Pulse nightclub massacre: Evidence for distal stress responses. *Comprehensive Psychoneuroendocrinology*, *10*, 100129. https://doi.org/10.1016/j.cpnec.2022.100129

Paul, J. (2018). *Under the radar: Exploring support for lesbian, gay, bisexual transgender, queer and questioning (LGBTQ) young people transitioning from foster care to emerging adulthood.* (Doctoral dissertation). University of Wisconsin-Madison.

Paul, J. (2020). Exploring support for LGBTQ youth transitioning from foster care to emerging adulthood. *Child & Youth Services Review*, *119*, 105481. https://doi.org/10.1016/j.childyouth.2020.105481

Paul, J. C., & Cruys, C. (2024). "We should be treated like we are somebody": Building supportive relationships with LGBTQ foster youth. *Family Relations*, *73*(4), 2671–2689. https://doi.org/10.1111/fare.13020

Paul, J. C., & Monahan, E. K. (2019). Sexual minority status and child maltreatment: How do health outcomes among sexual minority young adults differ due to child maltreatment exposure? *Child Abuse & Neglect*, *96*, 104099. https://doi.org/10.1016/j.chiabu.2019.104099

Price-Feeney, M., Green, A. E., & Dorison, S. H. (2021). Impact of bathroom discrimination on mental health among transgender and nonbinary youth. *The Journal of Adolescent Health: Official Publication of the Society for Adolescent Medicine*, *68*(6), 1142–1147. https://doi.org/10.1016/j.jadohealth.2020.11.001

Ragg, D. M., Patrick, D., & Ziefert, M. (2006). Slamming the closet door: Working with gay and lesbian youth in care. *Child Welfare*, *85*(2), 243–265.

Robinson, B. A. (2018). Child welfare systems and LGBTQ youth homelessness: Gender segregation, instability, and intersectionality. *Child Welfare*, *96*(2), 29–45.

Rosenwald, M. (2009). A glimpse within: An exploratory study of child welfare agencies' practices with LGBTQ youth. *Journal of Gay & Lesbian Social Services*, *21*(4), 343–356. https://doi.org/10.1080/10538720802498124

Samuels, G. M., & Pryce, J. M. (2008). "What doesn't kill you makes you stronger": Survivalist self-reliance as resilience and risk among young adults aging out of foster care. *Children and Youth Services Review*, *30*(10), 1198–1210. https://doi.org/10.1016/j.childyouth.2008.03.005

Testa, R. J., Habarth, J., Peta, J., Balsam, K., & Bockting, W. (2015). Development of the gender minority stress and resilience measure. *Psychology of Sexual Orientation and Gender Diversity*, *2*(1), 65–67. https://doi.org/10.1037/sgd0000081

Wilson, B., Cooper, K., Kastanis, A., & Nezhad, S. (2014). *Sexual and gender minority youth in foster care: Addressing disproportionality and disparities in Los Angeles*. The Williams Institute.

Wilson, B. D. M., & Kastanis, A. A. (2015). Sexual and gender minority disproportionality and disparities in child welfare: A population-based study. *Children and Youth Services Review*, *58*, 11–17. https://doi.org/10.1016/j.childyouth.2015.08.016

13 Is Anyone There?

Supports Available for Unaccompanied Migrant and Non-Migrant Residential Care Leavers in Spain

Federica Gullo, Laura García-Alba, Iriana Santos and Jorge F. del Valle

Introduction

According to the most recent data (Observatorio de la Infancia, 2024), residential care accounts for 49% of the total out-of-home care population of 51,972 children and young people in Spain. This type of placement has become the main alternative for addressing the needs of some specific subgroups of children and young people within childcare. Notably, it serves adolescents nearing the age of 18 who lack the option to reunite with their families, children and young people grappling with particularly complex emotional and behavioral challenges, as well as those with a migratory background (Bravo & Del Valle, 2009; Del Valle et al., 2012). This subgroup of young people represents 45% of placements in residential care and 12% of placements in family foster care settings in Spain (Observatorio de la Infancia, 2024). It includes both young people who previously lived with their families in Spain and those who arrived unaccompanied, lacking the guardianship of a responsible adult. The latter subset, often referred to as Unaccompanied Young Migrants (UYM), has significantly influenced the Spanish child welfare system since their arrival in the 1990s, being placed in residential care almost exclusively. According to recent data, 73% of migrants in residential care and 12% of those in family foster care were UYM. Remarkably, young people in this group remain primarily situated in residential care settings (96%), constituting 34% of the population in this type of arrangement, while comprising only 1% in family foster care (Observatorio de la Infancia, 2024). This group exhibits significant heterogeneity in terms of life experiences and backgrounds. However, they share common threads of uprooting experiences, including separation from their families and familiar surroundings, migration journeys, cultural adjustment challenges, and a resilient determination to pursue a better life from a very young age (Bravo & Santos, 2017). On the other hand, regardless of their diverse profiles, almost 5,000 young people, representing nearly 9% of those in care, exit the system upon reaching the age of majority (Observatorio de la Infancia, 2024). Every year,

DOI: 10.4324/9781003424468-18

numerous young people embark on their journey to independent living, carrying a heavy bag full of challenges that set them apart from their peers.

Social Support and Social Networks of Care Leavers

The journey toward adulthood has been subjected to multiple social and economic transformations over the past century, turning into an extended and unpredictable path (Mann-Feder, 2019). In Spain, the average age at which young people leave their family home is 30.4 years (Eurostat, 2024), with parents serving as the primary source of emotional and instrumental support throughout much of their youth. In stark contrast, care-experienced young people are forced into a swifter, riskier, less-supported transition from care to independent living (Stein, 2008), usually occurring immediately after they turn 18 and cease out-of-home placements (Rogers, 2011).

During this period, care-experienced young people often receive limited support from their families (Sulimani-Aidan, 2018), as the absence or inadequacy of their family relations is a common factor leading to children entering care (Arnett, 2019). In such circumstances, alternative sources of informal and formal support become crucial for facilitating their social integration and aiding them in coping with the challenges of everyday life (Hedin, 2016). Moreover, social support has consistently been linked to improved self-esteem, well-being, and mental health throughout the transition to adulthood (Galambos et al., 2006).

However, research has shown that the social networks of care leavers are often limited, with many relying heavily on practitioners and staff associated with the child welfare system (Marion et al., 2017; Rosenberg, 2019; Sulimani-Aidan, 2018) for both emotional and instrumental support (Hiles et al., 2013). While such support can yield positive effects and improved outcomes for young people (Mendes & Purtell, 2020), its inherent limitations and temporary nature contribute to the lack of a robust and stable support network, thus heightening the vulnerability of young people leaving care (Mendes & Snow, 2016).

Various researchers have highlighted that these young people are not only more likely to have fragile social networks but also to struggle to achieve success in critical areas such as education, employment stability, and mental and physical health (Gypen et al., 2017), placing them at a heightened risk of social exclusion (Stein, 2008). Among them, certain groups face an even more complex transition. For instance, girls (Heerde et al., 2016) may experience compromised psychological well-being due to increased exposure to maltreatment during childhood, which can persist into young adulthood (Van Vugt et al., 2014). Similarly, UYM encounter additional hurdles stemming from their challenging migratory experiences, lack of support, language barriers, and legal obstacles associated with undocumented status (Del Valle & Bravo, 2013; López-Reillo, 2013). Moreover, some scholars have suggested that the years following arrival can be particularly complicated due to culture shock and the challenges of establishing a new support network, often requiring about four years to achieve stability and effective adaptation to the new culture (Keles et al., 2018).

However, the pathways to adulthood for young people leaving care can be as diverse as their unique needs and experiences (Van Breda & Pinkerton, 2020). Available support networks play a significant role in explaining a large portion of this variance and serve as crucial protective factors for the success of young people transitioning from care (Neves et al., 2019). There is a strong consensus in the scientific community regarding the importance of providing formal support to these young people before, during, and after their transition from care (Harder et al., 2011). Since 2015, Spanish child welfare legislation has mandated local authorities to offer preparation for independent living to young people in care, starting from the age of 16 and continuing after they turn 18 until it is no longer needed. However, due to regional administrations being responsible for funding, designing, and implementing such services, the support care leavers receive can vary significantly from one region to another.

Therefore, this chapter, based on semi-structured interviews with 224 care leavers, aims to explore the composition and quality of both formal and informal support networks among young people exiting residential care in Spain. Additionally, it aims to examine the potential contribution of such support networks on various dimensions, while also considering potential differences that may be explained by the intersection of young people's characteristics, such as gender and migratory background. Our analysis will be guided by an ecological systemic perspective, with a focus on identifying support providers within the microsystem to which they belong: family, community, child welfare services, or care leaving services (Bronfenbrenner, 1979).

Method

Participants

Data were collected from 224 care leavers, with an average age of 19 years, who had been in care across various regions in Spain, including Catalonia, Cantabria, Basque Country, Castile and Leon, Madrid, Castilla-La Mancha, and Galicia. These individuals had either benefited from or were currently receiving different types of transitional support services for leaving care. The participants' backgrounds were diverse, including national Spanish young people (44.2%), UYM (33%), and young people from migrant families residing in Spain (22.8%). Among the UYM, the majority originated from Africa, especially from the Maghreb region (70.3%; Morocco and Argelia), followed by sub-Saharan Africa (25.7%; Senegal, Guinea, Ghana, and Ivory Coast), with only a small percentage originating from Asia (4.1%). In contrast, young people from resident migrant families primarily hailed from South America (52.9%; Brazil, Dominican Republic, or Argentina), followed by

Africa (35.3%), Eastern Europe (7.8%), or Asia (3.9%). The gender distribution skewed toward men (62.9%) compared to women (37.1%), largely influenced by the overwhelmingly male identification among UYM participants (91.9%), aligning with trends observed in the Spanish child welfare system (Observatorio de la Infancia, 2024). Excluding the UYM subgroup, the proportion of women would stand at 51.3%.

Instruments

For this study, a qualitative semi-structured interview was devised to collect relevant information regarding the participants' profiles, including characteristics such as gender (female/male), age (in years), origins, and UYM status (yes/no), as well as their experiences while in care (age upon entry in years, duration of care in terms of years, and number of placement changes). Additionally, potential risk factors were explored, including issues related to substance use, psychological challenges affecting daily functioning such as depression or anxiety, and any instances of self-harm or suicidal behaviors such as ideation, planning, or attempts. Furthermore, the interview delved into domains related to social integration, such as participants' educational and employment statuses. Moreover, the nature and characteristics of participants' social relationships and networks were examined in depth. This involved assessing both informal and formal support received from various individuals, including family members, friends, partners, and other influential figures. Additionally, the interview explored the transitional support services provided to participants, investigating the types and extent of benefits they were receiving. The information gleaned from the interviews was then categorized into dichotomous variables, according to the absence or presence of the issues explored (as is the case of variables related to risk factors, the support received from different figures, and the aftercare benefits received) or polytomous variables (as is the case of the educational and employment situations) based on their nature, facilitating subsequent analysis.

Procedure

This study was approved by the Responsible Research and Innovation Subcommittee at the Ethic Committee of the University of Oviedo. To engage potential participants, the research team contacted local authorities' child welfare services, providing detailed information about the study's objectives and methodologies. Upon obtaining their authorization, agencies offering transitional support services in each region were approached. Upon agreement to participate in the study, these agencies disseminated invitations to young people receiving care leaving support from them. Prior to participation, participants were provided with thorough information about the study's aims and procedures, emphasizing the voluntary and confidential nature of their involvement. The interviews, lasting approximately one hour on average, were conducted individually and face-to-face. The researchers traveled to various autonomous communities and cities where participants lived, ensuring interviews took place in locations chosen by participants and conducive to their comfort. Prior to commencing the interview, explicit informed consent was obtained from each participant.

Data Analysis

The collected data underwent a categorization and coding process before analysis, using SPSS Statistics software (v. 26). Descriptive statistics were used to depict participants' characteristics. Various statistical tests, including Chi-square, Student's t-tests, and analysis of variance, were conducted based on the type of the variables, aiming to examine potential associations and differences between participant groups. To account for the heterogeneity in participants' sociodemographic profiles, separate analyses were conducted with respect to gender. It should be noted that UYM were excluded from the examination of gender differences, while girls were excluded from the investigation focusing on differences related to the UYM condition. The reason for that is related to the unequal distribution of these characteristics, being female UYM scarcely present in both the Spanish child protection system and among our participants. Moreover, the investigation delved deeper into the participants' social support relationships and networks through qualitative methodologies. Content analysis, following the guidelines proposed by Bardin (1996), was employed. This method entails three chronological stages: *pre-analysis*, in which the material is prepared, and the initial ideas are operationalized and systematized; the *material exploitation*, consisting of coding, decomposing, or enumerating the initial material; and the *results treatment*, involving inference and interpretation.

Results

Participants' General Characteristics

Table 13.1 provides a comprehensive overview of the participants' characteristics, encompassing their current status, mental well-being, risk behaviors, and involvement with the child welfare system. The results show that the majority of participants were mainly focused on their studies or balancing academic pursuits with employment. More than half of the participants had been receiving mental health treatment (58.5%), 27% reported issues related to drug consumption, and almost a quarter (24.4%) displayed self-harming behaviors. Furthermore, women were more likely to show poorer psychological well-being and have become young parents. The UYM reported lower rates of poor psychological adjustment, drug abuse, and self-harming or suicidal behavior compared to their counterparts without similar backgrounds.

Table 13.1 Participants' characteristics and differences according to gender and UYM condition

Variables	*Total*	*Gender*		*UYM Condition*	
	% or M*(SD)*	*% or* M*(SD)*		*% or* M*(SD)*	
	N = *224*	*Women* n = *77*	*Men* n = *73*	*No* n = *73*	*Yes* n = *68*
Occupation					
NEET	12.1	11.7	13.7	13.7	11.8
Studying	54.0	50.6	45.2	45.2	64.7*
Working	13.8	9.1	16.4	16.4	16.2
EET	20.1	28.6	24.7	24.7	7.4*
Mental health treatments	58.5	85.7	75.3	75.3	8.8***
Drug consumption	27.2	37.7	35.6	35.6	8.8***
Psychological problems	8.9	19.5**	5.5	5.5	0.0*
Self-harming and suicidal behaviors	24.4	37.7	28.8	28.8	6.0***
Being a parent	2.3	5.2*	0.0	0.0	1.5
Age of entry in childcare	12.5(4.8)	11.4(4.5)	10.2(5.3)	10.2(5.3)	15.9(1.7)**
Time spent in childcare (years)	5.5(4.8)	6.6(4.5)	7.8(5.3)	7.8(5.3)	2.1(1.7)**
Changes of placement (numbers)	1.4(1.6)	1.2(1.4)	1.4(1.6)	1.4(1.6)	1.7(1.6)
Aftercare support (years)	1.4(1.6)	1.4(1.0)	1.5(1.1)	1.5(1.1)	1.2(1.4)

Note: M = mean; *SD* = standard deviation; UYM = unaccompanied young migrants; NEET = not in education, employment, or training; EET = in education, employment, and training; * = $p < .05$, ** = $p < .01$, *** = $p < .001$.

UYM were less likely to engage in a combination of training and work, opting instead for vocational training aimed at swiftly securing employment. They also tended to enter care at a later stage and remained in the system for shorter periods.

Participants' Support Networks

Regarding the informal support available to these young people, almost all participants maintained contact with some family members, albeit to a lesser extent with their parents (Table 13.2). While most participants valued positively their familial relationships, fewer considered them as a significant source of support:

> I don't count on the support of anyone in my family. Although I have a good relationship with my sisters, being far from them for so long has made me lose the confidence to talk about my problems. It's as if time has chilled the relationship: we do see each other and talk about stuff,

Table 13.2 Participants' social support by gender and UYM condition

Variables	*Total*	*Gender*		*UYM Condition*	
	% *or* M(SD)	% *or* M(SD)		% *or* M(SD)	
	N = 224	*Girls* n = 77	*Boys* n = 73	*No* n = 73	*Yes* n = 68
Contact with family	94.0	89.6	97.2	97.2	98.4
Contact with parents	75.6	67.5	69.4	69.4	95.2***
Contact with siblings	74.5	68.8	62.0	62.0	96.8***
Quality of relationship					
Positive	72.8	55.8	72.2	72.2	95.2***
Negative	27.2	44.2*	27.8	27.8	4.8
Family support	52.5	45.8	60.3	60.3	50.8
Friends support	85.9	89.6	93.2	93.2	75.90**
Partner support	34.4	48.1**	27.4	27.4	27.7
Reference adult support	76.0	74.0	79.5	79.5	72.3
Reference adult					
Social educators	63.1	61.4	44.8	44.8	83.0***
Parents	6.0	5.3	12.1	12.1	0.0
Other relatives	15.5	19.3	20.7	20.7	6.4
Acquaintances	15.5	14.0	22.4	20.7	10.6
Social education support	82.6	79.2	83.6	83.3	85.9
Housing	61.6	68.8*	52.1	52.1	63.2
Labor integration	55.6	45.9	62.0*	62.0	60.9
Financial help	42.9	54.5	50.7	50.7	17.6***
Legal assistance	45.9	31.6	23.3	23.3	85.7***
Psychological support	19.2	37.7**	13.7	13.7	4.4

Note: *M* = mean; *SD* = standard deviation; UYM = unaccompanied young migrants; * = $p < .05$, ** = $p < .01$, *** = $p < .001$.

> but when there is a moment when I'm feeling down, I don't think of calling them. The same goes for my parents and brothers, of course.
>
> (female, 19 years old, from a migrant family)

> I don't count on any of them for support...because I haven't lived at home with them these years. I believe they could help me, but I do not trust them enough to lean on them.
>
> (male, 19 years old, from a non-migrant background)

Girls tended to provide the least favorable evaluations of their family relationships. They were also more inclined to have a partner who, at times, was seen as an important source of support, as evidenced by the following comment:

> My partner was super essential because he helped me with money, or came shopping with me, stuff like that. I think that, especially at the

beginning, you need someone willing to go with you to do certain things, so you don't feel alone.

(female, 19 years old, from a migrant family)

On the other hand, UYM maintained closer ties with their families and placed higher value on their relationships. Despite the strong connection, they hesitated to share their challenges due to the geographical distance and their reluctance to burden their families with their concerns:

> I have my parents and three siblings. All living in Morocco. We keep in contact and have a good relationship – we don't speak every day, but often –. We get along well, but honestly, I don't usually count on them because there is no point in telling them my stuff if we don't live together. I would only make them feel bad for me too.
>
> (male, 19 years old, UYM)

> I came to Spain alone, my family lives in Morocco. I have my parents, three brothers and two sisters. I speak with them weekly but haven't seen them since I arrived here. We have a good relationship, but I don't tell them my stuff because I don't want them to be worried about me.
>
> (male, 18 years old, UYM)

> I prefer not to disturb my parents with my problems, so they don't get worried about me being so far.
>
> (male, 19 years old, UYM)

Moreover, while most participants reported being able to count on support from peers, UYM relied on this kind of support to a lesser extent, as illustrated by the following:

> I do have friends, but I consider them acquaintances more than real friends. I do not count on them at all if I need something.
>
> (male, 19 years old, UYM)

Conversely, most young people reported that they had a trusted adult to count on, often identifying this figure as a social educator from one of the residential settings they had lived in or from the transition support services from which they benefited, as evidenced by the following comments:

> I keep in touch with some social educators from the children's homes where I lived and call them if I need something. I like having them because they help me grow a bit more.
>
> (female, 19 years old, from a migrant family)

> The social educators supported me a lot in the past, and I still keep in contact with them. I know I can trust them.
>
> (male, 19 years old, from a non-migrant background)

> I developed a family-like bond with the educators. I used to speak to them, and each time I had a problem, they supported me. Emotionally, they were my family.
>
> (male, 20 years old, from a migrant family)

Other participants identified a trusted adult figure outside the social educator role, such as their partners' or friends' parents, teachers, or members of their extended family (e.g., uncles and aunts, grandparents), as illustrated by the following comment:

> I think that family is someone you love and can count on, so for me, my family is my partner, his family, a primary school teacher that I had [...]. I also keep in contact with my parents, but I feel that I'm the one who plays the parental role there. They are people I love, they are family, but I don't feel I can count on them. I love them, but I can't resort to them.
>
> (female, 21 years old, from a non-migrant background)

These views were particularly evident among UYM, who almost exclusively relied on service workers for support. In rare instances, they mentioned acquaintances or extended family members, and never their parents. In contrast, other young people also leaned on additional trusted figures, albeit primarily receiving support from practitioners.

Table 13.2 further outlines the prevalence of various aftercare formal support services care leavers received from transition to adulthood services. They benefited, on average, from three types of support concurrently, with psychological support being less commonly received.

Gender disparities were notable, with a higher proportion of girls residing in a flat for care leavers or receiving psychological support. Conversely, UYM received more legal support but less economic assistance. Additionally, both girls and UYM received more benefits simultaneously compared to other care leavers.

The potential association between receiving different sources of support and the young people's situation was also explored (Table 13.3). The lack of family support was associated with higher rates of mental health treatments ($\chi^2 = 4.642$, $p = .031$) and psychological distress ($\chi^2 = 4.486$, $p = .034$), less support from peers ($\chi^2 = 5.963$, $p = .015$) and other adult figures of reference ($\chi^2 = 4.743$, $p = .029$), a late entry ($t = 2.162$, $p = .032$) and shorter stay in care ($t = -2.162$, $p = .032$). The presence of support by a reference adult was associated with lower rates of drug consumption ($\chi^2 = 5.484$, $p = .019$), higher support by peers ($\chi^2 = 9.263$, $p = .002$), entering the childcare system younger ($t = 5.474$, $p = <.001$), and staying longer ($t =-5.474$, $p = <.001$). Finally, an association was found between the lack of peer support and

Table 13.3 Chi-Square and Student's t-test to explore associations between sources of support and participants' profile characteristics and care experiences

Variables	*Family Support % or M(SD)*		*Friends Support % or M(SD)*		*Reference Adult Support % or M(SD)*	
	No	Yes	No	Yes	No	Yes
Characteristics						
Occupation			*			
NEET	9.7	14.9	22.6	10.6	15.1	11.3
Studying	50.5	54.4	48.4	54.0	52.8	53.6
Working	17.5	11.4	22.6	12.7	17.0	13.1
EET	22.3	19.3	6.5	22.8	15.1	22.0
Mental health treatments (yes)	32.0*	19.3	25.8	25.4	24.5	25.6
Drug consumption (yes)	26.2	24.6	25.8	25.4	39.6*	23.2
Psychological problems (yes)	13.6*	5.3	6.5	9.5	11.3	8.3
Autolytic behaviors (yes)	30.7	19.5	27.6	23.9	30.8	22.3
Being a parent (yes)	1.9	2.7	9.7**	1.1	0.0	3.0
Care experiences						
Age of entry in childcare (years)	13.12(4.5)*	11.72(5.0)	14.97(2.5)***	11.96(4.9)	14.71(2.7)**	11.70(5.1)
Time spent in childcare (years)	4.88(4.5)*	6.28(5.0)	3.03(2.5)***	6.04(4.9)	3.29(2.7)**	6.30(5.1)
Changes of placement (numbers)	1.39(1.7)	1.39(1.6)	2.06(1.9)***	1.28(1.5)	1.37(1.8)	1.39(1.5)
Aftercare support (years)	1.44(1.3)	1.38(1.0)	0.95(0.7)*	1.49(1.2)	1.34(1.1)	1.43(1.2)
Source of support						
Family support (no)	-	-	67.7*	44.1	60.8*	43.4
Friends support (no)	20.4*	8.8	-	-	26.9**	10.1
Reference adult support (no)	30.1*	17.5	45.2**	20.1	-	-

Note. This table summarizes the associations and the degree of significance found between the mentioned variables through Chi-Square analysis or Student's T-Test according to their nature. * = $p < .05$, ** = $p < .01$, *** = $p < .001$.

having a poorer academic situation (χ^2 = 8.585, p = .035), being a young parent (χ^2 = 8.792, p = .003), entering later in the childcare system (t = 5.264, p = <.001), and having a shorter (t = -5.264, p = <.001), more unstable (t = 2.583, p = .010) trajectory in care. On the other hand, reporting friends as a source of support was associated with having access to transitional support services for longer (t = -3.478, p = .001).

Discussion

Nature of Care Leavers' Support Networks

This chapter explored the nature of the support networks of young people leaving care by collecting information about the different sources of support they perceived to be available for them within their respective contexts, including parents and other family members, friends, other trusted adults, or aftercare support services. Firstly, we have observed the infrequent listing of family context as a supportive resource for care leavers, in line with previous research findings among care-experienced young people compared to their peers (Sulimani-Aidan, 2018). This could probably be related to the complex dynamics characterizing the relationships between care-experienced young people and their families, which might have been eroded, deteriorated, or even become a source of problems for them over time (Gradaílle et al., 2018).

However, most participants could rely on support from friends and other trusted adults (Campos et al., 2020), often identified as social educators (Bravo & Del Valle, 2003; Campos et al., 2020; Rosenberg, 2019) from both residential care facilities and transitional support services. While practitioners can serve as an essential source of emotional and instrumental support for care leavers (Hiles et al., 2013; Mendes & Purtell, 2020), sustaining this support over time poses challenges (Sulimani-Aidan, 2017, 2018), highlighting the need to invest in expanding young people's support networks (Stein, 2008; Van Breda, 2018).

Moreover, care leavers were more likely to receive formal support services addressing practical issues such as education, housing, and employment compared to psychological support. Nonetheless, this does not necessarily indicate lesser need, as it may stem from the discontinuity of therapeutic interventions they received while in care (Munro & Simkiss, 2020). Young people might discontinue therapy due to financial constraints or difficulties in establishing rapport with a new therapist, thereby increasing their vulnerability, particularly since transitioning from care can aggravate existing problems and introduce new challenges (Dixon, 2008).

Care Leavers' Differential Support Needs

This study also highlighted how the support networks of young people leaving care could vary based on certain profile variables and their intersections, such as migratory background or gender. Interestingly, UYM were likelier to maintain better relationships with their families of origin than other youth, confirming the enduring emotional support families can still provide across distances (Santana-Vega et al., 2018), despite the absence of instrumental support indicated in their comments. This finding could potentially be attributed to the fact that this group typically enters care not due to traumatic experiences within their family context, but rather as a result of their status of UYM, while other young people often experience separation from their families due to experiences of abuse or neglect (Gullo et al., 2021; Söderqvist, 2013). The disparity in family experiences between UYM and other young people in care may also elucidate why UYM reported lower levels of emotional problems compared to other participants in this study. However, these findings need to be taken with caution, considering that UYM may be less likely to identify and report adverse experiences in the family, and instruments may not be sensitive or specific enough to assess sources of emotional distress directly related to their migratory experiences (Bravo & Santos, 2017).

However, UYM's support network appeared to be more restricted compared to other care leavers, relying less on friends for support and returning almost exclusively to social educators as trusted adults. Some authors have highlighted how UYM's migratory experiences might make them more reluctant to share personal information (Bravo & Santos, 2017) and how cultural shock can negatively affect their adjustment period until they manage to adapt and establish a new support network in the host country (Keles et al., 2018), which could explain our findings. It has also been observed that UYM were more likely to receive legal support for care leavers but less likely to receive financial support compared to other care leavers, potentially stemming from their administrative and legal status and the obstacles associated with being migrants. In light of this, it prompts reflection on how legal barriers related to UYM's immigrant status may overshadow their status as care leavers, affecting their access to public services. This phenomenon has already been described as potentially detrimental to their readiness for independent living (Wade, 2011) and social integration (Gimeno-Monterde & Gutiérrez-Sánchez, 2019).

It was also observed that girls were more likely to receive psychological support than boys, which may align with their potentially greater psychological needs (Dunning & Worthington, 2013; Van Vugt et al., 2014). Additionally, girls tended to benefit more from supported accommodation provided by care leaving support services. This finding could be attributed to their possibly enhanced capacity for adaptation to new environments, including residential and educational settings, as suggested by Martín (2015). Conversely, it might also be linked to a lower prevalence of externalizing issues compared to boys (Schiff, 2006), making their acceptance into and retention within such programs more feasible, despite potentially higher rates of internalizing issues (Ortuño-Sierra et al., 2016). Furthermore, the observation that women and UYM received more simultaneous benefits could underscore the complexity and challenges inherent in their paths toward independence.

It is also essential to highlight the higher prevalence of romantic partners as sources of support for girls. While relying on support from a partner can have a protective effect (Stubbs et al., 2023), it is necessary to acknowledge the potential risks associated with this dynamic. Care-experienced young girls might be more prone to engage in romantic relationships and assign them more importance than boys (Hlungwani & Van Breda, 2020; Schiff, 2006). Moreover, the unavailability of other sources of support may lead them to depend heavily on their partners (Sala-Roca et al., 2012), potentially rendering them more vulnerable in the event of being involved in an abusive relationship. In this context, several studies found a higher incidence of risky sexual behaviors and early or unintended pregnancies among care-experienced girls (Kääriäläa et al., 2019; Martín, 2015; Schiff, 2006). These findings highlight the importance of supporting care-experienced youth, especially girls, who need to navigate sexism and be supported to experience their sexuality from a standpoint of safety, autonomy, and equality, enabling them to make informed decisions about establishing healthy romantic relationships or starting families according to their own desires.

The Protective Role of Support

Our findings affirm the association between receiving greater support and attaining higher levels of adjustment, manifesting in improved well-being and reduced engagement in risky behaviors. Such outcomes are crucial for a successful transition from care (Hiles et al., 2013). Positive associations between support from friends and continued participation in education or training have also been described in previous research (Groinig & Sting, 2019), alongside the negative associations between such support and early parenthood (Stubbs et al., 2023).

Furthermore, our study revealed positive associations between receiving support from family and other sources such as friends and other trusted adults. These results may be related to the beneficial impact of the primary socialization context on the ability to develop interpersonal relationships and connections with others. Our results also show that receiving support from a reference adult was associated with a greater perception of support from friends. Such findings suggest that having a mentor can offset the effects of past adverse experiences, improving their relational models (Iwaniec & Sneddon, 2001) and helping them in strengthening relationships with peers (Sulimani-Aidan, 2017).

Regarding the length of stay in care, it may seem unexpected that those who spent more time in childcare and entered at a younger age perceived more support from different sources. This finding could be related to the notion that an early entry into childcare might entail shorter exposure to adverse experiences within the family context. Longer exposure to traumatic experiences during childhood has been identified as a risk factor for long-term adjustment issues (Egeland, 1997). Hence, a delayed entry into childcare can have negative repercussions on the adjustment of young individuals and their attachment processes (Tarren-Sweeney, 2008; Tarren-Sweeney, 2017). Moreover, those with more stable trajectories tended to perceive more support from friends, aligning with previous studies indicating the negative effects of instability on the integration (Moreira da Silva & Montserrat, 2014) and relationships (Dunning & Worthington, 2013) of these young people.

Lastly, the duration of aftercare support was positively associated with receiving support from friends, suggesting that prolonged formal support from services could also facilitate informal support networks (Stein, 2019). This extended support duration may afford individuals the time and resources needed to cultivate these networks, rather than solely focusing on self-sustenance tasks upon leaving care. This underscores the importance of providing continuity of support both during and after care as it serves as a catalyst for resilience and improved outcomes (Del Valle et al., 2003; Stein, 2019).

Conclusions and Implications for Practice

The present chapter discussed the compromised robustness of the support networks of young people leaving care, particularly highlighting the heightened vulnerability of UYM's networks (see also, Marion et al., 2017; Manzani & Arnoso-Martínez, 2014). According to our results, UYM tend to maintain better relationships with their parents compared to other care leavers, although this does not imply that they consider them as a source of support. Moreover, their networks can be smaller or lack diversity in terms of sources of support. They may face challenges in establishing connections with peers or accessing various forms of support beyond their familial relationships, which could elevate the risk of social exclusion (Santana-Vega et al., 2018). Implementing strategies to broaden the support networks of care-experienced youth, especially UYM, throughout their journey in out-of-home care could be crucial for ensuring a successful transition from care.

One strategy that could potentially benefit UYM is the use of mentoring programs that are particularly tailored for them, given their limited support networks and geographical distance from their family of origin. Multiple studies have illustrated the positive effects of mentorship on young individuals, leading to improved outcomes across various life domains (Bruce & Bridgeland, 2014; Marino et al., 2020; Mendes & Snow, 2016) particularly when working with at-risk youth (Du Bois et al., 2002). Mentors can help expand care leavers' social networks by facilitating connections with others they know, such as family members, friends, and acquaintances (Hiles et al., 2013). However, there is still a long road ahead to raise awareness and garner interest among public institutions and society regarding the efficacy of such intervention strategies, as mentoring programs remain limited in number and scope in Spain. The inclusion of the necessity for developing mentoring programs and promoting the presence of mentors as enduring support figures in national and regional legislation would present a significant advancement in this regard. It is imperative to promote the continuity of relationships forged during young people's time in care, enabling practitioners to carry out their roles effectively. Peer support and youth mentoring programs could possibly offer valuable avenues to expand young people's social networks. In this context, being connected with other care-experienced young people who have successfully overcome similar challenges can serve as a motivating force for individuals to cope with their own challenges.

It is also important not to overlook the potential benefits of thorough preparation for the transition out of care. Investing in the early development of social, decision-making, conflict management, problem-solving, and practical independent living skills – such as housekeeping, cooking, job search, and completing applications – could not only promote the development of new healthy relationships but also empower care leavers to better utilize aftercare support services. In this regard, Spain has introduced new programs and instruments such as the Planea Program (Del Valle & García-Alba, 2021), a web-based platform designed to enhance autonomy and life skills among young people in residential care. This program also includes a multi-informant tool for assessing young people's perceived life skills (García-Alba et al., 2021, 2022). It would be desirable to implement such tools or similar programs nationwide to streamline the efforts of professionals and improve the preparedness of this population.

The importance of birth families should also be considered in intervention strategies, as they often serve a significant presence in the lives of care-experienced young people, albeit not always as a source of support. Highlighting the need to include birth families in intervention scenarios is vital for enhancing the well-being and success of these young people (Dinisman et al., 2013). Moreover, UYM's families are often overlooked due to geographical distance, underscoring the need for specialized training in intercultural cooperation among staff (Gimeno-Monterde & Mendoza-Pérez, 2022).

Lastly, it is crucial to underline the importance of extending formal support (Harder et al., 2020), and ensuring access to available benefits for all care leavers who require assistance. This ensures that their transition to adulthood aligns as closely as possible with that of the general population. Moreover, assessing young people's individual needs and challenges based on their unique profiles and life experiences would enable services to operate more effectively and offer each young person with adequate resources.

Limitations and Implications for Future Research

The main limitation of this study lies in its non-random sampling method and potential bias associated with participants being affiliated with aftercare support services for care leavers. This could lead to an overrepresentation of young people with greater access to services, potentially overshadowing the experiences of those facing more complex situations upon leaving care (such as abrupt exits or ineligibility for aftercare services). It would be beneficial to carry out similar studies inclusive of young people who were unable or declined to participate in such services. Future research would also benefit from a more comprehensive analysis not only of the sources of support but also of the different types of support provided (e.g., instrumental, emotional). Longitudinal designs could further enrich our understanding by tracking the evolution of support networks over time and their influence on the well-being of care leavers.

An ongoing objective of the project that informed this chapter is to delve deeper into the intersectionality of being UYM and a female care leaver. Although this subgroup constitutes a small portion of the Spanish child welfare landscape, they may encounter specific challenges that warrant attention from policymakers and practitioners. However, due to methodological constraints, this chapter did not quantitatively analyze the experiences of this subgroup. Consequently, the UYM experiences examined in this chapter predominantly reflect those of male UYM, while the experiences of girls primarily represent non-UYM care-experienced young people. Nevertheless, conducting a qualitative comparative analysis of their experiences in relation to those of other care-experienced girls and male UYM remains a goal for future research publications stemming from this project.

Moreover, future research endeavors on this topic should examine broader inequalities in terms of gender and cultural backgrounds, while also considering and addressing various sexual orientations and gender identities and expressions. It could be valuable for future research to not only compare the overall experiences of young people leaving care across these sociodemographic categories and their intersections but also utilize instruments and methods that provide greater insight into their experiences of discrimination, exclusion, or victimization based on their migratory status, cultural background, sexual orientations, and gender identities and expressions.

Acknowledgments

The second author holds a post-doctoral scholarship funded by the Ministry of Universities through European Union NextGenerationEU funds (Margarita Salas).

References

Arnett, J.J. (2019). Foreword. In V.R. Mann-Feder, & M. Goyette (Eds.), *Leaving care and the transition to adulthood: International contributions to theory, research, and practice* (pp. xiii–xx). Oxford University Press. https://doi.org/10.1093/oso/9780190630485.001.0001

Bardin, L. (1996). *Análisis de contenido* [*Content analysis*]. Akal Ediciones.

Bravo, A., & Del Valle, J.F. (2003). Las redes de apoyo social de los adolescentes acogidos en residencias de protección: Un análisis comparativo con población normativa [Social support of adolescents in care]. *Psicothema*, *15*(1), 136–142.
Bravo, A., & Del Valle, J.F. (2009). Crisis y revisión del acogimiento residencial. Su papel en la protección infantil [Crisis and review of residential care]. *Papeles del Psicólogo*, *30*(1), 42–52.
Bravo, A., & Santos, I. (2017). Menores extranjeros no acompañados en España: Necesidades y modelos de intervención [Unaccompanied young migrant in Spain]. *Psychosocial Intervention*, *26*(1), 55–62. https://doi.org/10.1016/j.psi.2015.12.001
Bronfenbrenner, U. (1979). *The ecology of human development: Experiments by nature and design*. Harvard University.
Bruce, M., & Bridgeland, J.M. (2014). The mentoring effect: Young people's perspectives on the outcomes and availability of mentoring. A report for mentor: The national mentoring partnership. Civic Enterprises.
Campos, G., Goig, R., & Cuenca, E. (2020). La importancia de la red de apoyo social para la emancipación de jóvenes en acogimiento residencial [Importance of social support for the emancipation of young people in residential care]. *Electronic Journal of Research in Educational Psychology*, *18*(1), 27–54.
Del Valle, J.F., Álvarez, E., & Bravo, A. (2003). Evaluación de resultados a largo plazo en acogimiento residencial de protección a la infancia [Evaluation of long-term results in residential care]. *Infancia y Aprendizaje*, *26*(2), 235–249. https://doi.org/10.1174/021037003321827803
Del Valle, J.F., & Bravo, A. (2013). Current trends, figures and challenges in out of home child care: An international comparative analysis. *Psychosocial Intervention*, *22*(3), 251–257. https://doi.org/10.5093/in2013a28
Del Valle, J.F., & García-Alba, L. (2021). Manual del Programa Planea. Entrenamiento en habilidades para la vida independiente [Manual of Planea Program. Independent life skills training]. Consejería de Bienestar Social de la Junta de Comunidades de Castilla-La Mancha. https://infanciayfamilias.castillalamancha.es/sites/default/files/2021-07/Manual-Interactivo-Planea-CLM.pdf
Del Valle, J.F., Sainero-Rodríguez, A.M., & Bravo, A. (2012). Salud mental de menores en acogimiento residencial. Guía para la prevención e intervención en hogares y centros de la Comunidad Autónoma de Extremadura [Mental health of population in residential care]. Junta de Extremadura. Consejería de Sanidad y Dependencia. https://consaludmental.org/publicaciones/Saludmentalmenoresacogimientoresidencial.pdf
Dinisman, T., Zeira, A., Sulimani-Aidan, Y., & Benbenishty, R. (2013). The subjective well-being of young people aging out of care. *Children and Youth Services Review*, *35*(10), 1705–1711. https://doi.org/10.1016/j.childyouth.2013.07.011
Dixon, J. (2008). Young people leaving care: Health, well-being and outcomes. *Child and Family Social Work*, *13*(2), 207–217. https://doi.org/10.1111/j.1365-2206.2007.00538.x
Du Bois, D.L., Holloway, B.E., Valentine, J.C., & Cooper, H. (2002). Effectiveness of mentoring programs for youth: A meta-analytic review. *American Journal of Community Psychology*, *30*(2), 157–197. https://doi.org/10.1023/A:1014628810714
Dunning, K.B., & Worthington, K. (2013). Responding to the needs of adolescent girls in foster care. *Georgetown Journal on Poverty Law & Policy*, *20*(2), 321–349.
Egeland, B. (1997). Mediators of the effects of child maltreatment on developmental adaptation in adolescence. In D. Cicchetti, & S.L. Toth (Eds.), *Rochester symposium on developmental psychology*, Vol. 8. Developmental perspectives on trauma: Theory, research, and intervention (pp. 403–434). University of Rochester Press.
EUROSTAT. (2024). Estimated average age of young people leaving the parental home. https://ec.europa.eu/eurostat/web/products-eurostat-news/w/ddn-20240930-2

Galambos, N.L., Barker, E.T., & Krahn, H.J. (2006). Depression, self-esteem, and anger in emerging adulthood: Seven-year trajectories. *Developmental Psychology, 42*(2), 350–365. https://doi.org/10.1037/0012-1649.42.2.350

García-Alba, L., Postigo, Á., Gullo, F., Muñiz, J., & Del Valle, J.F. (2021). PLANEA independent life skills scale: Development and validation. *Psicothema, 33*(2), 268–278. https://doi.org/10.7334/psicothema2020.450

García-Alba, L., Postigo, Á., Gullo, F., Muñiz, J., & Del Valle, J.F. (2022). Assessing independent life skills of youth in child protection: A multi-informant approach. *European Journal of Psychology Applied to Legal Context, 14*(1), 1–10. https://doi.org/10.5093/ejpalc2022a1

Gimeno-Monterde, C., & Gutiérrez-Sánchez, J.D. (2019). Fostering unaccompanied migrating minors. A cross-border comparison. *Children and Youth Services Review, 99*, 36–42. https://doi.org/10.1016/j.childyouth.2019.01.035

Gimeno-Monterde, C. & Mendoza-Pérez, K. (2022): Making the family relationships of the unaccompanied youth visible: An opportunity to include a new actor in children care, *Residential Treatment for Children & Youth*. https://doi.org/10.1080/0886571X.2022.2101581

Gradaílle, R., Montserrat, C., & Ballester, L. (2018). Transition to adulthood from foster care in Spain: A biographical approach. *Children and Youth Services Review, 89*, 54–61. https://doi.org/10.1016/j.childyouth.2018.04.020

Groinig, M., & Sting, S. (2019). Educational pathways in and out of child and youth care. The importance of orientation frameworks that guide care leavers' actions along their educational pathway. *Children and Youth Services Review, 101*, 42–49. https://doi.org/10.1016/j.childyouth.2019.03.037

Gullo, F., García-Alba, L., Bravo, A., del Valle, J.F. (2021). Crossing countries and crossing ages: The difficult transition to adulthood of unaccompanied migrant care leavers. *International Journal of Environmental Research and Public Health, 18*(13), Article 6935. https://doi.org/10.3390/ijerph18136935

Gypen, L., Vanderfaeillie, J., De Maeyer, S., Belenger, L., & Van Holen, F. (2017). Outcomes of children who grew up in foster care: Systematic review. *Children and Youth Services Review, 76*, 74–83. https://doi.org/10.1016/j.childyouth.2017.02.035

Harder, A.T., Kongeter, S., Zeller, M., Knorth, E.J., & Dickscheit, J.K. (2011). Instruments for research on transition: Applied methods and approaches for exploring the transition of young care leavers to adulthood. *Children and Youth Services Review, 33*(12), 2432–2441. https://doi.org/10.1016/j.childyouth.2011.08.017

Harder, A.T., Mann-Feder, V., Oterholm, I., & Refaeli, T. (2020). Supporting transitions to adulthood for youth leaving care: Consensus based principles. *Children and Youth Services Review, 116*, Article 105260. https://doi.org/10.1016/j.childyouth.2020.105260

Hedin, L. (2016). Support and challenges in the process of leaving care: A Swedish qualitative follow-up study of foster youths' lived experiences. *Qualitative Social Work, 16*(4), 1–15. https://doi.org/10.1177/1473325015627384

Heerde, J.A., Hemphill, S.A., & Scholes-Balog, K.E. (2016). The impact of transitional programmes on post-transition outcomes for youth leaving out-of-home care: A metaanalysis. *Health and Social Care in the Community, 26*(1), 15–30. https://doi.org/10.1111/hsc.12348

Hiles, D., Moss, D., Wright, J., & Dallos, R. (2013). Young people's experience of social support during the process of leaving care: A review of the literature. *Children and Youth Services Review, 35*(12), 2059–2071. https://doi.org/10.1016/j.childyouth.2013.10.008

Hlungwani, J., & Van Breda, A.D. (2020). Female care leavers' journey to young adulthood from residential care in South Africa: Gender-specific psychosocial processes of resilience. *Child & Family Social Work, 25*(4), 915–923. https://doi.org/10.1111/cfs.12776

Iwaniec, D., & Sneddon, H. (2001). Attachment style in adults who failed to thrive as children: Outcomes of a 20-year follow-up study of factors influencing maintenance or change in attachment style. *British Journal of Social Work*, *31*(2), 179–195.

Kääriäläa, A., Haapakorva, P., Pekkarinen, E., & Sund, R. (2019). From care to education and work? Education and employment trajectories in early adulthood by children in out-of-home care. *Child Abuse & Neglect*, *98*, Article 104144. https://doi.org/10.1016/j.chiabu.2019.104144

Keles, S., Friborg, O., Idsøe, T., Sirin, S., & Oppedal, B. (2018). Resilience and acculturation among unaccompanied refugee minors. *International Journal of Behavioral Development*, *42*(1), 52–63. https://doi.org/10.1177/0165025416658136

López-Reillo, P. (2013). Young African migrants reinventing their lives in the Canary Islands. *The International Journal of Research into Island Cultures*, *7*(2), 39–54.

Mann-Feder, V. (2019). How can I be a real adult? Developmental theory as a framework for practice, policy and research on care leaving. In V. Mann-Feder y M. Goyette (Eds.), *Leaving care and the transition to adulthood: International contributions to theory, research, and practice* (pp. 31–49). Oxford University Press. https://doi.org/10.1093/oso/9780190630485.001.0001

Manzani, L., & Arnoso-Martínez, M. (2014). Psychosocial well-being in children and young immigrants without adult family referent: The risk and protective factors. *Norte de Salud Mental*, *12*(49), 33–45.

Marino, C., Santinello, M., Lenzi, M., Santoro, P., Bergamin, M., Gaboardi, M., Calcagnì, A., Altoè, G., & Perkins, D.D. (2020). Can mentoring promote self-esteem and school connectedness? An evaluation of the Mentor-UP Project. *Psychosocial Intervention*, *29*(1) 1–8. https://doi.org/10.5093/pi2019a13

Marion, E., Paulsen, V., & Goyette, M. (2017). Relationships matter: Understanding the role and impact of social networks at the edge of transition to adulthood from care. *Child and Adolescent Social Work*, *34*, 573–582. https://doi.org/10.1007/s10560-017-0494-4

Martín, E. (2015). Niños, niñas y adolescentes en acogimiento residencial: Un análisis en función del género [Population in residential care: Gender análisis]. *Revista Qurriculum*, *28*, 91–105.

Mendes P, & Purtell J. (2020). Relationship-based models for supporting young people transitioning from out-of-home care: Two case studies from Victoria, Australia. *Institutionalised Children Explorations and Beyond*, *8*(1), 120–132. https://doi.org/10.1177/2349300320967179

Mendes, P., & Snow, P. (2016). *Young people transitioning from out-of-home care: International research, policy and practice*. Palgrave Macmillan. https://doi.org/10.1057/978-1-137-55639-4

Moreira da Silva, L.A., & Montserrat, C. (2014). Jóvenes que estuvieron en el sistema de protección social a la Infancia. Reflexiones a partir de una investigación realizada en Girona, España. *Psicologia: Reflexão e Crítica*, *27*(1), 198–206.

Munro, E.R. & Simkiss, D. (2020). Transitions from care to adulthood: Messages to inform practice. *Paediatrics and Child Health*, *30*(5), 175–179. https://doi.org/10.1016/j.paed.2020.02.007

Neves, B.B., Dias de Carvalho, D., Serra, F., Torres, A., & Fraga, S. (2019). Social capital in transition(s) to early adulthood: A longitudinal and mixed-methods approach. *Journal of Adolescent Research*, *34*(1), 85–112. https://doi.org/10.1177/0743558418755685

Observatorio de la Infancia. (2024). Boletín de datos estadísticos de medidas de protección a la infancia. Boletín número 26. Datos 2023. Ministerio de Derechos Sociales y Agenda 2030. https://www.observatoriodelainfancia.es/oia/esp/descargar.aspx?id=8071&tipo=documento

Ortuño-Sierra, J., Fonseca-Pedrero, E., Inchausti, F., & Sastre i Riba, S. (2016). Assessing behavioural and emotional difficulties in the child-adolescent population: The strengths and difficulties questionnaire (SDQ). *Papeles del Psicólogo*, *37*(1), 14–26.

Rogers, R. (2011). 'I remember thinking, why isn't there someone to help me? Why isn't there someone who can help me make sense of what I'm going through?': 'Instant adulthood' and the transition of young people out of state care. *Journal of Sociology*, *47*(4), 411– 426. https://doi.org/10.1177/1440783311420793

Rosenberg, R. (2019). Social networks of youth transitioning from foster care to adulthood. *Children and Youth Services Review*, *107*, Article 104520. https://doi.org/10.1016/j.childyouth.2019.104520

Sala-Roca, J., Villalba-Biarnés, A., Jariot-García, M., & Arnau-Sabatés, L. (2012). Socialization process and social support networks of out-of-care youngsters. *Children and Youth Services Review*, *34*, 1015–1023. https://doi.org/10.1016/j.childyouth.2012.02.002

Santana-Vega, L.E., Alonso-Bello, E., & Feliciano-García, L. (2018). Trayectorias laborales y competencias de empleabilidad de jóvenes nacionales e inmigrantes en riesgo de exclusión social. *Revista Complutense de Educación*, *29*(2), 355–369. https://doi.org/10.5209/RCED.52444

Schiff, M. (2006). Leaving care: Retrospective reports by alumni of Israeli group homes. *National Association of Social Worker*, *51*(4), 343–353. https://doi.org/10.1093/sw/51.4.343

Söderqvist, Å. (2013). Leaving care with "cultural baggage": The development of an identity within a transnational space. *Australian Social Work*, *67*(1), 39–54. https://doi.org/10.1080/0312407X.2013.863955

Stein, M. (2008). Transition from care to adulthood: Messages from research for policy and practice. In M. Stein & E. Munro (Eds.), *Young people's transition from care to adulthood: International research and practice* (pp. 289–306). Jessica Kingsley.

Stein, M. (2019). Supporting young people from care to adulthood: International practice. *Child & Family Social Work*, *24*(3), 400–405. https://doi.org/10.1111/cfs.12473

Stubbs, A., Baidawi, S., & Mendes, P. (2023). Young people transitioning from out-of-home care: Their experience of informal support. A scoping review. *Children and Youth Services Review*, *144*, Article 106735. https://doi.org/10.1016/j.childyouth.2022.106735

Sulimani-Aidan, Y. (2017). Barriers and resources in transition to adulthood among at-risk young adults. *Children and Youth Services Review*, *77*, 147–152. https://doi.org/10.1016/j.childyouth.2017.04.015

Sulimani-Aidan, Y. (2018). Qualitative exploration of supporting figures in the lives of emerging adults who left care compared with their noncare-leaving peers. *Child & Family Social Work*, *24*(2), 247–255. https://doi.org/10.1111/cfs.12609

Tarren-Sweeney, M. (2008). The mental health of children in out-of-home care. *Current Opinion in Psychiatry*, *21*(4), 345–349. https://doi.org/10.1097/YCO.0b013e32830321fa

Tarren-Sweeney, M. (2017). Rates of meaningful change in the mental health of children in long-term out-of-home care: A seven- to nine-year prospective study. *Child Abuse & Neglect*, 72, 1–9. https://doi.org/10.1016/j.chiabu.2017.07.002

Van Breda, A.D. (2018). Research review: Aging out of residential care in South Africa. *Child and Family Social Work*, *23*(3), 513–521. https://doi.org/10.1111/cfs.12431

Van Breda, A.D., & Pinkerton, J. (2020). Raising African voices in the global dialogue on care-leaving and emerging adulthood. *Emerging Adulthood*, *8*(1), 6–15. https://doi.org/10.1177/2167696819870356

Van Vugt, E., Lanctôt, N., Paquette, G., Collin-Vézina, D., & Lemieux, A. (2014). Girls in residential care: From child maltreatment to trauma-related symptoms in emerging adulthood. *Child Abuse & Neglect*, *38*(1), 114–122. https://doi.org/10.1016/j.chiabu.2013.10.015

Wade, J. (2011). Preparation and transition planning for unaccompanied asylum-seeking and refugee young people: A review of evidence in England. *Children and Youth Services Review*, *33*, 2424–2430. https://doi.org/10.1016/j.childyouth.2011.08.027

Part 5

Interventions and Services for Fostering Social Support

14 Social Support of Young People During and After Residential Youth Care in the Netherlands

The Role of the Family, Care Workers, and Residential Group

Erik J. Knorth, Annemiek T. Harder and Jonathan D. Leipoldt

Introduction

Although the Netherlands ranks the highest in children's mental well-being, physical health, and academic and social skills of the world's 41 richest countries (UNICEF, 2020), 9.3% of all Dutch youth (aged zero to 23) are using child and youth care services (Knorth & Harder, 2023). Around 10% of those using these services stay in out-of-home care. Just over 50% of these children and young people (approximately 25,000) are placed in residential youth care (RYC) each year (Harder et al., 2020a). The main reasons for placement *regarding the child* include very serious emotional and behavioral problems, dangerous or threatening behavior directed to family members, and/or decreased contact with reality (e.g., psychosis and self-mutilation). *Regarding the family*, placement reasons include high risks of serious long-lasting abuse and neglect, major deficiencies regarding parental competencies, and/or huge unsafety in the child–parent relationship (e.g., unsafe or disorganized attachment). The problems are so grave that a family foster care placement is ruled out (Knorth & Harder, 2023). The RYC settings consist of therapeutic open residential care centers, including independent living programs (corresponding to 77.6% of the children and young people in RYC), family-like group care provisions (22.8%), and specialized secure residential care units (8.8%) (Harder & Knorth, 2022, p. 4). Government policy has been aimed to avoid out-of-home placements in general and RYC in particular for decades but has had limited success in reducing the number of children placed in care (Knorth & Harder, 2023).

In the 1980s and 1990s, an *ecological paradigm* became dominant in the field of child and family welfare, including an appeal to residential services (Whittaker et al., 1986). Treatment programs were developed to improve the family-like environment of youth in care. More attention was given to the residential group as a pedagogical-therapeutic environment (Van der Ploeg, 1984) for youth in RYC settings. The ecological paradigm also recognized the need to mobilize sources of social support (Whittaker, 1992). Thus, about 30 to 40 years ago, there was what might be called a "reconceptualization" of RYC.

DOI: 10.4324/9781003424468-20

In addition, the notion of *social climate* emerged as an environmental arrangement in care in which the provision of affection, structure, and the creation of space for personal growth can be varied (Van der Ploeg, 1981; see further below). At about the same time, research was initiated in (residential) youth care around the concept of *social support* – first in the United States (Whittaker & Garbarino, 1983), later also in the Netherlands and other Western European countries (Van der Ploeg et al., 1992; Whittaker, 1992). Social support is succinctly defined by Cohen et al. (1985) as "… all resources that are provided by other persons" (p. 73). This is also described as "enacted support", or social support that is actually offered; this is to distinguish it from "perceived support", or social support as experienced by a person (Smit & Laird, 1992).

Related to the concept of social support is the concept of *social network*. This refers to the composition of and the number of people in the group with whom a person has or believes to have contact (Whittaker, 1992). Some aspects that can be distinguished in a social network are, for example, the size, the composition, the frequency of contact, and the support received.

First, this chapter provides an overview of the social support needs of young people in Dutch RYC, including the support they receive. Based on the literature, it investigates whether and in what way parents and other family members are a source of support for young people during their stay, and how professionals can effectively promote this. The same question will be addressed regarding care workers/mentors in their one-on-one contact with young people: how can they best provide support? It also examines the facilitating qualities of the social group climate, which can be seen as a basis for more specific forms of support. Finally, it examines the post-RYC period, that is the need for social support among former residents and the importance of departure preparation and aftercare services.

Social support needs and received support of young people

Social support needs

According to self-determination theory (SDT) (Deci & Ryan, 2015; Harder, 2018), the social environment in which young people reside – whether it is the home environment or the environment of a residential group – should support or respond to three basic psychological needs: the need for autonomy, relatedness, and competence.

> The need for *autonomy* refers to the experience of a sense of choice or psychological freedom, the need for *relatedness* to the desire to feel connected to others, and the need for *competence* to the ability to affect the environment and to attain desired outcomes within it.
>
> (Harder, 2018, p. 323)

The SDT mentioned here formed the basis for a recently completed PhD study of the support needs of adolescents (13–18 years) admitted into a Dutch secure RYC setting (Sonderman, 2023). Based on individual, extensive in-depth interviews with young people from a gender-mixed residential living group (*N*=8), several issues emerged that "color" the experience of receiving social support.

Regarding the need for relatedness, the young people talk about "being consoled" by other inhabitants, about showing compassion and understanding for each other's suffering, and about being proud to have someone to take care for, but at the same time about their damaged ability to relate to other (young) people as a result of a lack of trust; "... all adolescents said that they are cautious in relating to the other adolescents" (p. 220). Each adolescent felt supported by at least one of the group workers, usually the mentor, but the relationship calls for continuity if it is to be beneficial to the youth; if there is discontinuity, for example, because the mentor changes jobs, it can be very "unsettling" for young people and feed "trust issues". All interviewees talked about the importance of contact with parents and family who were involved in their trajectories in different ways, depending on the individual needs. Contact with friends is also important for young people. The staff is sometimes concerned about what happens outside the door of the center during these contacts. Several inhabitants responded "... that you need to learn from mistakes" (p. 221).

Regarding the need for autonomy, it is important for young people to receive (individual) therapy where the choice to do so is experienced by them as a *shared decision*; then "... it felt right" (p. 221). When youth were given more freedom to go where they wanted, this was highly appreciated; it made them feel they were on the road to recovery and on their way out. When staff restricted freedom, for example to prevent self-harm, young people often felt that they needed the restrictions in retrospect. This is also the case with other forms of restriction, such as the use of random urine testing for drugs; inhabitants accept it if they have the impression that "... it was for their good" (p. 222) or is "meaningful" (Sonderman, 2023).

Regarding the need for competence, we see two themes in the results: the need for and success in therapy and the transition to adulthood. Young people want their (individual) treatment to give them progress in dealing with their personal problems, such as anxiety. One girl pointed out the amazing effect of Eye Movement Desensitization and Reprocessing (EMDR) therapy on her fears of dark rooms and basements. Young people can look forward to the time when they leave care and use the skills that they have learned, for example, in the catering industry or woodworking. On the other hand, we also know how much pressure young people are under when they are too unprepared to enter "full life" and have to stand on their own feet (Harder et al., 2020b; Smit, 1991).

Received social support

In the Netherlands, the first empirical research on social support for young people admitted to RYC was conducted in the 1990s (Van der Ploeg, 1992). In her PhD research, Buysse compared the support received by these young people (12–16 years) with that of a comparison group of young people, matched on age, gender, and educational level and approached through regular schools for secondary education, who had no contact with care (both groups *N*=63; Buysse, 1997). The size of the network from which social support is derived averaged 15 people in the first group and 20 people in the second group. Young people in care therefore have a relatively smaller social network (see also Bravo & Del Valle, 2003; Singstad, 2021).

The most important network members are members of the own family, especially mothers and siblings (*M*=3.16; SD=1.59; this means that on average young people mention over three persons in the family context as important support figures), and the extended family (*M*=3.33; SD=3.77) but also friends (*M*=3.76; SD=3.67). Care workers (*M*=1.83; SD=2.20) are also mentioned (for comparable results, see Ferreira et al., 2019). The frequency of contact with family, friends, and care workers is on average about once a week; with the extended family once every three to four weeks. Young people report receiving more support than they give from all network members, but this is clearly most true for contact with care workers. Even though mothers are at the top of the hierarchy of support providers (cf. Pinchover & Attar-Schwartz, 2018), young people also experience the most stress and conflict when in contact with their mothers, according to this study.

Social support by the family

A basic condition for young people to experience social support from their families is that (one of) the parents, but also siblings or other important members of the extended family are involved in some way in the treatment process in the center (Geurts et al., 2012; Pinchover & Attar-Schwartz, 2018; Simons, 2018).

One of the first large-scale empirical studies conducted in the Netherlands on parental involvement in RYC is the PhD study by Geurts (2010). Using a quasi-experimental design, she investigated whether a method of involving parents as much as possible in the treatment process – the Jeugdzorg in Context method (JIC; Youth care in Context in English) – actually worked, and whether this contributed to better outcomes; all this compared to (residential) care as usual (CAU). Both parents and professionals of a total of 173 young people (8–18 years) commented on the degree of family orientation of the help.

In terms of *treatment goals*, family-oriented goals are more common in the JIC condition (84% JIC vs. 67% CAU). In particular, "promoting the parent-child relationship", "improving/restoring family relationships", "developing a future perspective for the family", but also "promoting the detachment process between parents and young people" are the goals that are mentioned significantly more often in the JIC condition than in the CAU condition. Regarding the *operationalization* of a family orientation in treatment, parents experience that they are significantly more involved in the JIC program during the admission process, that they receive more support from the residential team, and that they value their guidance more overall than in CAU. According to the care workers, parents also have a greater say in treatment arrangements and more responsibility in JIC than in CAU. There is no difference between the two conditions in terms of accessibility/openness for parents of the residential group or of treatment plan discussions. It is striking that the second aspect is rated relatively low (unfavorable) by both parents and care workers. The conclusion is that the JIC program has a more family-oriented, parent-supportive approach than CAU. Whether young people feel better supported by and in their relationship with their parents as a result was not investigated.

In terms of *outcomes*, we see that in the JIC condition 74% of the young people completed their residential stay according to the arrangements in the treatment plan; the other 26% dropped out prematurely. The corresponding figures in CAU were 62% and 38%, respectively. According to the parents, their child's externalizing behavioral problems in the JIC condition are substantially reduced for almost half of the young people (47%); in the CAU condition, it's 33% (measured by application of the Reliable Change Index on CBCL-data at the start and the end of the treatment trajectory). For internalizing behavior problems, the figures are 36% in both conditions. Parents of children who return home after the JIC program report on average less parenting stress (effect size: +0.82, which means a large effect). According to care providers, the quality of the (family) environment has improved somewhat after the treatment, especially in the JIC condition (effect size JIC: +0.43, meaning a medium effect). At the same time, about half of the parents still experience parenting stress after the treatment, sometimes even more than before. This is consistent with Blankestein's (2022) findings that a higher degree of family-oriented work in secure RYC is also associated with more parenting stress among parents "during the ride". It is noteworthy that in almost half of the cases (47%), no aftercare is provided in the JIC condition (33% in the CAU).

Other, more recent research also shows positive outcomes of family-oriented work. Research by Blankestein (2022) in secure RYC settings shows that more family-oriented work in the care center is associated with shorter lengths of stay (see Simons, 2018, for the same finding). Blankestein's research reveals another interesting finding: when RYC workers have fewer obstructive thoughts about (the benefits of) family-oriented work, the likelihood that a (family) system intervention will be used increases. In this way, group workers can, perhaps unconsciously, influence the professional support that the child and parents receive in relation to each other.

Social support by the care workers

Social support for youth in RYC is often provided by group care workers because they interact with the youth on a daily basis (Knorth et al., 2010). The relationship between group care workers and youth in RYC can be considered as a key factor in successful RYC practice (Harder et al., 2013; Knorth et al., 2010). More specifically, the individual relationship between a young person and one of the group care workers, known as a coach or mentor, can be considered a mentoring relationship. A mentor is "a supportive adult who is significant to the child, who provides guidance, emotional and practical support, and who can serve as a role model and advocate in addition to or regardless of parents" (Sulimani-Aidan, 2017, p. 862). In the Netherlands, it is common for group care workers to be "formal" mentors and to be involved the individual treatment planning for young people (Harder et al., 2013).

Several studies have focused on the relationship between young people and care workers in (secure) RYC in the Netherlands. Schuengel (2002) and Zegers et al. (2006) examined the adolescent–care worker relationship in a juvenile justice institution. They defined the relationship in terms of attachment, that is, the affective bond between the adolescent and the adolescent's primary group care worker; that is his/her mentor, who was considered as a potential secure attachment figure. Schuengel (2002) found that adolescents did not seem to use their mentor as a secure attachment figure because the adolescents did not use the mentors as a secure base (i.e., seek direct contact with or proximity to their mentors). However, there did seem to be an affective bond between the adolescents and the mentors. The affective bond was also the only relationship aspect that showed a significant increase for those youth in residential care who did not switch between residential groups and from one mentor to another during their stay at the center (Schuengel, 2002).

While focusing on the same center, Zegers et al. (2006) found that more securely attached youth more often used care workers as a secure base and less often avoided contact with care workers compared to less securely attached adolescents. These findings suggest that youth with insecure attachment styles have poorer attachment relationships with staff than youth with secure attachment styles. In another study, Zegers (2007) showed that adolescents who experienced high emotional and social support from group care workers showed a decrease in delinquent incidents during care, whereas adolescents who perceived low support showed an increase in incidents.

In the context of secure RYC, Harder et al. (2013) found that youth and group care workers experienced a limited affective bond in their relationship two months after youth were admitted. Youth tended to use care workers and teachers as a secure attachment figure, suggesting that an affective bond is not a prerequisite for youth to experience staff as a secure base. Positive treatment skills of group care workers, such as being reliable and showing commitment, were the most important predictors of a good relationship according to both youth and care workers (Harder et al., 2013).

In a qualitative study, Harder et al. (2022) explored the experiences and needs of 11 adolescents and 12 RYC workers regarding their mentoring relationship in terms of their individual one-on-one conversations. Both the youth and the RYC workers were quite satisfied with their conversations, which were often focused on achieving improvement with the youth, such as feeling better. However, most youth did not have a need for these conversations. They preferred a mentor who was calm, respectful, listening, and reluctant to give advice. Although improvement in the well-being of the young person is often the goal with youth, most youth report that they do not show change or do not know if they show change as a result of these conversations. Only one RYC worker feels that his or her primary task is to change the behavior of the youth. According to the RYC workers, conversations with youth are often aimed at building a good relationship, coaching, setting treatment goals, and gaining insight into the youth.

These findings suggest that the social support provided by RYC workers is important for achieving positive relationships with youth. They also point to the need for training for care workers so that they are better prepared to work with youth (Eenshuistra et al., 2019; Harder et al., 2013). Adequate knowledge and skills of youth care workers can prevent common RYC problems such as staff burnout and turnover (Jongepier & Struijk, 2008). Several Dutch studies show that professional competence and consequently the quality and effectiveness of RYC can be improved by providing training to youth care workers (cf. Eenshuistra et al., 2016).

Recently, Eenshuistra and colleagues evaluated the Up2U training program developed specifically for RYC workers (Eenshuistra et al., 2021, 2022). Based on Motivational Interviewing (MI) and Solution-Focused Therapy, Up2U aims to establish a positive individual relationship with the youth and increase youths' intrinsic motivation for change. In a qualitative study, 12 care workers and nine adolescents showed that they were both satisfied with Up2U (Eenshuistra et al., 2022). Care workers identified the clarity, conciseness, and sample questions as positive elements and the extensiveness and implementation of Up2U as less positive. In another study, Eenshuistra et al. (2021) found that the 13 included RYC workers used MI skills significantly more after participating in an MI training program than before the training. In addition, there was a trend toward less use of MI non-adherent behaviors after training.

Social climate as a facilitator

Research on RYC has traditionally addressed the question of *what is achieved* (treatment effectiveness), such as the reduction of behavioral problems. Various meta-analyses (e.g., De Swart et al., 2012; Gutterswijk et al., 2020; Knorth et al., 2008) examining the treatment effects of RYC have found small to moderate improvements in behavioral problems in the short-term, but the longer the follow-up period, the less convincing the treatment effects are (Gutterswijk et al., 2023; Harder & Knorth, 2015). In addition, recidivism after RYC is high (Knorth et al., 2008; Van der Helm et al., 2012), with rates ranging from 30 to 60% (Leipoldt, 2021). By focusing on these questions of effectiveness, we tend to overlook the question of *how* (or whether) treatment effects are achieved. Because youth in RYC do not only engage in individual therapy but also live their lives and are cared for and supported by group care workers, we need to know more about "the other 23 hours" (Trieschman et al., 1969) and contextual factors affecting RYC treatment as this can explain between 30 and 50% of the variance in treatment outcomes (Attar-Schwartz, 2017). One important aspect of contextual characteristics is the daily living environment, hereafter referred to as social climate (SC) in RYC.

In general, SC has been established as a key factor necessary to achieve positive treatment outcomes (Leipoldt et al., 2019), such as reduced behavioral problems (Castro et al., 2023), improved quality of life (Leipoldt et al., 2022), and increased treatment satisfaction (Mesman Schultz, 1992). SC can be defined as:

> ...the quality of the social and physical environment in terms of the provision of sufficient and necessary conditions for the physical and mental health, well-being, and personal growth of the residents, with respect for their human dignity and human rights as well as (if not restricted by judicial measures) their personal autonomy, aimed at participation in society.
>
> (Stams & Van der Helm, 2017, p. 4)

This broad definition of SC has a clear relationship with the aforementioned SDT, where relatedness, autonomy, and competence are considered primary needs for personal growth and treatment motivation (Deci & Ryan, 2015; Van der Helm et al., 2018). Furthermore, treatment motivation itself is positively associated with treatment outcomes in RYC (Harder et al., 2012; Heynen et al., 2017). Therefore, a positive SC is considered a critical aspect for change and development of young people in RYC (Attar-Schwartz, 2017; Huefner & Ainsworth, 2021).

There are various operationalizations of SC and associated measurement tools (see Tonkin, 2016 for a review). However, key aspects of SC relevant to positive treatment outcomes in RYC include *perceptions of* involvement, support, autonomy, clarity, and structure/control (or strictness) (e.g., Leipoldt, 2021; Scholte & Van der Ploeg, 2000; Van der Helm et al., 2018). These aspects have been shown to be positively associated with SDT-relatedness (Nagpaul & Chen, 2019).

RYC settings that consist of high levels of perceived support and autonomy, low levels of repression (strictness), and a clear and structured environment are considered to have an "open climate" (Van der Helm et al., 2009). A basis for such an open climate is that there are positive peer relationships (especially for girls), in essence that "it takes a positive climate to make a positive climate" (Sonderman et al., 2022, p. 484). Studies examining SC in Dutch secure RYC have shown that this open climate is positively associated with less aggression among youth (Eltink et al., 2015; Sonderman et al., 2022), better coping strategies (Van der Helm et al., 2014), higher levels of empathy (Heynen et al., 2017), and more treatment motivation (Van der Helm et al., 2018). In addition, Scholte and Van der Ploeg (2000) showed that a balance between a therapeutic climate of firm, but not harsh, control and consistent non-obtrusive emotional support is key to promoting healthy development in young people with behavioral problems in RYC. These findings are also in line with Attar-Schwartz (2017), who showed that a positive, less strict, more friendly, and more supportive perceived SC was related to lower levels of peer and staff violence in RYC.

The above discussion illustrates the importance of an overarching basic positive therapeutic milieu in RYC (Reime & Tysnes, 2021). Such a perceived positive supportive milieu can create the right conditions for the further development of social supportive relationships among youth and between youth and staff members, which in turn can contribute to sustained behavior change and positive treatment outcomes (e.g., Attar-Schwartz, 2017; Harder, 2018). Ongoing monitoring of an RYC setting's SC, ensuring that staff and youth can regularly discuss the living environment in an open dialog and decide together when adjustments are needed, will ensure that the SC remains a core aspect of RYC in which youth feel empowered in their autonomy and connection to one another (Leipoldt & Strijbosch, 2020).

Social support after RYC

Several Dutch studies show that youth still have a need for support after RYC. For example, in Smit's PhD research, 67 former RYC residents (ages 12–21) were interviewed about the final phase of their residential stay: the preparation for this and the aftercare they subsequently received (Smit, 1991, 1993; Smit & Laird, 1992). The study found that just before a young person leaves, the institution carries out an assessment of the social support resources in 70% of the cases. This assessment takes place more often for young people who start living independently (80%) than for young people who return to their parental family (60%). In 30% of all cases, there is very little support available.

Regarding the size and nature of the network from which support is derived, Smit's results are comparable to those of Buysse (1997): mothers, siblings, and friends are more important sources of support than fathers. Smit calculated a so-called *support index*. This index expresses the ratio between the total number of people in a given relationship to young people (e.g., grandparents) mentioned and the number of people (e.g. grandparents) from whom they perceive they receive support. An index between 67 and 100 expresses the most supportive people and an index between 0 and 33 corresponds to a majority of non-supportive people. Smit also distinguished three types of social support[1]:

- *appraisal* (or emotional) support involves the expression of affection, empathy, care for, and the like.
- *belonging* (or companionship) support contributes to a sense of belonging and involves the presence or availability of other people with whom someone is connected.
- *tangible* support (or concrete help) means actively supporting a person and, if necessary, taking over some responsibility for solving a problem.

Appraisal support is relatively most received from the mothers, but the index is only 63 (for fathers 50). The same is true for tangible support (for fathers 45). The most belonging support is received from friends; the index is 76. For mothers, fathers, and siblings, the latter index is 51, 40, and 59, respectively. We can clearly see here that admitted young people do not always receive clear social support from their own families. This needs to be taken into account in the assistance process.

In another more recent study, Harder et al. (2011b) focused on the care needs of youth after leaving secure RYC. The results of the interviews with the 24 adolescents in the study indicate that many adolescents experience problems during the transition from secure care, particularly with finances, school and employment, and housing. In contrast to other studies, most adolescents report receiving support in the year after leaving care. Relatively few adolescents move to independence after leaving care, suggesting that many youth are not ready to make a true transition to adulthood.

Although young people often have a need for support after leaving RYC, the support provided by Dutch youth care organizations generally ends at the age of 18 (Van Breda et al., 2020). Regarding the organization of aftercare, there are several bottlenecks in the Dutch support for youth who turn 18 (Steketee et al., 2009). There is a lack of adequate support for foster care and RYC youth with psychiatric problems or mild mental disability or who have experienced homelessness. Other bottlenecks are the lack of expertise for this group of youth in care in terms of outreach support to develop practical skills and a social network, the voluntary approach of adult care, poor fit between youth and adult care, and lack of clarity about who is responsible for caring for this group (Steketee et al., 2009).

To prevent homelessness and stimulate independence after leaving care, in the 1990s the Exit Training program was developed in the Netherlands. The Exit Training is a ten-week program aimed at the preparation of young people for leaving RYC. Dutch studies that focused on the Exit Training program show promising results, including comparable or higher adjustment (e.g., stability of living circumstances or reasons for leaving the residential care setting) for youth who participated in the program compared to youth who did not participate in the program (Spanjaard et al., 1999; Harder et al., 2011a).

Conclusions

Our overview makes it clear that the concept of social support is of great value in the guidance and treatment of residentially admitted young people. The most important sources of support from which to draw are family and friends, care workers, and peers. Young people in RYC have a smaller social network than their nonresidential peers. The support they receive from their own family comes primarily from their mother – in the form of appraisal support and tangible support – while the mother figure can also be a major source of stress. It is also often stressful for parents to be involved in the care and treatment offered by the RYC center. It is not always possible for children and parents to be reunited. This is another reason why customization needs to be made. It is important that at the beginning of the process, a careful assessment of the possibilities and obstacles is made (Geurts et al., 2012). Belonging support comes mainly from friends and peers in the group. However, the latter can also play a negative role, for example, through bullying or aggressive behavior.

The quality of the SC in the group is important here. If this is negative, with a lot of animosity between the group members, it puts pressure on the leadership to change the atmosphere and mutual relations for the better (Eltink et al., 2015). This requires a professional approach in which it may sometimes be necessary to adjust the composition of the team of care workers (Sonderman, 2023). It is important to implement good monitoring of the group climate in which care workers and young people regularly check with each other whether and what is needed to improve the climate (Leipoldt, 2021). In a positive SC, there is also more room to offer support to individual young people, for example, in the form of mentoring conversations. Research shows that these conversations are seen as important by young people, not so much as a way to help them change their behavior, but as a way to be heard (Harder et al., 2022). A good relationship with a mentor is supportive for young people. There is a risk of staff turnover and discontinuation of positive alliances (Sonderman, 2023).

A challenge is preparing young people to leave care, including their transition to independent functioning in society. Research shows that this transition is stressful for young people and requires more attention and support from professionals, both inside and outside the residential setting. Not all residents are well prepared and receive adequate aftercare after leaving care, while there are clear indications that aftercare programs can be effective, for example, in preventing youth homelessness (Spanjaard et al., 1999). In this context, it is widely advocated that the age at which young people turn 18 should not be used as a criterion for enforced leaving care; most of them need (much) longer the support of adults who are/remain accessible to them (Van Breda et al., 2020).

Our overview does not yet provide much information about the conditions under which young people receive optimal support from their *peers* in the group. As mentioned earlier, the SC will be important but the composition and size of the group will also influence this. More research is needed in this area. The same applies to the role of education; in the Netherlands, there has been no meaningful research into the extent to which, and the way in which, young people can draw support from the education they receive, inside or outside the residential setting. If the trend in our country continues to offer RYC in small-scale units (Nijhof et al., 2020), it is foreseeable that young people will more often participate in education outside the care institution. It would be desirable to study the incriminating or supportive aspects of this in more detail.

Note

1 Actually, she discerns still two other types of social support, namely *cognitive* (or information) support [aimed at helping someone to understand something (better), for example, by providing information] and *self-esteem* support [this is providing a positive image of a person when (s)he compares her/himself to others]. These two types have not been included in Smit's research.

References

Attar-Schwartz, S. (2017). Experiences of victimization by peers and staff in residential care for children at risk in Israel from an ecological perspective. In A.V. Rus, S.R. Parris, & E. Stativa (Eds.), *Child maltreatment in residential care* (pp. 269–299). Springer International Publishing AG. https://doi.org/10.1007/978-3-319-57990-0_13

Blankestein, A. (2022). New applications of system interventions: Researching the question what works for serious behavioral problems of youth. *Tijdschrift voor Orthopedagogiek*, *61*(3),48–56 (in Dutch).

Bravo, A., & Del Valle, J.F. (2003). Social support networks of adolescents in residential care: A comparative analysis with normative population. *Psicothema*, *15*, 136–142. https://doi.org/10.1002/jcop.20348

Buysse, W.H. (1997). *Personal social networks and behavior problems in adolescence. An explorative study in three samples: A residential sample, a day treatment sample, and a reference sample* (Doctoral dissertation). Leiden: Leiden University.

Castro, E., Magalhães, E., & Del Valle, J.F. (2023). A systematic review of non-specific and specific treatment factors associated with lower or greater internalising and externalising symptoms in therapeutic residential care. *Children and Youth Services Review*, *147*, Article 106840. https://doi.org/10.1016/j.childyouth.2023.106840

Cohen, S., Mermelstein, R., Kamarck, T., & Hoberman, H.M. (1985). Measuring the functional components of social support. In I.G. Sarason & B.R. Sarason (Eds.), *Social support: Theory, research, and applications* (pp. 73–94). Martinus Nijhoff.

De Swart, J.J.W., Van den Broek, H., Stams, G.J., Asscher, J.J., Van der Laan, P.H., Holsbrink-Engels, G.A., & Van der Helm, G.H.P. (2012). The effectiveness of institutional youth care over the past three decades: A meta-analysis. *Children and Youth Services Review*, *34*(9),1818–1824. https://doi.org/10.1016/j.childyouth.2012.05.015

Deci, E.L., & Ryan, R.M. (2015). *Self-determination theory*. International encyclopedia of the social and behavioural sciences, 2nd ed. (Vol. 21). Elsevier.

Eenshuistra, A., Bhola, P.M., Hoek-Dekker, A., Knorth, E.J., & Harder, A.T. (2022). To change or not to change? A study regarding the satisfaction of care workers and adolescents with the Motivational Interviewing based residential youth care training program Up2U. *Child and Youth Services*, *43*, 1–28. https://doi.org/10.1080/0145935X.2022.2113870

Eenshuistra, A., Harder, A.T., & Knorth, E.J. (2019). One size does not fit all: A systematic review of training outcomes on residential youth care professionals' skills. *Children and Youth Services Review*, *103*, 135–147. https://doi.org/10.1016/j.childyouth.2019.05.010

Eenshuistra, A., Harder, A.T., & Knorth, E.J. (2021). Professionalizing care workers: Outcomes of a 'Motivational Interviewing' training in residential youth care. *Residential Treatment for Children and Youth*, *38*(3),248–268. https://doi.org/10.1080/0886571X.2020.1739597

Eenshuistra, A., Harder, A.T., Van Zonneveld, N.L., & Knorth, E.J. (2016). Look who's talking: A Motivational Interviewing based observation study of one-on-one conversations between residential care workers and adolescents. *International Journal of Child and Family Welfare*, *17*(1/2),64–84. https://ugp.rug.nl/IJCFW/article/view/37872

Eltink, E.M.A., Van der Helm, P., Wissink, I.B., & Stams, G.J.J.M. (2015). The relation between living group climate and reactions to social problem situations in detained adolescents: "I stabbed him because he looked mean at me". *International Journal of Forensic Mental Health*, *14*(2),101–109. https://doi.org/10.1080/14999013.2015.1033110

Ferreira, S., Magalhães, E., & Prioste, A. (2019). Social support and mental health of young people in residential care: A qualitative study. *Anuario de Psicología Jurídica*, *30*, 29–34. https://doi.org/10.5093/apj2019a12

Geurts, E.M.W. (2010). *Involving parents in residential youth care: A study of content and outcome of family-context oriented care and treatment* (Doctoral dissertation). Groningen: University of Groningen (in Dutch).

Geurts, E.M.W., Boddy, J., Noom, M.J., & Knorth, E.J. (2012). Family-centred residential care: The new reality? *Child and Family Social Work*, *17*(2),170–179. https://doi.org/10.1111/j.1365-2206.2012.00838.x

Gutterswijk, R.V., Kuiper, C.H.Z., Harder, A.T., Bocanegra, B.R., Van der Horst, F.C.P., & Prinzie, P. (2023). Associations between secure residential care and positive behavioral change in adolescent boys and girls. *Residential Treatment for Children and Youth*, *40*(2),173–196. https://doi.org/10.1080/0886571X.2022.2100561

Gutterswijk, R.V., Kuiper, C.H.Z., Lautan, N., Kunst, E.G., Van der Horst, F.C.P., Stams, G.J.J.M., & Prinzie, P. (2020). The outcome of non-residential youth care compared to residential youth care: A multilevel meta-analysis. *Children and Youth Services Review*, *113*, Article 104950. https://doi.org/10.1016/j.childyouth.2020.104950

Harder, A.T. (2018). Residential care and cure: Achieving enduring behavior change with youth by using a self-determination, common factors and motivational interviewing approach. *Residential Treatment for Children and Youth*, *35*(4),317–335. https://doi.org/10.1080/0886571X.2018.1460006

Harder, A.T., Eenshuistra, A., & Knorth, E.J. (2022). Feeling better: Experiences and needs of adolescents and professionals regarding their mentoring relationship in residential youth care. *Child and Youth Care Forum*, *51*, 613–631. https://doi.org/10.1007/s10566-021-09645-x

Harder, A.T., Kalverboer, M.E., & Knorth, E.J. (2011a). They have left the building: A review of aftercare services' outcomes for adolescents following residential youth care. *International Journal of Child and Family Welfare*, *14*(3/4),86–104. https://ugp.rug.nl/IJCFW/article/view/37848/35437

Harder, A.T., & Knorth, E.J. (2015). Uncovering what is inside the "black box" of effective therapeutic residential youth care. In J.K. Whittaker, J.F. Del Valle, & L. Holmes (Eds.), *Therapeutic residential care with children and youth: Developing evidence-based international practice* (pp. 217–228). Jessica Kingsley Publishers.

Harder, A.T., & Knorth, E.J. (2022). *Youth placed in out-of-home care in the Netherlands: Definitions and numbers – Version 3*. Erasmus University Rotterdam/ University of Groningen. https://research.rug.nl/en/publications/uithuisgeplaatste-jeugdigen-in-nederland-definitie-en-cijfers-ver (in Dutch).

Harder, A.T., Knorth, E.J., & Kalverboer, M.E. (2011b). Transition secured? A follow-up study of adolescents who have left secure residential care. *Children and Youth Services Review*, *33*(12), 2482–2488. https://doi.org/10.1016/j.childyouth.2011.08.022

Harder, A.T., Knorth, E.J., & Kalverboer, M.E. (2012). Securing the downside up: Client and care factors associated with outcomes of secure residential youth care. *Child and Youth Care Forum*, *41*(3),259–276. https://doi.org/10.1007/s10566-011-9159-1

Harder, A.T., Knorth, E.J., & Kalverboer, M.E. (2013). A secure base? The adolescent-staff relationship in secure residential youth care. *Child and Family Social Work*, *18*(3),305–317. https://doi.org/10.1111/j.1365-2206.2012.00846.x

Harder, A.T., Knorth, E.J., & Kuiper, C.H.Z. (2020a). Out-of-home placement of youth: What, for whom, and when? In A.T. Harder, E.J. Knorth & C.H.Z. Kuiper (Eds.), *Uithuisgeplaatste jeugdigen: Sleutels tot succes in behandeling en onderwijs* (pp. 13–30). SWP (in Dutch).

Harder, A.T., Mann-Feder, V., Oterholm, I., & Refaeli, T. (2020b). Supporting transitions to adulthood for youth leaving care: Consensus based principles. *Children and Youth Services Review*, *116*, 1–9. https://doi.org/10.1016/j.childyouth.2020.105260

Heynen, E.J.E., Van der Helm, P., & Stams, G.J.J.M. (2017). Treatment motivation and living group climate in German youth prison: A validation of the German adolescent treatment motivation questionnaire. *Residential Treatment for Children and Youth*, *34*(1),49–60. https://doi.org/10.1080/0886571X.2016.1251373

Huefner, J., & Ainsworth, F. (2021). Commentary: Recognizing the value of the milieu in therapeutic residential care for children and youth. *Residential Treatment for Children and Youth*, *38*(3),324–335. https://doi.org/10.1080/0886571X.2021.1915225

Jongepier, N., & Struijk, M. (2008). Time for re-evaluation of the pedagogical basic climate. *Jeugd en Co Kennis*, 2(4),19–25. https://doi.org/10.1007/BF03085940 (in Dutch).

Knorth, E.J., & Harder, A.T. (2023). Residential care for children and youth in the Netherlands: High difficulties in low lands. In J.K. Whittaker, L. Holmes, J. Del Valle, & S. James (Eds.), *Revitalizing residential care for children and youth: Cross-national trends and challenges* (pp. 193–208). Oxford University Press.

Knorth, E.J., Harder, A.T., Huyghen, A.M.N., Kalverboer, M.E., & Zandberg, T. (2010). Residential youth care and treatment research: Care workers as key factor in outcomes? *International Journal of Child and Family Welfare*, *13*(1/2),49–67. https://ugp.rug.nl/IJCFW/article/view/37822/35406

Knorth, E.J., Harder, A.T., Zandberg, T., & Kendrick, A.J. (2008). Under one roof: A review and selective meta-analysis on the outcomes of residential child and youth care. *Children and Youth Services Review*, *30*(2),123–140. https://doi.org/10.1016/j.childyouth.2007.09.001

Leipoldt, J.D. (2021). *Give me the environment that I need: The importance of social climate for the well-being of adolescents in therapeutic residential youth care* (Doctoral dissertation). University of Groningen. https:/doi.org/10.33612/diss.183547001

Leipoldt, J.D., Harder, A.T., Kayed, N.S., Grietens, H., & Rimehaug, T. (2019). Determinants and outcomes of social climate in therapeutic residential youth care: A systematic review. *Children and Youth Services Review*, *99*, 429–440. https://doi.org/10.1016/j.childyouth.2019.02.010

Leipoldt, J.D., Harder, A.T., Kayed, N.S., Knorth, E.J., & Rimehaug, T. (2022). The mediating role of social climate in the association of youth and residential service characteristics and quality of life. *American Journal of Orthopsychiatry*, *92*(2),203–216. https://doi.org/10.1037/ort0000598

Leipoldt, J.D., & Strijbosch, E.L.L. (2020). A positive climate in family-style group care and residential youth care. In A.T. Harder, E.J. Knorth, & C. Kuiper (Eds.), *Uithuisgeplaatste jeugdigen. Sleutels tot succes in behandeling en onderwijs* (pp. 109–117). SWP (in Dutch).

Mesman Schultz, K. (1992). Social climate, client satisfaction and quality of residential treatment programs. In J.D. van der Ploeg, P.M. van den Bergh, M. Klomp, E.J. Knorth, & M. Smit (Eds.), *Vulnerable youth in residential care. Part I: Social competence, social support and social climate* (pp. 249–260). Garant.

Nagpaul, T., & Chen, J. (2019). Self-determination theory as a framework for understanding needs of youth at-risk: Perspectives of social service professionals and the youth themselves. *Children and Youth Services Review*, *99*, 328–342. https://doi.org/10.1016/j.childyouth.2019.02.015

Nijhof, K.S., Laninga-Wijnen, L., Mulder, E., Van Domburgh, L., Popma, A., & Konijn, C. (2020). Small-scale groups in child and youth care: A first exploration. *Kind en Adolescent*, *41*(2),187–204. https://doi.org/10.1007/s12453-020-00236-6 (in Dutch).

Pinchover, S., & Attar-Schwartz, S. (2018). Is someone there for you? Social support of youth in educational residential care from family, peers and staff. *British Journal of Social Work*, *48*(8),2195–2214. https://doi.org/10.1093/bjsw/bcx164

Reime, M.A., & Tysnes, I.B. (2021). Youth experiences of and views on un-locked coercive placement in residential child care. *Young*, *29*(1),12–27. https://doi.org/10.1177/1103308820937560

Scholte, E.M., & Van der Ploeg, J.D. (2000). Exploring factors governing successful residential treatment of youngsters with serious behavioural difficulties: Findings from a longitudinal study in Holland. *Childhood, a Global Journal of Child Research*, *7*(2),129–153. https://doi.org/10.1177/0907568200007002002

Schuengel, C. (2002). Residential care: Safety and practice-based research. In M.H. van IJzendoorn, & H. de Frankrijker (Eds.), *Pedagogiek in beeld: Een inleiding in de pedagogische studie van opleiding, onderwijs en hulpverlening* (pp. 239–251). Bohn Stafleu van Loghum (in Dutch).

Simons, I. (2018). *Improving family-centered care in Juvenile Justice Institutions* (Doctoral dissertation). Leiden: Leiden University.

Singstad, M.T. (2021). *Perceived social support among adolescents in residential youth care: Prevalence and associations with symptom loads of psychiatric disorders and quality of life* (Doctoral dissertation). Trondheim, Norway: Norwegian University of Science and Technology.

Smit, M. (1991). Leaving residential care: A stressful experience. In W. Hellinckx, E. Broekaert, A. Vanden Berge, & M. Colton (Eds.), *Innovations in residential care* (pp. 211–225). Acco.

Smit, M. (1993). *Everything comes to an end. A study on ending of residential child care* (Doctoral dissertation). Leiden: Leiden University (in Dutch).

Smit, M., & Laird, E. (1992). The availability of social support after residential care. In J.D. van der Ploeg, P.M. van den Bergh, M. Klomp, E.J. Knorth, & M. Smit (Eds.), *Vulnerable youth in residential care. Part I: Social competence, social support, and social climate* (pp. 193–206). Garant.

Sonderman, J. (2023). *Heart shaped bruises: Residential group climate and effectiveness of treatment for girls in (secure) residential youth care* (Doctoral dissertation). Tilburg: Tilburg University.

Sonderman, J., Kuiper, C., Van der Helm, P., & Van de Mheen, D. (2022). With connection, less correction: Gender-specific needs of girls' residential group climate – A mixed method non-randomized case-study. *Child and Youth Care Forum, 51*(3),465–494. https://doi.org/10.1007/s10566-021-09628-y

Spanjaard, H.J.M., Van der Veldt, M.C.A.E., & Van den Bogaart, P.H.M. (1999). Exit training for youngsters in residential care: Treatment to prevent homelessness. *International Journal of Child and Family Welfare*, 4(2),130–148. https://ugp.rug.nl/IJCFW/article/view/37498

Stams, G.J., & Van der Helm, P. (2017). What works in residential programs for aggressive and violent youth? In P. Sturney (Ed.), *The Wiley handbook of violence and aggression* (pp. 1–12). John Wiley & Sons, Ltd. https://doi.org/10.1002/9781119057574.whbva116

Steketee, M., Vandenbroucke, M., & Rijkschroeff, R. (2009). *Care (for youth) doesn't stop at 18 years.* Verwey-Jonker Instituut (in Dutch).

Sulimani-Aidan, Y. (2017). To dream the impossible dream: Care leavers' challenges and barriers in pursuing their future expectations and goals. *Children and Youth Services Review, 81*, 332–339. https://doi.org/10.1016/j.childyouth.2017.08.025

Tonkin, M. (2016). A review of questionnaire measures for assessing the social climate in prisons and forensic psychiatric hospitals. *International Journal of Offender Therapy and Comparative Criminology, 60*(12),1376–1405. https://doi.org/10.1177/0306624X15578834

Trieschman, A.E., Whittaker, J.K., & Brendtro, L.K. (1969). *The other 23 hours. Child care work with emotionally disturbed children in a therapeutic milieu.* Aldine.

UNICEF. (2020). *Worlds of influence: Understanding what shapes child well-being in rich countries.* https://www.unicef.org/reports/worlds-influence-what-shapes-child-well-being-rich-countries-2020

Van Breda, A.D., Munro, E.R., Gilligan, R., Anghel, R., Harder, A.T., Incarnato, M., Mann-Feder, V., Refaeli, T., Stohler, R., & Storø, J. (2020). Extended care: Global dialogue on policy, practice and research. *Children and Youth Services Review, 119*, 1–14. https://doi.org/10.1016/j.childyouth.2020.105596

Van der Helm, G.H.P., Kuiper, C.H.Z., & Stams, G.J.J.M. (2018). Group climate and treatment motivation in secure residential and forensic youth care from the perspective of self determination theory. *Children and Youth Services Review, 93*, 339–344. https://doi.org/10.1016/j.childyouth.2018.07.028

Van der Helm, G.H.P., Stams, G.J.J.M., Van der Stel, J.C., Van Langen, M.A.M., & Van der Laan, P.H. (2012). Group climate and empathy in a sample of incarcerated boys. *International Journal of Offender Therapy and Comparative Criminology, 56*(8),1149–1160. https://doi.org/10.1177/0306624X11421649

Van der Helm, P., Beunk, L., Stams, G.J., & Van der Laan, P. (2014). The relationship between detention length, living group climate, coping, and treatment motivation among juvenile delinquents in a youth correctional facility. *The Prison Journal, 94*(2),260–275. https://doi.org/10.1177/0032885514524884

Van der Helm, P., Klapwijk, M., Stams, G.J., & Van der Laan, P. (2009). 'What works' for juvenile prisoners: The role of group climate in a youth prison. *Journal of Children's Services*, 4(2),36–48. https://doi.org/10.1108/17466660200900011

Van der Ploeg, J.D. (1981). The group climate. In J.D. van der Ploeg (Ed.), *Jeugd (z) onder dak. Deel 2: Opvoeding, organisatie en onderzoek in de residentiële hulpverlening* (pp. 280–296). Samsom (in Dutch).

Van der Ploeg, J.D. (1984). The residential setting as a damaging or supporting environment. In P.M. van den Bergh, J.D. van der Ploeg, & M. Smit (Eds.), *Grenzen van de residentiële hulpverlening* (pp. 10–39). VUGA (in Dutch).
Van der Ploeg, J.D. (1992). Social competence and social support in residential care. In J.D. van der Ploeg et al. (Eds.), *Vulnerable youth in residential care. Part I: Social competence, social support and social climate* (pp. 19–34). Garant.
Van der Ploeg, J.D., Van den Bergh, P.M., Klomp, M., Knorth, E.J., & Smit, M. (Eds.). (1992). *Vulnerable youth in residential care. Part I: Social competence, social support and social climate*. Garant.
Whittaker, J.K. (1992). Enhancing social support for high-risk youth and their families following residential care. In J.D. van der Ploeg et al. (Eds.), *Vulnerable youth in residential care. Part I: Social competence, social support and social climate* (pp. 81–100). Garant.
Whittaker, J.K., & Garbarino, J. (1983). *Social support networks: Informal helping in the human services*. Aldine Publishing Company.
Whittaker, J.K., Schinke, S., & Gilchrist, L. (1986). The ecological paradigm in child, youth and family services: Implications for policy and practice. *Social Service Review*, *60*, 483–503. https://doi.org/10.1086/644395
Zegers, M.A.M. (2007). *Attachment among institutionalized adolescents: Mental representations, therapeutic relationships and problem behavior* (Doctoral dissertation). Amsterdam: University of Amsterdam.
Zegers, M.A.M., Schuengel, C., Van IJzendoorn, M.H., & Janssens, J.M.A.M. (2006). Attachment representations of institutionalized adolescents and their professional caregivers: Predicting the development of therapeutic relationships. *American Journal of Orthopsychiatry*, *76*(3),325–334. https://doi.org/10.1037/0002-9432.76.3.325

15 Caring for the Caregivers

Evaluating Brazil's "Cuida" Program Aiming at Promoting Skills for Building Caring Relationships with Children and Youth

Bruna Wendt and Débora Dalbosco Dell'Aglio

Introduction

This chapter discusses the role of caregivers (referred to as social educators in Brazil) in the support network of children and adolescents in residential care. It highlights the importance of providing care, support, and skills to these professionals to enhance the quality of their educational and caregiving practices. The chapter also presents the qualitative results of an intervention called the "Cuida", which was carried out with caregivers from residential care institutions in southern Brazil.

Since the colonial period (beginning in 1500), placing vulnerable children in residential care institutions has been the primary means of childcare in Brazil. However, from the 1980s onward, with the mobilization of civil society and the promulgation of the Constitution of Federative Republic of Brazil (Brasil, 1988) and the Statute of the Child and Adolescent (Brasil, 1990), new approaches of conceiving childhood and protecting maltreated children have been articulated. These include "Casas-lares" (homes housing up to ten children) and "Famílias acolhedoras" (foster families).

Residential care institutions in Brazil aim to provide special therapeutic care to children and adolescents who are victims of abuse, neglect, or other risks in their home environments. These institutions offer protection and support to these vulnerable populations. According to the National Council of Justice (2020), approximately 34,157 children and adolescents are currently in Brazilian residential care institutions. Although there are legal initiatives at both the national (Brasil, 2009a) and state (Rio Grande do Sul, 2018) levels to implement programs such as "*Famílias Acolhedoras*" (Foster Families), the majority of children and youth in out-of-home care (96%) remaining in residential care institutions is still large (96%) compared with a small proportion (4%) in family foster care (National Council of Justice, 2020).

Regardless of the duration of their stay, residential care should provide children and adolescents with support, protection, and high-quality interactions with caregivers (Ferreira et al., 2020; Moré & Sperancetta, 2010; Steels & Simpson, 2017). Therefore, it is essential to direct efforts toward improving

DOI: 10.4324/9781003424468-21

the institutional infrastructure, climate, and professional practices aligned with current legal norms and guidelines. These improvements should aim to enhance the protection, well-being, and comprehensive development of children and adolescents. The caregivers in residential care play a central role in the life of the child in residential care, becoming his/her main source of protection, emotional support, and educational guidance (Ferreira et al., 2020; Kappler & Mendes, 2019; Marzol et al., 2012). Emotional bonds and positive interactions with caregivers are important protective factors in the face of adversities in the lives of children and adolescents in residential care (Ferreira et al., 2020; Kappler & Mendes, 2019). However, recent studies on interactions between caregivers and children in residential care have highlighted that often physical contact was avoided by caregivers, and emotional bonds were limited, due to various reasons, including institutional guidelines (Kappler & Mendes, 2019; Moura et al., 2022).

According to the Technical Guidelines for Residential Care Services (Brazil, 2009b), in addition to being responsible for basic care related to diet and hygiene, caregivers have several key responsibilities. These included building bonds, organizing the institutional environment, helping children and adolescents process their life stories, strengthening their self-esteem, and aiding in the development of their identities. Caregivers must also ensure that the children's health needs are covered, among other duties. Although institutional care is intended to be temporary (up to 18 months in Brazil), the bonds formed during this time are essential for the children's perception of protection and safety and their ability to rehabilitate from adverse pre-placement experiences.

Recent national and international studies have shown that affectionate and respectful relationships between children in residential care and caregivers are associated with higher levels of self-esteem (Schavarem & Toni, 2019), optimism and resilience (Weber et al., 2018), subjective well-being, and quality of life in youth (Ferreira et al., 2020). Additionally, such positive relationships seem to be associated with lower levels of depressive symptoms (Weber, 2017), behavioral and emotional adjustment difficulties (Hoffnung-Assouline & Attar-Schwartz, 2020), and youth risk behaviors such as substance use (Weber, 2017).

For example, in a qualitative study conducted with adolescents in residential care in Portugal, Ferreira et al. (2020) found that the teenagers recognized the positive impact of social support received in the residential care setting on their psychological functioning, especially in terms of self-efficacy. They noted that this support helped them develop new skills and autonomy. The adolescents also highlighted that such support was crucial for them to become sources of social support for others. Studies have also shown that there was a variance in staff support among children and youth in residential care based on personal characteristics. For instance, in a study of more than 1,400 adolescents in residential care in Israel, Hoffnung Assouline and Attar-Schwartz (2020) found that boys perceived lower levels of social support compared to girls.

It seems, therefore, that the role of caregivers is crucial for the well-being of children and youth in residential care. It is a complex and demanding role that requires dedication and responsibility, as well as ongoing training, support, and qualification. Daily exposure to stressful situations and a lack of institutional support can lead to burnout and health issues. Some studies report somatic complaints, insomnia, fatigue, irritability, sadness, and poor concentration among these professionals (e.g., Romero et al., 2016). Though these symptoms may not meet the criteria for mental disorders diagnoses (classified by ICD-10 or DSM-V), they can cause functional disabilities at work (Romero et al., 2016). In São Paulo, Brazil, Pagnota and Prebianchi (2021) identified, for example, a correlation between higher levels of stress and the use of maladaptive coping strategies (such as avoidance) among caregivers from philanthropic residential care institutions, particularly those with long working hours. Additionally, feelings of being unsupported among care workers were linked to frustration, insecurity, and dissatisfaction (Avoglia et al., 2012), all of which can interfere with the educational practices provided to the children and youth in residential care.

A caregiver experiencing stress and burnout incurs high social and economic costs, as the demand for health services increases. This also leads to absenteeism and staff turnover and decreases motivation for work, making it difficult to build positive relationships with both the children and colleagues (Romero et al., 2016). Thus, preventive and systematic care for these caregivers is essential. Promoting adequate training, along with listening spaces and guidance, is crucial to increasing their well-being and improving their care practices for children and adolescents in residential care.

Internationally recognized programs such as ACT-Raising Safe Kids (ACT-RSK) (Silva, 2009) and Triple P (Positive Parenting Program) (Sanders et al., 1999), originally developed for working with parents, can also be used to train other caregivers, such as residential care professionals. In Brazil, although many findings have pointed to the importance of training these professionals (Guerra & Del Prette, 2018; Halpern et al., 2015), there are few evaluation studies of such programs (Prada, 2007; Bersch, 2017), making it difficult to replicate or construct new evidence-based interventions. In this context, the "Cuida Program" was developed to support and enhance the positive educational practices of caregivers who work in residential care settings in Brazil. Along with its implementation in these settings, the program aimed to evaluate the implementation process and produce qualitative results, which will be discussed in this chapter.

The "Cuida" Program

The "Cuida" program is theoretically based on the principles of positive parenting, defined as the behavior of primary parents and caregivers that fosters the full development of children and ensures their rights through non-violent practices of discipline, guidance, empowerment, and recognition (Council of Europe,

2006). Given the intensive care relationship that caregivers in residential care have with the children and the fact that the setting acts as *in loco parentis*, the program fits the aim of improving the care practices of the caregivers.

Martín-Quintana and Rodrigo-López (2013) pointed out that the principle of positive parenting highlights the central role of children and adolescents in the acquisition, construction, and socialization of norms and values, facilitated by mutual collaboration between parents and children. Several studies have shown that the use of positive parenting is associated with higher levels of emotional well-being and a lower incidence of depressive symptoms, eating disorders, and drug abuse (Chen et al., 2019). Similarly, positive parenting practices seem to serve as a protective factor in the face of adverse childhood experiences (Yamaoka & Bard, 2019). While positive parenting programs are widely implemented in Europe and supported by the Council of Europe (Rodrigo, 2016), they are still limited in Brazil, typically arising from specific academic initiatives primarily aimed at parents. These programs have not yet been directed toward caregivers in residential care.

The "Cuida" program was implemented based on experiential methodology, which presupposes that knowledge is constructed collectively through the exchange of experiences. This approach respects the prior experiences and knowledge of group members, emphasizing their active participation (Martín-Quintana et al., 2009). The basic assumption of the program is that each experience will generate different reflections and outcomes. This methodology has been employed in other interventions with groups of parents (Máiquez-Chavez et al., 2000; Martín-Quintana et al., 2009) and institutional caregivers (Bersch, 2017).

The program was structured into eight weekly group meetings, each lasting two hours, for a total of 16 hours. The first and last meetings were primarily dedicated to administering pre- and post-intervention evaluation instruments to assess the program's effectiveness. The sessions, based on participants' experiences, covered themes such as positive educational practices, emotional regulation strategies, assertive communication techniques, conflict resolution methods, and self-care/self-efficacy strategies. This multicomponent format included psychoeducation practices and role-play activities. The content was selected based on national and international programs in positive parenting and institutional caregiver education (Bersch, 2017; Martínez-González, 2009; Prada, 2007; Sanders et al., 1999; Smith, 2009). Each meeting was facilitated by a moderator, who is a psychologist with prior experience in residential care, and accompanied by two trained observers. This chapter provides an overview of the evaluation study of the "Cuida" program's implementation process, emphasizing its significance in offering safe listening spaces and support to professionals, enabling them to serve as protective figures to those in care. Based on qualitative data and data triangulation, gathered from observations, moderator records, and participant questionnaires, we sought to evaluate participant satisfaction with the program, as well as assess their main learnings and the impacts on the daily institutional practices.

Methods

Participants

A total of 47 caregivers participated in this study (*M*=44.28 years; *SD*=9.34), including 37 women and 10 men; 73.3% had incomplete higher education. They worked an average of 39.47 hours a week (*SD* = 6.43) and had been working in this position for 10 years on average (*SD* = 10.47). All the participants worked in residential care settings in southern Brazil and completed all stages of the "Cuida" program. The inclusion criteria were: a) having at least a high school degree; b) having served as a caregiver in a residential care setting for children and adolescents for at least six months; and c) agreeing to participate in the evaluations before (T1) and after the program (T2).

Instruments

Socio-demographic Questionnaire

Participants were asked to report on their age, gender, marital status, level of education, time of employment in the residential care setting, and previous training courses they had completed.

Observers' Registration Form

This form was completed by two trained observers who were present at each session. They recorded the engagement of the participants with the dynamics and techniques suggested during the sessions, reported significant events, participants' comments and expressions, emerging themes, and other relevant observations.

A Participant Satisfaction Survey (Adapted from Durgante, 2019)

This survey included 14 questions to assess satisfaction with the program, clarity and understanding of the program content, and the generalization of learning after the end of the program's conclusion.

A Field Diary

This form was completed by the moderator to record observations, interpretations, and inferences at the end of each session of the program.

Procedure

The research team included a moderator and six trained observers who alternated in pairs throughout the eight meetings of each of the seven groups. The recruitment process for caregivers included disseminating information about the program in residential care settings throughout the city and on social media.

The meetings took place from October 2018 to October 2019 at the Institute of Psychology of the Federal University in Rio Grande do Sul. During the first meeting, the participants were asked to complete the informed consent form and the socio-demographic questionnaire. At the end of the last meeting, the participants filled out a satisfaction survey. Meanwhile, the trained observers filled out the moderator performance evaluation forms at each session to improve the program for future replication studies, ensuring greater control over possible methodological bias and greater data credibility (Levitt et al., 2018).

We analyzed 47 participant satisfaction surveys, 112 moderator performance evaluation forms completed by the observer pairs (excluding the eighth meeting, which was solely for closing and mingling), and the notes of the moderator's field diary. The qualitative data, based on observations, field diaries, questionnaires, and participants' reports, were examined using content analysis (Bardin, 2004). After the descriptive and content analyses of the data, we used data triangulation, including different information sources (including, the perceptions of the participating caregivers, the observers, and the moderator) and different time points (before, during, and after the program). Such a strategy enhances the internal validity and scientific rigor of qualitative research (Santos et al., 2018), which is essential for evaluating the implementation process of interventions (Steckler & Linnan, 2002).

The study was approved by the Research Ethics Committee of the Federal University in Rio Grande do Sul, under legal opinion 2,723,700. It follows the guidelines and norms outlined in Resolution No. 510/2016 for ethical research involving human subjects (Conselho Nacional de Saúde, 2016).

Results

Evaluation of the Implementation Process by Qualitative Indicators: Perspectives from Participants, Observers, and the Moderator

For qualitative data analysis, we considered the descriptive sections of the satisfaction surveys (completed by participants), observers' records, and the moderator's field diary. Content analysis was conducted, according to the three stages suggested by Bardin (2004): pre-analysis, exploration of the material, and inferential interpretation. The categories and subcategories, defined *a posteriori*, were organized as follows: (1) Impact of the program; (2) Interpersonal relationships (encompassing relationships with children and adolescents in care and with colleagues); and (3) General impressions, suggestions, and challenges.

The first category, *Impact of the Program*, encompassed the perceptions of participants, observers, and the moderator about the changes observed as a result of participating in the "Cuida" program. The participants noted improvements across various areas covered by the program, including emotional regulation, assertive communication, conflict resolution strategies, and self-care/self-efficacy strategies. Regarding *emotional regulation*, the participants reported adopting more adaptive strategies for managing their emotions, as reflected in comments such as "I think more before I act", "I act more calmly", and "I am more tolerant and patient in situations in general". As for *assertive communication*, the caregivers used praise and encouragement as positive communication strategies with children and adolescents. Regarding *conflict resolution strategies*, responses such as "I learned to listen more", "I learned to dialogue more", and "I realized the importance of negotiation and arrangements with children and adolescents in care" demonstrated that caregivers incorporated new conflict resolution methods in their daily interactions, both with children and adolescents in residential care and with colleagues. Regarding *self-care/self-efficacy*, most responses indicated an increased ability to critically assess oneself and one's work, along with a greater sense of competence and confidence.

The observers recorded several positive statements from the participants regarding the impacts of the program, such as: "improvement in communication", "promoting a space for dialogue", "dealing better with conflicts", "the role-plays helped me to consider other strategies", and "the weekly tasks encouraged me to rethink my daily work practices". However, they also reported challenges faced by caregivers in applying the program's techniques within their institutions, particularly because not all of their colleagues had participated in the intervention or possessed the same knowledge.

The moderator recorded in the field diary that participants frequently expressed throughout the intervention the importance of reflecting collectively on alternative approaches to managing conflicts based on peer feedback. They also highlighted the importance of implementing self-care strategies, which assisted them in setting deadlines and establishing more flexible goals.

The second category, *Interpersonal Relationships*, gathered all remarks related to perceived changes in interactions within the institutional context. In the subcategory Relationship with Children and Adolescents in care, participants highlighted improvements such as: "I learned that it is important to increase the children's self-esteem", "I tried to create and strengthen the bonds with them", "I've become more flexible with them", and "I am more protective of them". These comments emphasize the significance of the caregiver's protective and supportive role. In the subcategory *Relationship with Colleagues*, participants noted improvements such as "I've become more aware of my colleagues' difficulties and needs", "I feel more supported by my colleagues", and "I seek help from my colleagues more often". These responses illustrate the enhanced teamwork and the development of more empathetic and respectful relationships. The observers and the moderator also highlighted the value of interactions between caregivers from different shifts and the exploration of diverse points of view. These exchanges likely contributed to the improved quality of relationships with colleagues.

The third category, *General Impressions of the Program, Suggestions and Challenges*, included overall perceptions of the program, insights gained throughout the intervention, and suggestions for its expansion or improvement. The participants shared remarks such as "the program guided my work", "day-to-day tasks became easier", "I realized I was apathetic", and "I found hope again".

According to the observers, participants considered the program innovative, noting that interventions specifically aimed at caregivers were rare. The caregivers appreciated the program for offering a fresh perspective on their practices, as well as for providing a safe and confidential space to share experiences and feelings and to be heard. The observers also highlighted that participants frequently mentioned the moderator's prior experience in residential care as a significant and beneficial aspect of the program. Regarding the suggestions, the participants expressed a desire to "continue the program with other themes", "increase the course workload", "a greater dissemination", "provide evening classes", "extend the program to technical and directive teams of the residential care institutions", and "add new modules". In addition, the moderator recorded in the field diary a suggestion to include more specific themes, such as sexuality and drug addiction, which were areas of concern for the caregivers. As for the challenges, participants indicated the need for better time management during each meeting and noted the difficulty of including all caregivers in the city's care network.

Discussion

Caregivers play a key role in the social support network for children and adolescents in residential care, ensuring they receive comprehensive support and care. Studies indicate that supportive and nurturing relationships in care can significantly enhance the mental health and well-being of children and youth both during their time in care (Hoffnung Assouline & Attar-Schwartz, 2020) and after leaving care (Gallagher & Green, 2012).

Therefore, qualifying caregivers in residential care settings is essential to promote more positive and protective relationships with children in care. Initiatives such as the "Cuida" program are particularly valuable, as pointed out by the participants. These programs provide a safe and confidential space for caregivers to rethink their practices and share their struggles, uncertainties, and experiences—activities that are often rare in their daily routines. Regarding participant satisfaction, the analysis of the records showed that most of the caregivers who participated in the "Cuida" program were satisfied with the program content and their learning experiences, as well as with the moderator. Berkel et al. (2011) emphasized that while participant satisfaction alone is not sufficient, it is a key indicator of the success of interventions.

Regarding *perceived changes*, all of the themes addressed in the meetings were mentioned by participants. The subcategories of *assertive communication* and *conflict resolution strategies* were the most frequently cited by caregivers. This indicates the positive impact of the intervention on how they began to communicate with children and colleagues and seek more adaptive outcomes for conflicts. It is notable that both assertive communication and conflict resolution are social skills (Del Prette & Del Prette, 1996) that can be learned and are deeply related.

A theoretical review conducted by Del Prette and Del Prette (2005) identified that assertive communication, which emphasizes the respectful and empathetic sharing of opinions, produces both individual and collective benefits. It aids in the more adaptive resolution of conflicts arising from social interactions, specifically within the institutional context with children, adolescents in care, and colleagues (e.g., other caregivers, administrators, or coordinators). Some specific activities such as role-play (staging everyday situations), exploring solutions (Martínez-González, 2009), and negotiation likely facilitated the changes reported by the caregivers. In particular, the role-play technique, widely used in cognitive-behavioral therapy (Beck, 2014) and recommended by experiential methodology (Máiquez-Chavez et al., 2000), required caregivers—many with over 10 years of experience—to rethink their practices and ways of solving problems. Through this activity, coercive educational strategies like shouting were identified and reconsidered. According to Beck (2014), simulating experiences, exchanging roles, and other modes of interaction enable participants to share automatic thoughts, work on more adaptive responses, and develop new social skills. The methods of exploring solutions and negotiation are designed to encourage the use of dialog and flexibility in decision-making. This approach highlights the possibility of setting limits through democratic and bidirectional communication, developing educational practices more aligned with the principles of positive parenting.

The development of assertive communication skills and positive conflict resolution strategies may also have reflected on the quality of interpersonal relationships, especially with colleagues, as pointed out by the participants, the moderator, and observers. This improvement in relationships among caregivers is a significant outcome, especially since one of the most frequent complaints from caregivers was the difficulty in communicating with colleagues from other shifts. In an intervention with institutional caregivers, Bersch (2017) also identified conflicts between colleagues as a central issue, noting that misunderstanding about the routines of other shifts often led to disagreements and quarrels. Therefore, improving these relationships not only strengthens the social support network for caregivers but also enhances the support system for the children and adolescents in care.

Regarding the relationship with the children and adolescents in residential care, the professionals perceived themselves as more protective, flexible, and open to dialog. They also showed greater willingness to build and strengthen bonds with the children and adolescents. This topic was widely explored in the groups, as many caregivers previously avoided creating bonds due to the impermanent nature of the job. Cahill et al. (2016) highlight that developing quality relationships between children in care and residential care staff is recognized as an essential aspect of effective interventions. These relationships can serve as a significant protective factor in the face of adversity experienced by children in care.

At the end of the program, caregivers reported that the "Cuida" program guided their work and was useful in their institutional routine, promoting several reflections and providing practical tools. These perceptions demonstrate that the intervention in general successfully achieved its objectives of offering both theoretical and practical knowledge about positive educational practices. Remarks such as "daily life has become easier" and "the days have become lighter" point to the supportive role of the program in the daily activities of caregivers. It is notable that other theoretical studies have identified emotional overload, physical exhaustion, and feelings of guilt and powerlessness (Medeiros & Martins, 2018) as factors associated with a high incidence of symptoms of common mental disorders (CMD) such as insomnia, irritability, fatigue, and somatic complaints (Romero et al., 2016). One participant highlighted this by stating, "the caregiver is seen as a superhero, but they also have flaws". These human flaws can be addressed in spaces dedicated to listening and sharing of emotions, such as supervision, training, and psychotherapeutic care. Such support aims to improve the quality of life for these professionals and, consequently, enhance the quality of care provided to those they serve.

Although illness and frustration were frequently mentioned in their complaints, it was evident that most professionals found creative ways to build more positive relationships and promote greater well-being for those in care, even at their own financial expense. For instance, they organized cinema nights with popcorn and soda and created individual notebooks to preserve the stories and memories of children in care, especially those in the process of adoption or family reunification. Avoidance behaviors and authoritarian practices were gradually replaced by exchanges of praise, respectful dialogs, and seeking support from colleagues when necessary. A caregiver who feels cared for and recognized can offer the same level and recognition of those in their care.

Participants suggested expanding the program by adding new modules and increasing its promotion, which should be considered for future implementations. These suggestions highlight that caregivers recognize the program's relevance and effectiveness in their daily work, as well as the ongoing need for training aimed at enhancing their professional development. Some limitations should be noted, including the lack of a follow-up study, the small sample size, and the fact that the evaluators were part of the team conducting the meetings. Future studies should address these limitations by incorporating follow-up evaluations, using larger samples, and training additional moderators to replicate the program, thereby minimizing the risk of social desirability bias.

Final Considerations

This chapter discussed the role of caregivers in supporting children and adolescents in residential care and presented qualitative data on the implementation of the "Cuida" program, developed for these caregivers in southern Brazil.

While residential care cannot replace family care, the emotional support offered by these caregivers helps to meet, at least to a certain extent, the emotional needs of children in care, alleviating some of the negative impacts of family separation and institutionalization. Beyond offering protection, these bonds enhance personal growth and optimize a more adaptive psychological functioning (Ferreira et al., 2020). Therefore, caring for and training these caregivers is essential for enabling them to fulfill their important role within the social support network of children and adolescents in residential care.

Most of the caregivers who completed the "Cuida" program expressed high satisfaction with the program content, their learning experiences, and the moderator's performance. The caregivers reported important improvements in their educational practices, especially regarding assertive communication and conflict resolution strategies. They also noted becoming more protective, flexible, and engaged in building and strengthening bonds with the children in their care. Although these relationships may be temporary, they play a crucial role in enhancing the child's sense of security and providing a foundation for healthy development. As Bronfenbrenner famously said, "Every child needs at least one adult who is irrationally crazy about him or her" (Sadownik, 2023). We can conclude that the intervention was developed with socially valid objectives and acceptable procedures, significantly contributing to the improvement of positive educational practices among caregivers of residential care settings. While social validity alone does not guarantee successful outcomes, it is a crucial prerequisite for effective implementation and broader dissemination of interventions in real-world settings (Barbosa & Murta, 2019).

The gaps in Brazilian public policies supporting residential care settings are particularly apparent in the areas of training and professional development for caregivers. To address these deficiencies, it is crucial to systematically develop and evaluate preventive programs that promote positive practices among these professionals. Such initiatives are essential for enhancing service quality and ensuring that principles of care and protection are fully realized. Ensuring the rights of children and adolescents also necessitated investing in the resources and training of the professionals who support them. Focusing on the well-being and development of caregivers is key to sustaining positive care practices and support over the long term.

References

Avoglia, H.R.C., Silva, A.M., & Mattos, P.M. (2012). Educador social: Imagem e relações com crianças em situação de acolhimento institucional [Social educator: Image and relationship with children in shelter institutions]. *Revista Mal-Estar e Subjetividade*, *12*(1–2), 265–292. Retrieved from http://pepsic.bvsalud.org/scielo.php?script=sci_arttext&pid=S1518-61482012000100010&lng=pt&tlng=pt

Barbosa, L.M., & Murta, S.G. (2019). Social validity of a contextual behavioral science-based intervention for retirement education. *Psicologia: Reflexão e Crítica*, *32*, 24. https://doi.org/10.1186/s41155-019-0137-0

Bardin, L. (2004). *Análise de conteúdo* (3ª ed). [*Content analysis*]. Lisboa: Edições Setenta.
Beck, J. (2014). *Terapia Cognitivo-Comportamental: Teoria e prática.* [*Cognitive behavior therapy: Basics and beyond*]. Porto Alegre: Artmed.
Berkel, C., Mauricio, A.M., Schoenfelder, E., & Sandler, I.N. (2011). Putting the pieces together: An integrated model of program implementation. *Prevention Science*, *12*, 23–33. https://doi.org/10.1007/s11121-010-0186-1
Bersch, A.A.S. (2017). *Resiliência profissional e a Educação Ambiental: Promoção de ambientes de desenvolvimento em instituição de acolhimento.* [Professional resilience and Environmental Education: Promotion of development environments in residential care institutions]. Tese (Doutorado) – Universidade Federal do Rio Grande, FURG. Rio Grande, Rio Grande do Sul. Retrieved from https://sistemas.furg.br/sistemas/sab/arquivos/bdtd/0000011532.pdf
Brasil. (1988). *Constituição da República Federativa do Brasil de 1988.* [Federal Constitution of Federative Republic of Brazil]. Promulgada em 5 de outubro de 1988. Brasília, DF. Retrieved from https://www.planalto.gov.br/ccivil_03/Constituicao/Constituicao.htm
Brasil. (1990). *Estatuto da criança e do adolescente.* [*Statute of the child and adolescent*]. Diário Oficial da União. Lei nº 8.069, de 13 de julho de 1990. Brasília, DF. Retrieved from http://www.planalto.gov.br/ccivil_03/Leis/l8069.htm
Brasil. (2009a). *Nova lei nacional da adoção.* [*New national adoption law*]. Lei nº 12.010, de 3 de agosto de 2009. Brasília, DF. Retrieved from http://www.planalto.gov.br/ccivil_03/_Ato2007-2010/2009/Lei/L12010.htm
Brasil. (2009b). *Orientações técnicas para serviços de acolhimento para crianças e adolescentes.* [*Technical guidelines for residential care*]. Brasília, DF: Conanda.
Cahill, O., Holt, S., & Kirwan, G. (2016). Keyworking in residential child care: Lessons from research. *Children and Youth Services Review*, *65*, 216–223. https://doi.org/10.1016/j.childyouth.2016.04.014
Chen, Y., Haines, J., Charlton, B.M., & VanderWeele, T.J. (2019). Positive parenting improves multiple aspects of health and well-being in young adulthood. *Nature Human Behaviour*, *3*(7), 684–691. https://doi.org/10.1038/s41562-019-0602-x
Conselho Nacional de Justiça, C.N.J. (2020). *Diagnóstico sobre o Sistema Nacional de Adoção e Acolhimento.* [*Diagnosis of the national adoption and residential care system*]. Brasília, DF. Retrieved from https://www.neca.org.br/wp-content/uploads/SNA_Relatorio_Diagnostico-Sistema-Nacional-Adocao-Acolhimento_2020.pdf
Conselho Nacional de Saúde. (2016). *Resolução nº 510/2016.* [*Resolution nº 510/2016*]. Dispõe sobre a pesquisa em Ciências Humanas e Sociais. Brasil: Ministério da Saúde, Brasília, DF. Retrieved from http://conselho.saude.gov.br/resolucoes/2016/Reso510.pdf
Council of Europe. (2006). *Recommendation Rec(2006)19 of the Committee of Ministers to Member States on Policy to Support Positive Parenting.* (Adopted by the Committee of Ministers on 13 December 2006 at the 983rd meeting of the Ministers' Deputies). Retrieved from https://search.coe.int/cm/Pages/result_details.aspx?ObjectID=09000016805d6dda
Del Prette, Z.A.P., & Del Prette, A. (1996). Habilidades sociais: Uma área em desenvolvimento. [Social skills: a developing area]. *Psicologia: Reflexão e Crítica*, *9*(2), 233–255.
Del Prette, Z.A.P., & Del Prette, A. (2005). *Psicologia das habilidades sociais na infância: Teoria e prática.* [*Psychology of early childhood social skills: Theory and practice*]. Petrópolis: Vozes.
Durgante, H. (2019). *Desenvolvimento, implementação e avaliação do Programa Vem Ser: Programa de psicologia positiva para a promoção de saúde de aposentados.* [*Development, implementation and evaluation of "Vem Ser Program": A positive psychology program to health promotion of retirees*]. Tese (Doutorado) – Universidade Federal do Rio Grande do Sul, UFRGS, Porto Alegre, RS. Retrieved from https://lume.ufrgs.br/handle/10183/194393

Ferreira, S., Magalhães, E., & Prioste, A. (2020). Social support and mental health of young people in residential care: a qualitative study. *Anuario de Psicologia Juridica, 30*(1), 29–34. https://doi.org/10.5093/apj2019a12

Gallagher, B., & Green, A. (2012). In, out and after care: Young adults' views on their lives, as children, in a therapeutic residential establishment. *Children and Youth Services Review, 34*(2), 437–450. https://doi.org/10.1016/j.childyouth.2011.11.014

Guerra, L.L., & Del Prette, Z.P. (2018). Habilidades sociais educativas de cuidadores de crianças institucionalizadas. [Educative social skills of caregivers of institutionalized children]. *Arquivos Brasileiros de Psicologia, 70*(3), 98–112. Retrieved from http://pepsic.bvsalud.org/scielo.php?script=sci_arttext&pid=S1809-52672018000300008&lng=pt&tlng=pt

Halpern, E.E., Leite, L.M.C., & Moraes, M.C.M.B. (2015). Seleção, capacitação e formação da equipe de profissionais dos abrigos: O hiato entre o prescrito e o real. [Shelter professional selection, capacity building, and training: the gap between what is prescribed and reality]. *Trabalho, Educação e Saúde, 13*(supl. 1), 91–113. https://doi.org/10.1590/1981-7746-sip00033

Hoffnung Assouline, A.A., & Attar-Schwartz, S. (2020). Staff support and adolescent adjustment difficulties: The moderating role of length of stay in the residential care setting. *Children and Youth Services Review, 110*, Article 104761. https://doi.org/10.1016/j.childyouth.2020.104761

Kappler, S.R., & Mendes, D.M.L.F. (2019). Trocas afetivas de crianças em acolhimento institucional. [Affective exchanges of children in institutional care]. *Psicologia: Ciência e Profissão, 39*, e184527. https://doi.org/10.1590/1982-3703003184527

Levitt, H.M., Bamberg, M., Creswell, J.W., Frost, D.M., Josselson, R., & Suárez-Orozco, C. (2018). Journal article reporting standards for qualitative primary, qualitative meta-analytic, and mixed methods research in psychology: The APA Publications and Communications Board task force report. *American Psychologist, 73*(1), 26–46. https://doi.org/10.1037/amp0000151

Máiquez-Chavez, M.L., Rodrigo-López, M.J., Capote, C., & Vermaes, I. (2000). *Aprender en la vida cotidiana*: Un programa para padres. [*Learning in daily life: An experiential parenting program*]. Madri: Visor.

Martínez-González, R.A. (2009). *Programa-Guía para el Desarrollo de Competencias Emocionales, Educativas y Parentales.* [*Program guide to development emotional, educational and parental competencies*]. Madrid: Ministerio de Sanidad y Política Social

Martín-Quintana, J.C., Máiquez-Chavez, M.L., Rodrigo-López, M.J., Byme, S., Rodríguez-Ruiz, B., & Rodríguez-Suárez, G. (2009). Programas de Educación Parental. [Parenting programs]. *Psychosocial Intervention, 18*(2), 121–133. Retrieved from http://scielo.isciii.es/scielo.php?script=sci_arttext&pid=S1132-05592009000200004&lng=es&tlng=es

Martín-Quintana, J.C., & Rodrigo-López, M.J. (2013). La promoción de la parentalidad positiva. [Promote positive parenting]. *Revista Educação, Ciência e Cultura, 18*(1), 77–88. https://doi.org/10.18316/1090

Marzol, R. M., Bonafé, L., & Yunes, M. A. M. (2012). As perspectivas de crianças e adolescentes em situação de acolhimento sobre os cuidadores protetores. [The perceptions of children and adolescents in shelter institutions on the protective caretakers]. *Revista Psico, 43*(3), 317–324. Retrieved from http://revistaseletronicas.pucrs.br/ojs/index.php/revistapsico/article/viewFile/7988/823

Medeiros, B.C.D. de, & Martins, J.B. (2018). O estabelecimento de vínculos entre cuidadores e crianças no contexto das instituições de acolhimento: um estudo teórico. [The establishment of bond between caregivers and children in the context of fostering institutions: A theoretical study]. *Psicologia: Ciência e Profissão, 38*(1), 74–87. https://doi.org/10.1590/1982-3703002882017

Moré, C.L.O.O., & Sperancetta, A. (2010). Práticas de pais sociais em instituições de acolhimento de crianças e adolescentes. [Practices developed by social parents in institutions for shelter of children and adolescents]. *Psicologia & Sociedade*, *22*(3), 519–528. https://doi.org/10.1590/S0102-71822010000300012

Moura, G.G., Amorim, K.S., & Rossetti-Ferreira, M.C.T. (2022). "Quem não pega, não se apega"? Interações e vínculos com bebês acolhidos. ["Who doesn't pick-up, doesn't get attached"? Interactions and bonds with foster infants]. *Psicologia: Teoria e Pesquisa*, *38*, e38322. Epub November 07, 2022. https://doi.org/10.1590/0102.3772e38322.pt

Pagnota, R.M.N.F., & Prebianchi, H.B. (2021). Estresse e estratégias de enfrentamento em profissionais de abrigos institucionais. [Stress and coping strategies in shelter professionals]. *Psicologia: Ciência e Profissão*, *41*(spe2). https://doi.org/10.1590/1982-3703003193180

Prada, C.G. (2007). *Avaliação de um programa de práticas educativas para monitoras de um abrigo infantil*. [Assessment of one program of educative practices for caregivers of foster care for children]. Tese (Doutorado) – Universidade Federal de São Carlos, UFSCar, São Carlos, São Paulo. Retrieved from https://repositorio.ufscar.br/bitstream/handle/ufscar/2828/TeseCGP.pdf?sequence=1&isAllowed=y

Rio Grande do Sul. (2018). Lei n° 15.210, de 25 de julho de 2018. *Institui o Programa de Guarda Temporária de Crianças e Adolescentes – Família Acolhedora*. [Establishes the temporary custody program for children and adolescents – Foster families]. Retrieved from http://www.al.rs.gov.br/filerepository/repLegis/arquivos/LEI%2015.210.pdf

Rodrigo, M.J. (2016). Quality of implementation in evidence-based positive parenting programs in Spain: Introduction to the special issue. *Psychosocial Intervention*, *25*(2), 63–68. https://doi.org/10.1016/j.psi.2016.02.004

Romero, D.L., Akiba, H.T., Dias, A.M., & Serafim, A.P. (2016). Transtornos mentais comuns em educadores sociais. [Common mental disorders in social educators]. *Jornal Brasileiro de Psiquiatria [online]*, *65*(4), 322–329. https://doi.org/10.1590/0047-2085000000140

Sadownik, A. (2023). Bronfenbrenner: Ecology of human development in ecology of collaboration. In: A. R. Sadownik, A. Višnjić Jevtić (eds.), *(Re)theorising more-than-parental involvement in early childhood education and care*, (pp. 83–95), International perspectives on early childhood education and development, Springer, 40. https://doi.org/10.1007/978-3-031-38762-3

Sanders, M.R., Markie-Dadds, C., & Turner, K.M.T. (1999). *Practitioner's manual for Enhanced Triple P*. Brisbane, Australia: Families International Publishing.

Santos, K.S., Ribeiro, M.C., Queiroga, D.E.U., Silva, I.A.P., & Ferreira, S.M.S. (2018). O uso de triangulação múltipla como estratégia de validação em um estudo qualitativo. [The use of multiple triangulation as a validation strategy in a qualitative study]. *Ciência eSaúdeColetiva*,*25*(2),655–664.https://doi.org/10.1590/1413-81232020252.12302018

Schavarem, L.N., & Toni, C.G.S. (2019). A relação entre as práticas educativas parentais e a autoestima da criança. [The relationship between parenting style and children's self-esteem]. *Pensando Familias*, *23*(2), 147–161. Retrieved from http://pepsic.bvsalud.org/scielo.php?script=sci_arttext&pid=S1679-494X2019000200012&lng=pt&tlng=pt

Silva, J. (2009). *Parents raising safe kids: ACT 8-week program for parents*. Washington, DC: American Psychological Association.

Smith, M. (2009). *Rethinking residential child care: Positive perspectives*. Bristol, UK: Policy Press.

Steckler, A., & Linnan, L. (Eds.). (2002). *Process evaluation for public health interventions and research*. San Francisco, CA: Jossey Bass.

Steels, S. & Simpson, H. (2017). Perceptions of children in residential care homes: A critical review of the literature. *The British Journal of Social Work*, 47(6), 1704–1722. https://doi.org/10.1093/bjsw/bcx107

Weber, L.N.D. (2017). Relações entre práticas educativas parentais percebidas e a autoestima, sinais de depressão e o uso de substâncias por adolescentes. [Relationships between perceived parenting practices and self-esteem, signs of depression and substance use by adolescents]. *Revista INFAD de Psicología. International Journal of Developmental and Educational Psychology*, 2(1), 157–168. https://doi.org/10.17060/ijodaep.2017.n1.v2.928

Weber, L.N.D., Dias, A.Y.M.S., Gomes, L.C., & Pasqualotto, R.A. (2018). Práticas parentais percebidas, autoestima, otimismo e resiliência em futuros professores. [Perceived parenting practices, self-esteem, optimism and resilience in future teachers]. *Revista INFAD de Psicología. International Journal of Developmental and Educational Psychology*, 1(1), 193–202. Retrieved from http://www.infad.eu/RevistaINFAD/OJS/index.php/IJODAEP/article/view/1188

Yamaoka, Y., & Bard, D.E. (2019). Positive parenting matters in the face of early adversity. *American Journal of Preventive Medicine*, 56(4), 530–539. https://doi.org/10.1016/j.amepre.2018.11.018

Conclusion

Shalhevet Attar-Schwartz and Eunice Magalhães

This book makes both empirical and theoretical contributions to the literature on social support for young people in residential care. Social support is widely recognized as a protective factor for mental health, especially for those who have experienced adversity and risk (Attar-Schwartz & Fridman-Teutsch, 2018; Magalhães & Calheiros, 2017). Children and young people in residential care are particularly vulnerable due to histories of abuse and neglect, ongoing mental health challenges (Magalhães & Camilo, 2023), and the difficulties associated with living in institutional settings and transitioning out of the system. Ensuring supportive, secure relationships during and after care is therefore essential.

In Part 1 of this book, we examine the theoretical foundations that guide research into social support for young people in residential care and across their life course. Attar-Schwartz et al. highlight how the literature offers a broad range of conceptualizations and definitions of social support, including frameworks like social capital theories, the life course perspective, and interdependence theory. They emphasize the need to conceptualize and measure social support for young people in residential care by recognizing sources beyond staff or parents—such as siblings, grandparents, and peers—as essential for children and youth who often experience emotional deprivation and relational challenges with primary caregivers. Additionally, rather than solely considering network size, the authors underscore the importance of assessing young people's capacity to effectively mobilize these support networks (Melkman, 2017). A combined approach, incorporating trauma-informed, relational, and interdependence theories, offers a pathway to help youth in residential care not only to address past challenges but also to build meaningful, lasting relationships. Beyond preparing youth for independence, the focus should be on fostering interdependence by cultivating supportive relationships (Antle et al., 2009) and expanding beyond their current connections within the care system to promote a sustainable, long-term network of support.

Building on the perspective of the long-term impact of supportive relationships, Gilligan presents cases of young people who have overcome the challenges of residential care, highlighting the enduring influence of social support

DOI: 10.4324/9781003424468-22

into adulthood. These cases illustrate how transformative a young person's trajectory can be when they have access to resources, consistent support, and a sense of recognition. Gilligan emphasizes the importance of not only fostering supportive relationships within the care setting but also encouraging connections with external individuals who enhance young people's self-determination and agency. By offering diverse opportunities to build capacities and meaningful relationships, the author suggests, we can create a positive, transformative impact with lasting benefits for youth as they transition to adulthood.

Chapters three through seven highlight the positive role of social support on a variety of outcomes for young people in residential care, linking it with reduced psychopathology, improved well-being (Attar-Schwartz et al.; Magalhães & Calheiros; Gallitto et al.; Singstad), enhanced quality of life (Singstad), and better academic performance (Magalhães & Calheiros). These studies, conducted in Portugal, Canada, Israel, Norway, and Australia, highlight the critical role of caregivers both within and outside of care settings, along with other sources such as parents, friends, siblings, and grandparents. In the Portuguese context, the findings emphasize the buffering effects of caregiver support within residential care (Magalhães & Calheiros), an effect mirrored in the Australian context, where strong relationships with care workers were perceived as central to addressing young people's needs (Moore et al.). Moore and colleagues argue that a children's rights approach in residential care—where youth feel loved, respected, and have their rights upheld—enhances their protection and overall well-being. Evidence also suggests that strong support from staff can mitigate the impact of stressors (Calheiros et al., 2020; Magalhães et al., 2021), challenging the assumption that stress inevitably results in negative outcomes. Instead, responsive and supportive relationships with staff can function as both therapeutic and protective factors for youth in care (Assouline & Attar-Schwartz, 2020). Out-of-home caregivers play a significant role in reducing negative outcomes and enhancing well-being (Gallitto et al.; Singstad), complemented by the positive influence of maternal support, especially noted in the Norwegian context. Additionally, a longitudinal U.S. study by Park and colleagues found that family members and other relatives remained the most frequently cited sources of support among care leavers, highlighting the enduring significance of family connections even after leaving care.

It is essential to provide training and supervision for residential care staff while also supporting and monitoring meaningful contact between young people and significant others, both within the residential care setting and from their original environments (Attar-Schwartz et al.). Supportive peer relationships are key for some young people in care, particularly for girls, as they correlate with higher quality of life, as noted by Singstad. Adolescents' mental health in residential care appears to benefit from diverse, supportive relationships, including those with staff, peers, and birth nuclear and extended families (Assouline & Attar-Schwartz, 2020; Attar-Schwartz & Huri, 2019;

Pinchover & Attar-Schwartz, 2018; Pinheiro et al., 2022a; Pinheiro et al., 2024). This was similarly emphasized by the chapters of Knorth and colleagues and Attar-Schwartz and colleagues, who found that parents, siblings, grandparents, care workers, and peers were the primary sources of support for young people in residential care. These findings highlight the importance of residential care systems in helping young people to mobilize and strengthen their support networks. Such efforts can not only enhance their mental health and well-being during their time in residential care but also support a smoother, more effective transition into life after care. From an interdependence perspective, young people should be given the opportunity to sustain and develop meaningful, supportive, and warm relationships, which play a crucial role in their long-term success beyond the care setting.

The findings also highlight the importance of examining the context in which support contributes to young people's well-being, as well as the specific circumstances under which it is most beneficial, as illustrated in the chapter by Attar-Schwartz et al. For example, the Israeli data indicate that when youth perceive staff attitudes towards their parents as more favorable, the link between parental contact and reduced emotional and behavioral difficulties is strengthened. These insights underscore the need for targeted training of residential care staff to foster supportive and constructive family interactions.

Social support from various sources serves as a protective factor for young people's psychological adjustment not only in out-of-home care but also during their transition to life after care. This support is essential for mobilizing critical resources, such as career and housing opportunities, which facilitate better social integration (as discussed in Sulimani-Aidan's chapter). Care leavers often face challenges with limited networks and fewer resources compared to peers without congregate care histories (as noted by Park and colleagues). Findings from CalYOUTH—a longitudinal study of care leavers in the U.S. (2012–2020) detailed by Park et al.—indicate that as these young people age, both their positive evaluations of supportive relationships and the size of their networks tend to decrease. This decline is more pronounced with family and institutional support than with peer support, which remains relatively consistent across ages (see Park's chapter for further insights). The reduction in available support over time presents ongoing challenges for residential care settings and post-care services aiming to provide continuous and stable assistance. These services face significant challenges in supporting young people's transition to independent living, particularly in contexts like Ghana (as discussed by Frimpong-Manso) and India (see Modi et al.). Given the barriers young people often face in accessing support, it is crucial for governments in these settings to allocate additional human and financial resources to the out-of-home care system, ensuring post-care assistance, as suggested by Frimpong-Manso. Moreover, Modi and colleagues highlight the need for tailored approaches that address the specific needs of young people leaving care, emphasizing the development and implementation of policies and practices aimed at breaking the cycle of risk and social exclusion often faced by care leavers.

Although much emphasis is placed on preparing young people for independence after leaving care, some authors argue that policies should focus on promoting interdependence instead (Antle et al., 2009). This shift is not just a change in practice but a fundamental rethinking of the transition from out-of-home care. It involves ensuring that "bridge relationships" (Antle et al., 2009, p. 312)—such as helping professionals, mentors, and extended family members—are in place to help youth maintain supportive relationships that can aid them in living autonomously after leaving care. When young people develop skills to seek and receive support from close relationships, they can better rely on these connections during their transition. Therefore, a practice framework centered on interdependence is essential to prevent social exclusion and psychological challenges for youth with histories of out-of-home care (Antle et al., 2009). In line with this approach, Sulimani-Aidan's chapter emphasizes the importance of both formal and informal support in enhancing the chances of success and opportunities for care leavers. Specifically, residential care services should encourage youth to engage with extended family, friends, and other support networks to strengthen their social ties.

Designing effective post-care support services should also adopt an intersectional perspective. Vulnerability increases when young people in care belong to specific groups, such as LGBTQIA+ individuals or migrants. LGBTQIA+ youth, often report multiple forms of oppression, indicating that their needs were unmet in care settings and highlighting significant physical and mental health challenges (Lopez Lopez et al.). LGBTQIA+ youth are overrepresented in the out-of-home care system and are more likely to experience inequalities in their physical, mental, and social well-being (Alvarez et al., 2022; Schaub et al., 2022). From an intersectional perspective, factors such as ethnicity, sexual orientation, and gender identity introduce additional challenges for these youth and must be considered when addressing their mental health needs in care (Schaub et al., 2022). The lack of specialized training and cultural competence among staff working in residential care is a critical issue, as it undermines the delivery of appropriate services that address the needs of LGBTQIA+ youth, including their educational needs and a successful transition out of care (Schaub et al., 2022).

Similarly, unaccompanied migrant youth often report limited support networks and face difficulties accessing formal assistance (Gullo et al.). Recent studies have shown that unaccompanied young migrants are at a higher risk for clinical levels of PTSD, depression, and anxiety (Hornfeck et al., 2023). Despite these challenges, research also indicates that these vulnerable groups may demonstrate resilient trajectories (Alvarez et al., 2022). In the chapter by Gullo and colleagues, findings suggest that greater support is linked to better psychological functioning and well-being, aligning with evidence that culturally sensitive placements can improve health outcomes (O'Higgins et al., 2018). Therefore, it is crucial to develop policies and practices that ensure young people have access to multiple sources of social support throughout their time in residential care, during their transition, and after leaving care, while also addressing the specific needs of groups particularly vulnerable to social exclusion, such as LGBTQIA+ youth and migrants.

Implications for practice and policy in residential care

The findings presented in this book emphasize the need for innovative services and policies for young people in residential care. This includes providing lifelong training opportunities and promoting interdependence by fostering and maintaining social connections over time. Programs that focus on staff communication skills, emotional regulation, self-care, and self-efficacy are essential for equipping staff with the tools to provide safe, supportive relationships for young people, as Wendt and Dell'Aglio highlight in their chapter. A recent systematic review emphasizes the critical role of staff attributes and skills in fostering quality relationships in care (Pinheiro et al., 2022b), underscoring the importance of recruiting qualified staff with empathy and compassion (Magalhães et al., 2024). Additionally, providing supervision and supporting staff self-care is vital, as the nature of this work often leads to burnout and disengagement (Magalhães & Cerdeira, 2024; McNamara, 2010; Travis et al., 2016), particularly when caring for clients with significant emotional and behavioral needs (Castro et al., 2023, 2024; Magalhães & Camilo, 2023; Pinchover et al., 2015).

Moore and colleagues stress the importance of encouraging staff reflection, both individually and within teams, fostering an organizational culture where child-centered leadership ensures ethical and relational practices. Singstad also underscores the importance of high-quality caring environments, while Knorth and colleagues argue that contextual factors, such as social climate, significantly impact treatment outcomes in residential care. Consistent with Magalhães and Calheiros' findings, a positive organizational climate improves both staff motivation and youth engagement, leading to stronger, more responsive relationships. A supportive social and physical environment is essential for safeguarding the physical and mental health of youth in care (Pinchover & Attar-Schwartz, 2014; Stams & Van der Helm, 2017), and Knorth and colleagues advocate for the systematic monitoring of group climate to maintain supportive relationships.

Furthermore, interventions addressing trauma are critical for helping youth recover from attachment disturbances and trust issues. Positive, trusting relationships are enhanced by inclusive, trauma-informed care environments that offer stability and predictability for staff, reducing turnover and fostering consistent support (as discussed by Singstad). In sum, effective interventions in residential care settings require collaboration between researchers, practitioners, and other stakeholders to foster meaningful, quality relationships, which in turn improve youth outcomes, as Gallitto and Flynn also suggest.

The insights and recommendations in this book make valuable contributions to both literature and practice, offering guidance for child welfare researchers and practitioners. The editors commend the authors' high-quality contributions, which hold significant potential to advance policies and practices in this field.

References

Álvarez, R. G., Parra, L. A., Ten Brummelaar, M., Avraamidou, L., & López, M. L. (2022). Resilience among LGBTQIA+ youth in out-of-home care: A scoping review. *Child Abuse & Neglect*, *129*, 105660. https://doi.org/10.1016/j.chiabu.2022.105660

Antle, B. F., Johnson, L., Barbee, A., & Sullivan, D. (2009). Fostering interdependent versus independent living in youth aging out of care through healthy relationships. *Families in Society*, *90*(3), 309–315. https://doi.org/10.1606/1044-3894.3890

Assouline, A. H., & Attar-Schwartz, S. (2020). Staff social support and adolescent adjustment difficulties: The moderating role of length of stay in the residential care setting. *Children and Youth Services Review*, *110*,104761. https://doi.org/10.1016/j.childyouth.2020.104761

Attar-Schwartz, S., & Fridman-Teutsch, A.(2018). Father support and adjustment difficulties among youth in residential settings: The moderating role of victimization by peers and gender. *American Journal of Orthopsychiatry*, *88*, 701–712.

Attar-Schwartz, S., & Huri, Y. (2019). Grandparental support and life satisfaction among adolescents in residential care. *Children and Youth Services Review*, *96*, 70–78. https://doi.org/10.1016/j.childyouth.2018.11.033

Calheiros, M. M., Patrício J. N., & Silva, C. (2020). Social support as a moderator of associations between youth's perceptions of their social images and self-representations in residential care. *Children and Youth Services Review*, *119*(105667). https://doi.org/10.1016/j.childyouth.2020.105667

Castro, E., Magalhães, E. & Del Valle, J. (2023). A systematic review of non-specific and specific treatment factors associated with lower or greater internalising and externalising symptoms in therapeutic residential care. *Children and Youth Services Review*, *147*. https://doi.org/10.1016/j.childyouth.2023.106840

Castro, E., Magalhães, E. & Del Valle, J. (2024). A systematic review of quality indicators in therapeutic residential care drawn from young people´s beliefs and experiences. *Child Indicators Research*. https://doi.org/10.1007/s12187-024-10118-5

Hornfeck, F., Eglinsky, J., Garbade, M., Rosner, R., Kindler, H., Pfeiffer, E., & Sachser, C. (2023). Mental health problems in unaccompanied young refugees and the impact of post-flight factors on PTSS, depression and anxiety – A secondary analysis of the better care study. *Frontiers in Psychology*, *14*, 1149634.

Magalhães, E. & Calheiros, M. M. (2017). A dual-factor model of mental health and social support: Evidence with adolescents in residential care. *Children and Youth Services Review*, *79*, 442–449. https://doi.org/10.1016/j.childyouth.2017.06.041

Magalhães, E., Calheiros, M. M., Costa, P. & Ferreira, S. (2021). Youth's rights and mental health: The role of supportive relations in care. *Journal of Social and Personal Relationships*, *38*(3), 848–864. https://doi.org/10.1177/0265407520975507

Magalhães, E. & Camilo, C. (2023). Maltreatment history and internalizing and externalizing in out-of-home care: A three-level meta-analysis. *European Journal of Psychology Applied to Legal Context*, *15*(2), 89–103. https://doi.org/10.5093/ejpalc2023a10

Magalhães, E., & Cerdeira, J. (2024). Professionals' insights on supervision in Portuguese residential care. *Child & Family Social Work*. https://doi.org/10.1111/cfs.13235

Magalhães, E., Ferreira, M., Ornelas, S., Silva, C., Camilo, C. & Calheiros, M. (2024). Youth-caregiver relationship quality in residential youth care: Professionals' perceptions and experiences. *Journal of Social and Personal Relationships*, *41*(4), 822–845. https://doi.org/10.1177/02654075231215824

McNamara, P. M. (2010). Staff support and supervision in residential youth justice: An Australian model. *Residential Treatment for Children & Youth*, *27*(3), 214–240. https://doi.org/10.1080/0886571X.2010.501630

Melkman, E. (2017). Childhood adversity, social support networks and well-being among youth aging out of care: An exploratory study of mediation. *Child Abuse and Neglect*, *72*, 85–97. https://doi.org/10.1016/j.chiabu.2017.07.02

Melkman, E.P., & Benbenishty, R. (2018). Social support networks of care leavers: Mediating between childhood adversity and adult functioning. *Children and Youth Services Review*, 86, 176–187. https://doi.org/10.1016/j.childyouth.2018.01.040

O'Higgins, A., Ott, E. M., & Shea, M. W. (2018). What is the impact of placement type on educational and health outcomes of unaccompanied refugee minors? A systematic review of the evidence. *Clinical Child and Family Psychology Review*, *21*, 354–365. https://doi.org/10.1007/s10567-018-0256-7

Pinchover, S., & Attar-Schwartz, S. (2014). Institutional social climate and adjustment difficulties of adolescents in residential care: The mediating role of victimization by peers. *Children and Youth Services Review*, *44*, 393–399. https://doi.org/10.1016/j.childyouth.2014.07.005

Pinchover, S., & Attar-Schwartz, S. (2018). Is someone there for you? Social support of youth in educational residential care from family, peers, and staff. *British Journal of Social Work*, 48, 2195–2214. https://doi.org/10.1093/bjsw/bcx164

Pinchover, S., Attar-Schwartz, S., & Matattov-Sekeles, H. (2015). Director's leadership and burnout among residential child care workers: Possible implications for practice. *Scottish Journal of Residential Child Care*, *14*(2), 2–11.

Pinheiro, M., Magalhães, E. & Baptista, J. (2022a). Adolescents' resilience in residential care: A systematic review of factors related to healthy adaptation. *Child Indicators Research*, *15*, 819–837 https://doi.org/10.1007/s12187-021-09883-4

Pinheiro, M., Magalhães, E. & Baptista, J. (2024). Resilience in residential care: A qualitative study based on the voices of adolescents. *Children and Youth Services Review*, *162*, 107694 https://doi.org/10.1016/j.childyouth.2024.107694

Pinheiro, M., Magalhães, E., Calheiros, M. M. & Macdonald, D. (2022b). Quality of relationships between residential staff and youth: A systematic review. *Child and Adolescent Social Work Journal*. https://doi.org/10.1007/s10560-022-00909-6

Schaub, J., Stander, W. J., & Montgomery, P. (2022). LGBTQ+ young people's health and well-being experiences in out-of-home social care: A scoping review. *Children and Youth Services Review*, *143*, 106682. https://doi.org/10.1016/j.childyouth.2022.106682

Stams, G.J., & Van der Helm, P. (2017). What works in residential programs for aggressive and violent youth? In P. Sturney (Ed.), *The Wiley Handbook of Violence and Aggression* (pp.1–12). John Wiley & Sons, Ltd. https://doi.org/10.1002/9781119057574.whbva116

Travis, D. J., Lizano, E. L., & Mor Barak, M. E. (2016). 'I'm so stressed!': A longitudinal model of stress, burnout and engagement among social workers in child welfare settings. *The British Journal of Social Work*, *46*(4), 1076–1095. https://doi.org/10.1093/bjsw/bct205

Index

Pages in *italics* refer to figures, pages in **bold** refer to tables, and pages followed by "n" refer to notes.

For Product Safety Concerns and Information please contact our EU
representative GPSR@taylorandfrancis.com
Taylor & Francis Verlag GmbH, Kaufingerstraße 24, 80331 München, Germany

www.ingramcontent.com/pod-product-compliance
Ingram Content Group UK Ltd.
Pitfield, Milton Keynes, MK11 3LW, UK
UKHW021829101126
477531UK00020B/552

* 9 7 8 1 0 3 2 5 4 3 5 3 6 *